NATIONAL GEOGRAPHIC

TRAVELER

New Orleans

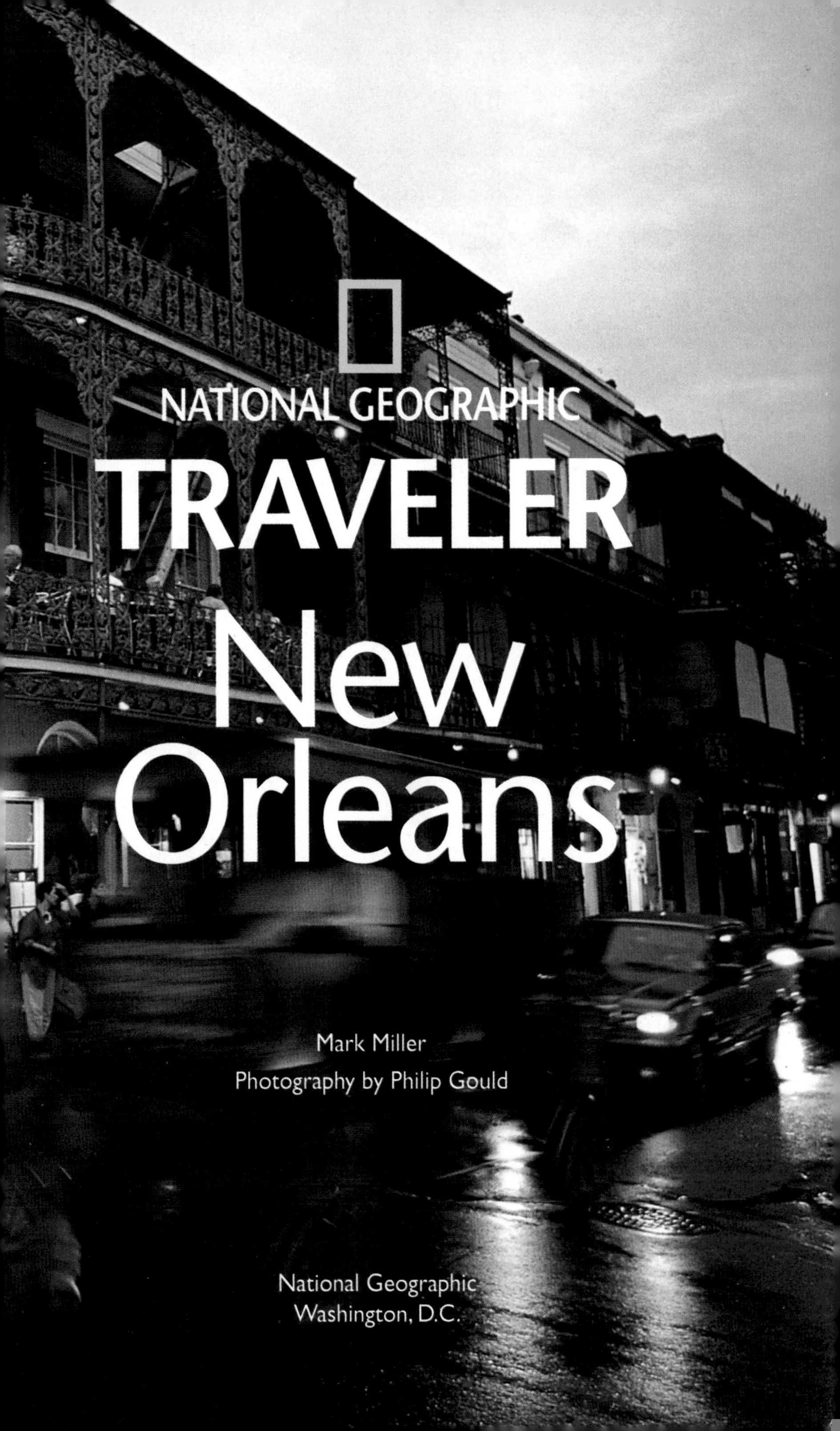

NATIONAL GEOGRAPHIC

TRAVELER

New Orleans

Mark Miller

Photography by Philip Gould

National Geographic
Washington, D.C.

Contents

Page 1: Marching band musician
Pages 2–3: Evening in the French Quarter
Left: St. Louis Cathedral in early morning fog

How to use this guide

See back flap for keys to text and map symbols

The National Geographic Traveler brings you the best of New Orleans in text, pictures, and maps. Divided into three sections, the guide begins with an overview of history and culture. Following are five area chapters with featured sites chosen by the author for their particular interest and treated in depth. Each chapter opens with its own contents list for easy reference. A final chapter suggests possible excursions from New Orleans.

A map introduces each area of the city, highlighting the featured sites and locating other places of interest. Walks and drives, plotted on their own maps, suggest routes for discovering the most about an area. Features and sidebars offer intriguing detail on history, culture, or contemporary life.

The final section, Travelwise, lists essential information for the traveler—pre-trip planning, getting around, and emergencies—plus a selection of hotels and restaurants arranged by area, shops, and entertainment possibilities.

To the best of our knowledge, site information is accurate as of the press date. However, it's always advisable to call ahead whenever possible.

66

Color coding

Each area of the city is color coded for easy reference. Find the area you want on the map on the front flap, and look for the color flash at the top of the pages of the relevant chapter. Hotel and restaurant listings in **Travelwise** are also color coded to each area.

St. Louis Cathedral
www.stlouiscathedral.org
Map p. 51 (or Map 171 C2)
Chartres St. facing Jackson Sq.
504-525-9585
Daily services
Donation

Visitor information

Practical information is given in the side column next to each major site (see key to symbols on back flap). The map reference gives the page number where the site is shown on a map; in Chapters 6 & 7, grid coordinates are provided as well. Further details include the site's address, telephone number, days closed, entrance fee ranging from $ (under $5), $$ (between $5 and $10), and $$$ (over $10). Visitor information for smaller sites is listed in parentheses within the text.

TRAVELWISE

Hotel & restaurant prices

An explanation of the price ranges used in entries is given in the Hotels & Restaurants section beginning on p. 236.

AREA MAPS

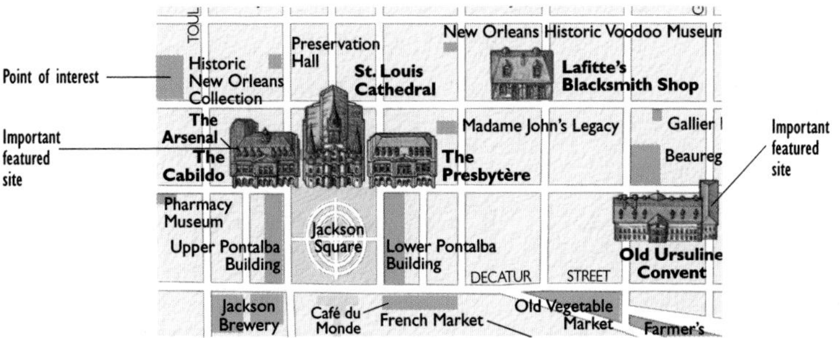

- A locator map accompanies each area map and shows the location of that area in the city.

WALKING TOURS

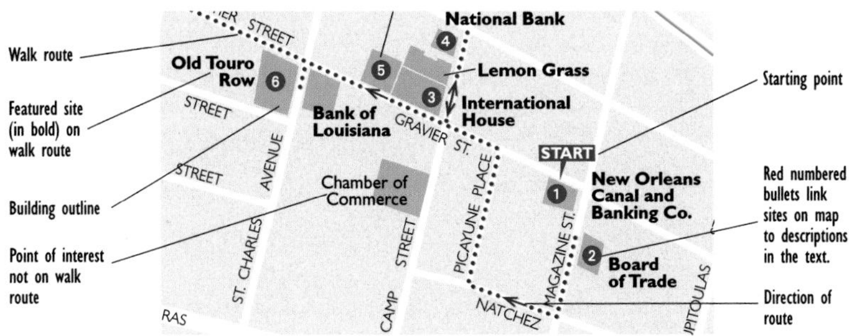

- An information box gives the starting and ending points, time and length of walk, and places not to miss along the route.

GREATER NEW ORLEANS & EXCURSION MAPS

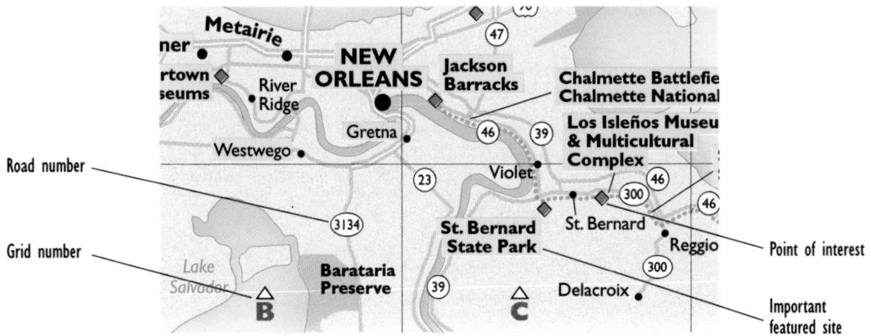

- Towns and cities described in the Greater New Orleans (p. 171) and the Excursions (pp. 206–207) chapters are highlighted in yellow on the map. Other suggested places to visit are also highlighted and are shown with a red diamond symbol.

NATIONAL GEOGRAPHIC

TRAVELER New Orleans

About the authors & photographers

Author Mark Miller is a Contributing Editor of *National Geographic Traveler* magazine. He earned a degree in American Social History from Stanford University and subsequently reported for Reuters and the CBS Radio network He has contributed to Society books and publications, including NATIONAL GEOGRAPHIC, since 1977, his assignments ranging across North America from Alaska to Florida, as well as to the Hawaiian Islands, the Caribbean, and Europe. He wrote the *National Geographic Traveler: Miami & the Keys.* A resident of Los Angeles, he is a partner of 12 Films, a documentary film production company.

Philip Gould is a documentary photographer who has made Louisiana his home and favorite subject for more than two decades. Based in Lafayette, he has photographed throughout the state, the South, the nation, and beyond. Gould has published numerous books about Louisiana and has also contributed to a variety of other publications, including *National Geographic Traveler* magazine. In 1996 he received the Louisiana Governor's Arts Award for Professional Arts of the Year.

Author and freelance travel journalist James Gaffney wrote the "New Orleans today" and the "Hotels & restaurants" sections. He currently resides in New Orleans with his wife, Cathy.

The "Food & drink," "Shopping," and "Entertainment & activities" sections, as well as the 2005 hotel and restaurant updates, are by Becky Retz. A native New Orleanian who grew up along the shores of Bayou St. John, she has related the charming quirkiness of her hometown in her writings, as a local tour guide, and as a stand-up comic.

History & Culture

Union ships fight their way to New Orleans in 1862.

New Orleans today

IT'S A SURE BET THIS MYSTERIOUS CREOLE CHILD OF THE MOONLIT swamp was born in the midnight hour. Little else can account for the city's jazzy, free-wheeling soul. New Orleans at once bewitches and befuddles outsiders accustomed to living their days and nights close to the mainstream.

A 300-year-old melting-pot heritage, sprung from early French, Spanish, West African, and Caribbean settlers, guarantees this is not your father's Southern city. "Let the good times roll" is more credo than motto for this sultry, near tropical town aptly dubbed the Big Easy—languorous and eccentric to a fault.

New Orleanians make no excuses when it comes to living life with gusto. Don a pair of rose-colored glasses and this rock-around-the-clock party town tucked on a crescent of the Mississippi River looks like a long-lost Huck Finn acquaintance. Merrymakers unfamiliar with the local turf are both stunned and

jubilant to discover the city's abstinence-challenged culture has spawned drive-through daiquiri shops, bars open 24-7, and plastic "go-cups" for patrons wishing to take their high spirits onward.

Meantime, the mere mention of food triggers a Pavlovian response among locals. With little prodding, they'll launch into a sweeping discourse about the hottest new culinary kid on the block or rave about a recently savored soft-shell crab meunière or an oyster-stuffed roasted quail. Slip a spoon into New Orleans's spicy gumbo for a taste of a multiethnic cooking tradition that has been refined to perfection by chefs ranked among the finest on the planet. Simply put, with more than 1,200 restaurants and 650 bars, only the determined ever go to bed hungry—or thirsty.

Downtown New Orleans with Harrah's casino in the foreground

Homespun quirkiness branded with tradition has long set the city apart from the rest of the country. The Monday staple of red beans and rice, for example, dates from an era when homemakers worked the backyard clothesline on wash day while pots of slow-cooking red beans simmered on the kitchen stove. And helping to cool sweltering brows during the summertime, family-owned sno-ball stands—every local has a favorite—serve the shaved-ice-and-simple-syrup treat, customarily crowned with a coat of velvety condensed milk.

At Christmastime, families flock to the Fairmont Hotel, where a phalanx of Bethlehem mangers, towering fir trees, and real gingerbread houses decorate the block-long lobby. Nostalgia takes the shape of a snowman named Mr. Bingle, an ice-cream-cone-hatted character created by a now-defunct department store to hawk toys. For sheer extravagance, little can compare with "Celebration in the Oaks," when more than a million twinkling lights, fanciful ornaments, and mirrored objets d'art adorn City Park's centuries-old oak trees.

Colorful colloquialisms add spice to a "Nawlins" accent that is typically far more reminiscent of Brooklynese than anything so predictable as a Southern drawl. In some circles, "How are you?" has been transformed into "Where y'at?" Terms of agreement include "Yeah, you right." And "gone by my mama's" probably means you're heading off to the folks' house Sunday for a pot roast dinner. Median strips are called neutral grounds, the weekly supermarket ritual is "making groceries," and where you went to high school is more important than "Watcha' daddy do?"

Even when it's not hurricane season, this flood-prone town tucked below sea level and surrounded by water can be a precarious place to live. The solution is simply to embrace the sensual pleasures of life with joyful abandon, whether it's impromptu second-line dancing, fried shrimp po-boys, or the revelry of Mardi

Gras when, among other antics, dog lovers take to the streets with their satirically costumed canines for the Krewe of Barkus parade.

Serendipity and contradiction have long been joined in New Orleans. Today this former French colony moves to its own rhythm against a backdrop of wild nightlife and Catholic worship, of potholed streets and manicured gardens blooming with night jasmine, of thriving blue bloods and a striving underclass, of poorly funded public schools and grown-ups who spend thousands of dollars to throw beads from Carnival floats.

Joyful decadence tells only part of the story though. The multicultural population added immigrants from Ireland, Germany, and Italy in the 1800s, and, during the last half of the 20th century, from Latin America and Vietnam. The economy is fueled largely by oil and gas, health care, higher education, and a flourishing

convention and tourism industry. Recently, the city has seen the opening of the Ogden Museum of Southern Art, Louisiana Artworks, the National D-Day Museum, the 300,000-square-foot phase III addition to the Ernest N. Morial Convention Center, Six Flags New Orleans, Harrah's Casino, the 18,500-seat New Orleans Arena for NBA basketball, and Zephyr Field for AAA baseball.

Yet progress for all its promise has always

Couples dance to Cajun music at New Orleans's annual Jazz & Heritage Festival.

seemed to run a poor second to the simple pleasures of life. Hop aboard a green streetcar for a ride along St. Charles Avenue, passing stately columned homes as well as Tulane and Loyola Universities. Arm yourself with a bag of popcorn and an antique walking cane from M.S. Rau on Royal Street and go feed the

ducks near the lagoon in City Park; afterward, stroll through the newly opened Sculpture Garden. Or take the Canal Street Ferry to Algiers Point. Gaze across Old Man River. Feel the tug yet? People may leave their hearts in San Francisco, but souls belong to New Orleans.

Earthly delights in the birthplace of jazz—America's only truly original art form, historians believe—include Preservation Hall, the no-frills traditional-jazz palace. Step inside to hear the rollicking sound born in New Orleans's bars and bordellos in the wee hours of the 20th century—still the rhythmic pulse of the city that gave the world Louis Armstrong and Jelly Roll Morton.

On a blissfully cloudless and breezy day the French Quarter is a captivating journey of the senses through paradise found. As you stroll centuries-old streets, the ghosts of Creole gentry quietly observe from wrought-

Visitors and locals alike find favorite treats at the lively French Market.

iron balconies. The jingle-jangle of street musicians fill air redolent with the seductive aromas of seafood joints and old-guard dining dens. If you prefer not to linger, grab a frank from a corner Lucky Dog vendor and head over to Jackson Square to see St. Louis Cathedral, one of the country's most beautiful houses of worship.

Try passing a stormy night in the French Quarter, on a mahogany four-poster bed, the past echoing in the hypnotic rain dance on lace-curtained French doors. As Blanche DuBois in Tennessee Williams's *A Streetcar Named Desire* observed, "Don't you just love these long rainy afternoons in New Orleans when an hour isn't just an hour—but a little piece of eternity dropped into your hands…?" ■

Food & drink

IN A CITY THAT STILL BOWS TO AN ENTRENCHED CLASS SYSTEM, NOTHING draws people of all backgrounds together like a spicy seafood gumbo or a hot roast beef po-boy sandwich, dripping gravy and oozing mayonnaise. This is a town where lunch conversation is much less likely to be about current events or lofty ideas than it is to be about dinner. And whether that dinner is served in an antebellum mansion in the Garden District or a cozy shotgun house in Mid-City, if it's Monday, there's a good chance creamy red beans and rice will be on the table.

Ask transplants to the area how they ended up in New Orleans, and the response will likely sound something like this: "I came here for a vacation, started eating, and just never went back home."

Anecdotal evidence of the lure of Crescent City cuisine can be seen everywhere; visitors would be hard pressed to miss the city's girth. From the porky politicians to the heavyset housewives, New Orleans is a fat town. In fact, a national study a few years ago found the Big Easy to be the fattest city in America. No surprise here. Locals could be heard laughing about it in restaurants all over town.

In the beginning, food brought the city's population together out of necessity. The earliest European settlers, the French, had a natural flair for cooking, but no knowledge of how to use the indigenous foodstuffs found in this new world. To learn the secrets of the strange ingredients, they eventually turned to the Native Americans (among them the Choctaw and the Houma).

Chief among the newfound foodstuffs were corn—ground into cornmeal and made into corn bread—and filé (pronounced fee-LAY), a fine powder made from ground sassafras leaves and used by the Indians for both culinary and medicinal purposes.

Filé became an essential ingredient in the development of gumbo, one of Creole cooking's mainstays. To create the gastronomic wonder that is Creole cooking, however, took more than the efforts of just the French and Indians. Along the way, the Spanish, Germans, Italians, and, more important, the city's enslaved Africans added their own touches, employing the wide variety of local produce as well as the shrimp, crabs, oysters, and crawfish pulled from the surrounding waters.

To the rich sauces of the French and the Indians' expertise with local ingredients, the Spanish added spice in the peppers they brought from Latin America. They also introduced paella, the rice and meat dish that provided the early inspiration for jambalaya.

The Africans introduced a new vegetable to the region in their native okra. Additionally, black New Orleanians have played a major role in developing the splendid and savory dishes for which the city is famous.

The arrival of the Germans in the mid-1700s also marked the arrival of fine sausage-making, as well as the region's first steady supply of milk and butter from German cows. Following the 1803 Louisiana Purchase, Italian immigrants made their contribution in the form of tomato sauces and the muffuletta sandwich. As Chef John Folse has written in *The Evolution of Cajun & Creole Cuisine,* "Creole cuisine is indebted to many unique people and diverse cultures who were willing to contribute and share their cooking styles, ingredients and talent."

The cuisine of the Cajuns (or Acadians), on the other hand, the Creoles' country cousins, though served in abundance throughout the city, is not a product of New Orleans. The Cajuns, who were also of French heritage, made their way to Louisiana after the British expelled them from Nova Scotia in 1755. These farmers and fishermen settled in the southern portion of the state's bayou country, a region that became known as Acadiana.

The Cajuns developed a style of cooking that reflected their environment. Generally, the food is more robust and less sophisticated than traditional Creole cuisine, satisfying diners' taste buds with hearty versions of

Enticing bait attracts customers to a Creole restaurant in the French Quarter.

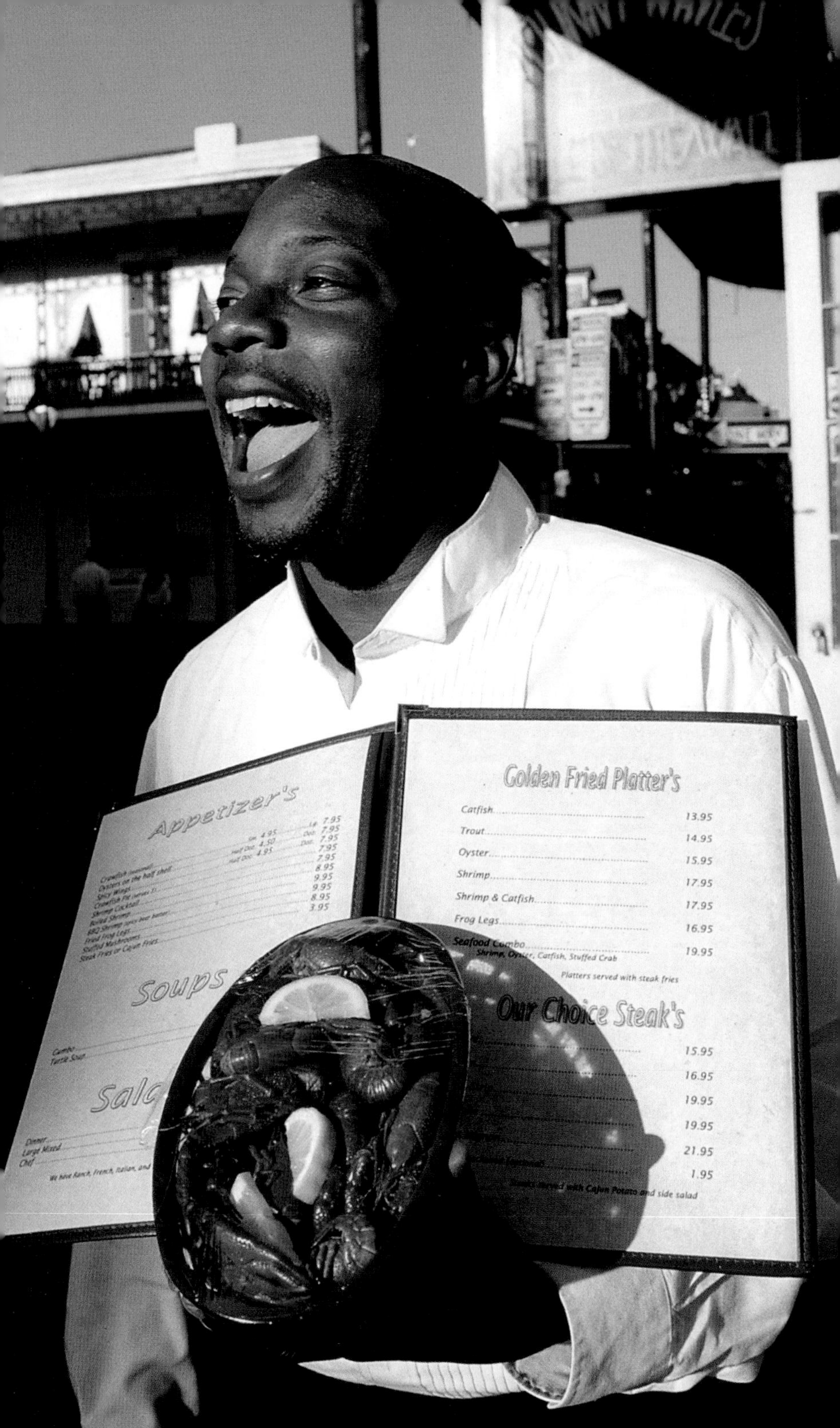

Appetizer's
Soups
Golden Fried Platter's
Catfish 13.95
Trout 14.95
Oyster 15.95
Shrimp 17.95
Shrimp & Catfish 17.95
Frog Legs 16.95
Seafood Combo 19.95
Shrimp, Oyster, Catfish, Stuffed Crab
Platters served with steak fries
Our Choice Steak's
15.95
16.95
19.95
19.95
21.95
1.95
Steaks served with Cajun Potato and side salad

Famed for French-Creole fare, Galatoire's has changed little since 1905.

jambalaya or grillades and grits. Spices and peppers are amply used, ingredients that have come to represent the Cajuns' zest for life. Its simple "one pot" dishes, such as andouille gumbo, are often characterized by the use of sausages, chicken, duck, pork, wild game, seafood, or wild greens. Unlike Creole cooking, Folse writes in his book, "no attempt was made to re-create the classical cuisine of Europe. None of the exotic spices and ingredients available to the Creoles were to be found by the Cajuns in bayou country. They were happy to live off the land, a land abundant with fish, shellfish and wild game."

Over the years, Creole and Cajun foods have been served side by side, and today diners often find it difficult to tell one from the other. In fact, Chef Paul Prudhomme, famed for his K-Paul's Louisiana Kitchen restaurant, his cookbooks, and his own line of spices, says that for all practical purposes Creole and Cajun have blended to become a new hybrid he calls "Louisiana food."

Rice is a mainstay of both cuisines. Creole and Cajun chefs typically begin one of their culinary treats by making a roux of flour and oil. (A roux acts as a thickening agent and also provides flavoring, usually a nutty one.) From there, things can get quite interesting. Gumbo, for instance, can be created from hundreds of recipes, and the prevailing attitude is that all of them have their virtues.

The recipes for some of the most popular dishes in the city's most popular restaurants have never been written down; most of the chefs carry on an oral tradition, letting their protégés learn by doing. Here, innovation is constant. For example, the "blackening" of chicken, fish, and meat—popularized by Chef Prudhomme—is a relatively recent practice. By cataloging the various cuisines and providing instruction in them, the Culinary Institute of New Orleans is preserving an important part of this region's unique cultural heritage.

Diners today find more variety than ever before. While traditionalists enjoy Antoine's soufflé potatoes, served much the same as they were when Antoine Alciatore opened his famous restaurant in 1840, blocks away Chef Susan Spicer is redefining New Orleans cuisine at her Bayona restaurant with such dishes as grilled shrimp and black bean cakes with coriander sauce. Either way, no visitor should miss a chance to experience one of the city's highest art forms. ■

Lexicon of culinary terms

ANDOUILLE (ahn-DOO-ee) — A spicy pork sausage, andouille often accompanies red beans and rice, jambalaya, and many other local dishes.

BEIGNET (bin-YAY) — Sprinkled with powdered sugar, this doughnut is square in shape and has no hole. The Café du Monde is famous for such treats.

BOUDIN (BOO-dan) — Cooked rice, herbs, spices, and onions are added to ground pork; this hot, spicy mixture is then stuffed into a sausage casing.

CAFÉ AU LAIT — Dark-roasted New Orleans-style chickory coffee and hot milk traditionally mixed in equal measures.

CAFÉ BRÛLOT (caf-AY broo-loh) — Ordered after dinner, it is hot coffee blended with liqueurs, spices, and orange peel in a chafing dish, then ignited.

CHICORY (CHICK-ory) — A common flavoring in New Orleans coffee, chicory comes from an herb root that is dried, ground, and roasted.

COURT BOUILLON (coo-BOO-yon) — This rich and spicy stew or soup contains fish fillets (usually redfish), lemon slices, a bay leaf, tomatoes, onions, and perhaps other vegetables as well.

DRESSED — It is a term used to describe sandwiches. If you order a sandwich "dressed," it will come with lettuce, tomatoes, and just about everything else.

ÉTOUFFÉE (ay-too-FAY) — This tomato-based sauce is frequently used to prepare such Crescent City favorites as shrimp étouffée and crawfish étouffée.

FILÉ (fee-LAY) — Made from ground sassafras leaves, filé is a traditional seasoning and thickening agent for gumbo.

GRILLADES (GREE-yads) — Squares of broiled veal or beef are stewed in a zesty tomato sauce and usually served with grits.

GRITS — Coarsely ground hominy, this dish is similar in appearance to mashed potatoes, but its taste more closely resembles corn.

Red beans and barbecued ribs at Jazz Fest

JAMBALAYA (jum-buh-LIE-yah) — Lavishly seasoned, this eclectic mixture is prepared from whatever happens to be on hand in the kitchen. In New Orleans such things are usually cooked rice, tomatoes, shrimp, chicken, ham, onions, and celery.

MUFFULETTA (muff-uh-LET-uh) — A phonebook-thick sandwich, a muffuletta is a hearty helping of Italian meats, cheeses, olive salad, and Italian bread.

PO-BOY — Called a poorboy in other parts of the country, this regional variation is a sandwich whose name mimics the New Orleans accent; typically, it is filled with something fried and served between slices of French bread.

PRALINE (PRAH-leen) — A candy in the shape of a patty, this sticky confection is made from pecans, butter, sugar, and water. You'll find pralines sold virtually everywhere in New Orleans.

RED BEANS & RICE — Kidney beans are boldly spiced, seasoned, and mixed with pickled pork; veal or smoked sausage usually accompanies this popular dish. ■

History

ON THE EVE OF THE EUROPEANS' ARRIVAL IN NORTH AMERICA, SOUTHEASTERN Louisiana had a diverse population, ranging from small hunting clans to large agrarian societies like the Choctaw, the Mississippi Valley's most successful farmers. Among the many native groups who made their homes in this region were the Natchez, Atakapa, Opelousa, Caddo, Tunica, Yazoo, Houma, Okelousa, Chitimacha, Washa, and Chawasha. Most maintained extensive cultural and economic ties with other groups, some of whom may have lived as far away as Central America or the Caribbean.

Robert Cavelier, Sieur de La Salle, claimed the Mississippi watershed for France in 1682.

ANTIQUITY

Within early Louisiana's native groups, families probably organized their daily activities according to clearly defined roles. Men governed, defended, hunted, fished, and built shelters—palmetto-thatched and beehive-shaped grass huts, wood-frame and wattle-and-daub houses—and also canoes and tools. Women cared for the young and the elderly, farmed, made clothing and utensils, prepared food (usually boiled, roasted, or parched), and decorated their homes and religious places. Hunting of deer, bears, bison, and a multitude of smaller game animals provided not only protein but also clothing of leather and fur decorated with feathers, freshwater pearls, and carved bone amulets.

Religious rituals varied, but most native peoples sought a harmony with nature and the world. The Natchez, Acolapissa, Caddo, Houma, Taensa, and Tunica constructed sacred buildings, some raised on truncated pyramidal earth mounds that were similar to Mesoamerican temples. There they honored their dead with celebrations of dance, song, and food that reminded some early French

Above: Jean Baptiste Le Moyne, city founder
Opposite: John Law, Scottish financier

explorers of All Saints' Day. Family members also gathered at burial grounds to weep over boxes containing ancestors' bones; then they held feasts of remembrance. Many groups observed an early November holiday called the feast of souls, during which they venerated their departed relatives.

People wore ornaments such as necklaces, bracelets, armbands, rings, and ear and nose plugs made of shells, pearls, and copper traded from distant tribes. They competed in games and sports. They made music, and they sang and danced for entertainment and for religious ceremony, sometimes performing individually, at times in pairs and groups. In most respects, their lives were peaceful and comfortable, and their initial reaction to newcomers usually was one of accommodation. Yet most of them survive today only as place-names on road maps. Over time, populations were decimated by European diseases and by eventual wars of resistance to settlement by the newcomers.

FIRST SIGHTINGS

In 1682 the French explorer Robert Cavelier, whose title was Sieur de La Salle, voyaged down the Mississippi to the Gulf of Mexico and claimed the river's entire watershed for his country and its king, Louis XIV. Though the assertion was presumptuous, France was Europe's most powerful nation at that time, and the attitude in its royal circles was that a French presence in this part of North America was essential—given the Spanish colonial presence to the south and west, and the English and Dutch beachhead on the East Coast.

In 1698 an expedition of several small ships led by two French-Canadian brothers, 38-year-old Pierre Le Moyne, Sieur d'Iberville, and 19-year-old Jean Baptiste Le Moyne, Sieur de Bienville, was sent by King Louis XIV to establish a colony on the Mississippi River Delta. The brothers encamped on Ship Island (today part of the Gulf Islands National Seashore) and then crossed to the mainland, where they stopped briefly at what is now Ocean Springs, Mississippi. On the second day of March 1699, they sailed up the stream from the Gulf, the first Europeans to enter the river from the sea. The following day—Fat Tuesday, the last day before Lent—the older brother ordered his party to the west bank some 60 miles below what would become New Orleans, near the present-day hamlet of Venice. In honor of the holiday he named the campsite Pointe du Mardi Gras and a nearby waterway Bayou Mardi Gras.

As the explorers voyaged upriver, their Choctaw guides showed them a portage trail across the narrows between the river and Lake Pontchartrain, land associated with the Chickasaw Indians. The footpath started where New Orleans's French Market is today, and it ran north through tall, coarse grasses and over cypress swampland to Bayou St. John, a stream flowing some 4 miles north into the lake. (Part of the trail's route is traced today by Bayou Road, which runs diagonally south toward the river, conspicuously at variance with the French surveyors' subsequent grid of streets.) The portage site impressed Jean Baptiste Le Moyne, who pronounced it ideal for a city, situated as it was on a beautiful bend or "crescent" of the river—the origin of New Orleans's nickname Crescent City.

SETTLEMENT OF NEW ORLEANS

French officials wanted settlers to farm, but most of the ones who came first spent their time searching for gold and silver, and pearl fisheries. By 1712 there were barely 380 colonists, and in messages they sent to France most complained bitterly about the dearth of support. But Paris ignored them; the French treasury was nearly bankrupt, and so was the royal Bourbon dynasty, which had spent the country's gold in military adventures and colonial schemes. Fed up with the Louisianians' fortune-hunting and expense—the colony was deep in the red—the French ministry ignored them.

Spotting an opportunity, Scottish financier John Law came to Paris with a scheme to create a development bank funded by investors who were lured by the claim that Louisiana was full of riches. Law convinced the French to grant his Company of the West a monopoly on trade and government in Louisiana. His business was in fact a pyramid scheme to sell investors land, paying "dividends" with money invested by new buyers. Law, however, was a friend of Philippe II, duc d'Orléans, regent of France—the political mind behind the child-king Louis XV, who was not yet old enough to rule. In 1718 Law instructed Jean Baptiste Le Moyne (whose brother had died of yellow fever in Cuba) to build at the head of the trail to Lake Pontchartrain. The colony was christened La Nouvelle Orléans for his patron.

The settlers cleared land while complaining about the absence of women. To stop the grumbling, prostitutes and other female inmates were taken from Parisian jails and shipped to the colony. It was a dreary destination; the town was a dismal collection of wooden shacks. Meanwhile, Law's scheme collapsed. The French government took over the colony and put Jean Baptiste Le Moyne in charge of it. A more enlightened program sent "Casket Girls" from Paris, each selected for housewifely skills and given a small case—cassette—of things she needed to start her new life. Also sent were the Ursuline Sisters, who arrived in 1727 to found a convent.

By the 1730s the city was shipping meat, hides, bricks, and lumber to the Caribbean and sending sugar and rum to France. But growing hostilities with the Chickasaw, who viewed the Europeans' agrarian and mercantile ambitions as a threat to their ancient world, led to war. The French eventually put down the resistance in 1740, but the fighting discouraged Le Moyne, who resigned as governor and retired in 1743. The colony continued to grow: A 1761 census counted some 3,000, including African-American slaves and free people of color.

SPANISH ERA

In 1762, anticipating defeat in the Seven Years' War (1756–1763)—a conflict pitting Britain and Prussia against Austria, France, Russia, Saxony, Sweden, and Spain—Louis XV persuaded his Spanish cousin Carlos III to let him cede much of Louisiana to Spain. The deal, called the Treaty of Fontainebleau, was a ploy; Louis correctly surmised that victorious Britain would demand the French territory in North America in exchange for peace. When Britain did make the demand, Louis revealed he had previously ceded Louisiana to Spain—an ally still too strong to be bullied by London.

To spur Louisiana's growth, France offered trousseau chests and passage to marriageable women.

The new Spanish governor, Antonio de Ulloa, arrived in New Orleans with some 90 soldiers, but he got such a hostile reception from the French Creoles that he eventually fled to Havana and governed from there for most of the next 30 months. He rankled locals by instituting strict commercial regulations—New Orleans was a circus of corrupt business practices—and by replacing Creole officials with Spaniards. In 1768, the colonists revolted. In response, Spain sent 24 ships and some 2,600 troops under the command of a tough Irish-born Spanish subject named Alexander O'Reilly, who crushed the rebellion. Several of the ringleaders were shot, and others were imprisoned or exiled. Ironically, the stern Spanish administration that followed brought order to the poorly run colony and ushered in a prosperous and peaceful period.

The outbreak of the Revolutionary War in the 13 Colonies in 1775, and their Declaration of Independence from the British the next year, had little affect on New Orleans short of drawing away skilled laborers. The city faced many problems—hurricanes, floods, levee breaks, slave revolts—but all paled beside a devastating fire that broke out on a windy Good Friday, 1788, when an altar candle in a private chapel fell, igniting draperies. When it was over, some 856 buildings out of 1,100 were ashes, and the French provincial look of the original city was gone. The city built in its place was, architecturally speaking, Spanish. Another fire in 1794 claimed about 200 buildings and brought even stricter building codes; wood was replaced with adobe and shingled roofs with tile, giving the city an even more Mediterranean face. Although Spanish administration proved beneficial to New Orleans—it wisely focused primarily on business, commerce, law enforcement, and maintenance while leaving Creole French institutions alone—behind its new Iberian facade the city remained essentially French.

LOUISIANA PURCHASE

The twilight of the Spanish era commenced with Napoleon Bonaparte's rise to power in France. Envisioning a New World empire to match his European one, he pressured Spain

An 18th-century slave auction unfolds in the rotunda of the opulent St. Louis Exchange Hotel.

into returning Louisiana to France in October 1800, via the Treaty of San Ildefonso. By April 1803, however, his thinking had changed. He no longer believed that the colony could be administered from abroad, but he did not want the British to have an opportunity to try to do so. President Thomas Jefferson and James Monroe, a former minister to France, also feared British adventures in the West. Napoleon, who believed France and Britain were destined to fight, was very concerned about his inability to finance a war.

The offer to sell came during a dinner party for Monroe, upon his mid-April arrival in Paris. Two weeks of negotiation produced a deal, even though Monroe did not have the authority to guarantee it. Because the age of sail made immediate consultation with Washington impossible, Monroe gambled on his belief that the arrangement—$15,000,000 for a tract extending from the Gulf of Mexico to Canada and west to the Rockies—would win approval at home. Some New England congressmen tried to kill the deal, correctly pointing out that the U.S. Treasury didn't have $15,000,000, but Jefferson cajoled enough votes anyway.

Before Napoleon's rise, most New Orleanians would have been delighted to become part of a French colony again. Of some 8,000 people who lived in Greater New Orleans, about half were Creoles of French descent, and barely a quarter were Spanish, most of them officials and their families. But with Napoleon's ascent had come anti-Catholic regulations that worried the mostly Catholic colonials. They feared repression, ironically, from a return to administration by the French. The city, after all, had done well under Spanish rule. It now had sawmills, distilleries, cordage factories, cotton mills, sugar refineries, a small rice mill, and hundreds of new fire-resistant buildings. Expanding waterfront commerce employed an army of stevedores, dockworkers, and drayers. New Orleans was practically booming.

The lowering of the Tricolor and raising of the Stars and Stripes was uneventful. At that time, only a few Americans were in the city, and most of them were river men. William C.

Claiborne, Governor of the Mississippi Territory, became governor of the Territory of Orleans in 1805.

WAR OF 1812

In 1805 the City of New Orleans was formally incorporated, and a census counted 8,212 residents—3,551 Caucasians, 1,556 free people of color, and 3,105 slaves. Each year, more and more ships were tying up to posts and wharves along the levee, where hordes of longshoremen carried sacks of grain, barrels, and crates up and down gangways. At the new waterfront meat market a 12½-cent coin known as an *escalius* could buy a pound of Indian-raised beef. Workmen lunched on hot rice cakes and *pain patate,* a cold sweet potato pie. Ever increasing federal custom revenues from river commerce were not lost on the U.S. Congress, which admitted Louisiana into the Union on April 30, 1812. It was a heady milestone, but militarily Louisiana's river delta country was a back door left open, and the nation was once again at war.

Seven weeks earlier, the United States had invaded Canada over a variety of grievances including a British trade war that was throttling American commerce. The British were still occupying American territory in the Great Lakes region, supplying Indians with weapons to fight settlers, and occasionally impressing Yankee merchant mariners into the British Navy by snatching them from U.S. ships at sea. For the next two years the war went badly for American forces. In the summer of 1814 Washington, D.C., was sacked and the White House torched. By the end of 1814, however, both sides were stalemated and weary of war. The United States and Great Britain ended the conflict by signing the Treaty of Ghent in Belgium on the day before Christmas.

But an invasion force of some 10,000 crack British troops, unaware of the treaty activities, was marching toward New Orleans from downriver. Augmenting his regular U.S. soldiers with volunteers from every walk of

Chalmette Battlefield national historic site

life, including the outlaws of pirate Jean Lafitte, Maj. Gen. Andrew Jackson (also unaware of the peace) chose to make his stand at Chalmette Plantation, on a narrow neck of land between the Mississippi and a boggy cypress swamp about 9 miles downriver from the city. A brilliant decision, it left the British no option but a frontal assault into Jackson's Pennsylvania long rifles, accurate to distances far beyond the range of British muskets, and a shredding hail of cannon-fired grapeshot.

On the morning of January 8, 1815, the American force of some 4,000 men decimated the attacking British troops. The British had advanced en masse through sheer force of will and discipline, an Old World tactic that was tragically outdated and symbolized the differences between the two nations.

The Battle of New Orleans, an unnecessary last clash in the last war between Britain and the United States, ushered in a new era of American confidence, further reinforcing the image of the United States as a nation able and willing to defend its territory.

ANTEBELLUM ERA

The War of 1812 was a passage for the United States and New Orleans. Both entered a period of prosperity fueled by America's abundant resources and a mercantile zeitgeist bordering on secular religion. Despite floods and an ever shifting channel, the Mississippi was the main commercial highway of the interior, and New Orleans was its portal to world markets. Beset with mosquitoes and epidemics—yellow fever killed some 8,000 in 1853—and coping with levee breaks, hurricanes, and sweltering summers with oppressive humidity, it was, as one observer sagely noted, an inevitable city in an impossible place.

The advent of the steamboat turned the Mississippi into a two-way street; goods could be shipped upriver with relative ease. Ships also went to Europe, unloaded cargo, and returned crowded with immigrants; between 1812 and the outbreak of the Civil War about 500,000 newcomers, mostly Irish and French, passed through en route to new lives as upriver farmers. Anglo-Americans arrived in droves, attracted by the city's phenomenal growth. By 1820 New Orleans's population surpassed 40,000—five times what it had been at the time of the Louisiana Purchase. By 1840 it was over 80,000.

Better educated than the previous century's roughshod river men, the influx of Americans included commodities brokers, commercial agents, shippers, attorneys, physicians, warehouse builders, and entrepreneurs. Many of them lived in an ambitious English-speaking enclave upriver from the French Quarter. Few spoke French, however, and despite a general civility the Americans and the Creoles had little in common. The French speakers felt invaded, considering their culture to be antithetical to Anglo-American ways.

Creole attempts to monopolize the city government thwarted Yankee progress, but the era of Creole dominance was ending. In 1836 the American community forced the city to split into three gerrymandered municipalities: one French, one American, and the third with too many nationalities to be dominated by any one. In 1852 they reunited, but by then the balance of power had moved upriver from the Quarter, across Canal Street to the new American-dominated Central Business District.

Meanwhile prosperity brought stone-paved streets, the St. Charles streetcar line, railroads, coal-gas street lamps, and ornate, luxurious hotels and theaters. By 1860 New Orleans was not only the cotton capital of the world but also the wealthiest city, per capita, in America. Commercially tied to exchanges in New York and London, it watched with mixed emotions as the Southern states drifted toward secession; New Orleans had little to gain from war, and its great river road to the Gulf left it exposed to invasion by sea.

CIVIL WAR & RECONSTRUCTION

On January 26, 1861, the Louisiana State Legislature voted to secede from the Union, leaving many New Orleanians confused and anxious about where their interests lay. The city's commercial elite stood to lose the most if trade was interrupted or complicated by new international regulations. A serious threat to old ways was the Union's push to abolish slavery and provide free public education and voting rights to all. So ingrained was slavery as a load-bearing column of the Southern economy that even the 750 or so free people of color who owned some of New Orleans's 12,000 slaves were ambivalent. It all became moot on April 12, 1861, when a Louisiana regiment commanded by Pierre Gustave Toutant Beauregard, a New Orleans-bred Creole and Confederate general, fired on the Union's Fort Sumter in Charleston Harbor, sparking the bloodiest war in U.S. history.

Within six weeks Union ships blockaded the mouth of the Mississippi River, cutting off shipping and depriving the city of basics like flour. By the spring of 1862 New Orleans was hungry and guessing when Federal forces

1880s New Orleans, shown depicted in an engraving, prospered from cotton and shipping.

would attack. Forts Jackson and St. Philip flanked the river downstream, but the U.S. Navy sent a flotilla under the command of David Farragut, a calculating strategist who employed stealth and daring to move nearly all of his ships and sailors past the Confederate outposts with relatively few losses. He linked up with ground forces in the city on May 1, 1862, and New Orleans fell quickly, the only real violence resulting from widespread panic that devolved into a looting rampage.

The Union grip on New Orleans and the river's mouth hobbled the Confederacy, splitting it in two and depriving the Rebels of their main southern port. Benjamin Butler, a dour Army general from Massachusetts, was put in charge of the occupation force—a martial law situation that would outlive the war itself by 12 years, ending in 1877. It was a peculiar limbo for the once flourishing city, which was used to governing itself. Offended by the contempt and surliness of the locals, Butler imposed draconian measures, including the confiscation of personal property from those who did not swear allegiance to the Union. His troops, as some soldiers are wont to do, did not endear themselves to the city's Creole women, who did everything they could to insult the Northerners.

"Reconstruction," a bad joke to most New Orleanians, ended with the city in economic doldrums. Most blamed Union occupation, but the real cause was historical; the steamboat era had passed, leaving New Orleans without rail links to domestic markets. America's commercial mainstream, like the fickle Mississippi, had changed its course.

GILDED AGE

The Gilded Age, a satirical novel published in 1873 by Mark Twain and Charles Dudley Warner, gave America's post-Civil War period its ironic name. For most working people in smokestack cities, this was not a golden time at all; instead, it was a difficult era of rapid industrialization characterized by the ruthless pursuit of profit and the exploitation of workers. The industries that Twain and Warner decried bypassed New Orleans, however, while expanded railroads and the Erie Canal cut into the Mississippi Valley commerce that the city had depended upon for a living.

New Orleans languished until the 1880s, when growing international trade, followed by direct rail links to domestic markets, once again made the city a strategic commercial hub. Southern Louisiana's cotton and sugar producers achieved record yields, and in the Central Business District brick warehouses and commercial buildings sprang up to store goods and house banks, brokerages, machine shops, barrel makers, ironworks, and other trades linked to local enterprises. Hoping to attract major industries, in 1884–85 the city hosted what it billed as the World's Industrial and Cotton Centennial Exposition. The idea was good but poorly executed. The Exposition opened late and unfinished, received only a quarter of the visitors boosters had predicted, closed early with a half-million-dollar debt, and lured no new commerce. What it did do, however, was introduce New Orleans to those who did attend. Thousands went home with unanticipated memories of a surprisingly exotic city with fine hotels, extraordinary restaurants, top-talent theaters, elegant houses, impressive commercial buildings, beautiful boulevards, and genuine European refinement. The seeds of the tourism that would have a worldwide constituency of admirers and create an entirely new economy had been planted.

An offshoot of early tourism was a thriving trade in flesh. Councilman Sidney Story got an ordinance passed that restricted prostitution

W. A. Walker painted this 1883 panorama of New Orleans's riverside commerce.

to a red-light district just lakeside of the Quarter, a neighborhood that to his chagrin was dubbed Storyville. It lasted only two decades—the U.S. Navy threatened to leave unless Storyville was shut down—but in those 20 years the tradition of hiring piano players to entertain brothel patrons greenhoused a new style of improvisational music. Nurtured in the neighborhoods and streets of New Orleans, this new music traveled under the city's name until a disapproving Chicago critic dredged up "jass," an archaic English word meaning "to chase" but used colloquially to imply a promiscuous nature. We now know this unique form of music as "jazz."

JAZZ AGE

American short-story writer and novelist F. Scott Fitzgerald coined the phrase that would characterize the Roaring Twenties: the jazz age. In New Orleans, however, that age actually commenced just before the turn of the century. Among its musician progenitors was Ferdinand Joseph La Menthe Morton, a piano-playing Creole of color who was known by his nickname, Jelly Roll. His practice of transcribing what he played led jazz historians to anoint him as the world's first significant jazz composer. Like some of his compatriots, Jelly Roll Morton had logged many hours at the keyboard in Storyville, and like them he would make New Orleans synonymous with American musical innovation.

The moody music reflected the city's bittersweet entry into the 20th century. Although the maritime industry experienced an economic boom during World War I, New Orleans's waterfront prosperity did not reach far beyond the levees. The French Quarter declined into a slum, its once elegant Creole town houses now crowded with struggling immigrant Italian families. The Quarter was so poor, in fact, that the fine old ironwork decorating its galleries was sold to raise extra money. And if the economic malaise was not discouraging enough, just after the Armistice in Europe an influenza epidemic ravaged the population, killing some 35,000 people in the city alone.

By the 1920s New Orleans was known as a place where artists, musicians, writers, and other creative types could live inexpensively, dine excellently, and be entertained by locals such as the young jazz trumpeter Louis Armstrong. For would-be bohemians who did not have enough money to pay for a transatlantic passage, the city was a good alternative to Paris's Left Bank.

In January 1922, the writer Sherwood Anderson took an apartment in the French Quarter and declared that New Orleans ought to be the winter home of every serious American artist. Soon the young William Faulkner was a sojourner, penning his first novel in a garret off Jackson Square and throwing parties featuring bootleg gin. A bohemian attitude helped; despite a new pump-powered drainage system that worked so well the Dutch adopted it, the city was frequently shut down by flooding caused by the region's torrential rains or the Mississippi River's colossal surges.

Not surprisingly, Louisianians appreciated a politician who could keep the levees intact and the streets dry. In 1928 they elected a Democratic governor who promised that and a whole lot more. His name was Huey P. Long, an attorney whose "share the wealth" oratory was seductive to many, particularly after the Depression left millions with so little.

Louis Armstrong and his band played at New Orleans's Suburban Gardens nightclub in 1931.

THE BIG CHANGE

Governor Huey Long, Jr., roared into the 1930s, promising Louisianians concrete highways, free bridges, and many other things. He funded a medical school at Louisiana State University in New Orleans, allegedly rejecting nearby Tulane in retaliation for its refusal to award him an honorary degree. Personality politics ruled, replacing the Creole cronyism of the previous century with the political machine of the Long organization.

In 1932, New Orleans's renown as a source of new music spread overseas when trumpeter Louis Armstrong made his first European tour. In London, admiring critic Percy Brooks wrote down the young musician's moniker—"Satchelmouth"—the way that his sidemen pronounced it, thus codifying Armstrong's trademark as "Satchmo."

On January 1, 1935, Tulane University defeated Temple University by a score of 20 to 14 in the first Sugar Bowl game, and in 1938 the new Huey P. Long Bridge spanned the Mississippi River 9 miles above the city, replacing time-consuming train ferries and winning back much of the commerce that had fled New Orleans decades earlier when railroads replaced steamboats. Thomas Lanier Williams, a 27-year-old playwright from St. Louis, arrived by bus in 1938 and moved into a French Quarter boardinghouse on Toulouse Street, hoping to find work with the Federal Writers' Project. He didn't, but he stayed anyway, signing his manuscripts with his nickname "Tennessee." More than any other 20th-century writer, Tennessee Williams would use the city as a palette, making one of its streetcar lines a symbol of the human desire for love in one of America's most enduring modern dramas.

In 1941, far away in Los Angeles, Jelly Roll Morton died at age 55, worn out by a life of excess. His New Orleans-style jazz had been eclipsed by the dance-happy Swing Era, and his mind was tormented by the belief that he had been placed under a voodoo curse.

That same year, as World War II continued to darken the world, local inventor Andrew Higgins started testing a new kind of military boat, known as a landing craft, at his factory on New Orleans's Magazine Street.

German U-boats began positioning themselves off the mouth of the Mississippi soon after the United States entered the war, and early in 1942 the German craft made their first sinking of a ship in the Gulf. More than a dozen vessels would be lost at sea south of New Orleans in the first year of the war, during which Higgins Industries employed some 30,000 New Orleanians to build its blunt-bowed landing craft, giving jobs to many blacks and women. The war revived the city's shipbuilding industry—its yards also produced high-speed PT boats—and spurred the development of Louisiana's offshore oil-drilling industry, putting thousands to work and creating a tradition in Cajun communities of skilled labor in the oil industry.

In 1940, New Orleans had made an initial purchase of some 650 acres in Kenner as the site of Moisant Airport. During World War II, however, that land was requisitioned by the U.S. government and used for a military base. In 1946, a year after the war ended, Moisant Airport began providing commercial service out of the government-built wartime facilities. (Aviation Board Chairman Edward Rapier urged New Orleans to build a new terminal and tower to replace the old facilities.) The opening schedule of arrivals and departures at Moisant listed six airlines and fifty flights daily, and by 1947 it was one of the nation's largest commercial airports in area, sprawling across 1,360 acres. Nearby Kenner—the city at its edge—felt squeezed, and its city councilmen began to voice their concerns about the growth of the airport.

In general, the region's good times rolled on until the 1980s, when a collapse in oil prices dispersed many who worked in the petroleum industry, cutting property tax revenues and patronage of the arts. One ripple effect was a flight of middle-class families that cost New Orleans a U.S. Congressional seat; another has been a chronic economic anemia. Despite a fancy and affluent elite society, New Orleans is one of America's poorest big cities in terms of per capita income, and it suffers the usual social ills—crime and homelessness in particular—associated with urban poverty.

Huey Long's political machine outlived him.

The city, however, has a fiercely loyal and involved cadre of residents who have taken the lead in architectural restoration and cultural revitalization. Tourism has become a pillar of the economy while traditional commerce has declined in importance over the years. What lies ahead is anyone's surmise. What is certain is that New Orleans remains an interesting, vibrant, attractive, and sophisticated city. It has a remarkably exotic setting on the nation's most important river, with a historical pageant as fascinating and romantic as any found elsewhere in the United States. It is a city cherished by many who live in it, and it enjoys their protection. What changes will come are likely to include many positive ones. ■

The arts

PERHAPS NO OTHER AMERICAN CITY OR REGION IS MORE DOWN-TO-THE-BONE musical than New Orleans and southern Louisiana. Jazz evolved here, and so did the careers of many well-known musicians. Literary and artistic careers began here, as writers and artists found inspiration and acceptance. The benefits of all this creativity are seen and heard throughout the city—in its streets, concert halls, theaters, museums, and architecture.

MUSIC

Jazz may be New Orleans's musical signature, but the city is also a venue for a remarkable variety of locally evolved music including Cajun, zydeco, and rhythm-and-bluesy swamp pop. This diversity is easy to understand when you consider the unique ethnic recipe that gave rise to the region's culture.

By the time the United States acquired Louisiana in 1803, people of African descent accounted for nearly half the city's population, a community that cherished its Old World music and dancing traditions. By the turn of the century, German and Irish immigrants were living in neighborhoods alongside the African Americans. Acadians—French-speaking rural folk from Nova Scotia, run out of Canada by the British in the mid-1700s—had settled the swampy wilderness to the west and southwest and evolved a subsistence culture the Indians called Cajun. In their isolated world, Cajuns entertained themselves using violins and later accordions, singing songs in a rhythmic patois.

In most other American cities, musical performances and parades were infrequent; in New Orleans they occurred often. During Carnival, African Americans masquerading as Indians took to the streets, parading in costume and singing and drumming in ways reflecting traditions of West African and Caribbean call-and-response chanting. Creoles flocked to the Quarter's French Opera House, which also presented recitals and symphonic performances. Anglo-Americans contributed the military-style brass band, whose musicians typically could read and write music; they adopted the syncopated rhythms of African-American cakewalks and minstrel tunes along with Gypsy, Jewish, Celtic, Viennese, Mexican, and Cuban musicology. By the 1880s, marching bands were a national vogue.

The following decade produced syncopated piano compositions called ragtime, which delighted audiences. Brass bands took notice and began to mix traditional marches with ragtime numbers. African-American "mutual aid and benevolent societies" adopted the marching band as well—now a staple of Carnival parades, public concerts, political rallies, and funerals. They added the fancy stepping and call-and-response intricacies from their own heritage, with results both crowd-pleasing and musically advanced.

New Orleans music took a long step forward in the 1890s as a result of new and repressive segregation laws that unified the city's African Americans and Creoles of color, who tended to remain aloof from each other. They had markedly different approaches to music, and their coming together was catalytic; when the generally improvisational African-American musicians sat down to play alongside formally trained Creoles, both groups' musical horizons changed. One gained structure, the other freedom. The same phenomenon occurred among the city's Euro-American bands, when mostly self-taught Italians joined the spit-and-polish Germans whose music was written down and strictly followed.

Jazz

When the 20th century arrived, the Central Business District was chockablock with legitimate theaters, vaudeville houses, music-publishing firms, and instrument stores. Lake Pontchartrain's resorts and amusement parks employed bands, and in the neighborhoods' community social halls, corner saloons, and mutual aid and benevolent societies, dances were held almost nightly. In Storyville's piano parlors, keyboardists improvised freely, combining the city's diverse influences to produce music never heard before. Riverboat orchestras took it to the heartland, where audiences generally applauded. Promoters

Above: King Oliver's Creole Jazz Band
Below: Uptown's Maple Leaf Bar

in distant cities beckoned, and many of New Orleans's leading artists hit the road. Chicago and New York became the penultimate venues for ambitious jazzmen like Italian-American Nick LaRocca and his Original Dixieland Jazz Band, who went there in 1916. At New York's Victor studios in 1917, the group made the first commercial jazz recording, a novelty coming on top of the new seductive music that electrified the nation. Almost overnight, New Orleans jazz became a coast-to-coast sensation.

In hindsight, perhaps the most significant departure occurred in 1922, when Louis Armstrong was summoned to Chicago by cornet player Joe "King" Oliver, his mentor. Oliver's Creole Jazz Band was the first black ensemble to be recorded (in 1923), and under his guidance the young Armstrong emerged as a brilliantly innovative musician who almost single-handedly pioneered the jazz soloist tradition. (Up to then, musicians rarely took individual turns.) Armstrong's debut dovetailed with improvements in recording quality,

making him the first jazz artist to win an international following.

In the 1930s, New Orleans jazz—referred to today as traditional jazz—was replaced by swing and then, in the war years, by bebop. But jazz fans and critics realized that the New Orleans sound was not merely a transitory music; it is a fully dimensioned genre worthy of study and preservation. In New Orleans public schools, a jazz education program now introduces selected students to basic traditional melodies and the music's history. Local colleges have added traditional jazz studies to their music programs, ensuring that the music will not be lost.

Cajun music

When their wanderings ended in southern Louisiana some 250 years ago, Acadians brought with them a musical heritage rooted in medieval France, but the only instruments they had were a few violins. Poverty and the loneliness of rural life infused their songs with a heartbroken, what's-the-use-of-living sentiment. Influenced by the music of Creoles of African descent, in the late 19th century they adopted inexpensive and durable small accordions sold by hardware stores and mail-order catalogs, creating a music so unique that in the 1920s phonograph companies began to record it. The discovery of oil in south Louisiana brought an influx of Anglo-American workers who favored country and western music, and augmented Cajun string bands with guitar and fiddle, and later steel guitars, bass, drums, banjos, and mandolins. Cajun went national in 1964 when audiences cheered it at the Newport Folk Festival, and the music has grown in popularity ever since.

Zydeco

Because its basic instrument is the accordion, zydeco is often taken for a brand of Cajun music; in fact, it arose among southern Louisiana's Creoles of color after World War II. Critical turf wars aside, it does owe much to Cajun. But today zydeco draws on diverse pop music sources, including soul, disco, rap, and reggae, and it is increasingly performed in English instead of Creole dialect. Purists rue its adoption by the music industry, which favors it over Cajun for use in films and commercials. In New Orleans and out in rural regions you can hear it performed the old-fashioned way, backed up by wheezy accordions and propelled by an irresistibly rhythmic beat.

Swamp pop

This musical gumbo of New Orleans-style rhythm and blues, country and western, and Cajun and black Creole music was born in southern Louisiana's Acadian country in the mid-1950s. It began with teenage Cajun and black Creole musicians who had become infatuated with the styles of artists such as Elvis Presley, Little Richard, and New Orleans's cultural treasure Fats Domino. You can recognize swamp pop by its emotional singing style, simple and often bilingual lyrics, honky-tonk piano, bellowing saxophones, and strong rhythm-and-blues backbeat.

LITERATURE

Tennessee Williams and Truman Capote saw their careers catch fire in New Orleans and later remembered the city for both inspiration and acceptance. Samuel Clemens, recalling his five years as a riverboat pilot in *Life on the Mississippi,* credited the city's antebellum commerce for the early success that gave him the confidence to attempt a literary career.

Underlying New Orleans's appeal is its aura of tolerance and permissiveness (local liquor laws do not require bars to close; they also permit on-street drinking from nonbreakable containers). In 1921, when small-town life struck many creative types as inhibiting, Ernest Hemingway sailed for Paris on the advice of Sherwood Anderson, who in 1922 moved to New Orleans. It was often said then that the French Quarter was the best alternative for a writer without the money for a Left Bank sojourn, but New Orleans was far more than a consolation prize. Its iconoclastic magazine *Double Dealer,* which launched in 1921 (and then folded five years later), won a national readership by offering liberal opinions and avant-garde literature.

Among the city's more recent notables is short-story writer and novelist Richard Ford, who made his home in the French Quarter for

Zydeco sound features the washboard-like *frottier,* shown at the Jazz & Heritage Fest.

a while. His fifth novel, *Independence Day,* won the 1996 Pulitzer Prize and the PEN/Faulkner Award for fiction. The 1981 Pulitzer Prize for fiction was awarded to *A Confederacy of Dunces,* John Kennedy Toole's comic romp through New Orleans. The honor was a bittersweet reprise to one of the most tragic of New Orleans's literary lives. Disheartened in 1969, after years of being unable to find a publisher for his manuscript, Toole killed himself. His mother, believing in his work, enlisted the help of writer Walker Percy, who lived across Lake Pontchartrain in Covington. Percy was a deep-thinking existentialist who laid the white Southern soul bare and regarded slavery as the South's "original sin" and tragic flaw. Established by *The Moviegoer* (1961) and *Love in the Ruins* (1971), he persuaded the Louisiana State University Press in 1980 to publish Toole's manuscript, for many the penultimate portrait of the city's eccentricity.

New Orleans's best-known living writer is probably Anne Rice, who launched her career in 1976 with the best-selling novel *Interview with the Vampire.* Born in the city in 1941, she was raised in the Garden District and in Texas. After achieving literary success, Rice returned to the district in 1989. She immersed herself in historical preservation, buying and refurbishing what was once St. Elizabeth's Orphanage at 1314 Napoleon Avenue, and helping restore her childhood parish church, St. Alphonsus, at 2045 Constance Street. She has since moved to a nearby suburb, having sold her New Orleans residence, an imposing old manse at 1239 First Street. Rice is a phenomenon unto herself, as her Web site *(www.annerice.com)* makes clear.

New Orleans inspired writers Tennessee Williams (left) and Truman Capote (right).

Until the mid-19th century, New Orleans's literary voices had been mostly French and under the thrall of François-Auguste-de-René Chateaubriand, standard-bearer of the French Romantics. He set two novels—*Atala* (1801) and *René* (1802)—in Louisiana, inspiring Adrien and Dominique Rouquette, sons of a prosperous New Orleans merchant, to take up the pen. Schooled in France in the 1830s, they returned to Louisiana to publish verse extolling the region's beauty and Creole culture.

In terms of sheer improbability, no New Orleans literary life can match that of Lafcadio Hearn, born in the Greek Ionian Islands in 1850 to a British father and Greek mother and educated in England. At age 19, minus an eye lost during a boyhood mishap, he immigrated to America. He reported for the Cincinnati *Commercial* until 1877, then moved to New Orleans, supporting himself by freelance writing and working odd jobs while renting at 516 Bourbon Street (now an apparel store). Hearn eventually became chief editorial writer and cartoonist of the New Orleans *Item* and a man about town, recognized by his long hair and wide-brimmed black planter's hat. He wrote articles opposing corruption, child labor, white slavery, and gang violence; published translations of Creole and gypsy folktales; and won acclaim with his 1889 novel *Chita*, about a tidal wave that hit near New Orleans in 1856. In 1890 he sailed to Japan on assignment from *Harper's*, married a woman from a samurai family, and became a Japanese citizen named Koizumi Yakumo. His supernatural yarns and Japanese fairy tales fascinated his adopted countrymen until his death in 1904. (His ashes are interred in a Buddhist cemetery.) An anthology of his writings, *Lafcadio Hearn's Japan*, was recently published.

Former Garden District resident Anne Rice, famed for vampire sagas, at Lafayette Cemetery

Hearn might never have come to New Orleans if he had not read a story about Creole culture published in the May 1875 *Scribner's Magazine*. The author was George Washington Cable, who had struck literary gold two years earlier when the magazine published his story "Sieur George." Cable and Bret Harte came into instant vogue as the creators of "local color" fiction, in which authors reproduced regional dialects. George Washington Cable's depictions of the Creole elite did not always go over well, but he became a national celebrity anyway, enjoying friendships with Mark Twain and Oscar Wilde.

In the first half of the 20th century, New Orleans's literary reputation attracted many bright lights, including Gertrude Stein, John Dos Passos, Thornton Wilder, Erskine Caldwell, and the young Katherine Anne Porter. In the 1930s, the city's premier literary salon was that of star *Times-Picayune* reporter Lyle Saxon, a Louisiana native who became a noted regional writer, penning books about state politics and historical fiction. He championed architectural preservation, restoring 536 Royal Street and a 16-room town house at 612 Royal, both sites of his soirées. While state director of Louisiana's Federal Writers' Project, Saxon oversaw the writing of the *New Orleans City Guide*, published in 1938 and still one of the most intriguing portraits of the city in print.

There are others whose writings are notable for insights into southern Louisiana life. Shirley Ann Grau, a Sophie Newcomb College graduate, was a 1965 Pulitzer honoree for her novel *The Keepers of the House.* Frances Parkinson Keyes (rhymes with "eyes") wrote *Madame Castel's Lodger,* a novel that conjures up New Orleans's postbellum world. Playwright Lillian Hellman debuted as a voice against injustice with *The Children's Hour* in 1934 and *The Little Foxes* in 1939. She set her last drama, *Toys in the Attic* (1960), in the Garden District boardinghouse at 1718 Prytania Street, where she was born in 1905. When her father's shoe-manufacturing business failed in 1911, Hellman returned with her family to New York, but from age 6 to 16 she spent six months of every year with her aunts, who owned the boardinghouse and fussed over their precocious niece, taking her on adventures around town that made life in Manhattan dull by comparison.

Who knows what F. Scott Fitzgerald might have written about New Orleans if he had taken to it? In January 1920 he arrived on a train from St. Paul, Minnesota, and rented the small white house at 2900 Prytania Street, where he started correcting page proofs of his first novel, *This Side of Paradise.* Pining for his fiancée Zelda Sayre, a high-strung debutante in Montgomery, Alabama, he twice interrupted his work to visit her. Convinced that he had a future, they made plans for a wedding in New York City. Before leaving New Orleans only weeks after his arrival, he sent pages to *Scribner's* editor Maxwell Perkins, ending his cover letter with a postscript: "O. Henry said this was a story town—but it's too consciously that."

THEATER

In 1916 a group of amateur actors calling themselves The Drawing Room Players rented space in the Lower Pontalba Building (for $17.50 a month) and launched Le Petit Théâtre du Vieux Carré. It is still going, now located at the corner of St. Peter and Chartres Streets, and recognized as one of America's finest nonprofessional community theaters. The playbill generally relies on the tried and true—favorite musicals, favorite plays—but the actors here are passionate and dedicated, and the productions have a reputation for ingenuity and flair.

Big-budget traveling Broadway productions are featured at the opulent Saenger Theater *(143 N. Rampart St. 504-524-2490),* the sole survivor of a dozen houses that once made up New Orleans's theater district around Canal and Basin Streets. Vaudeville built downtown's Orpheum Theater *(129 University Place. 504-524-3285).* Completed in 1921, it is the home of the Louisiana Philharmonic Orchestra. The interior is fantastic; the city's largest terra-cotta frieze decorates a design more vertical than horizontal, bringing the 1,783 seats close to the stage and within the embrace of great acoustics.

The city's theatrical avant-garde includes the Contemporary Arts Center *(900 Camp St. 504-528-3800),* the Southern Repertory Theater *(365 Canal St. 504-522-6545),* Tulane University's Dixon Hall and McAlister Auditorium *(Dept. of Theatre and Dance, 6823 St. Charles Ave. 504-314-7760),* and the University of New Orleans Performing Arts Center *(Dept. of Drama and Communications, Lakefront. 504-280-6000).*

The multidisciplinary Contemporary Arts Center presents new plays, performance art, musical concerts, and dance in a gallery complex housed in a refurbished old brick building in the Warehouse District. If Tennessee Williams were starting out today, he would probably be featured in the Southern Repertory's New Playwrights series, slumped in the back row and biting his nails while gauging the audience response. The theater—warm and intimate, in contrast to the glitzy mall around it—looks for the best work by regional writers and mounts four productions a year, including modern classics by the likes of Arthur Miller, Tennessee Williams, Lillian Hellman, Sheila Bosworth, Athol Fugard, Carson McCullers, Oscar Wilde, and Horton Foote.

Tulane University presents classics along with works by faculty, students, artists-in-residence, and others. They vary widely, but this is a university of high quality, and the offerings reflect that. Among the city's most popular small stages is the True Brew Theatre *(200 Julia St. 504-524-8440).* It presents original work by local writers and durable fare from crowd-pleasers like Neil Simon. Visit the Best of New Orleans Web site *(www.bestofneworleans.com)* for up-to-the-minute information.

***Cat on a Hot Tin Roof,* by Tennessee Williams, at Le Petit Théâtre**

DANCE

The current standard-bearer of classical movement in the Crescent City is the New Orleans Ballet Association *(504-522-0996),* whose dancers take the stage at the Mahalia Jackson Theatre of the Performing Arts in Armstrong Park. The association's repertoire has tended to be traditional—*The Nutcracker* and *Swan Lake* have been regulars in the September to May season. Recently, however, the company became affiliated with the highly regarded Cincinnati Ballet. The new relationship with the Ohio-based troupe and the association's announced intention to "present diverse top-quality performances reflecting the spectrum of styles and the racial and ethnic population of the Greater New Orleans area" bode well for the future.

The first regular dance performances in the city occurred not among the French, whose dancing was limited to private balls, but on the banks of Bayou St. John. The colony's *code noir* granted slaves a Sunday of rest, and until the mid-19th century hundreds of enslaved people gathered at the Place des Negres, mixing with *gens de couleur libre*—free people of color—to sing, dance, and socialize. That heritage is preserved through performances by the N'Kafu Traditional African Dance Company *(Mariama J. Curry, 4233 Palmyra St.),*

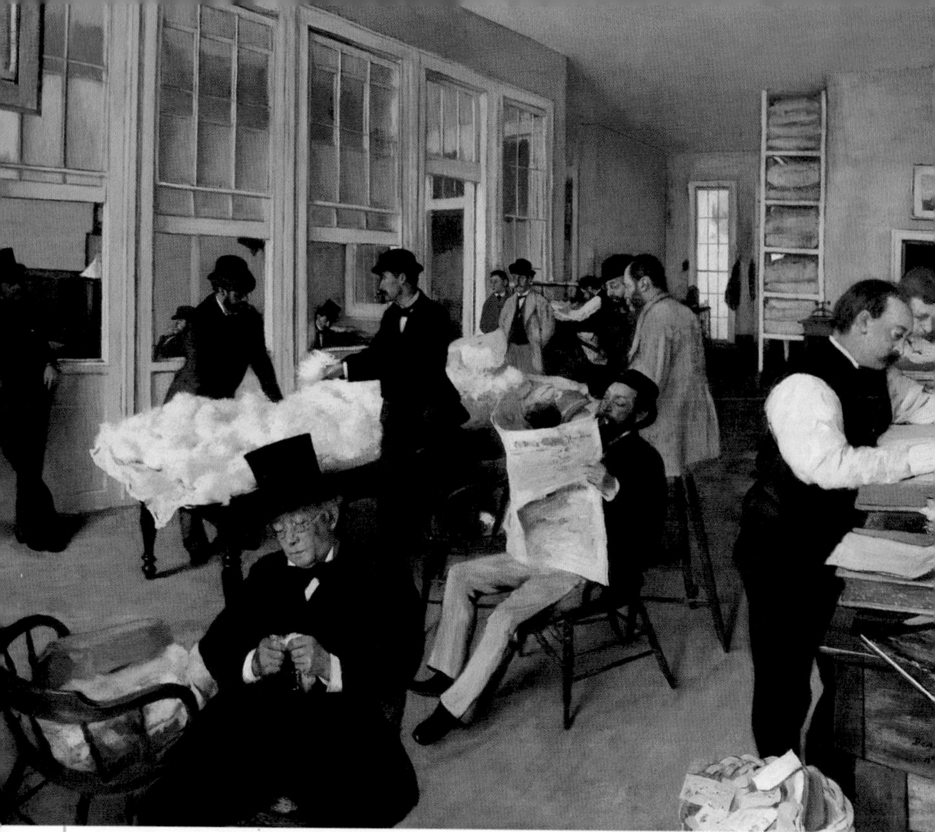

Edgar Degas created "Portrait in an Office: The New Orleans Cotton Exchange," a painting of his uncle's cotton brokerage office, in 1883.

an association of dancers, singers, and musicians who re-create Old World rituals. The troupe does not have a permanent home, but New Orleans's alternative newspapers and informational Web sites note when N'Kafu is scheduled to perform, listing the locations and times. The city's leading modern dance repertory company is New Orleans Dance *(825 Webster St. 504-394-7761),* directed by Barbara Hayley. Since 1987 it has presented the choreography of local, regional, and nationally recognized dance artists. Like N'Kafu, this company is an itinerant troupe whose performances are intermittent and remarkably polished.

FINE ARTS

If the founders of New Orleans had not been French, it is unlikely that they would have set out so early to civilize their mosquito-ridden, subtropical outpost—situated at about the same latitude as the Great Pyramids of Egypt—through art and music. They brought with them shiploads of objets d'art—fine porcelains in particular—along with the peculiarly European mix of refinement and brutality that characterized the age. The French staged operas and fancy balls and drank fine wines while slicing one another up with dueling swords, dodging cutthroat pirates downriver, and torturing prisoners. Riots were frequent, thugs and outlaws were everywhere, and residences were built like forts. Artists were not what this outpost needed in the beginning; newcomers who found their way there usually possessed more utilitarian skills as well—the architect who painted, the soldier who played the violin.

Painting

There was, reportedly, a painter named Miguel Garcia accompanying the Le Moyne brothers when they made their first voyage up the Mississippi in 1699, but New Orleans's first image-makers devoted their talents to hand-colored drawings and architectural views of the city's low skyline to inform colonial officials, impress investors, or illustrate books. The first noted artist is thought to have been Ferdinand Salazar, whose splendid full-length portrait of wealthy landowner Don Andres Almonester y Roxas, painted in the late 1700s, hangs in the Presbytère on Jackson Square. Most people could afford only miniatures, usually of loved ones. After the United States annexed Louisiana, the city's prosperity attracted dozens of painters and engravers from the East Coast and Europe; they earned their livings creating likenesses, many of them displayed in New Orleans's museums and historic public buildings.

Among the portrait painters was the artist-naturalist John James Audubon, who came to New Orleans in 1821 while working on his monumental series *Birds of America.* He rented a studio at 706 Barracks Street for ten dollars a month and, like his colleagues, supported himself by commissions. Audubon did well enough at it to make time for his personal project, and by the autumn his diary noted the completion of "62 drawings of Birds & Plants, 3 Quadrupeds, 2 snakes, and 50 Portraits of all sorts."

In the 1840s, George Catlin, known for his paintings of Native Americans, paid several visits to New Orleans. Some art historians credit him with an oft-reproduced Catlin-style portrait of the influential hairdresser-turned-voodoo-queen, Marie Laveau.

During the winter of 1872–73, French Impressionist Edgar Degas sojourned in New Orleans, where he lived at the Esplanade Avenue home of his Creole relatives. Degas found the subtropical sunlight oppressive and retreated indoors to paint, creating several of his finest early works in the offices of his uncle's cotton brokerage firm.

In the mid-19th century, a surge in the construction of grand public buildings offered commissions for murals and decorated panels that attracted dozens of artists to the city. There they produced images of virtually everybody and everything, and many of these creations now reside in the collection of the New Orleans Museum of Art in City Park. Established in 1910 by Isaac Delgado, a Jamaican immigrant who became a millionaire sugar broker in New Orleans, it is generally regarded as the premier public collection in the Gulf South.

Among the pieces at the Museum of Art are examples of Newcomb Pottery, created between 1894 and 1940 by women studying at the city's H. Sophie Newcomb Memorial College, now affiliated with Tulane University. The college's experimental program provided employment for its graduates in times when there were few careers for women beyond nursing and secretarial work. The studio—it was never a factory—produced approximately 70,000 pieces designed by about 90 student artists (all female). Men were always the potters, and the pieces, usually with nature-oriented motifs, became the quintessential wedding gift in the Crescent City. Today some of the Newcomb vases fetch $30,000; few are available for under $1,000.

The city's unusual mix of European and West Indian architectural styles, ethnicities, and social classes inevitably drew the attention of early photographers. Arnold Genthe was one of them, and he set up his tripod in the 1920s to compose moody, soft-focus sepia-toned scenes of the French Quarter. Storyville prostitutes are the subjects of the city's most famous photographic images, which were made early in the 20th century by commercial photographer Ernest James Bellocq. Those striking photographs were not exhibited until 1970, 21 years after Bellocq's death, and to many who saw them, they instantly revealed the unassuming documentarian to be an American master.

In recent years artists and dealers have been drawn to New Orleans by the availability of old commercial buildings. As a result, the Central Business District's once moribund Warehouse District and Julia Row have been transformed into a thriving community of studios and fine art galleries that attract collectors and buyers from around the United States. The work spans the definition of art, from the familiar to the avant-garde, from folk to academic, from mud to multimedia. New Orleans has always been a city indifferent to imported trends, and this still young part of town exemplifies that in a sophisticated but unpretentious way.

ARCHITECTURE

Heritage, heat, and humidity shaped the face of New Orleans: France, Spain, Africa, the West Indies, and Anglo-America contributed building styles; the subtropical latitude and low-lying terrain provided the heat and humidity. Fires had destroyed much of the city's European colonial character by the end of the 18th century; thereafter the dominant influence came from the industrial Eastern states, where classical motifs were in vogue. What has survived in the old neighborhoods is a virtual living museum of architectural styles, many unique to this region, some to New Orleans exclusively.

The first structures built by the settlers were temporary, but the rapidity of their rotting, warping, and subsidence into New Orleans's soggy alluvial soil—hastened by hurricane-force winds and Mississippi River flooding—and the discomfort of the region's steamy summer weather spurred architects to creative improvisation.

When you look at old New Orleans buildings, the practical ingenuity of an age before air-conditioning is evident. Raised residences rest on piers to escape heat and dampness and to catch breezes; lofty ceilings permit hot air to rise above people; windows and doors off commodious porches or galleries are set far back so they can be left open during downpours and at night. You also see reflected in their types (meaning their shapes and room arrangements) and their styles (referring to trim and decoration) the endeavors, economic levels, social arrangements, and technology of their respective eras.

Cypress was the most frequently used wood, hewed into massive beams that were assembled into sturdy frames filled in with brick. New Orleans's local brick, typically soft, had to be encased in stucco or covered with siding to prevent deterioration caused by airborne moisture. Because stone was scarce in southern Louisiana, it became a luxury import. In later, more prosperous years barges would float great blocks of Indiana limestone down the Mississippi, and ships would arrive from Massachusetts with Quincy granite for public buildings and the mansions of the city's elite.

Among the architectural vestiges of life in old New Orleans are its inviting porte cochere town houses, built in the Quarter from about 1800 to 1830 and distinguished by a carriageway entrance leading to a rear enclosed courtyard. The ground floor was typically a commercial space, with residences beginning on the floors above. When you duck through their passageways, look for the servants' wing, usually attached to one side of the rear of the house to form a wall of the courtyard.

In an age of slaves and domestic help, such outbuildings were common, sometimes rising three stories. Heat and the danger posed by flames from wood-fired cooking led to the practice of placing kitchens in outbuildings; the main houses had only fireplaces to create warmth. Outbuildings held storage areas and slaves' and servants' quarters; sometimes they had rooms for the owners' older male children.

If New Orleans has an architectural trademark, it is the shotgun house, a long, narrow, rectangular building with its rooms arranged one behind the other in a straight line, front to back; sometimes the rooms open onto a corridor running the length of the building. The design was ideally suited to New Orleans, and such houses were built here from the mid-19th century until just before World War II.

After two devastating fires, in 1788 and 1794, wood-shingle roofs were outlawed and wooden "colombage" frames had to be plastered in. The transfer of the territory to the United States in 1803 brought Yankees who built houses and commercial buildings according to what they were used to back East. Row houses were an Anglo-American trademark, sometimes a dozen shoulder to shoulder, sharing walls and exterior arrangements.

The city's high period came between 1830 and 1862 at the peak of the cotton and sugar trade. During this era New Orleans acquired its most beautiful houses and public buildings, in a time when quarried stone was imported, custom-designed furnishings and cast ironwork were commissioned, and tile roofs were replaced with slate. European motifs were eclipsed by classical ones, particularly Greek Revival, and then Victorian styles, which would remain in vogue into the 20th century.

Flood and fire robbed New Orleans of its youthful skyline, but misfortune has also

Stairway in Mid-City's Longue Vue House

New Orleans houses

The Crescent City's most visible and cherished links to the past are its unique residences. Some are grand; most are modest. They combine classical architectural styles with local whimsy and the requirements of a subtropical clime. Built mainly of soft brick—New Orleans has no suitable native stone—and durable woods such as cypress and longleaf pine from the north shore of Lake Pontchartrain, they reflect a complex cultural heritage and the city's evolution from a French colonial outpost to 19th-century America's leading commercial window on the world.

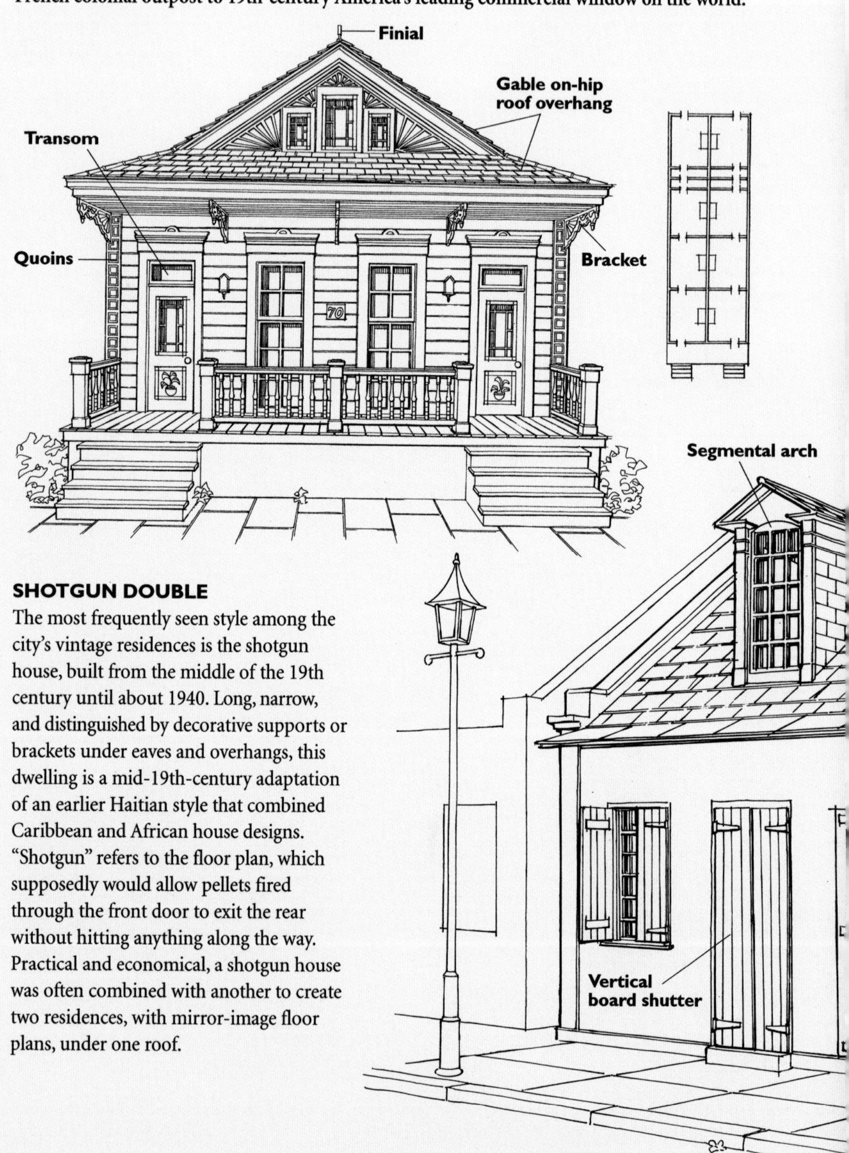

SHOTGUN DOUBLE

The most frequently seen style among the city's vintage residences is the shotgun house, built from the middle of the 19th century until about 1940. Long, narrow, and distinguished by decorative supports or brackets under eaves and overhangs, this dwelling is a mid-19th-century adaptation of an earlier Haitian style that combined Caribbean and African house designs. "Shotgun" refers to the floor plan, which supposedly would allow pellets fired through the front door to exit the rear without hitting anything along the way. Practical and economical, a shotgun house was often combined with another to create two residences, with mirror-image floor plans, under one roof.

DOUBLE-GALLERY HOUSE

Seen throughout the Garden District and Uptown, this is a refinement of the American town house built in the first half of the 19th century. Raised on low brick piers to escape flooding, set back from the street, decorated with Greek Revival columns or Italianate embellishments such as cast-iron grillwork, double-gallery houses featured deep porches and upper-floor balconies. Built of wood and brick (often stuccoed), with front doors set to the side (presaging the Victorian style), they were often the city homes of wealthy cotton and sugarcane planters.

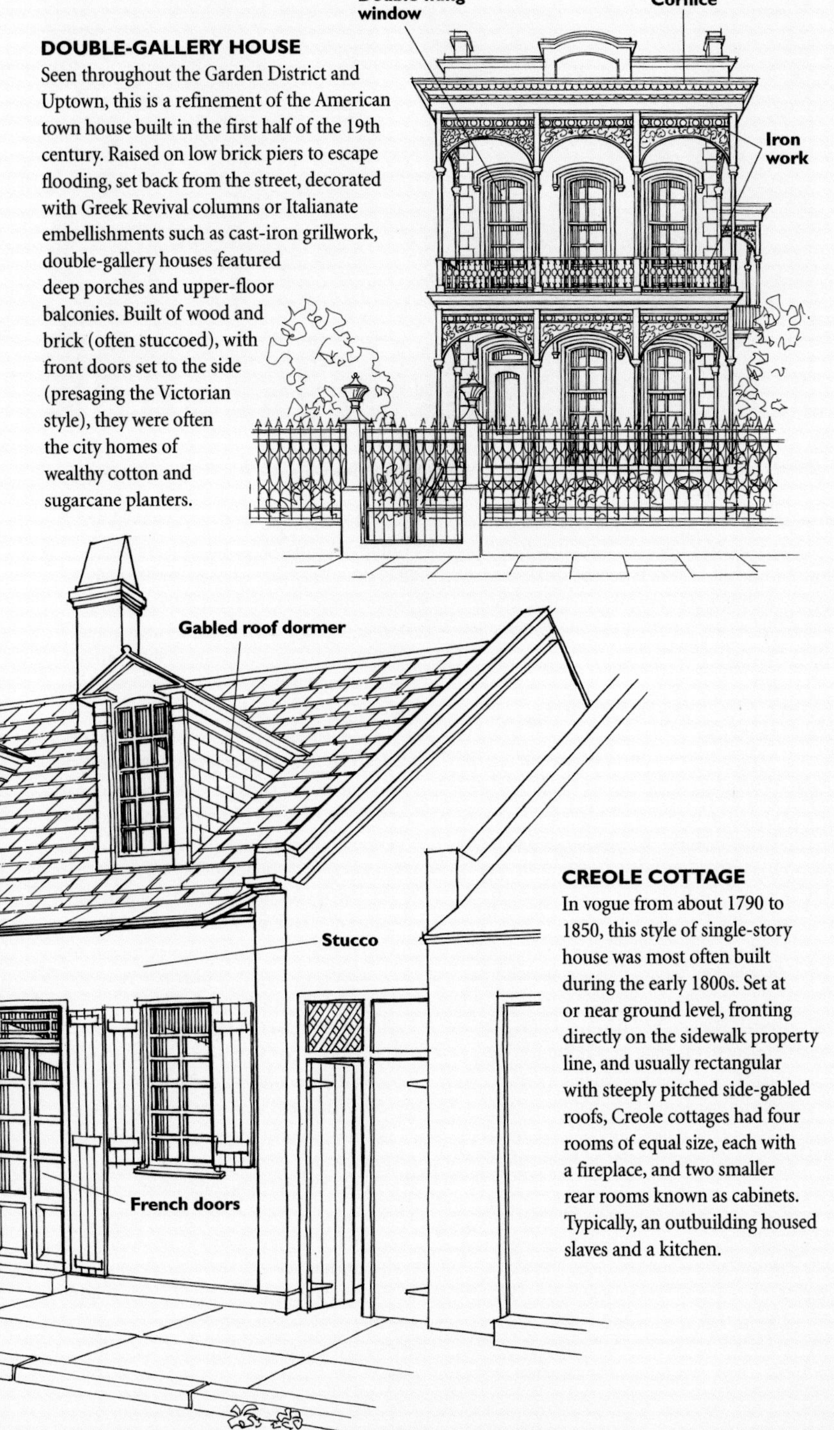

CREOLE COTTAGE

In vogue from about 1790 to 1850, this style of single-story house was most often built during the early 1800s. Set at or near ground level, fronting directly on the sidewalk property line, and usually rectangular with steeply pitched side-gabled roofs, Creole cottages had four rooms of equal size, each with a fireplace, and two smaller rear rooms known as cabinets. Typically, an outbuilding housed slaves and a kitchen.

Lovely old houses dot the Garden District, where New Orleans's restoration movement began.

preserved what survived; periods of economic depression since the Civil War often stayed the wrecking ball. In times past, editorials rued the lack of civic funds for redevelopment. Today the rallying cry is restoration and preservation of a rare architectural treasury.

HISTORIC PRESERVATION MOVEMENT

In 1907 New Orleans razed an entire block of historic buildings in the Vieux Carré to make room for the Civil Courts building. There was talk of tearing down the Cabildo, and a zoning consultant recommended the demolition of ten square French Quarter blocks between Rampart and Dauphine. Unease among city residents who cherished these old streets led to a 1932 ban on French Quarter demolition. A grass roots movement largely started by Elizabeth Werlein (1887–1946) produced an amendment to the state constitution creating the Vieux Carré Commission in 1936, an agency with the power to forbid the razing or inappropriate remodeling of buildings that were deemed historically or architecturally significant—the first in America.

Today the fight to save New Orleans's oldest neighborhoods is led by the Preservation Resource Center. Founded in 1974 as a citywide, not-for-profit organization, the PRC initiated the rescue of the Warehouse District, once a virtual ghost town and now a desirable address. The PRC's Operation Comeback program sponsors workshops that show prospective buyers how to identify vacant properties suitable for renovation, negotiate their purchase, get financing, and complete a successful fix-up on their own or find the right people to do it. The Operation office *(923 Tchoupitoulas St. 504-581-7032)* is open Monday through Friday. Its photographic displays, as well as those on the PRC's Web site *(www.prcno.org)*, survey the city's 16 national register districts and historic neighborhoods. An electronic scrapbook lists the available properties. You'll find information about financing, workshops, architectural tours, and training programs for first-time home buyers. A reference library holds books and magazines on restoration techniques, historic architecture, interior design, gardening, and local lore.

Members point out that renters are never displaced—targeted properties must be vacant (many are abandoned)—and the PRC is not merely a club dedicated to self-interest. One of the most popular programs, Christmas in October, enlists members and volunteers to make essential and often substantial repairs for low-income elderly and handicapped homeowners. By any standard, the PRC is a phenomenal success—in large measure because New Orleans has a lot of people who love the city enough to undertake the hard work and expense of urban pioneering. ■

Introduce yourself first to the French Quarter, the site of New Orleans's original settlement. It grew from a few houses in a clearing hacked out of riverside palmetto groves into the city's architectural centerpiece and cultural heart.

French Quarter

Rebirth Brass Band at the Maple Leaf Bar

French Quarter

THIS FABLED 6-BY-13-BLOCK RECTANGLE OF HISTORY AND CULTURE along the Mississippi River is for most of the world synonymous with New Orleans, the most widely known of its diverse districts and neighborhoods. The French Quarter, or Vieux Carré (Old Square), was laid out not long after the French founded the city in 1718 and, using a grid pattern, drafted a formal street plan.

The historical heart of New Orleans, the French Quarter was originally enclosed by ramparts. Fires swept through in 1788 and again in 1794, razing much of the original French Creole architecture. Under Spanish rule at the time, the city's replacement buildings took on a Spanish flair, complete with the beloved wrought-iron galleries,

A street musician holds forth.

shuttered doors, and rear courtyards that have become so quintessentially Vieux Carré. The French Quarter is both a residential and business district, its streets lined with historic landmarks, elegantly restored residences, shops whose prices and wares span the range of tastes and pocketbooks, world-renowned restaurants, and discreetly situated offices. Save for Bourbon Street's brash entertainment strip, the French Quarter permits no neon signs. City laws decree that its buildings conform to the architectural styles of the late 1700s to mid-1800s, the period when New Orleans asserted itself as the mercantile and

cultural hub of the Mississippi Delta region. In the center of the Quarter sprawls Jackson Square, strikingly European in the formality of its architecture and landscaping.

An essential stop before you roam far is the **Jean Lafitte National Historical Park and Preserve French Quarter Visitor Center** *(419 Decatur St., bet. Conti & St. Louis Sts. 504-589-2636)*. Its exhibits offer an excellent introduction to the region's history and its complex culture. A short video, "Mississippi in Motion," surveys how the river has changed through the decades. A free, ranger-led walking tour of the French Quarter leaves from the center daily at 9:30 a.m. and 11:30 a.m.

Whether you join the group or explore on your own, be sure to acquire a map of the Quarter here, for no neighborhood in America offers a greater concentration of historical exotica. Wander at the slow and relaxed pace for which New Orleans—the Big Easy—is known. ■

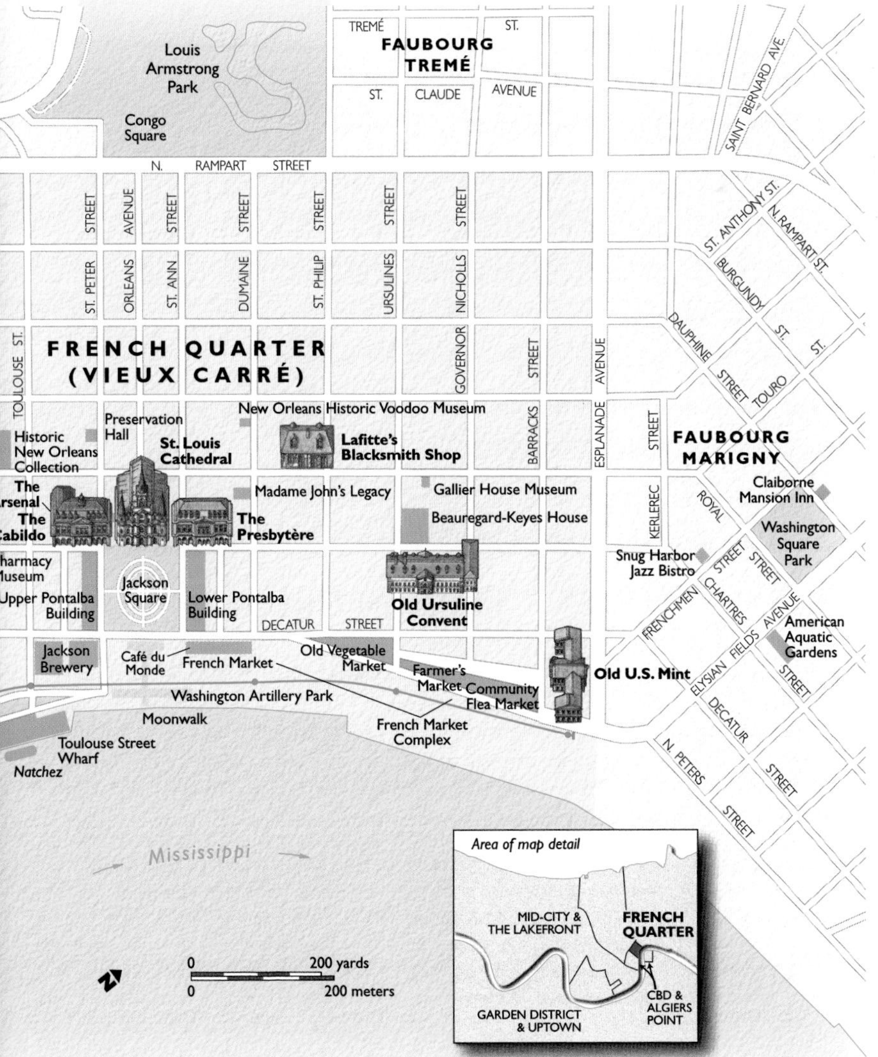

European rules of architecture and landscaping shaped New Orleans's first and still foremost public place. The 1855 lithograph is by J. Durler.

Jackson Square

HERE IS WHERE NEW ORLEANS WAS FOUNDED NEARLY 300 years ago, in a canebrake at a bend in the Mississippi. Giving French sentries a view upriver and down, the spot was also the head of an Indian portage trail leading to Bayou St. John, a stream that afforded easier passage through the difficult thickets and bogs separating the colony from Lake Pontchartrain.

Jackson Square

Map pp. 50–51

At the foot of Jackson Square, the Mississippi elbows north, for 2.5 miles turning its "east bank" into its westernmost shore. Consequently, the square faces southeast, disorienting newcomers by seeming in conflict with a river known for flowing south. Thus New Orleanians give directions relative to the river's flow, creating places like Uptown (upriver) and the Lower (downriver) French Quarter.

Laid out in 1721 by military engineer Adrien de Pauger, the Place d'Armes, as the square was originally called, was a dirt field

where soldiers and militiamen drilled and mustered in emergencies, where proclamations were posted, and where slaves and criminals were punished. In the town plan drawn up by Louisiana's engineer-in-chief, Pierre le Blond de la Tour, the plaza, bounded by Chartres, Decatur, St. Peter, and St. Ann Streets, was the center of the city. Its name would change twice—to the Plaza de Armas when the Spanish took control of the Louisiana Territory in the 1760s, and in 1848 to Jackson Square, in honor of Gen. Andrew Jackson's defense of the city at the Battle of New Orleans in 1815. The square's current look dates from 1853, when the Baroness Micaëla Pontalba cut down the bordering allée of sycamores to make way for her Pontalba Buildings. She fenced in the square with elaborate cast iron and landscaped it in a solar pattern honoring France's Sun King, Louis XIV; each of its four corners is commanded by a statue representing one of the four seasons. The square retains a 19th-century European formality. Its ambience, however, is casual. You'll see lunchtime readers, mothers and children, musicians, jugglers, artists, fortune-tellers, and the never ending traffic of camera-toting tourists. ■

St. Louis Cathedral

St. Louis Cathedral
www.stlouiscathedral.org
Map pp. 50–51
Chartres St. facing Jackson Sq.
504-525-9585
Daily services
Donation

IN 1720 THE FRENCH GARRISON ERECTED A WOODEN chapel on the Place d'Armes, but a powerful gale blew it down. A replacement, completed in 1727, burned along with much of the city in the Good Friday fire of 1788. A year later work commenced on a third place of worship, replaced in 1851 by the Cathedral of St. Louis, America's oldest continuously active cathedral.

The cathedral's three slate-roofed neoclassic steeples were the signature of architect J.N.B. de Pouilly, who was fired during construction when the center one collapsed. Architect Alexander Sampson finished the job, which was tinkered with in 1872 by Erasmus Hurnbrecht. He added a mural above the main altar depicting St. Louis, the King of France, proclaiming the seventh crusade. Belgium's Louis Gille designed the baroque altar screen, hand carved in 1852 in Ghent.

To live in the Quarter is to have your hours marked by the cathedral's bell, cast in Paris in 1819. (Two lesser ones mark quarter hours.) Highlighting the interior, says William Faulkner in his novel *Absalom, Absalom!,* are its "beautiful saints and handsome angels," some of whom watch over the tabernacle's ornate door amid a flurry of cherubs. To the left of the main altar is a statue of the patroness of New Orleans, Our Lady of Prompt Succor—to whom parishioners prayed repeatedly in this once epidemic-prone parish. To be christened at the gorgeously carved marble baptismal font was (and still is) a socially notable way to commence your life as a New Orleanian.

Behind the cathedral, at the foot of Orleans Street, is **Saint Anthony's Garden,** laid out in 1848 and shaded by oaks, sycamores, and magnolias. Though closed to the public, it can be viewed through its wrought-iron fence. The central urn-topped white-marble obelisk commemorates 30 officers and men of the 80-man Imperial French Navy corvette *Tonnerre;* they died of yellow fever during an epidemic in August 1857. The dead mariners' ship-mates raised 400 francs for the monument, which stood for over half a century at the French Quarantine Station 70 miles downriver before being moved here in 1914. ■

Below: Clark Mills's bronze equestrian statue of Andrew Jackson, unveiled in the square in 1856, replicates statues in Washington, D.C., and Nashville, Tennessee. Opposite: Court maids prepare for the Spring Fiesta Queen's coronation. The traditional event showcases houses.

The Cabildo

The Cabildo
http://lsm.crt.state.la.us
Map pp. 50–51
701 Chartres St.
504-568-6968 or 800-568-6968
Closed Mon.
$

HERE, ON DECEMBER 20, 1803, FRENCH OFFICIALS transferred the Louisiana Territory to the United States, thereby doubling the size of the young nation and ending France's New World ambitions. A survivor of war and fire, the Cabildo symbolizes New Orleans's unique history as a prize once coveted by three nations.

Napoleon's death mask. Sympathy for the deposed emperor ran deep in early New Orleans.

Begun in 1795 and completed four years later, the Cabildo's Tuscan columns, arcades, brickwork, and masonry are often seen in 18th-century Spanish colonial outposts. The building took its name from the Spanish town council, the "Illustrious Cabildo," which met here in the "capitol house" or Casa Capitular. Following the Louisiana Purchase, it served until 1853 as New Orleans's city hall and the meeting place of the territorial legislature. The indefatigable Baroness Pontalba persuaded the City Council to finance the construction of a cupola and mansard roofline in 1847 to match the plans to her own buildings, which edged two sides of Jackson Square (see p. 59).

The Cabildo is filled with exhibits tracing the state's odyssey from a French outpost to a languishing captive of the Union following the Civil War. Note the portraits of important persons that line the grand staircase, each individually labeled. Of special interest are the room where the Louisiana Purchase was consummated and a bronze death mask of Napoleon Bonaparte, one of only three known to exist. Other second-floor exhibits trace Louisiana history from the 1700s to the years just before the Civil War. Displays on the third floor address the realities of slavery and plantation life and describe life in New Orleans during the Civil War and Reconstruction. ■

Combination tickets

The Louisiana State Museum operates five properties in the French Quarter: the Cabildo/Arsenal, Presbytère, 1850 House, Old U.S. Mint, and Madame John's Legacy. Combination tickets, good for three days, are available. Each building displays works from the museum's collection of over 2,000 Louisiana-related paintings and prints. For more information, visit http://lsm.crt.state.la.us. ■

The Arsenal

A FORBIDDING NAME BELIES ITS FUNCTION AS ONE OF the five historic New Orleans landmarks owned and operated as a museum by the State of Louisiana. Built next to the Cabildo in 1839 by architect James Dakin, and considered part of that site, the Arsenal took its name from its predecessor, an arsenal built here by the Spanish in 1769. What some New Orleanians would rather forget is the civil strife that made it a symbol of the city's growing pains.

The Arsenal
http://lsm.crt.state.la.us
Map pp. 50–51
600 St. Peter St. (enter through the Cabildo)
504-568-6968 or 800-568-6968
Closed Mon.
$

Reconstruction was not a happy time in New Orleans, which had lost its thriving economy early in the conflict and languished under Union occupation. Despite many shining examples of reconciliation and cooperation between the races, the town's people of color and their white allies were menaced by white supremacist bands. In 1874 an attempt by the police to round them up escalated into a shootout known as the Battle of Liberty Place. Initially the lawmen were forced to retreat into the Custom House and the Cabildo. Commanding the Arsenal, the police used the cannon stored there to blast cannonballs toward Chartres Street, sending the thugs packing.

Today the Arsenal contains special exhibits on state and local history, plus a permanent exhibit entitled "Louisiana and the Mighty Mississippi." The theme is transportation, but this is not dry stuff. It is a *Gone With the Wind* pageant of ambitions, wealth, and adventure played out in Louisiana's odd melding of raucous frontier life and effete European sophistication. Among the prints and paintings are images of flatboats scudding down the river, of opulent saloons and dining rooms aboard paddle wheelers, and the Currier and Ives print depicting "The Great Mississippi Steamboat Race" between the *Natchez VI* and the *Robert E. Lee* in 1870. ■

French Quarter ironwork

The French Quarter's elaborate iron balconies and grilles were introduced by Spanish masters between 1762 and 1800. Originally they were hand-wrought according to metalworking traditions that spread to Europe from North Africa. The most ambitious and grandiose of the cast-iron work is found in the Pontalba Buildings (see p. 59). Under the Baroness Micaëla Pontalba's patronage, her artisans developed techniques for casting their intricate designs, a significant advance that reduced the time and expense required to produce them. ■

Ironwork came from local foundries, the East, and Europe.

The Presbytère

The Presbytère
http://lsm.crt.state.la.us
Map pp. 50–51
751 Chartres St.
504-568-6968 or 800-568-6968
Closed Mon.
$

ON JACKSON SQUARE DOWNRIVER FROM ST. LOUIS Cathedral is the Cabildo's twin, commenced in 1797 to serve as quarters for the cathedral's platoon of priests. Initially bankrolled by the Spanish beneficent Don Andres Almonester y Roxas, the construction outlived him and his pocketbook, and it wasn't completed until 1813. By that time, the Stars and Stripes flew over New Orleans.

Don Andres Almonester y Roxas

Born in Andalucia in 1725, the don came to Louisiana in 1769 as a Spanish colonial official and made a fortune, acquiring much of the land surrounding the Place d'Armes. He endeared himself to the city's faithful by paying for a cathedral following the 1788 fire, then went on to finance the Cabildo (where a splendid, full-length portrait of him hangs) and begin the Presbytère. His marble tomb lies inside St. Louis Cathedral. His daughter, Micaëla, became the Baroness Pontalba and carried on the family tradition, commissioning the redbrick Pontalba Buildings that adjoin her father's edifices. ■

Originally called the Casa Curial ("Ecclesiastical House"), the Presbytère got its present name from its location on the former site of a residence, or *presbytère,* of Capuchin monks, whose light brown robes inspired the name of the coffee drink cappuccino. When Almonester's endowment was spent, the wardens of the cathedral took responsibility for the project's completion. The building never housed priests, however, and was used instead for commercial endeavors until 1834. In 1848 Almonester's daughter, the Baroness Pontalba, pushed for the addition of a mansard roof to match her makeover of the Cabildo. The handsome edifice housed the city's municipal courts until 1911, when it joined the museum's collection of historic properties.

It is nearly a mirror image of the Cabildo: Both share graceful ground-level arches, a motif repeated on their second floors by expansive, high-arched windows, and again by dormer-style windows on their mansardlike third-floor roofs. The Presbytère is a lovely place inside as well, with its permanent exhibition entitled "Mardi Gras: It's Carnival Time in Louisiana." This interactive exploration of the history, evolution, and celebration of Carnival throughout Louisiana features audio and video exhibits as well as exquisite artifacts. Keep an eye out for the crown jewels worn by Carnival "royalty." ■

Pontalba Buildings

EVEN TODAY THESE GREEK REVIVAL ROWHOUSES EXUDE an exclusive air, which was precisely the intent of their builder, the Baroness Pontalba. Inspired by her apartments of Paris, they were conceived as part of the Baroness's plan to create a neighborhood of upwardly mobile New Orleanians that might serve as a gentrified rampart against the swelling American presence in the commercial district across Canal Street.

1850 House
http://lsm.crt.state.la.us
Map pp. 50–51
523 St. Ann St.
504-568-6968 or 800-568-6968
Closed Mon.
$

Baroness Pontalba's determination to create beautiful buildings followed a disastrous marriage to a deranged French aristocrat, whose father attempted to murder her at the family villa on the outskirts of Paris, injuring her badly. She recovered, only to find her cherished haven in the world of New Orleans's Catholic Creole elite threatened by the Yankees Protestant antipathy for their fancy ways. A century and a half later, the apartments in her buildings are some of the most sought after in New Orleans. Former tenants include some of the city's most notable literary sojourners—Sherwood Anderson and Katherine Anne Porter among them. The Baroness's Parisian home, the Hotel Pontalba, is now the residence of the American ambassador.

Three years of construction, completed in 1851, produced these high-style residences and ground-level shops (and rear slave quarters) in a pair of block-long redbrick structures designed to give Jackson Square an architectural unity. Finished first were 16 rowhouses on St. Peter Street (where the Baroness briefly resided), called the Upper Pontalba, followed by a similar collection, the Lower Pontalba Building, across the plaza facing St. Ann Street. One of the three-story townhouses in the lower Pontalba has been restored to its antebellum appearance by the Louisiana State Museum and is open to the public.

The Pontalba Buildings were constructed with a second-floor gallery sheltering a public sidewalk below.

Complete with period furnishings, decorative artifacts, and art of the era, the **1850 House** re-creates upper-middle-class family life during the city's most prosperous period. There are tours, but you're welcome to explore on your own. ■

Walk: the Quarter's literary sites

Writers tend to congregate where rents are low, the culture is high, the citizenry tolerant, and the worship of commerce not overpowering. New Orleans has always delivered that, along with a convivial café tradition that makes the solitary trade of writing less lonely.

So it's no wonder that many of the world's most famous writers have been drawn to the Big Easy—Ernest Hemingway, Tennessee Williams, Thornton Wilder, and W. Somerset Maugham among them. Exploring some of their haunts, this tour starts from the **Upper Pontalba Building** ❶ on Jackson Square's downtown side (see p. 59). Keep in mind that most of the sites are private residences and not open to the public.

After World War I, New Orleans had a reputation among writers for offering many of the sensual pleasures of Paris's Left Bank for the price of a train ticket. Among those lured to it was Sherwood Anderson, remembered for his 1919 story collection, *Winesburg, Ohio.* He visited Paris, then moved to New Orleans in early 1922 with his wife, Elizabeth, and rented a room in the Pontalba Buildings. Their Saturday night literary soirées became a tradition, attended by Thornton Wilder, W. Somerset Maugham (*Of Human Bondage*), Booth Tarkington (*The Magnificent Ambersons*), poet Edna St. Vincent Millay, a 1924 Pulitzer Prize-winner whose short, tight skirts and clinging sweaters shocked other Pontalba tenants, and future Nobel laureate William Faulkner, to whom Anderson became a mentor. In 1937 Katherine Anne Porter, remembered for her 1962 novel *Ship of Fools* and 1939 short story collection *Pale Horse, Pale Rider,* rented a 40-foot-long attic room in the Pontalba for $30 a month, telling her editor it was perfect for a beginning writer. She, too, would win a Pulitzer.

Walk to **624 Pirate's Alley** ❷, just upriver from St. Louis Cathedral between Chartres and Royal Streets. Here in a ground-floor apartment for six months in 1925–26, Faulkner worked on his first novel, *Soldiers' Pay,* for which Anderson found a publisher. This room is now **Faulkner House Books** *(504-524-2940),* home of the Pirate's Alley Faulkner Society, a literary group that supports and promotes Southern writers.

Backtrack to Chartres, turn right, walk to St. Peter Street, and turn right. At No. 616 is

Book lovers shop for used and rare volumes at Faulkner House Books.

Le Petit Théâtre du Vieux Carré (see p. 92), an amateur repertory company since 1916 (America's oldest), where Sherwood Anderson and visiting Sinclair Lewis, the first American to win the Nobel Prize in literature, once took the stage.

At 632 St. Peter, the **Avaret-Paretti House,** Tennessee Williams lived in 1946-47 in a third-floor room. There he wrote *Summer and Smoke* and his Pulitzer Prize-winning *A Streetcar Named Desire.* Through the skylight he remembered dreamy views of drifting clouds.

At the corner look for **711 Royal Street** ❸, which native son Truman Capote rented in 1945 after returning from New York City. In a "small hot bedroom almost entirely occupied by a brass bed" made "noisy as a steel mill" by streetcars below, the 21-year-old wrote part of his first novel, *Other Voices, Other Rooms,* a tale of alienated youth that rocketed him into literary orbit. (The *Breakfast at Tiffany's* author wrote fondly of New Orleans in his 1975 memoir *Music for Chameleons.*)

In 1961, in their apartment in the four-story **Pedesclaux-LeMonnier House** at 636-640 Royal, between St. Peter and Toulouse Streets, Jon and Louise Webb used a hand-operated press to print the premiere issue of their literary journal *Outsider;* they went on to publish Allen Ginsberg, Jack Kerouac, Henry Miller, and Lawrence Ferlinghetti. In 1965 they encouraged Charles Bukowski, a hard-drinking California poet then unknown, to come to New Orleans, get sober, and write. He stepped off a bus in March 1965, took an apartment near the Webbs on Royal, and penned *Crucifix in a Deathhand,* his first collection.

After arriving in December 1938 by bus from St. Louis, Tennessee Williams moved into a boardinghouse around the corner at **722 Toulouse Street,** between Royal and Bourbon. From here, walk up to Bourbon Street and turn right. In the 1920s, Thornton Wilder, whose *The Bridge of San Luis Rey* and *Our Town* won Pulitzers in 1927 and 1938, rented the townhouse at **623 Bourbon ❹.**

Return to Royal Street and walk three blocks upriver to the landmark **Hotel Monteleone ❺** at 214 Royal, where in September 1924 Arch Persons and his wife, Lillie Mae, rented a suite. Soon after, she gave birth to Truman Capote at the nearby Touro Infirmary. In 1915 Tennessee Williams treated his 94-year-old grandfather William Dakin to a stay at the Monteleone, and worked there on his still-controversial play *Camino Real.*

The walk ends here, unless you wish to pay tribute to Williams's last permanent New Orleans address, a mile away in the Lower Quarter. He owned an apartment complex at 1014 Dumaine Street and so loved his second-floor main apartment that he hoped to end his days there. But it was not to be; the city's preeminent 20th-century literary voice died in New York City at the Hotel Elysée on East 54th Street in 1983, aged 72. ■

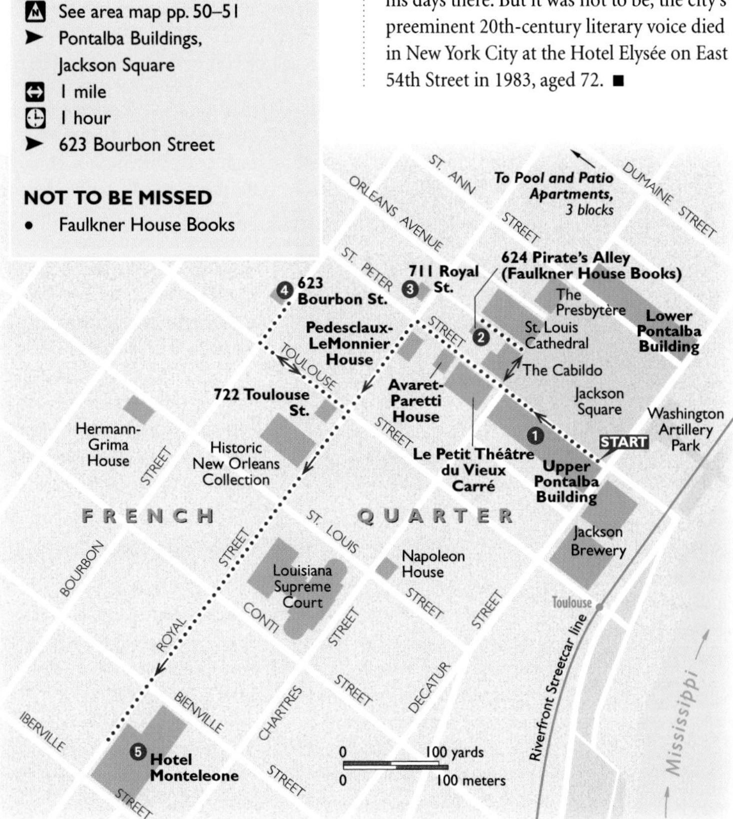

Madame John's Legacy

Madame John's Legacy
http://lsm.crt.state.la.us
Map pp. 50–51
632 Dumaine St.
504-568-6968 or 800-568-6968
Closed Mon.
$

ONE OF NEW ORLEANS'S FINEST EXAMPLES OF LATE 18TH-century Creole architecture, this curiously named residence was one of the few to barely escape the great fire of 1788 and to be completely spared the 1794 fire. Soon after, the Spanish government instituted building codes to make the French Quarter less incendiary. The result was an entirely new look for the city, leaving Madame John's Legacy a rare relic of its vanished past.

French emigrants built houses like this in Canada, the West Indies, and parts of Illinois, typically after they prospered and outgrew their original rude settlers' cabins. The residence consists of three buildings separated by an L-shaped courtyard: a main house, a kitchen with cook's quarters, and a two-story *garçonnière*—a separate apartment reserved for older brothers, children, or servants.

The first thing you'll notice about the main house is how it was built high above the ground, with a porch (gallery) running along the front and back of the house. This raised design removes occupants from the sunbaked streets and protects during flooding. The ground floor, with French doors for maximum ventilation, is a solid masonry basement of soft stuccoed brick to create space for storage and domestic functions; it also serves as a foundation for the living quarters above. The high, double-pitched roof and small dormers are signature details of Louisiana's 18th-century colonial houses. Though the thick-walled exterior suggests a cramped and dim space inside, instead you'll find a pleasant domestic enclave filled by the Louisiana State Museum with folk art, furnishings, and artifacts from the twilight of the 1700s.

The courtyard was a workplace for household chores. The detached kitchen, although inconvenient, reduced the risk of cooking fires spreading to the main house. ■

Schoolchildren tour Madame John's Legacy, one of New Orleans's oldest residences.

Madame John's legacies

Madame John's Legacy has a colorful past. The first owner of the property, Jean Pascal, was a French sea captain killed by Natchez Indians. Another owner, Dame Marie Anne Dotrange Seghers, lived the high life; upon her death in 1819, her estate included 34 dresses, 100 bottles of imported wine, and four female slaves. Madame John, however, never existed. The house takes its name from a short story published in the late 1800s about a free woman of color who became the mistress of a Creole gentleman; having never married, the man bequeathed the house to her. ■

Once the center of the city's furnituremaking trade, Royal Street still deals in furnishings and finery.

Royal Street

FROM THE BEGINNING RUE ROYALE WAS THE PREEMINENT street of the French Quarter, its name a nod of respect to the King of France. As New Orleans prospered in the early 1800s, banking houses opened around its intersection with Conti Street, and leading entrepreneurs built their houses along it. This is a street to stroll at leisure, for it embodies the city's most cherished historical themes, displaying the decorative architecture and early 19th-century ambience that charms so many French Quarter visitors.

Royal Street

Map pp. 50–51

New Orleans's commerce in antiques—furniture, porcelain, and jewelry especially—is centered in shops lining Royal and Chartres Streets. Among the city's early master furnituremakers was Frenchman François Seignouret, who also traded in imported wine out of the **Maison Seignouret** at 520 Royal, which he built in 1816. All his furniture creations, including pieces in the White House, discreetly display a carved initial *S*. His maison's central carriage tunnel leads to a stone-laid courtyard where you can relax on a bench by a fountain. Note the architectural details that make this an oft painted, oft photographed building. The arches, wood pillars, and curving stairway are all quintessentially Vieux Carré.

Another typical scene can be found at **Le Monde Creole** *(624 Royal St. 504-568-1801)*, a shop noted not only for its elegant oddities but also for the serene courtyard within its 170-year-old, three-story, Creole-style townhouse. Guided walks featuring New Orleans's Creole heritage depart daily from the shop to explore secret courtyards throughout the Quarter. ■

Historic New Orleans Collection

Historic New Orleans Collection
www.hnoc.org
Map pp. 50–51
533 Royal St.
504-523-4662
Closed Sun.–Mon. Tours offered at 10 and 11 a.m. & 2 and 3 p.m.
Free. Guided tours: $

IN THE 500 BLOCK OF ROYAL STREET YOU'LL FIND ONE OF the city's most fascinating history museums. Although its official address is No. 533, the Historic New Orleans Collection is actually housed in seven adjacent 18th- and 19th-century buildings. Embracing three intimate courtyards, the building's galleries and a museum mount changing exhibitions that treat some 300 years of Louisiana's saga, with special attention to the city's distinctive stories.

At the Collection's center is the **Merieult House,** completed in 1792 and one of only a few buildings to survive the devastating fire that swept the French Quarter in 1794, making it a rare survivor from the city's Spanish colonial era. The first floor is taken up by the **Williams Gallery,** which hosts changing exhibitions on the history and culture of Louisiana.

From here, tours lead through the second floor's ten rooms, each devoted to a different period of Louisiana's history. Documents, maps, furniture, artifacts, photographs, books, and paintings illustrate singular aspects of New Orleans life since the city's founding—not only documenting every era but re-creating their domestic appearance.

The first room you come to, the **French Colonial Gallery,** recalls the city's founding in 1718 under French rule; prominently displayed is a portrait of Jean Baptiste Le Moyne, Sieur de Bienville, the founder of New Orleans, along with a Louisiana-made refectory table (1740) and an engraved map of New Orleans, dating from 1764. The **Spanish Colonial Gallery** remembers the days when Spaniards ruled the Louisiana Territory, between 1763 and 1803. Of special note are several land treaties between the Spanish governors and Indians, as well as famous portraits by Spanish colonial artist Salazar y Mendoza; be sure to seek out the lovely "Clara de la Molte" (1795).

The **Louisiana Purchase Gallery** recalls the transaction between President Thomas Jefferson and Napoleon I in 1803, which doubled the size of the United States; at less than three cents an acre for 828,000 square miles, it was also the greatest land bargain in U.S. history. Here, don't miss the original documents that finalized the deal. In the **Battle of New Orleans Gallery,** there's no doubt as to the hero of this 1815 battle, with two portraits of Andrew Jackson dominating the colorful room. The **Empire Gallery** re-creates the years from 1820 to 1840 using exquisite examples of period furniture, paintings, and documents. Among the relics in the **Victorian Galleries,** representing the years 1850 to 1900, are a pair of American Rococo Revival settees and a wonderful French Second Empire chandelier (ca 1855). Here, too, you'll find early Mardi Gras mementos, since this celebration evolved during this time. The **Plantation Gallery,** covering 1830 to 1900, traces the saga of the Louisiana plantations from antebellum days through Reconstruction, paying special attention to the lives of slaves

Opposite: A shade frame displays 19th-century clothing accessories.

and free people of color. The last rooms you come to, the **River Galleries** primarily concern activities on the Mississippi River from the mid-19th century to the present.

WILLIAMS RESIDENCE MUSEUM

The house is the legacy of Leila and Gen. L. Kemper Williams, whose shared determination ensured that their trove of artifacts and historic properties were kept intact and made available to the public. The old 1889 Trapolin townhouse they purchased in 1938 and restored in the early 1940s is now the Williams Residence Museum. Tucked behind the Merieult House off the Collection's central courtyard, their "hidden house," surrounded by three beautiful courtyards, offers an intimate glimpse into the acquisitive passion peculiar to dedicated collectors with means.

The home is beautiful and a must-see for those intrigued by the city's last formal era—and, perhaps, America's as well. Its furnishings reflect mid-20th-century American decorating trends favored by the wealthy—white-on-white and pastel color schemes, fabric-covered walls, bleached wood treatments, 18th-century English antiques, and walls covered with paintings and prints. You'll also see early maps of Louisiana and the Gulf South from the Collection.

WILLIAMS RESEARCH CENTER

A scholar's paradise, the Collection's elegant Williams Research Center *(410 Chartres St. 504-598-7171. Closed Sun.–Mon.)* is located in a handsome beaux arts-style building. It houses more than a million items—Louisiana maps, letters, documents,

photographs, family papers, and one-of-a-kind historic artifacts—composing the region's leading collection of materials on Louisiana and the Gulf South. The repository is precious and requests must be made to view its contents in the spacious reading room. ■

As summer approaches, Gallier House docents alter furnishings as 19th-century residents did, seeking relief from heat and humidity.

Gallier House Museum

Gallier House Museum
www.gnofn.org/~hggh/
Map pp. 50–51
1118-1132 Royal St.
504-525-5661
Mon.–Sat. 10 a.m. to 3:30 p.m. (guided tours only)
$$

MORE SUCCESSFUL THAN MOST WHO CAME TO NEW Orleans from the Emerald Isle was the Gallier family. Both father and son trained as architects; the son built this beautiful townhouse between 1857 and 1860 on a lot where the resolute nuns of the Ursuline Convent had once planted an orchard.

In a calculated move James Gallagher changed his family's name to Gallier before leaving Ireland, believing a more Gallic-flavored appellation would facilitate their acceptance into the French-speaking city. (It did.) James Sr. and Jr. ran up a list of credits for an assortment of public and private buildings. (The magnificent 1858 French Opera House, which burned in 1919, was James Jr.'s crowning achievement; his 1866 Italian Renaissance-motif Bank of America building, still standing at 115 Exchange Alley, is believed to be New Orleans's first with a cast-iron facade.)

In 1857 James Jr. commenced construction of this expansive residence whose central skylight, flushing toilet, and hot running water made it the most modern building in town. An attached kitchen was another innovation; the recently introduced enclosed stove reduced the fire danger. Gallier decorated the facade himself, adding graceful ironwork arches to its second-floor gallery. This is a typical Louisiana townhouse in that nearly all its living rooms open onto porches, galleries, or balconies, maximizing ventilation.

What makes the Gallier House an unusually interesting museum is the attention to authentic period details changing with the season. In summer, for instance, furniture is fitted with cotton slipcovers and rugs are replaced with straw matting. The visit includes the home's lovely interior garden, elegant carriage way, and, in the rear, its restored slave quarters. ■

Beauregard-Keyes House

NOVELIST FRANCES PARKINSON KEYES WAS IN HER TIME the reigning queen of the New Orleans literati, and for 25 years, commencing in 1944, she used this porticoed Greek Revival home as her winter residence. She wrote many of her 51 books in its prim Victorian interior, earning the right, as its protector, to add her name to the old raised cottage.

Beauregard-Keyes House
- Map pp. 50–51
- 1113 Chartres St.
- 504-523-7257
- Mon.–Sat. (guided tours only)
- $

Architect François Correjolles built the house in 1826 for Joseph LeCarpentier, a prospering auctioneer. Seven years later, a Swiss diplomat purchased it and added the garden. The house went through many owners and by 1925 was a candidate for the wrecking ball. That horrified a group of patriotic ladies—patriotic, at least, to the Confederacy. They felt that the home of so illustrious a soldier as Confederate Gen. Pierre G.T. Beauregard ought to be saved, even though the man who had ordered the first cannon shot at the Union garrison of Fort Sumter had lived here for only a few months, in 1866 and 1868. The women bought it and raised enough money to partially restore it.

After Frances Parkinson Keyes acquired the house in 1944, she finished restoring it and moved in with her collection of antique dolls. Every winter until her death in 1970, she used its former slave quarters as a writing studio; sometimes she decided the fates of her characters in the interior courtyard.

Don't miss the Swiss consul's formal side garden, which retains its original 1830s design of ornamental shrubbery separated by paths resembling a sunburst, a French motif known as a parterre. ■

In winter, Keyes wrote in this comfortable study.

A mint julep, Your Majesty?

Born in 1885, Keyes was a best-selling author in the 1940s and 1950s, winning acclaim with novels including *Dinner at Antoine's*. Her position in New Orleans society was such that her engraved invitations, annotated in her precise handwriting, confirmed the recipients' acceptance among the city's elite. Among many guests she entertained were the Duke and Duchess of Windsor, whom she invited in 1950 to a black-tie mint julep party, followed by dinner at Antoine's. ■

The Ursuline nuns, as resourceful as they were pious, championed women's education.

Old Ursuline Convent & St. Mary's Church

THE FINEST EXAMPLE OF FRENCH COLONIAL PUBLIC architecture in the United States, the convent was one of the first three New Orleans buildings to earn national historic landmark status (in 1960, along with Jackson Square and the Cabildo).

Old Ursuline Convent
- Map pp. 50–51
- 1100 Chartres St.
- 504-529-3040
- Guided tours Tues.–Sun.
- $

St. Mary's Church
- Map pp. 50–51
- 1100 Chartres St.
- 504-529-2651
- Hourly guided tours & daily Masses
- Donation

Constructed in 1748–52, the convent escaped the 1788 fire undamaged, making it the city's only French-era survivor. It was constructed in the *briquettes-entre-poteaux* style—brick walls framed by massive cypress timbers.

The convent's founding Ursuline nuns dedicated themselves to the education of girls, the care of orphans, and the nursing of the poor. The school they founded upon their arrival from France in 1727 was one of America's first institutions of learning for women. Here the sisters also opened America's first charity hospital and, eventually, the nation's first free school devoted to Native and African Americans. In 1815 the sisters prayed on behalf of Andrew Jackson in the Battle of New Orleans, a gesture for which the future President came here to thank them. In 1824 the nuns retreated to a new convent 2 miles downriver, and the old convent became the archbishop's residence and offices (1824–1899). It was also a meeting place (1831–34) for the state legislature and, for much of the 20th century, a parish and elementary school complex.

In 2004 the Archdiocese of New Orleans refurbished the building and reopened it as part of the new Catholic Cultural Heritage Center. Displays include artifacts and artwork from area churches.

St. Mary's Church, also part of the new center, was completed in 1845 as the chapel of Archbishop Antoine Blanc and then, under various names, served a succession of congregations—French, Spanish, Creole, Irish, German, Slavonian, and Italian. Its simple exterior belies the decorative interior, where Masses (and tours) are offered daily. ■

Old U.S. Mint

TUCKED AWAY IN THE LOWER QUARTER, THE OLD U.S. MINT is the only place that struck coins for both the U.S. and the Confederacy. Andrew Jackson lobbied for its completion in 1835 to help fund development of the frontier. The building started sinking into the soft soil until stabilized by Army engineers in the 1850s.

Old U.S. Mint
http://lsm.crt.state.la.us
Map pp. 50–51
400 Esplanade Ave.
504-568-6968 or 800-568-6968
Closed Mon.
$

The Spanish fort of San Carlos stood on this site from 1792 until its dismantling in 1821—in late 1814 Andrew Jackson inspected his army here before marching them downriver to face the British in the Battle of New Orleans. Gray stone Doric columns front the redbrick Greek Revival structure, which minted its first gold and silver coins in 1838, using steam-powered stamping machines. After Louisiana seceded from the Union in 1861, state officials turned the building over to the Confederate Army, which quartered troops in it. During their residency, only four coins were minted due to a lack of bullion. In 1862 Federal forces occupied New Orleans, and soon after the Civil War the only money issued here bore the motto "E Pluribus Unum." Moneymaking ceased in 1909, after which the building served a variety of purposes; in 1932, for example, it was a federal prison. In 1981 it opened as a site of the Louisiana State Museums.

Just inside the Esplanade entrance you'll find the **Coin Vault** *(504-523-6468)*, which sells coins struck here between 1838 and 1909. The second-floor **New Orleans Jazz Museum** *(504-568-6968)* is filled with memorabilia recounting jazz's evolution. Scholars and devotees can make an appointment to study vintage sheet music and listen to rare recordings.

Visit the third-floor landing for a look at Xavier Gonzalez's 1940s-era mural, "Dixie's Bar of Music," portraying jazz luminaries of the thirties.

The third floor houses an archive of documents including French and Spanish colonial maps. The river view is splendid, and from here elevators lower you to the Barracks Street entrance, a side of the building ornamented with cast-iron galleries. ■

Mardi Gras Indians

Not Indians but mostly working-class African Americans, the Mardi Gras Indians are a highlight of Mardi Gras parades. Men sew their own costumes—fantastic displays of plumage and embroidered, bejeweled regalia that take up to a year to create—and join one of 20-odd tribes that march through the city. The tradition dates back more than a century, to a time when blacks were not included in the exclusive Anglo-American krewes, Mardi Gras organizations that allowed membership by invitation only. They developed their own style of celebrating by forming "tribes" and sporting feathers as a sign of respect and affinity for another oppressed group, the Native Americans. ■

A complex interweaving of history and folklore produced Carnival's African-American "Indians," here parading during Mardi Gras.

Musician with riverboat in background. Designed specifically for Mississippi navigation, flat-bottomed, steam-powered paddle wheelers were the river's commercial workhorses.

A walk along the river

This walk takes you along the Mississippi shoreline, where New Orleans began in a clearing hacked out of a palmetto grove. It sets off from the French Market and ends at the Spanish Plaza—symbolic landmarks of the city's past. Along the way you'll visit museums and markets, stroll riverside promenades, and drink in the spirit of the city's cultural trademarks, Mardi Gras and jazz.

Start at the historic **French Market ❶**, a complex of buildings that sprawls between Decatur and N. Peters Streets, and St. Ann and Barracks Streets just east of Jackson Square. Commerce here dates from the late 1700s, when the Spanish put up a permanent enclosed marketplace. It was replaced in 1813 by a French-built meat market housed in today's **Café du Monde** building, the oldest structure in the complex. (The Café du Monde, by the way, is traditionally the place to order your first chicory-laced café au lait and beignet.) For decades, the local trade was in fruits, vegetables, meat, poultry, fish, and wild game. John James Audubon would come here to purchase birds for mounting and careful study before he painted them. Ships loaded cargoes that could be preserved for ports across the world. Native American and African-American merchants did business here amid a babble of European tongues, French most of all. In the 1930s, workmen employed by the U.S. Government's Works Progress Administration swarmed in to renovate the market and install refrigeration. Another makeover in the 1970s installed cafés and shops, sending most of the food wholesalers and vendors moved to the smaller Farmer's Market between Governor Nicholls and Ursulines Streets. If you take this walk on a weekend, look for the flea market between Governor Nicholls and Barracks Streets.

Leaving the market, walk west along Decatur Street to **Washington Artillery Park** opposite Jackson Square and climb the stairs for a superb view of the square's "solar" motif—hedges and walkways splaying out like the sun's rays. For a close-up look at the Mississippi, take the stairs down the other side, walk through the flood wall gate, and

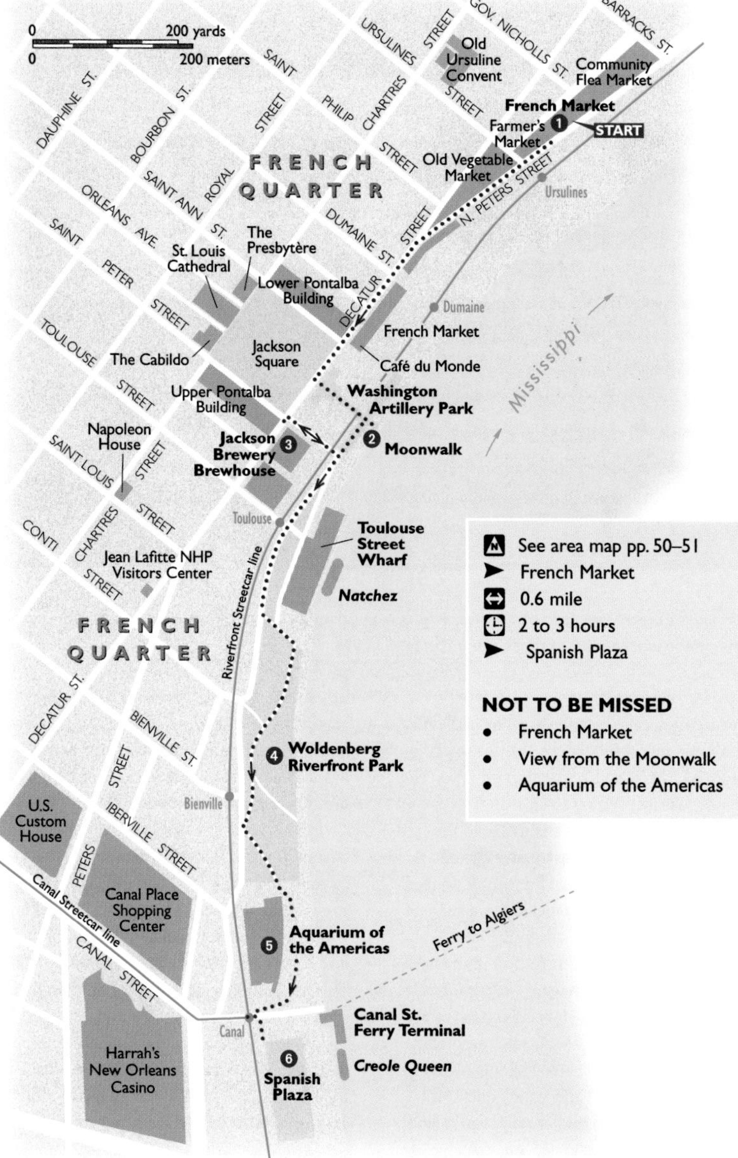

cross the streetcar tracks to stairs climbing to the top of the levee.

The best (and most convenient) place to put your hand in the most fabled of American rivers is along the **Moonwalk ❷,** a wooden promenade built in 1981 on the riverside slope of the levee paralleling the French Market complex. Part of Woldenberg Riverfront Park, it was named in honor of former Mayor Maurice "Moon" Landrieu. Its bleacherlike steps descend to the crescent bend of the Chippewas' *missi sipi*—"big water"—that inspired early residents to nickname this town the Crescent City. People

A French Market vendor sells seafood spices. Quarter residents have shopped for food and other delicacies at the market since the late 1700s.

have been coming here for a long time, because it's said to be a place where you can usually find a cooling breeze. In this relaxing place you can sit and watch ship traffic on the river or take an evening stroll.

Proceed right on St. Peter Street to the **Jackson Brewery Brewhouse** ❸ *(620 Decatur St.)*, nicknamed Jax Brewery. It was built in the late 1890s as the castlelike headquarters and brew house of the Jackson Brewing Company. An unusual renovation in the mid-1980s inserted a contemporary commercial complex within the five-story-high chess piece, built for Irishman David Jackson by a German architect. This is not old New Orleans—among the tenants are Planet Hollywood and a Hard Rock Café—but the modernization works, and the mall is a fine place to rest and refuel. Next door at 600 Decatur is the Jackson Brewery Millhouse, full of shops to browse.

Back along the river, look for the steamboat ***Natchez*** *(504-586-8777 or 800-233-BOAT. Fare)*, which departs in late morning and early afternoon from the **Toulouse Street Wharf** behind the Jax Brewery and makes a two-hour excursion up- and downriver. (At night, a dinner-and-jazz cruise is offered.) A voyage aboard this handsome antique evokes the romance of Mark Twain's *Life on the Mississippi*, a memoir of his career as a river pilot.

Farther upriver from the Moonwalk, beyond the wharf, is **Woldenberg Riverfront Park** ❹. This willow-lined promenade was once a bustling commercial wharf. The statue of a man giving advice to a boy commemorates the park's benefactor, New Orleans businessman Malcolm Woldenberg.

Walk upriver through the park toward the foot of Canal Street and the Audubon Institute's **Aquarium of the Americas** ❺ *(504-581-4629 or 800-774-7394. $$$)*; it is announced by sculptor Ida Kohlmeyer's depictions of marine life. As the name implies, the aquarium's range of interest is hemispheric, addressing underwater life and environments from the remote Arctic to the tip of South America. Within live thousands of fish, other underwater creatures, and an aviary of water birds. Major exhibits treat in detail the Mississippi River and the Gulf of Mexico. The huge screen in the adjacent Entergy IMAX

Sharks patrol relentlessly in the main fish tank at the Aquarium of the Americas.

Theatre (rising nearly six stories) shows wraparound documentaries on ocean life and science *(504-581-IMAX or 800-774-7394).*

From the plaza in front of the aquarium, continue on to the foot of Canal Street where, if you reconnoiter carefully, you will find concrete steps vaulting the streetcar tracks. They lead to the pedestrian portal for the **Canal Street Ferry** to **Algiers Point** (see pp. 117–124) across the Mississippi.

Beyond the terminal, descend the stairs into **Spanish Plaza ❻,** whose centerpiece is a fountain ringed by tiles symbolizing Iberian provinces. Back when warehouses formed an impenetrable wall between the French Quarter and the river, this was the only place where you could contemplate the Mississippi close-up. The ***Creole Queen*** riverboat is moored here, departing twice daily for two-and-a-half-hour cruises downriver to the Chalmette Battlefield (see pp. 180–183).

Towering above Spanish Plaza at the foot of Canal Street is **Harrah's New Orleans Casino** *(504-533-6000).* The 100,000-square-foot Greek Revival edifice, which opened here in 1999, has 3,000-odd slot machines and 120 gaming tables. It has adopted architectural touches traditionally seen in the Quarter, and its five huge indoor courtyards reflect the themes of New Orleans history.

To return to where you began, board either the Riverfront streetcar line or the Canal streetcar line at the Canal Street stop. ■

Riverfront streetcar line

Running between Esplanade Avenue in the Lower French Quarter to Thalia Street in the Warehouse District, the Riverfront line's Red Ladies include 1920s Perley Thomas streetcars like those on the St. Charles line (the Canal Street line includes streetcars designed to resemble the older models). There are ten stops: at Esplanade Avenue (the downriver turnaround), Ursulines, Dumaine, Toulouse, Bienville, Canal, Poydras, Julia, Calliope, and Thalia Streets (the upriver turnaround). To signal the driver that you want to get off, pull the bell cord running the length of the car. ■

The sun sets and lights go on along Bourbon Street, synonymous with New Orleans's musical heritage.

Bourbon Street

THOUGH ONLY 14 BLOCKS LONG, IT IS NEW ORLEANS'S BEST-known street, yet even those who would rather do anything than criticize their beloved Crescent City get rueful when you ask them what they think of "The Street" these days. Like Los Angeles's Hollywood Boulevard, it symbolizes more than it delivers. In any case, an evening on Bourbon Street is a must.

Bourbon Street
Map pp. 50–51

For some, Bourbon's clubs, bars, and neon-trimmed strip joints—it is the only French Quarter street where neon signs are allowed—is wonderfully exotic. Doorways breathe cigarette smoke and jazz. Look through parted curtains and see topless dancers slither and grind. Some bars shuck oysters; others fleece tourists. Named not for liquor but royalty—the Duke of Bourbon, an 18th-century Frenchman who invested in the colony—the street's public face is one of bars and sidewalk sipping. (Order your drink in a "go-cup" and you may sip as you stroll.)

Bourbon Street's sidewalks come alive after dark, when musicians often play into the early morning hours.

During Mardi Gras, the street—the heart of which are the 200–800 blocks—fills with go-cuppers, so many that it is difficult to move. The line between convivial imbibing and excess blurs, particularly among young out-of-towners who see Mardi Gras as equivalent to spring break in Fort Lauderdale.

The street, however, redeems itself through music. Nowhere in the world is there a greater concentration of music clubs, where many new musicians face their first audiences alongside veteran teacher-mentors. Some Bourbon Street clubs keep their doors open until daybreak. You can stand outside and audition several at once. You will hear old jazz and new jazz, Dixieland, blues, rhythm and blues, brass bands, soul, funk, world music, Cajun, and zydeco. There are banjos, thumbtacked pianos, harmonicas, accordions, trumpets, trombones, guitars, flutes, bones, string basses, and saxophones galore. Some of the players are self-taught octogenarians whose repertories are vast and who ought to be designated national treasures.

The **Famous Door** *(339 Bourbon St. 504-598-4334)* starts its evenings around the dinner hour with Dixieland, switching to rhythm and blues about nine. Gut-bucket blues wail and twang in the **Old Absinthe House** *(240 Bourbon St. 504-525-8108)*. Cajun music and food dominate at **Cajun Cabin** *(501 Bourbon St. 504-529-4256)*. Nightly live jazz is the rule at **Maison Bourbon** *(641 Bourbon St. 504-522-8818)*. Finally, **Fritzel's European Jazz Pub** *(733 Bourbon St. 504-561-0432)* is known for offering *très* cool jazz of the "Round Midnight" variety. ■

Mardi Gras

New Orleans is synonymous worldwide with the madcap celebration of the old European Christian tradition, transplanted here in 1699 when French-Canadian Sieur d'Iberville and his troupe of explorers encamped downriver on the last day before Lent.

In the Roman Catholic calendar (and some Protestants ones), Mardi Gras—literally Fat Tuesday—is the day before Ash Wednesday, the first day of the austere Lenten season, generally in February or early March. Since Lent is a time for penitence and fasting, Fat Tuesday traditionally provided one last opportunity to use up all of the fats in the home, to enjoy final hours of indulgence. Roman Catholic countries—especially Italy, France, and Brazil—are known for their merrymaking and festivities during this time, a weeks-long celebration known as Carnival.

New Orleans, of course, has fashioned the celebration into its own version of out-of-control, crazy merriment, featuring masquerade balls and uninhibited street processions. There isn't much evidence of any kind of celebration in the early 1700s, though by 1781 Carnival was established enough that straightlaced civic officials were sputtering that the celebration's free-spirited and tolerant abandon, during which "people of color" mixed easily with other celebrants, was endangering public morality. During the 1800s Mardi Gras was once outlawed; even masks, a key element of the fun, were briefly forbidden. But the "*bals masque*" continued with such relish—the "season" expanded to seven months—that it was deemed necessary to limit it to the weeks between January 1 and Fat Tuesday, lest locals celebrate all year long. Sometime in the 1830s the first processions took place; today some 60 parades crowd the Carnival calendar, most occurring in the last two weeks before Mardi Gras.

But the spirit of Mardi Gras commences early in New Orleans with the kickoff of the festive Carnival season on Twelfth Night, or January 6. Christmas trimmings vanish, Carnival decorations go up, and New Orleans krewes—social clubs that host parades and/or fancy balls—begin their celebrations. Carnival's grand finale is what the world knows as Mardi Gras, a four-day weekend of parades and festivities beginning on the Saturday before Ash Wednesday. Don't miss Saturday's Endymion parade, said to be one of the longest on Earth, and Sunday's Bacchus procession, which celebrates earthly pleasures, as its name suggests.

But the climax is on Fat Tuesday, when five parades sashay along St. Charles Avenue and Canal Street—including the famous parade of Rex, King of Carnival. (Check the "Mardi Gras Guide" or newspapers for information.) For these, spectators arrive before dawn; the sidewalk crowd resembles a well-equipped encampment, complete with portable grills. Expect to see people costumed, made up, or dressed up in ways you might not have seen before. The creativity is astonishing, often hilarious, and routinely bawdy. Marching clubs march, and decorated flatbed trucks convey hundreds of masked and costumed revelers.

A traditional practice of those who ride parade floats is to fling souvenirs to spectators who shout the traditional request: "Throw me something, Mister!" If you're fortunate, you might catch an imitation doubloon, or "gold" coin, bearing a krewe's insignia; more likely you'll receive a string of plastic beads. If you want to be favored by throwers, wear a costume that attracts. ■

Carnival Belle

Between 1937 and 1968, 17 different krewes chose the elegant and charming Germaine Cazenave Wells as their bal masque queen a record 22 times. Her father was Arnaud Cazenave, the maestro of highly acclaimed Arnaud's restaurant, where many of her gowns, along with costumes and accessories worn by her kin, are on display in its second-floor Germaine Wells Mardi Gras Museum, at 813 Bienville St. It's open daily in the mid-morning and at night after six. You enter through the restaurant, and there's no admission. Germaine wouldn't think of it. ■

Top: The venerable Rex parade, a hoary Mardi Gras tradition.
Above: A wave to a float may elicit the toss of "somethin'," usually a string of beads.
Right: History and fancy combine in a French Quarter celebrant's costume.

Preservation Hall

Preservation Hall
www.preservationhall.com
Map pp. 50–51
726 St. Peter St. (bet. Bourbon & Royal Sts.)
504-522-2841 (day) or 504-523-8939 (night)
$ (cash only)

THE GRANDDADDY OF ALL JAZZ CLUBS AND A LANDMARK of American music since the 1920s, Preservation Hall is as its name proclaims—an institution dedicated to the survival of traditional New Orleans jazz, one of the greatest American art forms. The performers here are among the finest anywhere.

Although it occupies an old building, Preservation Hall dates from only 1961, founded and opened by Philadelphians Allan and Sandra Jaffe. Some of its oldest performers played with local great Louis Armstrong, and they still make their fragile way here to play with the freewheeling improvisational flair that Armstrong introduced in New Orleans in the 1920s and 1930s, changing jazz forever. Like many shrines with larger-than-life reputations, this one can disconcert first-timers. Seating is casual, limited, and not very comfortable; you might have to sit on the floor. There is no air-conditioning, and there are no rest rooms. And it is not a hall in the usual sense, but actually a small front room with peeling paint and haphazard lighting. For a jazz lover, and for those who appreciate authenticity, however, an evening here can be the ultimate New Orleans experience.

Doors open nightly at 8 p.m. for five sets, each consisting of 30-minute performances by regular groups or bands. Lines form early and stretch around the corner.

Be sure to browse the Hall's collection of recordings offered for sale—currently a dozen CDs offering a comprehensive survey of New Orleans music. ■

Musicians young and old play together in this world-renowned shrine of traditional jazz.

Hermann-Grima House

ON ST. LOUIS STREET JUST OFF BOURBON IS AN EARLY 19TH-century architectural jewel, so well preserved that the last 170 years evaporate when you enter it. The rosy federal townhouse is a relic of living history: In its kitchen, New Orleans's only functioning 1830s-era cookery, volunteer docents demonstrate old-style Creole cooking from May to October. Throughout the manse, period furnishings evoke the prosperous social climate here between about 1830 and 1860, the twilight of the antebellum era.

Hermann-Grima House

www.gnofn.org/~hggh/

Map pp. 50–51

820 St. Louis St.

504-525-5661

Closed Sat.–Sun.

$$

Built in the 1830s for German immigrant businessman Samuel Hermann, the house mixes American and Creole elements—a central hall in front (an American convention) and a loggia in the rear, a feature common in Creole houses. Mortar has been stenciled on the pink brickwork to give the impression of the Pennsylvania bricks that had been ordered for construction but didn't arrive in time.

Inside, the parlor and formal dining room appear as they might have in 1833, when the Hermanns hosted some 350 people at a reception. Between 2 and 4 in the afternoon, dinner, the day's main repast, would be served in two or three courses, each comprised by as many as a dozen dishes. After each course, the tablecloth was removed to reveal a fresh one.

Details throughout the house reveal that it was one of the more comfortable households in antebellum New Orleans. Be sure to admire the marble tub in the bathing room, where servants brought hot water in painted tin kettles like those displayed here.

Be sure to look closely at the rooms when you visit. The staff delights in historically correct details that seem quaint today but were just good housekeeping when this home was new and Andrew Jackson was President. From mid-October until All Saints' Day (Nov. 1), for instance, the house is decorated in the manner of a mourning Creole household of the 1830s: A black wreath hangs on the front door; mirrors and portraits of the deceased are draped in black. From early December until New Year's Day, the rooms glitter with such Christmas decorations as greenery, velvet, and lace, and carved wooden angels and other figurines. ■

Courtyards like this one once separated the Quarter's residences from servants' quarters, detached kitchens, and garçonnières.

North of Rampart

North of the Quarter, on the other side of Rampart Street, sprawls an indistinct area called North of Rampart. Its upriver reach includes the Faubourg Tremé—subdivided in the early 1800s on what had been the cane fields of French Creole planter Claude Tremé—and part of its downriver sprawl is included in the district known as the Esplanade Ridge. Maps are generally blurry about the area's boundaries, and even residents differ over where one district ends and another begins. But few would argue with those who revere this part of New Orleans as the Cradle of Jazz.

Here on Sundays in the early 1800s, hundreds of West Africans gathered across Rampart to sing and dance on a circus ground that came to be known as Congo Square. Music sustained the enslaved Africans' sense of ethnic identity and community, becoming an established aspect of New Orleans's black Creole life when hundreds settled in the "Tremé" (still mostly African-American). They formed music-oriented social clubs whose tradition of musical innovation and public performances continues to this day.

Jazz pioneer Buddy Bolden poses with his band in 1902.

Within a century, what had been swamp and marsh was transformed into a vibrant, bawdy part of town known for its theaters and concert halls, cabarets, dance halls, and "fancy houses" (bordellos). This sophisticated musical scene was second only, if it was second at all, to New York's Tin Pan Alley.

Save for the social clubs, all that is gone now, and there is little to suggest the significance of Congo Square, now a public monument within Louis Armstrong Park—a large greensward with grassy knolls and ponds, named for native son and world-famous musician Louis Armstrong (1901–1971). ■

New Orleans Jazz National Historical Park

Plans are in the works to build a complex of buildings in Armstrong Park that will form the New Orleans Jazz National Historical Park. When completed it will include a visitor center complex with interpretive displays, exhibits, and historical artifacts; a performance area; and park headquarters. In addition, other significant jazz-related sites throughout New Orleans will be named and preserved; so far, 50 have been identified, many in the South Rampart Street area. Particularly important is South Rampart's 400 block, which contains several historic sites. Among them is the Odd Fellows Hall, which was used by various musical groups during the formative decade of New Orleans jazz—roughly, from 1900 to 1910—and the two-story Iroquois Theater, built in 1911. The Iroquois was an African-American vaudeville and movie house, and from 1912 to 1920 many local jazz vocalists and musicians went professional here. A temporary visitor center, with exhibits and a bookstore, is located at 916 N. Peters Street in the French Quarter; call 877-589-4041 for more information. ■

Louis Armstrong Park

Beyond the arched gateway lies the birthplace of jazz. Below: A bronze statue of music legend Armstrong greets park visitors.

ONE IRONY OF LOUIS ARMSTRONG PARK IS THAT DURING Armstrong's lifetime, there were clubs in town in which he could not play. Another is that, by the 1950s, most of the 19th-century African-American neighborhoods where jazz passed its infancy had been razed in the name of urban renewal. Perhaps saddest of all is that a park bearing the name of a man whose personality and music bridged cultural divides has been plagued by muggings.

Still, its 32 acres are hallowed ground. An arch spans the entrance where St. Ann Street meets Rampart. Just inside to the left is **Congo Square,** where jazz was conceived. In the 1700s, the French colonial Code Noir granted slaves a respite from labor on Sundays. By the early 1800s, they and free people of color were gathering by the hundreds here in the Place des Negres, speaking the languages of their African forebears, observing tribal and religious rituals, and making music, dancing, and singing. Here, too, in the mid-1800s, the witch queen of New Orleans, Marie Laveau, presided over voodoo rites until 1857.

Elizabeth Catlett's statue of Armstrong stands in the center of the park, adjacent to N. Rampart Street. Behind the square stands the **Morris F. X. Jeff, Sr., Municipal Auditorium** *(504-218-0150),* a venue with an eclectic playbill. Nearby, WWOZ-FM (90.7) broadcasts the music of New Orleans exclusively. The New Orleans Ballet and Opera companies share the **Mahalia Jackson Theatre for the Performing Arts** *(504-218-0150),* which honors the New Orleans-born diva, who died in 1972. ■

Louis Armstrong Park

- Map pp. 50–51
- Entrance at St. Ann & N. Rampart Sts.
- 504-218-0150
- Bus: Esplanade

Jazz hothouse

The seeds of New Orleans's musical tradition were planted at Congo Square, where on Sundays between 1817 and 1857, the city's "free people of color" and West African slaves made music with drums, banjo-like instruments, and rhythm-makers. Meanwhile, classical music flourished elsewhere in town, and inevitably these parallel musical styles—one African, West Indian, and Caribbean; the other West European—began to influence each other.

The proximity of venues for the two musical mainstreams was particularly stimulating to African-American and Creole musicians, whose improvisational ways made them more receptive to cross-cultural forays. Ferdinand Joseph Lamothe "Jelly Roll" Morton (1890-1941), for instance, considered the world's first significant jazz composer, credited his inspiration to learn piano to a recital he attended at the French Opera House.

After the Civil War, African-American neighborhood organizations known as social aid and pleasure clubs began to spring up around town. They mounted parades as expressions of community pride and also as a way to create work for musicians. Parading became so much a part of life here that it evolved into a training program for young musical talent.

Left: Jelly Roll Morton
Above: The Maple Leaf Bar on Oak Street

In the late 1800s, brass marching bands came into vogue across America as interest grew in syncopated musical styles influenced by African-American minstrel tunes and cakewalks. By the 1890s, ragtime's syncopated piano compositions were hugely popular, and brass bands began to add to their standard repertories. Meanwhile the blues, whose simple form enabled many to play it, created a legion of self-taught musicians for whom improvisation was second nature.

New Orleans thrived as the 20th century commenced. Legitimate theater, vaudeville, music-publishing houses, and instrument stores employed scores of musicians in the Central Business District. There is colorful folklore about jazz having evolved in the piano parlors in and around the "red-light" neighborhood near Canal and Rampart Streets, known as Storyville. Scholars, however, credit its popularity largely to the Quarter's bistros and saloons and the African-American self-help societies' frequent parades that introduced jazz to tourists. In Lake Pontchartrain's amusement parks and resorts, competition for audiences pushed bands to innovate. Community social halls and saloons held dances almost nightly. Elsewhere, however, the Crescent City sound met resistance. In 1915, when a white Dixieland band from New Orleans performed in Chicago, critics panned the music, calling it "jass," an archaic English term meaning at best "passion" and at worst "sexual abandon"—and meanwhile planting the seed of the new music's name. Several years later, hit recordings by Nick LaRocca's five-piece Original Dixieland Jazz Band of tunes such as "Tiger Rag" gave New Orleans a cachet among the avant-garde. Within a few years, "jazz" symbolized America's cultural ascendancy, and when writer F. Scott Fitzgerald proclaimed the boom years of the 1920s the Jazz Age, that seemed right to just about everybody.

For a time, Jelly Roll Morton enjoyed sole credit for the "invention" of jazz (a mistaken notion in itself). But others contributed greatly to the music during the early 20th century. Among them was Edward "Kid" Ory, a Creole born upriver on the San Francisco Plantation; he toured the country and in 1919 introduced "New Orleans" music to the West Coast. "Basin Street Blues" composer Spencer Williams, who wrote for Josephine Baker, took it to Paris in the 1920s. The most acclaimed of New Orleans's musical envoys, Louis Daniel Armstrong, is credited with infusing the blues with the sophistication of Tin Pan Alley tunes, and, through his masterful trumpet playing, establishing the convention of the jazz soloist. His innovations set musicians free to refine the great American art form, and they established Armstrong as arguably the 20th century's most influential American musician.

The Swing Era of the 1930s began the eclipse of traditional New Orleans-style jazz. In recent years, however, prominent musicians such as New Orleans-born trumpeter Wynton Marsalis have taken to reminding Americans of their most unique musical legacy simply by playing it. ■

An audience enjoys a live performance in Saenger Theater, the sole survivor of New Orleans's once lively theater scene.

Old theater district

BEFORE THE SECOND WORLD WAR, THE NEW ORLEANS theater district centered around Canal and Basin Streets, a nexus of major streetcar lines and a glittery neighborhood awash in dramas, comedies, vaudeville, and musical revues—a Southern cousin of Tin Pan Alley where publishing houses printed sheet music for a nation eager for the city's latest tunes.

Old theater district

Map pp. 50–51

Saenger Theater

143 N. Rampart St. at Iberville St.

504-524-2490 (tour information) or 504-522-5555 (tickets)

Streetcar: Canal

The music reverberated from resonant wood and plaster halls like the Lyric, Strand, Crescent, Plaza, and Trianon. One by one, however, they closed, burned, or fell to the wrecking ball. The only thriving survivor is the magnificent **Saenger Theater,** opened in 1927 as a movie house. Films are rarely shown here today; instead the hall presents top-billed entertainment of all kinds, including traveling Broadway shows, in its ornate, gorgeously restored interior designed by Emile Weil to look like a Renaissance palace's exterior facade. During performances, its dark blue ceiling twinkles with starlike pinpoints of light. Call to ask about tours or open hours.

The city's response to the decline of the theater district was redevelopment—which meant the tearing down of those grand performing arts halls and, in 1941, the building of the Iberville Housing Project. Nothing was revitalized, however, and much of this once wonderful neighborhood, including its share of Basin Street, remains blighted a half century hence, most of its storefronts shabby, many of its residents impoverished. Keep in mind that solitary strolls are not recommended in this neighborhood, particularly after hours.

BASIN STREET

Past glories and the song "Basin Street Blues" ("Where all the proud and elite folks meet/Heaven on earth, they call it Basin Street") limn its name with glamour, but the 20th century has been hard on Basin Street, which runs one block north of the French Quarter, between Armstrong Park and Canal Street. The street's name commemorates what was, from 1794 to 1927, the Quarter's seaport, a lakelike "turning basin" for barges and scows at the terminus of the Carondelet Canal from Bayou St. John and Lake Pontchartrain. The waterway followed the route of what is now Lafitte Street from the Bayou southeast to the French Quarter's rear wall, permitting boats to unload—mostly food and building materials—at the Quarter's foot. There is little left to testify to the street's history. A statue of the Latin American revolutionary Simón Bolívar marks Basin's terminus at Canal, where in the tree-shaded neutral ground it becomes Elk Place (commemorating a long-gone Elks Club hall that stood here). Even the offices of **Basin Street Records,** featuring New Orleans artists, no longer reside here; they moved to the 4100 block of Canal Street in 1997.

Other than that, the district's sites include two haunting cemeteries (see pp. 87 and 88–89) and the old "funeral church" (see p. 86). ■

Storyville & E. J. Bellocq

For a time Basin Street was the main artery of Storyville, a district where legalized prostitution flourished from 1897 to 1917, and the nightlife featured music and amateur street corner "spasm bands."

Many of the bordellos did good business, and in the vicinity of Basin and Bienville Streets they occupied imposing mansions advertising "real" oil paintings and other upscale amenities. Directories known as *Blue Books* listed over 700 "ladies." The bordellos' madams strained to affect airs of respectability. (One asserted that a prospective patron "must be of some importance, otherwise he cannot gain admittance.") Parlor pianists, employed to entertain patrons, made their livelihood here and developed their own style with their earnings. The best—Jelly Roll Morton for one—used the opportunity to experiment in the new genre of jazz. This produced the folklore that jazz owed its existence to Storyville—one implication being that the license of the houses somehow set the creative spirit free. In any event, Storyville lost its legal protections in 1917, and by World War II most of its grand houses were gone. Today the site lies mostly beneath the cheerless 1940s-era Iberville Housing Project.

Storyville's memories live on in the works of photographer Ernest James Bellocq, whose sensitive, nonerotic portraits of its prostitutes are masterpieces of American art. Born in 1883, Bellocq stood barely five feet tall. He lived in Storyville, supporting himself with commercial work and in his spare time photographing its social outcasts, winning their confidence with his respectful manner. His images, found on glass-plate negatives at his desk after his death in 1949, were exhibited for the first time in 1970 at New York's Museum of Modern Art. They immediately established him as a master of his medium. In 1978 French director Louis Malle's film, *Pretty Baby,* based on Bellocq's Storyville years, was released. ■

Candles flicker in the chapel's St. Jude shrine.

Our Lady of Guadalupe Chapel

IT IS THE CRESCENT CITY'S OLDEST SURVIVING CHURCH building. Completed in 1827, an era when cholera and yellow fever epidemics menaced the city, Our Lady of Guadalupe was designated a chapel and dedicated to St. Anthony. In that time of plague, it commenced its religious career doing grim duty as the Mortuary Chapel.

Our Lady of Guadalupe Chapel

http://saintjudeshrine.com

- Map pp. 50–51
- 411 N. Rampart St. at Conti St.
- 504-525-1551
- Daily Masses & Sun. services
- Donation

During epidemics, the St. Louis Cathedral was often overwhelmed by funeral requests, compelling its priests to direct the distraught to the new church, pointedly located just beyond the northwest rampart of the French Quarter, opposite St. Louis Cemetery No. 1. Here, victims—often hundreds weekly—received last blessings. Beyond its austere triple-arch entrance, within brick and stucco walls to the front left, the **St. Jude shrine** (St. Jude is the patron of the desperate and forlorn) flickers with candles that illuminate flowers and written requests for divine succor. Though its simple belfry and steeple are more pleasing than impressive, the chapel remains a necessary one, no longer dealing with cholera and fevers, but with hearts made heavy by the hopelessness and despair that dog the Tremé's sizable population of poor folk.

Remodeling has erased some of the charm within the sanctuary, a loss mitigated by the altar's lovely ecclesiastical furnishings and relics. In the side chapel of St. Jude, note the intricate tile mosaic depicting the Blessed Trinity; another chapel honors New Orleans's peace officers and firefighters. There's a curious bit of local folklore to the left of the entry doors: a statue of St. Expedite, supposedly a creation of misunderstanding that occurred in the 1800s when the unidentified figure arrived in a crate marked "EXPEDITE."

In the adjoining rectory building is a gift shop known for its inventory of holy cards, a selection said to be New Orleans's best. ■

St. Louis Cemetery No. 1

Believed by some to hold the ashes of voodoo queen Marie Laveau, this tomb is a shrine to the faithful.

MELANCHOLY AND PHOTOGENIC, THIS IS NEW ORLEANS'S oldest surviving burial ground. Its maze of mildewy, decaying tombs and wall vaults, benches, urns, and funerary sculpture—grieving lambs and distraught angels—engender a wistful awareness of time's passage. If you can visit only one cemetery, make it this one.

Founded in 1789 by the Spanish, its lots were sold out by 1820. Its high brick walls are buttressed inside by triple-tiered "oven" vaults, embracing a labyrinth of tombs arranged haphazardly along crooked narrow paths. The older tombs were built of local brick that was plastered and whitewashed. Newer ones employ carved stone, usually granite or marble. Their architecture is eclectic, including classical motifs such as Greek Revival and variations of baroque and Gothic—even faux Egyptian. There are barrel-vaulted crypts, pitched-roof tombs, pyramids, coffin-shaped stone sarcophagi, and mini-temples with columns and porticoes. Among the most impressive are freestanding "society tombs" for members of the professional or ethnic mutual aid societies common in old New Orleans. To design one for a prominent clan or group was a coveted commission.

Perhaps the most visited is the **Glapion family tomb,** which many believe holds the remains of voodoo queen Marie Laveau. (Her cabinetmaker husband was a Glapion.) Devotees mark it with red chalk *X*'s for good luck and leave offerings.

Also interred in the cemetery is Homer Plessy, convicted for refusing to sit in a railroad car designated by Louisiana law for blacks. He was infamously affirmed in 1896 by the Supreme Court in *Plessy v. Ferguson,* establishing the now discredited legal fiction that "separate but equal" treatment of minorities satisfied the Constitution. (Plessy, a moral ancestor of future civil rights figures, died in 1925 at age 63.) ■

St. Louis Cemetery No. 1

Map pp. 50–51

Bounded by Basin, St. Louis, Conti, and Tremé Sts.

Note: This cemetery is notorious for muggings. Visit with a tour, such as those offered on Sundays by Save Our Cemeteries (504-525-3377 or 888-721-7493).

St. Louis Cemetery No. 2

St. Louis Cemetery No. 2
Map pp. 50–51
Enter through the Bienville St. gate between N. Claiborne Ave. & N. Robertson Sts.

GROWING POPULATIONS OF THE DEPARTED DUE TO contagious diseases required the opening of St. Louis Cemetery No. 2, consecrated in 1823, four blocks away from No. 1. Its tombs are more ornate and architecturally diverse than those in its predecessor, and its formal paths give it a pleasing, classical European atmosphere despite the fallen fortunes of the surrounding neighborhood.

Exquisite mortuary architecture is seen here: multitiered wall vaults, ornate family crypts, elaborate "society" tombs of French, Italian, Portuguese, Spanish, and African-American mutual aid societies, and some of New Orleans's finest ironwork. No. 2 was staked out in swampland about a third of a mile from the French Quarter after officials concluded that "miasmas" arising from the corpses of fever victims buried in adjoining St. Louis Cemetery No. 1 were the cause of the city's epidemics. Modern drainage has banished the swamp but not No. 2's aura of the early 1800s.

Its location, however, is problematic. Bounded by N. Claiborne Avenue and St. Louis, N. Robertson, and Iberville Streets, the cemetery lies beneath I-10, which mars its classical layout, and adjoins the Iberville Housing Project, making it unsafe. That's a shame, because the cemetery's three walled squares are evocative relics of the customs, styles, and multicultural mix of old New Orleans.

If you go on your own, midmorning is generally safest. Once a year, on All Saints' Day (Nov. 1) by long-standing tradition, mounted police officers guard most of the city's burial grounds while family members and friends of the departed come out to whitewash tombs, repair damage, and leave flowers, candles, and other remembrances.

Otherwise, the best—and safest—way to visit the cemetery is with a tour group. You can arrange a tour through Historic New Orleans Walking Tours *(504-947-2120)*. Le'Ob's Tours *(504-288-3478. www.leobstours.com)* offers tours to large groups.

VISITING THE CEMETERY

Three squares compose the cemetery, though only two are worth visiting. Enter through the Bienville Street gate—going alone is not recommended—and proceed to **Square Two,** the central block,

Eternity: a year and a day

New Orleans's high water table and periodic flooding made underground burial impractical, and high ground was limited. Above-ground crypts, common in the city, solved the first problem; continual re-use the second. Local law requires that a body be interred for a year and a day before it may be moved—enough time for the heat to work a natural cremation. Thereafter, if space is needed, the prior remains are placed in an ash pit beneath or behind the crypt. Some consider the practice callous. Others feel that ashes mixed for all time symbolize families or friends forever united. ■

A procession at the cemetery honors Oscare James Dunn, America's first African-American lieutenant governor (1868–1871).

between Conti and Bienville Streets. This is the most architecturally interesting and complex section in the cemetery, with a cross axis called **Priest's Aisle,** around which are clustered many elaborate and historically significant tombs. Here you'll find the resting places of two old-time mayors, Nicholas Girod (see p. 93), and James Pitot, the first to preside over the city after its incorporation in the early 1800s.

But history takes a backseat to aesthetics; the tombs themselves are the stars here. Many of them are the work of the prolific J.N.B. de Pouilly, a graduate of Paris's École des Beaux-Arts, who arrived in New Orleans in the 1830s with a portfolio of drawings he had made of tombs in Paris's fabled Père Lachaise cemetery; he also designed the St. Louis Cathedral.

The Greek Revival style was in vogue at the time, and No. 2's crypts and tombs were built with classical columns, pediments, and pedestals. The New Orleans influence asserted itself in ornamental ironwork—some of the city's finest is found here—and the carved stone angels and cherubs inevitably slumped in mourning or were prostrate with grief. To see some of de Pouilly's most creative and affecting work, find your way to the communal tomb of the Orleans Cazadores, a benevolent society, and those of the Graihle, Miltenberger, and Peniston-Duplantier families.

Upriver across Bienville Street, in **Square Three,** tombs include a fascinating collection commissioned by African-American societies.

When Monsieur de Pouilly's time came to enter eternity, his mortal remains were interred here in a wall vault between Conti and St. Louis Streets. ■

Faubourg Marigny

Named for Bernard Xavier Philippe de Marigny de Mandeville, the Creole planter whose farmland this once was, New Orleans's first suburb (in French, "faubourg") sprouted in 1805 as a residential neighborhood just downriver from the French Quarter.

Roughly bounded by the Mississippi River, Esplanade Avenue, and Marais and Montegut Streets, the Marigny (mare-rin-yee) is home to a diverse collection of vintage architectures. You can tour the district safely on foot up to N. Rampart Street; lakeside of N. Rampart, you should tour by automobile. Warehouses built during an early 19th-century mercantile boom are coveted as studio space by the Marigny's many creative types, who impart to Frenchmen Street's cafés a genuine Bohemian flair. Mostly translated into English or changed altogether in the mid-1800s, some of the names de Marigny originally gave to his suburb's streets, like the Rue de Musique (today's Music Street) and the Rue de Poets (now St. Roch), seem to have anticipated its destiny as an artistic neighborhood.

An exodus of refugees fleeing Haiti's bloody revolution in the late 1700s quickly filled the planter's development with French families, free people of color, and escaped African slaves. The multiracial community got along well and lent its name to the next generation's light-skinned, reddish-haired African Americans, who (as did Malcolm X) referred to themselves as marignys.

A good many newcomers built Creole cottages, generally small houses with a raised main floor, an exterior staircase, and several shuttered doors facing the street. Esplanade Avenue's homes are noticeably larger than those just upriver in the Lower Quarter, and unlike them are mostly brick. Stroll **Esplanade Avenue's** leafy neutral ground from Royal Street toward the river, however, and you'll pass an architectural sampler of New Orleans-style residences built by prosperous Creole clans: the Greek Revival John Gauche/Matilda Grey Mansion at **704 Esplanade;** two lovely Creole cottages at **Nos. 640–638** dating from 1822; a pair of French Second Empire houses at **Nos. 634–632;** a striking 1890s-era Victorian at **No. 622;** and at **No. 616** an Italianate-style example of the shotgun cottage whose modest expense made it a favorite of working-class families.

Downriver from Esplanade, the district's personality changes again; this is where many feel the Marigny, with houses generally humbler than those on Esplanade, truly begins. Rue de François is today's **Frenchmen Street,** the Marigny's central commercial street, bisecting a neighborhood where low rents attracted the artistic community that now occupies most of its studiolike warehouse spaces. Preservationists consider the Marigny an architectural treasure in need of rescue, but Bohemian life goes on here, particularly in the 500 and 600 blocks, which hold an interesting array of music clubs, cafés, and bookstores. The **Praline Connection Restaurant and Candy Shop** *(542 Frenchmen St. 504-943-3934),* which occupies a former bank building, is one of New Orleans's top-rated Creole-style eateries. Among jazz aficionados the **Snug Harbor Jazz Bistro** *(626 Frenchmen St. 504-949-0696)* ranks high. Before or after a set, a cup of something and the evening air at a

Bernard Xavier Philippe de Marigny de Mandeville

De Marigny inherited his father's seven-million-dollar estate in 1800 and commenced to spend it freely—so freely that within a few years he was bankrupt and had to subdivide his plantation. An aesthete, he gave his new streets names such as Rue de Poets, Rue d'Amour, and Rue de Musique. Addicted to gambling—the Rue de Craps commemorates the dice game he is said to have introduced to America—he ran out of money in his 93rd year and died. Some called de Marigny a wastrel; others praised his timing. ■

nearby café is a very pleasant way to relax and enjoy the passing parade of Marigny folk. If you're feeling a bit footsore, take the #3 Vieux Carré bus from Royal and Touro back to the Quarter via Dauphine Street.

It's not a place to be after dark, but if by day **Washington Square Park** has a few people in it, the green offers a relaxing and safe respite. Between Dauphine and Royal, it fronts on Elysian Fields Avenue, laid out and named by de Marigny himself, who cherished the notion that it might someday rival the elegance of Paris's Champs-Elysées. Despite the avenue's name, taken from the famed Parisian boulevard, the architecture along this wide way has never lived up to de Marigny's vision of a "Paris of the New World." Enduring fame of a subtler kind attached to Elysian Fields, however, when playwright Tennessee Williams set *A Streetcar Named Desire* here. The streetcar is long gone; a bus with Williams's marquee now grinds through the neighborhood.

A new addition to the Marigny's list of places to stay is the upscale **Claiborne Mansion Inn** *(2111 Dauphine St. 504-949-7327)*, a handsome structure facing Washington Square and dating from 1859. With seven guest rooms, an enclosed garden, and a pool, its proportions reflect the prosperity New Orleans enjoyed before the Civil War. Just up the street is another pleasant hideaway—a commercial nursery doing business (for a long time) as **American Aquatic Gardens** *(621 Elysian Fields. 504-944-0410)*. Although it's a retailing concern, it's a serene place, where fountains trickle softly amid a watery garden of reeds, lilies, and grasses. ■

Praline Connection waiters display house specialties in front of the venerable restaurant.

More sites in the French Quarter

LAFITTE'S BLACKSMITH SHOP

A peaceful place for all ages to repair after an evening on upper Bourbon, this is one of the French Quarter's most unusual and pleasant watering holes, housed in a small swaybacked 1770s smithy supposedly used by pirates Jean and Pierre Lafitte to fence their ill-gotten booty and trade in slaves. Its soft brick-and-post construction—called *poteaux-en-terre* for its practice of setting the wooden beams directly on or in the ground—identifies it as French colonial and thus one of New Orleans's oldest buildings. Sometimes listed as a piano bar, the main attraction here is conversation on the candlelit patio.

Map pp. 50–51 ✉ 941 Bourbon St. ☎ 504-593-9761

LE PETIT THÉÂTRE DU VIEUX CARRÉ

A short stroll from Jackson Square is America's oldest continuously active community theater, here since 1916 in a building dating from 1789. Every spring it hosts the Tennessee Williams Festival, an event that attracts scholars, playwrights, and aficionados of the playwright's work. If you can attend a performance, do. In any case, find your way to the theater's lovely stone-laid patio, where a fountain trickles.

Map pp. 50–51 ✉ 616 St. Peter St. ☎ 504-522-9958 Season runs Sept.–June $ $$$

MUSÉE CONTI WAX MUSEUM

The costumes worn by the museum's lifelike figures evoke Louisiana's past with an unusual intimacy. The most senior in a tableau of more than 100 notables is the French explorer René-Robert La Salle, who in 1682 claimed this region for France. He shares the air-conditioned spotlight with Andrew Jackson, here in military garb, as he probably appeared at the Battle of New Orleans in 1815. The emperor Napoleon Bonaparte, curiously, idylls in his bath, and the pirate Jean Lafitte appears to be straining for a pose of respectability. A troupe of voodoo dancers, their gazes disconcertingly intense, includes Marie Laveau, New Orleans's preeminent voodoo priestess, who died in 1881.

Map pp. 50–51 ✉ 917 Conti St. ☎ 504-525-2605 $ $$

NAPOLEON HOUSE BAR AND CAFÉ

This favorite French Quarter watering hole offers an atmospheric interior and a peaceful courtyard. The tile roof is a rare original, one of only a few left in the Quarter. It enjoys a much-embroidered reputation as a house built in 1814 for New Orleans Mayor Nicholas Girod, who supposedly intended to rescue his fallen idol Napoleon Bonaparte from exile on the British island-colony of St. Helena and give him this three-story brick-and-beam building. Before the plot, if there was one, could be carried out, Bonaparte died (in 1821, probably from arsenic poisoning). Girod's plans, however, live on as local lore. The clientele is loyal, and the place is usually thronged. Don't be shy about ordering one of the trademark mixed drinks—a Pimm's Cup or a Sazerac cocktail—as regulars favor them, too. At this excellent watering hole, you can also order a staple of New Orleans's menus, the muffuletta sandwich, which

Audubon haunts

In 1821 naturalist-artist John James Audubon lived in Cottage No. 1 at 505 Dauphine Street while working on his Birds of America series. The one-story redbrick complex, now grandly furnished self-sufficiencies, is a perfect expression of the Creole cottage style: elegant, simple, sturdy, and practical. His studio was at 706 Barracks Street. Born in Haiti in 1785, the son of a French slave trader, Audubon lost his Creole mother to a slave rebellion. Shipped off to France, he later ducked army service by sneaking back to America, where he lived from hand to mouth until painting took hold of him at the age of 35 and he began to produce his romantically posed yet painstakingly accurate depictions of birds. New Orleans's affinity for dress-up and make-believe suited him; while dropping hints that he was the lost Dauphin of France, he alternatively struck the poses of an expatriate French aristocrat and a gentleman mountain man, drawing upon his trapping and hunting experiences with Daniel Boone. ■

Patrons relax at Napoleon House, a favorite of Tennessee Williams.

attempts to squeeze a lot of salami, ham, pastrami, cheese, and olive salad between slices of seeded bread.

Map pp. 50–51 500 Chartres St.
504-524-9752

NEW ORLEANS HISTORIC VOODOO MUSEUM

Enclosing an appropriately dusky ambience, the museum displays the paraphernalia of that mysterious branch of spiritualism born long ago in Africa. Here you'll find dolls and potions and powders, which mean little to nonpractitioners but are nonetheless exotic. The large portrait on the wall as you enter depicts the fabled Marie Laveau, a free woman of color who reigned as a powerful voodoo queen in the 1800s. You need not be shy or solemn, only respectful. Vodoun, after all, is a religion. Ask those on hand here about guided tours that focus on New Orleans's voodoo culture. Bloody Mary, the Poet Priestess, will guide you through both the history and mystery with walking tours of cemeteries, tours of ghost- and vampire-haunted sites, and even attendance of voodoo rituals; call the museum for further information.

Map pp. 50–51 724 Dumaine St
504-523-7684 $$

Voodoo Museum curator "Bloody Mary"

NEW ORLEANS PHARMACY MUSEUM

The home and workplace of America's first officially licensed apothecary, the New Orleans Pharmacy Museum also exemplifies the Creole townhouse architectural style. Louis Dufilho set up shop here after its completion in 1837, and his courtyard herbal garden is still growing. Be sure to admire the circa 1860, beautifully handcarved rosewood cabinets, made in Germany. The Belgian slate floor came across the Atlantic as ballast on sailing ships. You probably won't recognize the period paraphernalia and compounds that fill the apothecary bottles lining their shelves—crude drugs, medicinal herbs, gris-gris potions used by voodoo practitioners—since most of Dufilho's remedies have gone the way of his leeches, once kept alive in jars for blood-letting to rid the sick of illness-causing humors.

Map pp. 50–51 514 Chartres St. 504-565-8027 Closed Mon. $ ■

Jazz & Heritage Festival

Entering its fourth decade, this annual spring celebration of New Orleans music and culture runs for ten event-filled days. It features three components: the outdoor Louisiana Heritage Fair, the Evening Concert Series, and educational programs.

The outdoor Heritage Fair, which takes place daily from mid-morning to early evening at the Fair Grounds Race Course, mounts a dozen stages for musical performances. The playbill features local artists, including musicians from neighborhood social aid and pleasure clubs. The stages are surrounded by what appears to be a nomadic tented bazaar of food vendors, featuring the tantalizing specialties of Cajun, West African, and Caribbean cuisines. The Heritage Fair vigorously enforces against outside beverages. There are unlimited general admission ticket sales at the gate.

The Evening Concert Series features performances at selected venues around town. Seating at most Evening Concerts is reserved, making advance ticket purchases advisable. The festival's popularity has grown to the point where out-of-towners are advised to also make lodging reservations months ahead of time.

For festival tickets, write 1205 N. Rampart St., New Orleans, LA 70116; visit www.nojazzfest.com; or call Ticketmaster (800-488-5252). For schedules of performances, usually announced in mid-February, visit the festival's Web site. ■

An accordion, a washboard, and a fiddle produce the quintessential sound of rural Cajun music at Jazz Fest.

Full of architectural treasures, the Central Business District, or CBD, is the heart of commercial New Orleans. Its long shadows cast across the Mississippi to quiet residential Algiers Point, once a thriving shipbuilding hub.

Central Business District & Algiers Point

A granite angel guards the Whitney Bank building.

Central Business District & Algiers Point

THE DIFFERENCES BETWEEN THE FRENCH QUARTER AND NEW ORLEANS'S financial center lie in history, culture, and commerce. Unlike the French Quarter, the CBD is a creation of the Anglo-American mercantile community. It frequently keeps banker's hours and is most alive on weekdays. As its name declares, its primary purpose is business.

The CBD's skyline is modern, but its history as the American sector stretches back nearly two centuries. Among its office towers are very old streets with scores of handsome brick commercial structures built from the 1830s to the early 20th century to pursue all the trades and markets that propelled the city's growth. Roughly bounded by Canal Street, the

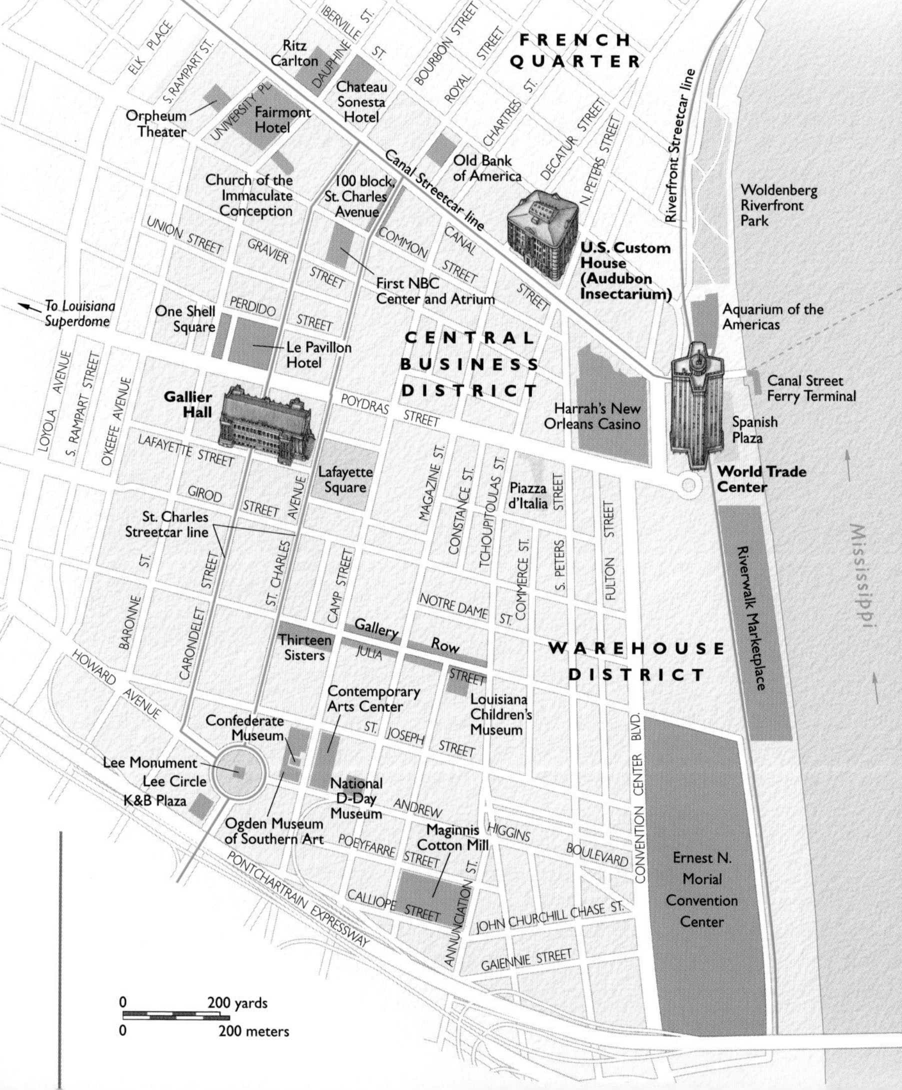

Convention Center, the Pontchartrain Expressway, and O'Keefe Avenue, the CBD includes in its upriver section the Warehouse Arts District. Here the city's leading fine arts dealers and auctioneers do business in renovated spaces, mostly in 19th- and early 20th-century buildings, where the printing and cotton bale-pressing trades once flourished. The retreat of traditional industries, followed recently by widespread conversion of lofts into living spaces, has attracted urban professionals, artists, architects, and others for whom aesthetics figure large in daily life.

PATTERSON DRIVE
MORGAN STREET
Seger-Rees House
VERRET STREET
OLIVIER STREET
Algiers Point Court House
Ferry landing
DELARONDE STREET
BERMUDA STREET
Mt. Olivet Episcopal
PELICAN AVE.
SEGUIN AVE.
ALIX ST.
PELICAN STREET
Holy Name of Mary
ALGIERS POINT
ELIZA ST.
Canal Street Ferry
House, Gardens & Gumbo
POWDER STREET
BOUNY STREET
EVELINA ST.
Jazz Centennial Walk of Fame
OPELOUSAS AVENUE
TECHE STREET
NUNEZ STREET
VERRET STREET
SLIDELL STREET
BROOKLYN STREET
HOMER STREET
NEWTON STREET
DIANA STREET
Blaine Kern's Mardi Gras World
DE ARMAS STREET
Area of map detail
MID-CITY & THE LAKEFRONT
FRENCH QUARTER
GARDEN DISTRICT & UPTOWN
CBD & ALGIERS POINT
NUNEZ STREET

In the early 1800s the first Yankees to arrive called this part of town the Faubourg Ste. Marie. The American community centered around Lafayette Square, where Old City Hall, the imposing Greek Revival masterwork by James Gallier, Sr., was flanked by federal townhouses and government offices. After the economic setbacks caused by the Civil War, shipping and railroad commerce revived to finance construction of many larger industrial buildings. Some, like the restored redbrick Maginnis Cotton Mill, built in 1882 on the block bounded by Annunciation, Calliope, Constance, and Poeyfarre Streets, survive as perfect expressions of American mercantile pride. Business still thrives here, but now the CBD's personality is permanently split between traditional enterprise and its post-industrial flowering as a vibrant and creative visual arts community.

Especially at night, when its office towers glitter, the CBD is often photographed from across the Mississippi at Algiers Point, an old residential neighborhood on a knob of land that points east toward the French Quarter. A commuter ferry provides a magical crossing. ■

A candy cart in the CBD recalls the heyday of horse- and mule-drawn commerce.

Canal Street

Harrah's New Orleans Casino
www.harrahs.com
- Map pp. 96–97
- Canal St. near the river
- 504-533-6000 or 800-HARRAHS
- Streetcar: Canal

IT WAS SURVEYED AS THE ROUTE OF A WATERWAY TO BE dug from the Mississippi to Lake Pontchartrain via the Carondelet Canal. But in 1812 a broad boulevard was laid out instead. Canal Street is said to be the nation's widest main street, and, at 171 feet across, the first to be illuminated with electric lights. New Orleanians, however, prize its role as the dividing line between downtown (18th-century French Quarter) and uptown (19th-century American sector). The Canal streetcar line recently reopened along this vital thoroughfare.

During Mardi Gras, parades march every day and night along the tree-lined commons extending from the Mississippi nearly to City Park (see p. 152).

Where flatboats would have turned inland from the Mississippi, had the canal been dug, the **World Trade Center** *(2 Canal St.)* rises 33 stories to overlook the great river bend that destined this piece of land to become a colonial beach-head. The revolving Club 360° *(504-522-9795)* takes 90 minutes to scan the city's horizons, justifying the pricey drinks with unbeatable bird's-eye views of every part of New Orleans.

At the foot of Canal Street is **Harrah's New Orleans Casino,** whose 100,000-square-foot Greek Revival building is an exception to a long-standing state prohibition against land-based gambling places. The 200-million-plus-dollar edifice opened with great fanfare in 1999 and features 3,000-odd slot machines and more than 120

Harrah's New Orleans Casino features a classical-revival style popular in the 19th century.

gaming tables. Its architectural touches suggest the French Quarter, while the design themes of its five huge courtyards reflect aspects of New Orleans history—including Mardi Gras, jazz, and pirate Jean Lafitte.

The somewhat down-at-heel stretch of Canal Street from the river to Rampart Street covers 0.7 mile, an easy and architecturally distinguished stroll. Now a shopping district, its outlets vary greatly in quality. Some occupy once impressive buildings, but the overall effect is in marked contrast to the boulevard's historic elegance. Initially lined by elegant townhouses and Protestant churches built in the styles of the American Northeast, by the mid-1800s Canal Street boasted dozens of narrow office buildings and luxury shops appropriate to one of the world's leading ports. Survivors include **No. 622,** completed in 1859 for the Merchants Mutual Insurance Company, and the white 13-story beaux arts Maison Blanche, now the **Ritz Carlton New Orleans** *(901 Canal St. 504-524-1331),* a former department store and office building, opened in 1909.

Among the few former residences surviving from the street's high period is the restored **Boston Club** *(824 Canal St.).* This three-story townhouse was built in 1844 for a plantation-owning physician named William Mercer. The ornate second-floor wrought-iron gallery is original. Typical of the department stores that catered to Canal's plutocrats is the 1913 beaux arts facade across the street, now part of the **Chateau Sonesta Hotel** *(504-586-0800),* whose main entrance is around the corner at Dauphine.

In the mid-1800s, the median strip where Canal Street and St. Charles Avenue intersect was old New Orleans's main public assembly place. Nearby, rare and ornate cast-iron galleries distinguish **123** and **125 St. Charles Avenue,** a pair of townhouses that went up in 1845 and, until recently, housed Old Kolb's Restaurant, a saloon dating back to 1898. The handsome Italianate home at **115 St. Charles Avenue,** built in 1826 and remodeled in 1874, houses the all-male Pickwick Club, whose members have participated in Mardi Gras for 150 years. A block away, at Carondelet and Canal Streets, is the **St. Charles Streetcar Zero Stop,** a convenient and usually less crowded place to board the famous trolley.

A rare survivor of the district's great banking houses is the **Old Bank of America,** just off Canal at 115 Exchange Alley. Its five stories, graced with Italianate details rising above Corinthian columns, date from 1866. ■

Neutral ground

Animosity between French Creoles and Anglo-American newcomers living upriver from Canal Street grew so intense that in 1836 the city was partitioned into three municipalities, each with its own police force. The border between the English- and French-speaking enclaves was Canal Street, whose median was proclaimed neutral ground as a buffer to discourage street fights. New Orleans reunited under one administration in 1852, but the term neutral ground survives as the name for all of the city's medians. ■

Chandeliers light the Baronne Street entrance to the Fairmont, where political hobnobbing and Carnival pageantry are traditions.

Fairmont Hotel
Map pp. 96–97
123 Baronne St.
504-529-7111
Streetcar: Canal

Fairmont Hotel

YOU WILL NOT FIND A GRANDER HOTEL LOBBY IN NEW Orleans than the great entry corridor of this opulent establishment. The doyen of old Crescent City lodgings is actually an assemblage of several buildings, the oldest dating from 1893, the youngest from 1923.

Now a Fairmont Hotels property, this elegant structure began as the Roosevelt Hotel, in honor of Theodore Roosevelt, the famous Rough Rider. It claims to be one of the first Southern hotels with air-conditioning. The hotel's Spanish Renaissance Revival building on Baronne Street was built in 1893. If its grand entry makes you feel a bit small, venture far enough down its corridor to find (on the left) the intimate and swanky **Sazerac Bar & Grill.** The *moderne* decor—the slick look of Hollywood sets that showcased the dancing of Fred Astaire—and the 1940s murals by Paul Ninas create an ambience of elegance and ease. The bar's specialty is the Sazerac cocktail, a drink of rye whiskey, Peychaud and Angostura bitters, lemon peel, and sugar, a libation identified with New Orleans. The restaurant favors Creole cuisine. During the high period of "Kingfish" Huey Long's political road show, the Fairmont was the governor's unofficial New Orleans headquarters, and remains the premier venue for political events and socializing, as well as exclusive Mardi Gras fetes. The hotel's beaux arts **University Place** building on the other side of the block, opened on New Year's Eve 1908, took in its first guests as the Hotel Grunewald.

OTHER NOTABLE BUILDINGS

Part of the Fairmont Complex, University Place was the site of the University of Louisiana until 1894, when the school moved uptown to a new campus on St. Charles Avenue and became Tulane (see p. 134).

Across the street from the hotel, at 129 University Place, is the **Orpheum Theater** *(504-524-3285. home.gnofn.org)*, opened in 1921 to stage vaudeville shows mounted by the Orpheum Circuit Company. Its ornate terra-cotta facade is original, and its beautiful interior, completely restored in 1981, is the home of the Louisiana Philharmonic Orchestra. ■

Church of the Immaculate Conception

WHO WOULD HAVE THOUGHT THAT THE JESUITS, SENT packing from New Orleans in 1763, would return and bequeath to it a church whose second incarnation, the Church of the Immaculate Conception, is one of the city's most architecturally interesting buildings?

To call its style Moorish is not quite enough; the redbrick church's architects embellished it with Venetian Gothic touches, German stained-glass windows, and green copper-clad, onion-shaped domes. It is all a reverberation from the structure's predecessor, the first church to rise here. The six-year project, completed in 1857, was designed by John Cambiaso, a Jesuit priest and architect who had lived in Spain and fallen under the romantic thrall of Iberian-Moorish building styles. Cambiaso specified more than 200 tons of decorative cast iron, including massive columns. Even the pews were iron.

The church probably could have survived anything but the wrecking ball, which swung its way in 1926. The columns and pews were saved, and again the Spanish-Moorish motif was employed to build a larger church whose plans called for two cast-iron towers, rising in a massive filigree some 18 stories. (The copper-domed spires you see were built instead.)

As you enter, take note of the three arches framing the church's heavy bronze front doors, which retract sideways into the walls. The vivid color of the huge rose window above becomes apparent in the interior, where spiral columns and pointed arches suggest a caliph's palace. Also salvaged from the original church was the bronze altar, clad in gold leaf, with its attendant arches and onion domes; it was fabricated in Lyons, France. The white marble statue of the Virgin Mary above the altar is a refugee from the French Revolution of 1848. Intended for a royal chapel, it was purchased with $5,000 donated by members of the congregation. The saga of the Jesuits who set all this in motion is depicted in the stained-glass windows, crafted in Munich. ■

Church of the Immaculate Conception

Map pp. 96–97
132 Baronne St.
504-529-1477
Masses daily & Sun. p.m.
Streetcar: Canal

A Madonna and Child stand in the soft light of German stained-glass windows.

Audubon Insectarium

Insectarium
Map pp. 96–97
www.audubonsinstitute.org
423 Canal St.
504-861-2537
$$
Streetcar: Canal

THE NEWEST GEM IN THE AUDUBON NATURE INSTITUTE is set to open in 2005 in the most imposing building on Canal Street: the former U.S. Custom House. More than 30,000 square feet of this late Greek Revival structure are filled with high-tech, interactive exhibits devoted to insects.

Three custom houses preceded the current building on this spot—the first, part of the old French Fort St. Louis, a defensive bastion; the second, a Spanish revenue house; the third, American, which burned in 1819. The cornerstone of this great gray marble edifice, covering one square block, was laid in 1848. Construction went forward in fits and starts, ceasing during the Civil War. Eventually, the work would take 33 years to finish. In an ironic twist of history, one of the construction superintendents was an Army captain named Pierre Beauregard, whose dubious destiny would be to rebel against the United States. In 1861 he commanded the artillery battery that fired the Confederacy's first shot against the Union garrison at Fort Sumter in the harbor at Charleston, South Carolina.

Massive and fortresslike, the Custom House still exudes the air of importance it possessed in the years before 1913, when the 16th Amendment to the U.S. Constitution imposed a permanent income tax. Its great blocks of marble were quarried in Quincy, Massachusetts, and freighted by ship and rail to New Orleans. There, successive troops of stonecutters carved them into classical shapes—four facades, each with four colossal fluted columns crowned with Egyptian capitals. The building rose from an excavation surrounded by a cofferdam built of cypress timbers and caulked with cotton, spawning a myth that it was built atop cotton bales. (It rests upon a massive layer of cypress beams, which is one of the reasons it has since sunk some three feet.)

The building was well enough along to permit the Union Army to set up a command post in it after occupying New Orleans in 1862 and, after the war, to briefly imprison some 2,000 Confederates within its somber walls. The last of many supervising architects signed off on the project in 1881.

Today the walls of the old U.S. Custom House enclose thousands and thousands of bugs. In Fall 2005, the Audubon Nature Institute will open the doors to its newest facility: a museum devoted to the million or so known species of insects, the most common creatures on Earth.

Exhibit highlights include the **Field Camp,** where visitors meet an "in-the-field" collector and get the chance to touch live insects; **Life Underground,** offering a bug's-eye view of a subterranean world teeming with giant animatronic insects; **Louisiana Swamp,** featuring creatures that make their homes in the state's famous swamps; **Termites,** a gallery focusing on the dangers of introduced species; **Butterflies in Flight,** a garden with free-flying butterflies; and the **Hall of Fame,** which displays the fastest and biggest bugs. Be sure to check out the **Cooking Show,** where celebrity chefs whip up tasty treats such as Chocolate Chirp Cookies and Mealworm Egg rolls. ■

Lafayette Square

PERHAPS NEW ORLEANS'S FRENCH-SPEAKING OLD GUARD, anxious over the growing Anglo-American dominance of the city's commerce, took heart in 1825 when the Yankees renamed Place Gravier as Lafayette Square in honor of the Marquis de Lafayette. At least the new name honored a French hero of the American Revolution.

Mardi Gras celebrants gather at Gallier Hall, a symbol of the Anglo-American takeover of antebellum New Orleans.

But in 1836 the *Américain* presence was boldly proclaimed when James Gallier, Sr., completed his imposing Greek Revival masterpiece, **Gallier Hall,** modeled on the Parthenon in Athens. The magnificent structure symbolized the English-speaking community's determination to run things their own way.

Staked out in 1788 by Spanish surveyor Carlos Laveau Trudeau, Lafayette Square became the hub of the American Second Municipality when the culturally fractious city was divided into three cities in 1836. After they were consolidated in 1852, Gallier Hall became the administrative center. The federal government put up a post office across the square, then federal offices, including the Fifth Circuit Court. Lawyers and bankers and bureaucrats are still here, and so are the homeless, in sad proximity to symbols of power and private wealth. The bronze statue of Benjamin Franklin offers none of the great statesman's wry advice, nor does that of Henry Clay, a frequent New Orleans visitor, whose fierce federalism earned him local admirers despite Southern disaffection with Washington. At least the 1898 statue of tycoon John McDonogh implies hope. Depicted are a boy and girl offering flowers of thanks to McDonogh, who financed the building of the city's free public schools. ■

Lafayette Square

Map pp. 96–97

Streetcar: St. Charles

Gallier Hall

Map pp. 96–97

545 St. Charles Ave.

Open Mon.–Fri.

Streetcar: St. Charles

A stroll among architectural treasures

This walk explores the heart of what began as the sugarcane plantation of New Orleans's founder Jean Baptiste Le Moyne, Sieur de Bienville, and grew to become America's cotton capital. Prosperity fled the district, but the redbrick East Coast-style townhouses and commercial buildings of the Yankees who founded it endure.

Above: A devilish detail decorates a column of a Camp Street building.
Opposite: Rusticated red granite blocks front the Egyptian-style Whitney National Bank Safety Deposit Vaults.

The money came from the ships that crowded the docks along the marshy riverbank. It attracted an army of business people who lined the riverfront with four- and five-story brick-and-timber buildings. Banks sprang up along Magazine Street, then Camp Street, then Carondelet Street. By the 1880s it seemed New Orleans might prosper forever, and, until the stock market crash of 1929, its mercantile temples grew ever larger and more opulent.

Start this walk in the 300 block of Magazine, where the three-story gray granite building, put up in 1843 for the **New Orleans Canal and Banking Company** ❶, survives at 301 Magazine Street in all its Greek Revival splendor. Its two Doric columns were salvaged from a predecessor erected here in 1829. The bank's mission was to finance the New Basin Canal from here to Lake Pontchartrain.

The old American banking district is centered around Natchez and Magazine Streets. At 336 Magazine is the **Board of Trade** ❷, a handsome remnant of what was once the block-long, glass-roofed Banks' Arcade. Note the building's burly granite pedestal and its fine upper-floor brickwork.

Turn right on Natchez Street, squeezed by lovely redbricks erected in the 1840s and 1850s. Then turn right onto **Picayune Place,** a humble alley but also a historic district that was once the center of New Orleans's newspaper and printing business. The buildings' original entrances have been mostly bricked or cemented over and they now open onto Camp Street.

At the end of Picayune Place, turn left on Gravier and follow it to No. 611, at the corner of Gravier and Camp. Here stands the old Louisiana Bank and Trust Company, a ten-story building completed in 1906. Now the **International House** ❸, its first three floors are wrapped in pale stone; the seven above are faced with red brick. Next door is the old Tutonia Insurance Company building, a Gilded Age relic from the 1880s. Its appealing details include the fine masonry of its stone base and polished granite columns supporting a central archway. Curious figures adorn the upper-floor windows and parapet, including caryatids on the third floor. It now houses the popular **Lemon Grass** restaurant *(504-523-1200).* The four-story brick-and-stone **Old New Orleans National Bank** ❹, at 201 Camp Street, was completed in 1888 and restored in 1995 by its owner, the Whitney National Bank. Note its lovely arches, massive red sandstone base, and the monumental red granite columns.

Returning to Gravier, you'll find the magnificent red granite **Whitney National Bank Safety Deposit Vaults** ❺ at 619 Gravier Street. Characterized by huge blocks of stone, burly granite columns, a mammoth entrance lintel, and bronze first-floor window grilles, the Whitney has instilled confidence in its depositors since 1888.

On the opposite side of the street, at the corner of Gravier and St. Charles, the two four-story Italianate brick-and-stucco buildings of

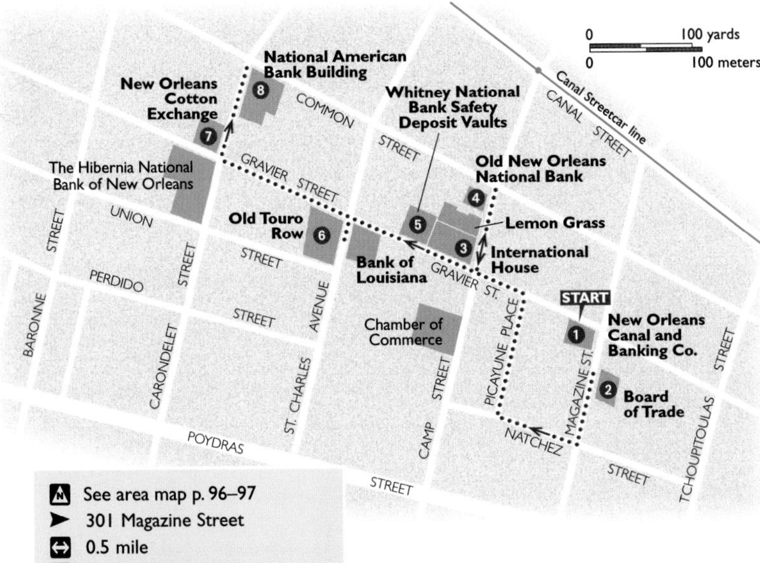

See area map p. 96–97
- ➤ 301 Magazine Street
- 0.5 mile
- 1 to 2 hours
- ➤ 200 Carondelet Street

NOT TO BE MISSED

- N.O. Canal & Banking Co.
- Old Touro Row

the **Bank of Louisiana** at 300 and 304 St. Charles boast cast-iron ground-floor piers, folding door-windows, and heavy iron lintels over upper-story windows. Across the street, at 301, 311, and 317 St. Charles, the **Old Touro Row** ❻ buildings, now occupied by Regions Bank, were originally stores. Their ironwork typifies the commercial houses built by the district's most successful entrepreneurs.

Follow Gravier to Carondelet Street. At 231 Carondelet, the old **New Orleans Cotton Exchange** ❼ lives on as a savings bank. Until 1962, when the exchange closed and New Orleans retired from the cotton trade, brokers worked on the double-height trading floor. The building's copper cornice, once common in the CBD, is rare today. The 1929 stock market crash ended the district's half-century-long construction boom, just after the **National American Bank Building** ❽ opened at 200 Carondelet. One of Louisiana's finest art deco masterpieces, this wonderfully flamboyant structure stands on a base of gleaming black granite, its upper walls of Indiana limestone. ■

Warehouse District

Warehouse District
Map pp. 96–97

IN THE 1980s, ARTISTS BEGAN MOVING INTO THE AREA known as the Warehouse District, lured by the low rents and light-filled spaces of the late 19th-century warehouses left over from the days when this area served as a port. Today, art galleries prosper—especially along Julia Street—earning the neighborhood the appellation "SoHo of the South."

Above: The Arthur Roger Gallery includes a temporary exhibit of glass sculpture by Dale Chihuly. Opposite: A gala marks an opening at the Contemporary Arts Center.

Roughly bordered by Poydras Street, Baronne Street, Higgins Boulevard, and the river, the area is also called the Arts District—with its share of trendy restaurants, shops, and art museums. To best experience the artsy flair of this area, leave your car and stroll Julia Street, paying special attention to the blocks between St. Charles Avenue and Tchoupitoulas Street that include the renowned Thirteen Sisters and houses Gallery Row. Here, galleries offer work that includes both the difficult and the sleek, the latter being the kind of art you would find in New York's SoHo. (See also p. 259.)

JULIA STREET

As the American community grew and prospered upriver from the Quarter in the mid-1800s, many impressive residences sprang up between Canal Street and Higgins Boulevard. Built with unstinting budgets, they reflected traditional New England tastes in architecture—particularly brick-and-stone Greek Revival, federal, and Italianate townhouses. Louisiana architect Henry Hobson Richardson (1838–1886) lived a comfortable childhood in the area, growing up to national renown as the creator of Richardsonian-Romanesque style.

Among the era's surviving architectural masterworks are the 13 contiguous three-story town-houses located in the 600 block of Julia Street and known as the **Thirteen Sisters.** Stolidly built of red brick during 1832 and 1833 as a speculative venture by the New Orleans Building Company, they represent the first significant assertion of Anglo-American

The Thirteen Sisters on Julia Street, an early expression of Anglo-American residential architecture in New Orleans

residential architecture in the CBD. Their lower rear buildings were originally slave quarters, but some of them now serve as guest houses, apartments, and studios; galleries now fill many of the fronts. Walking toward the river on Julia Street, you'll find among its galleries those of **George Schmidt** *(626 Julia St. 504-592-0206)*, a historical painter and self-proclaimed antimodernist, and **Jim Blanchard** *(608 Julia St. 504-522-4815)*, whose studio and gallery share the same address. Farther along Julia Street, in a section known as **Gallery Row,** awaits the **Ariodante Contemporary Craft Gallery** *(535 Julia St. 504-524-3233)*. It is known for fine decorative objets d'art. The **New Orleans Auction Galleries** *(510 Julia St. 504-566-1849)* holds antique estate sales on weekends. You will find a dozen more impeccable showcases here. An unusual one is the studio-showroom of **Christopher Maier Furniture Design** *(329 Julia St. 504-586-9079)*, whose custom-built pieces reflect architectural elements and classical art motifs.

Everything comes together at the **Contemporary Arts Center,** a dazzlingly redesigned 1905 warehouse located just off Lee Circle. Here, in 10,000 square feet of gallery space, some two dozen contemporary exhibitions are presented every year. The architects for the Arts Center worked with visual artists to create a captivating four-story atrium featuring a freestanding elevator shaft, a decorative ceiling, and a semicircular reception desk of colored glass plates by sculptor Gene Koss, who heads the glass studio at Tulane University. Performers stage plays, dance events, and concerts in the center's two theaters. A relaxing bookstore-café on the premises offers a superb inventory of art books and magazines. ■

Contemporary Arts Center

- Map pp. 96–97
- 900 Camp St.
- 504-528-3805 or 504-523-0990 (café)
- Closed Mon.
- $$, free on Thurs.
- Streetcar: St. Charles

Preservation Resource Center

www.prcno.org

- Map pp. 96–97
- 923 Tchoupitoulas St.
- 504-581-7032
- Open Mon.–Fri.
- Bus: Tchoupitoulas

Preservation Resource Center

The Warehouse District was in decline in 1974, when the nonprofit Preservation Resource Center (PRC) was founded to rescue the city's deteriorating architectural legacy. The idea was to involve citizens in preservation by encouraging them to buy and restore architectural and historical relics, many of them abandoned. Meanwhile PRC volunteers made essential repairs to the homes of elderly and disadvantaged homeowners, taking a leading role in the movement that would ultimately revive the Warehouse District, where over 3,000 people now live. Housed in the 1852 Gothic revival Leeds Foundry building, the PRC's visitor center is a perfect place to pick up brochures and guides to the city's historic neighborhoods as well as view exhibits on the unique architecture. ■

Louisiana Children's Museum

IF KIDS COULD DESIGN MUSEUMS, THIS WOULD BE THE result. Yet, despite its name, the Louisiana Children's Museum is a museum for adults as well—the intent being to engage parents and children through hands-on exhibits designed to enlarge a child's sense of personal capabilities and, by extension, life's possibilities.

What four-footer wouldn't gain confidence after piloting a tugboat or anchoring a television news show or lifting 500 pounds? There's just plain fun here, too, such as watching your shadow turn into a luminous ghostly silhouette, pedaling a bike with a skeleton, or trying to play catch while spinning around. Parents can do more than watch, because many activities are designed so grown-ups may take the role of teacher or facilitator, or simply participate alongside their children. If signs don't explain how, ask a docent for suggestions. It is all intended to engender questions, of course; to encourage the youthful curiosities that occasionally allow youngsters to discover an innate calling or a passion. But even if playing the role of waiters in the Kids' Café doesn't fire the culinary ambitions of a young Paul Prudhomme, the experiences are bound to expand a child's sense of the world. As a backup, there's bubble-blowing or perhaps the snack area.

The museum's building is a 45,000-square-foot warehouse dating from 1861, designed by New York architect James Loubat in the style of a Tuscan palazzo. It boasts broad, high-arched doorways and big windows. Raised brick details, known as string courses, outline the arches. Its brick is believed to be original, as are its great beams of longleaf pine, which once grew in abundance along the north shore of Lake Pontchartrain but is no longer commercially available. Care was taken to retain the building's wonderful, well-worn appearance by leaving beams and columns unpainted, refurbishing the original industrial scale near the front desk, and installing wooden shutter doors that match the originals. The Museum Store is a gift shop and educational resource. ■

Louisiana Children's Museum

- Map pp. 96–97
- 420 Julia St.
- 504-523-1357
- $$
- Bus: Tchoupitoulas

A bubble-making device enthralls a patron of this museum for kids.

Ogden Museum of Southern Art

Ogden Museum of Southern Art
www.ogdenmusem.org
Map pp. 96–97
925 Camp St.
504-539-9600
$$
Streetcar: St. Charles

FITTINGLY, THE ARTS DISTRICT HOLDS A NUMBER OF excellent art museums in addition to its sophisticated galleries. Among the finest and most innovative of these institutions is the Ogden Museum of Southern Art, which opened in the fall of 2001.

There is indeed such a thing as Southern American art—ranging from old-time folk art through 19th-century regional interpretations of classical genres (landscapes and portraiture, especially) to the very modern. The bulk of the museum's holdings—about 1,200 works by some 400 artists—came from New Orleans attorney and entrepreneur Roger H. Ogden; his eye for the elements that distinguish Southern American art from that of other American regions guided him in assembling one of the finest groupings of it anywhere.

The five-story, rectangular, ultra-modern building that houses the collection sharply contrasts the 19th-century red sandstone Richardsonian-Romanesque **Taylor Library** next door, which has been integrated into the museum complex. The intent is not only to display artifacts that illustrate the evolution of Southern visual art, but also to serve as an interactive, state-of-the-art learning center for students and casual visitors as well as scholars.

As you wander through the gallery at **925 Camp Street** *(Open Tues.–Sun.)*, keep in mind the question implicit in this place: What distinguishes this art from that produced elsewhere in America? Although most of the museum's older paintings depict Louisiana history, they also illustrate the evolution of styles associated with the region. Among vintage works are rural landscapes by 19th-century artists Clarence Millet, William Henry Buck, and Richard Clague, masters previously known mainly to scholars and local collectors. One of the Ogden's most unusual works is a monumental allegorical portrait of Louisiana by Dominico Canova, an Italian who settled in New Orleans in the 1800s. ■

Lulu King Saxon's "Uptown Street" (1890) hangs in the Ogden Museum of Southern Art.

National D-Day Museum

OPENED 56 YEARS TO THE DAY AFTER 175,000 ALLIED soldiers stormed Hitler's Atlantic Wall at Normandy, this museum is the first in the United States to focus specifically on the invasion.

The core of the museum's collection consists of some 3,500 artifacts from the Allied push into Europe, purchased from the Musée de la Libération in St. Lô, France. The items recall the political turmoil leading to World War II; America's home front mobilization and the profound impact it had; planning for the assault and its execution; the beaches; and the subsequent campaigns leading to the Allied victory over Germany.

Veterans and their families have contributed myriad personal souvenirs, such as a pocket Bible carried in combat and a helmet that stopped a bullet—items curators describe as some of the most important Normandy artifacts in the country. Interactive exhibits include oral histories from veterans on all sides, as well as documents, photographs, and never-before-seen film footage of the invasion.

Upon entering, you're greeted with the exhibit "War Clouds," which depicts the imbalance of military power among the United States, Japan, and Germany in the late 1930s. Models of aircraft, warships, and soldiers illustrate how meager were America's peace-time forces in comparison with those of the Axis powers. New Orleans was chosen for the museum's site because it was here that inventor Andrew Higgins (see pp. 112–113) built and tested the landing craft that made the invasion possible.

Housed in the renovated 1856 Louisiana Brewery, the display was designed by the firm that created the exhibits for New York's Ellis Island and Statue of Liberty Museums. ■

Opening ceremonies (above); founder Stephen Ambrose, the late historian, below

National D-Day Museum

www.ddaymuseum.org

✉ 945 Magazine St.

☎ 504-527-6012

$ $$

Andrew Jackson Higgins: shipbuilder

He was a builder of boats used by oil companies to explore Louisiana's backwaters, and he had a reputation as a hot-tempered Irish American who drank a bottle of whiskey a day. He was also credited by Dwight Eisenhower as the man most responsible for the Allied victory in World War II.

His given name implied savvy and resourcefulness, and Andrew Jackson Higgins exhibited both. Convinced war was coming, he foresaw the military's need for fast and maneuverable boats. Certain that steel would be in short supply, in 1939 he purchased the entire Philippine mahogany harvest and shipped it across the ocean to Louisiana.

Following Pearl Harbor, the Marines asked for landing craft, and the Navy invited boatbuilders to submit designs. They had to shield soldiers and crewmen from small arms fire during the assault, be durable enough to survive collisions with underwater obstacles and the stress of repeated high-speed landings, and have sufficient power to back off the sand, if necessary. Their engines and controls had to be reliable, and above all they had to be delivered at an affordable price. Higgins was ready. For years he had built a powerful shallow draft boat he called the *Eureka*. His military version was 36 feet long and nearly 11 feet wide, and it could be carried aboard transports for launching offshore. The front square ramp was metal, but most of the rest of the boat was wood. It could carry a platoon of 36 soldiers, or a Jeep and a squad of 12.

The Navy's reaction was cool. Higgins's declaration that the "Navy doesn't know one damn thing about small boats" did not win him friends in the Pentagon, where his use of wood was questioned. Moreover, his competition included established East Coast shipyards. Higgins's modest Gulf Coast operation did not impress visiting brass.

Nevertheless, he won a series of small contracts to deliver a "landing craft vehicle, personnel," the Navy acronym for which was LCVP. It rode rough even in moderate seas, bouncing hard and taking water over the gunwales. Its saving virtue was an ability to off-load soldiers and equipment in seconds. When the Marines reported that "Higgins boats" were superior to all others, the Navy awarded Higgins a major contract.

Demonstrating as much skill at mass production as in design, he set up assembly lines throughout New Orleans—the first ever for boatbuilding—some in tents. His biggest was the City Park plant, eventually employing some 30,000 workers. Operations were integrated and fair: All were paid top wages regardless of race or gender, the first time this had been done in the city. Workers labored around the clock seven days a week, beneath banners emblazoned with exhortations such as, "The

man who relaxes is helping the Axis!"

They also turned out landing craft for tanks and PT (patrol torpedo) boats. All were railroaded to Bayou St. John for sea trials on Lake Pontchartrain. By the end of the war Higgins's enterprise had produced over 20,000 LCVPs, which hit beaches from the Pacific to the Mediterranean. On June 6, 1944, hundreds of them delivered the D-Day invasion force to Normandy's deadly shores.

In a 1964 interview, former Allied Supreme Commander Dwight Eisenhower remarked, "If Higgins had not designed and built the LCVPs, we never could have landed over an open beach." "Without them," said Ike, "the whole strategy of the war would have been different." Now, more than 50 years after Higgins's boats made possible the invasion of Normandy Beach, the event remains etched in the national psyche as a prideful and pivotal moment in the Allied victory over the Germans. ■

Above: Andrew Higgins. Below: Assembly-line workers build landing craft.

Confederate Museum

Confederate Museum
www.confederatemuseum.com
Map pp. 96–97
929 Camp St.
504-523-4522
$
Closed Sun.
Streetcar: St. Charles

MANY OF THE MORE THAN 56,000 LOUISIANANS WHO fought in gray under the Stars and Bars founded this pressed brick archive in 1891, called it Memorial Hall, and filled it with personal souvenirs and memorabilia of the Civil War.

Visitors examine rifles used in America's bloodiest war.

They donated uniforms and battle flags, medals and insignia, diaries, maps, and Bibles, canteens, mess kits, rifles, swords, bayonets, and cap-and-ball revolvers. From desks, basements, and attics came some 90,000 documents—letters, official papers, photographs, newspaper clippings—creating one of the nation's largest museums dedicated to the Rebel view of America's bloodiest conflict.

It's said that no war is as bitterly contested as a civil war, and the poignant exhibits as well as the items displayed here—more than a thousand—bear witness to the fervor of the combatants. Among more than 125 battle flags is that of the infantry battalion led by Roberdeau Wheat, stained with his blood. Somber faces gaze from some 500 tintypes, ambrotypes, daguerreotypes, cartes de visite, and albumens—expressing the fatalism engendered by combat that was often hand to hand; tens of thousands of lives could be lost in a single day.

Here, too, are the personal affects of Confederate President Jefferson Davis, as well as Gen. Robert E. Lee's frock coat and Gen. P.G.T. Beauregard's tunic and sword. ■

Lee Circle & Lee Monument

Lee Circle

Map pp. 96–97

Streetcar: St. Charles

WHEN ROBERT E. LEE DIED IN 1870 AT AGE 64, NEW ORLEANS was still a city chafing under Reconstruction rule. Revered for his decency in war and his dignity in defeat, Lee's admirers were (and still are) many. So it's no wonder plans were quietly launched to commemorate the general's valiant effort to win independence for the Confederacy. It would take 14 years to raise the money. When in 1884 the unveiling took place, the sight of the most honored veterans at the ceremony evoked tears in the huge crowd.

Revered in defeat, Robert E. Lee keeps a vigil over his lost Confederacy.

Soaring 60 feet above that crowd stood their compatriot, resurrected in bronze by New York sculptor Alexander Doyle.

The statue tops a four-tiered pyramidal base of Georgia granite and a fluted Doric column of white Tennessee marble designed by architect John Roy. He stands nearly 17 feet tall, arms folded and boots planted in a heroic stance evoking his determined resolve. His northerly gaze symbolizes in the popular mind his determination never to be taken by surprise again.

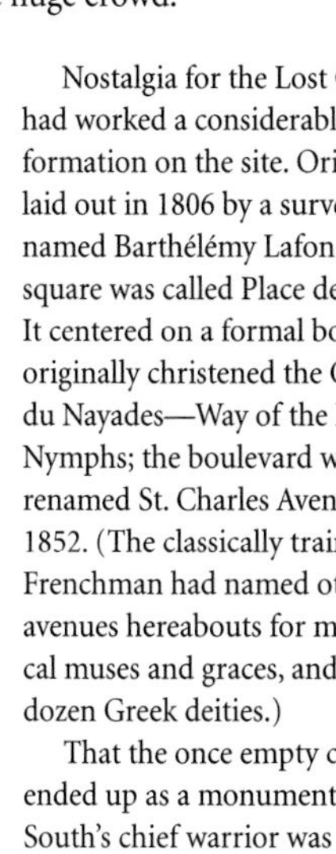

Nostalgia for the Lost Cause had worked a considerable transformation on the site. Originally laid out in 1806 by a surveyor named Barthélémy Lafon, the square was called Place de Tivoli. It centered on a formal boulevard originally christened the Cours du Nayades—Way of the River Nymphs; the boulevard was renamed St. Charles Avenue in 1852. (The classically trained Frenchman had named other avenues hereabouts for mythological muses and graces, and two dozen Greek deities.)

That the once empty circle had ended up as a monument to the South's chief warrior was no small irony, for during New Orleans's postwar occupation the site had served as the main encampment of the Union garrison. ■

J'accuse!

An anomaly among America's 49 other states, Louisiana's laws are modeled not on English Common Law but rather the Napoleonic Code. The differences between the practice of law here and elsewhere make out-of-state businesses thankful for the local attorneys who navigate them through the complexities of Louisiana's peculiar legalities. ■

More places to visit in the CBD

A violin-motif assemblage in the K&B Plaza sculpture garden

FIRST NBC CENTER & ATRIUM

Its height—53 stories—triggered fears of a colossal clash with New Orleans architectural harmony. But the pale pink granite-faced First NBC Center has won respect through its architects' incorporation of three Crescent City hallmarks—the gallery, roof dormers, and setbacks. It isn't the city's tallest building (One Shell Square reaches a bit higher), but it is certainly the most appealing of the CBD's newer skyscrapers, with a gallery on St. Charles that shelters sidewalk pedestrians from rain. Explore its tall atrium, an elegant space that connects with the hotel next door and Carondelet Street.

Map pp. 96–97
201 St. Charles Ave. Streetcar: St. Charles

K&B PLAZA

When New Orleanians watched their beloved 1908 beaux arts public library fall to the wrecking ball in 1960, they groused that whatever was going to replace it on this site had better be good. The John Hancock Mutual Life Insurance Company enlisted the architects of Skidmore, Owings, and Merrill, and when the doors of their building opened in 1963, New Orleans had entered the era of modern architecture with flying colors. The architects made a wise choice by asking the great Isamu Noguchi to create the building's fountain, a fluted granite column supporting a crescent and named "The Mississippi." Today the structure stands as the K&B building and boasts a contemporary sculpture garden on its elevated plaza.

Map pp. 96–97 1005 St. Charles Ave.
Streetcar: St. Charles

LOUISIANA SUPERDOME

Daily tours on the hour explore the home of the New Orleans Saints football team. The site of many Super Bowl and Sugar Bowl games, this behemoth seats 100,000, its eight-acre roof arcing 27 stories high. Out on the Poydras Street side, a bronze soldier guards the **Vietnam Veterans Memorial.** Across the street, Ida Kohlmeyer's abstract sculpture, "Krewe of Poydras," symbolizes Mardi Gras revelry.

Map pp. 96–97 1 Sugar Bowl Dr.
504-587-7713 $$

PIAZZA D'ITALIA

Much critical ballyhoo accompanied the ribbon-cutting that opened this Arts District outdoor urban plaza in 1979, and with good reason. Conceived by Los Angeles-based architect Charles Moore to honor New Orleans's Italian-American heritage, the 1.6-million-dollar project was a seminal event. Critics quickly dubbed its style "post-modern," and it is credited as a primary catalyst for the genre, now accepted as an original (not derivative) style of our time. For all its significance, the plaza has suffered from civic indifference, its pretty fountain and neon lighting turned off.

Poydras & Tchoupitoulas Sts.
Bus: Tchoupitoulas ■

Algiers Point

Directly across the Mississippi River from the CBD and the Quarter, but a world apart, is the west bank neighborhood of Algiers Point. Annexed to New Orleans in 1870, it feels pleasantly removed from the bustle of the city across the river, which here turns sharply around the right-angle Algiers Bend. Quiet, tree-shaded avenues and old Victorians create the ambience and look of a 19th-century small town.

Algiers Point refers to the 25-block area that juts out into the Mississippi, on maps pointing almost directly at the Quarter, or Vieux Carré. Its name is a vestige of the slave trade; in antebellum days Algiers was one of North Africa's most heavily trafficked slave ports, and this point of land was a waystation for the hapless hordes shipped from there and elsewhere on ships that moored along the west bank. Held here in pens until summoned by the Quarter's auction houses, the Africans were ferried across the river for sale.

An Algiers Point resident works in the yard of his Greek Revival cottage on Pelican Avenue.

Algiers Point was part of the original 1719 land grant given to New Orleans's founder, Jean Baptiste Le Moyne, Sieur de Bienville. Like most of the land adjoining the Quarter, it too came under the plow and became part of a family plantation. Shipbuilding took over the riverbank, and with the arrival of the Southern Pacific Railroad, the community experienced an economic boom as a regional shipping hub. The suburb's merchant princes built houses suited to their self-images, replacing Creole cottages with stately columned Greek Revival manses. Disaster struck in 1895 when a fire reduced more than 200 buildings and houses to a plain of ashes and broken chimneys. A determined no-nonsense rebuilding effort ensued, filling scorched lots mostly with long rectangular shotgun doubles, popular two-family residences built in great numbers in New Orleans from about 1840 until 1910. A new courthouse was built, and the vogue in Victorian architecture, in particular the turreted Queen Anne and formal Edwardian styles, decorated neighborhoods with veritable wedding cake residences rising two and three stories. Many of these have been restored, and some are bed-and-breakfasts, benefiting from the Point's relative somnolence and its ten-minute ferry ride to the Quarter. ■

Canal Street Ferry

Canal Street Ferry
Map pp. 96–97
Ferry landing at Canal Street Ferry Terminal
Free; $1 for vehicles crossing from Algiers Point to Canal St. terminal

In operation since 1827, the ferry must certainly be one of the most pleasant public conveyances in America. What's more, it is free for pedestrians and only a dollar for automobiles that cross from Algiers Point to the ferry's berth at the Canal Street Ferry Terminal. People who live across the river, but choose not to commute to the CBD by car, line up here early; the first ferry leaves for the Canal Street docks at 5:30 a.m.

But there are likely as many or more tourists lining the rail as regular commuters, because the view of New Orleans from the river is splendid. The experience of getting out into the flow of the Mississippi—here a half-mile wide and nearly 190 feet deep (the deepest point on the entire river)—is unforgettable. Ships head downriver at startling speeds and plow upriver against the current with ponderous effort, their great diesel-electric power plants rumbling, their bows cleaving the turgid, muddy stream.

The ferry runs every half-hour until midnight (every 15 minutes during rush hour). A round-trip takes about 30 minutes, although the actual crossing usually requires only 6 minutes. Make a back-and-forth voyage at dusk, when the city's lights sparkle on the water and skies can color up in vivid reds and blues and purples. From the ferry or atop the Algiers Point levee, the nighttime view of St. Louis Cathedral, rendered luminous by floodlights, marks this as truly one of New Orleans's most romantic urban adventures. ■

Blaine Kern's Mardi Gras World

Blaine Kern's Mardi Gras World
Map pp. 96–97
233 Newton St., Algiers Point
504-361-7821
$$

Opposite: Sculptures intended for Mardi Gras floats were created in artist Blaine Kern's Algiers Point warehouse studios.

For all its fame, true Mardi Gras is over within a week, leaving those who cannot travel to New Orleans during Carnival doomed to hear about it, over and over, from those who did. However, you can still experience a wonderful aspect of it at the Algiers Point operation of one of the best known creators of Mardi Gras floats. In a row of cavernous warehouses, artist Blaine Kern's workers assemble and decorate many of the moving fantasies that krewes proudly parade through New Orleans. When the festivities are over, they're stored here at Mardi Gras World, enabling you to inspect them close-up, watch artists and builders at work, and take photographs. Kids can slip into costumes, and the gift shop holds a trove of Carnival souvenirs. Your tour guide might be Kern himself, who probably knows more about Mardi Gras parades than anyone.

He grew up a few blocks away and at one time considered a job offer from the Disney empire. But he turned it down and embarked on a venture that has established his float-building company as the world's largest, supplying floats to about two-thirds of the city's roughly 60 major Mardi Gras organizations and to out-of-town clients, including Disney.

When you step off the Canal St. Ferry, look for the free Mardi Gras World shuttle van, which meets the ferry and takes you directly there. ■

Walk around Algiers Point Historic District

This is a leisurely walking tour, in keeping with the usual pace in this off-by-itself part of New Orleans. It will probably take you about two hours if you don't pause at one of the cafés or corner stores for a po-boy sandwich you'll pass en route, or browse in shops along the way. Don't be in a hurry; not many people here ever are.

The Algiers Point Courthouse faces the Mississippi in old Algiers.

The Algiers Point Historic District is officially bounded by the Mississippi River, Slidell Street, and Atlantic Avenue. However, much of the renovation accomplished so far is clustered within Morgan Street/Patterson Drive (locals often refer to them jointly as River Road) and Verret Street, Opelousas Avenue, and Power Street. Before fire swept through in 1895, the mix of architecture in the district was considerable. The Victorian vogue was in full force during the rebuilding period, and as a result these mostly residential streets are now chockablock with what architectural historians call "Anglo-American" buildings—in this case, mostly ornately trimmed cottages.

Starting from the Algiers Point ferry landing, make your way along Morgan Street to the 1896 Moorish-flavored **Algiers Point Courthouse** ❶ *(225 Morgan St. 504-368-4516. Open Mon.–Fri.)*. You undoubtedly noticed its twin crenelated turrets and clock while crossing the river. Two stories of arched windows look appropriately North African. Inside you'll find high ceilings, beautifully crafted wooden doors and trim, and a pleasant librarylike smell of old-time officialdom. The columned French colonial plantation house of the Duverje family stood here. Later, it served as the community courthouse until it burned down in 1895.

Backtrack from the courthouse entrance to Seguin Street, and turn left. Stroll down to Delaronde Street and turn left again into the 300 block, where you will find beautifully restored shotgun doubles and cottages from the last years of the 19th century. Continue on Delaronde and into the 400 block, where you'll come to the **Seger-Rees House** ❷**.** The finest Greek Revival example to escape the great fire, this structure now operates as a bed-and-breakfast *(405 Delaronde St. 504-362-2504)*. It looks like a single residence but is in fact a double townhouse, completed in 1849 for shipbuilding partners Augustin Seger and Thomas Rees. Continue downriver (east), turn right, and follow Verret Street south to Pelican Avenue and turn left. Here you'll find the **Mt. Olivet Episcopal Church** ❸ at No. 530, the oldest house of worship in Algiers. Built some time before the Civil War, it looks a bit austere, like a modest country church.

Two blocks farther, at 705 Pelican Avenue, is the **Vallette-Barrett House.** This privately owned plantation-style residence dates from about 1850, the twilight of Algiers's agrarian era. At 725 Pelican is an architectural gem, the Italianate **Algiers Point Library** ❹ *(504-596-2640. Closed Fri. & Sun.).* Dedicated on December 28, 1907, it opened along with four other New Orleans libraries funded by philanthropist Andrew Carnegie, a disciple of learning who established such facilities around the country. Only two of his gifts to New Orleans are still serving as libraries. Inside this one is a special collection of works about Louisiana, Algiers Point, and the historic district.

Backtrack on Pelican Avenue, turn left onto Vallette Street, and walk south (away from the Mississippi River) two blocks to the intersection of Vallette and Eliza. The 1940s art deco movie theater building at 446 Vallette was renovated by glassblower Mark Rosenbaum and his wife, Brenda, and reopened as their **Rosetree Glass Studio and Gallery** *(888-767-3873. Closed Sat.–Sun.).* This is one of the most appealing galleries in Algiers Point; it is full of gracefully shaped, richly colored blown-glass pieces.

Go west on Eliza and north on Verret Street for a close-hand look at the **Holy Name of Mary Church** ❺ *(500 Eliza St. 504-362-5511).* Built of brick in 1929, it is a beautiful Gothic structure dominating the block between Alix and Eliza Streets. It is also the Point's largest church.

When you're ready to make your way back toward the ferry landing, a stroll toward the river along Bermuda and Delaronde Streets brings more Victorian houses. Walk along the grassy levee's new promenade. Designated the **Jazz Centennial Walk of Fame** ❻ *(Along levee between ferry terminal and De Armas St.),* the paved walkway is dotted with benches and street lamps. Plaques honor the local musicians who gave birth to jazz a century ago. The promenade is one of the best spots in town to watch the endless parade of traffic on the Mississippi; it also offers an excellent vista of the New Orleans skyline.

Another fine place to await the return boat is the **Dry Dock Cafe** *(133 Delaronde St. 504-361-8240).* A casual place featuring home-style fare, its windows open wide onto the ferry landing. ■

See area map pp. 96–97
➤ Algiers Point Courthouse
1.25 miles
2 hours
➤ Jazz Centennial Walk of Fame

NOT TO BE MISSED
- Seger-Rees House
- Holy Name of Mary Church
- Jazz Centennial Walk of Fame

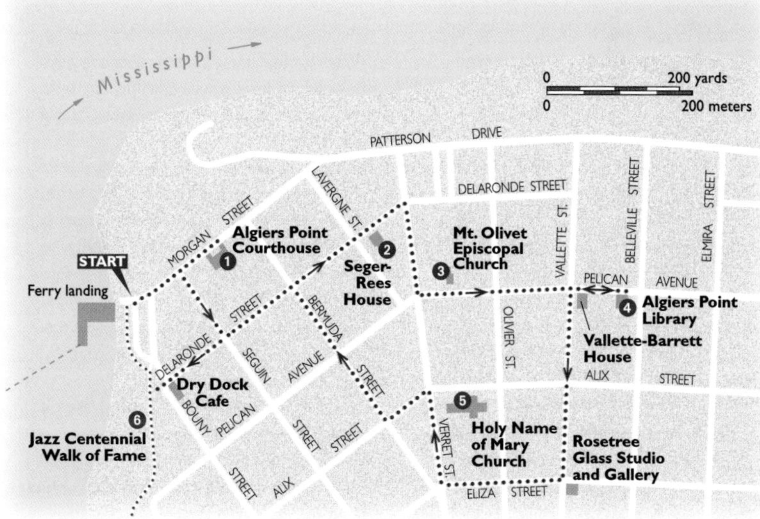

Navigating the Mississippi

No American stream challenges the skill of its mariners more than this great river, the world's fourth largest, after the Amazon, the Congo, and the Nile. With its tributary the Missouri, it follows a twisted 3,710-mile course to the Gulf of Mexico—mile zero—turning into a behemoth whose power can spin an oceangoing freighter like a top.

The Mississippi reaches its deepest level off Algiers Point, where the channel plunges nearly 200 feet and is from one-third to about one-half mile wide—enough room, you would think, to easily accommodate the heavy traffic in freighters, bulk carriers, barges, tugboats, cruise ships, and excursion boats. But in December 1996, the 763-foot grain carrier *Bright Field* lost power on a downriver run, slamming its 90,000 tons into the Riverwalk Marketplace near the Café du Monde in early afternoon, scattering the crowd in panic. Awareness of the river's perils was brought home to the 116 people injured, the owners of the 15 shops and 456 hotel rooms destroyed, and public safety officials.

Ships traveling downstream face a peculiar dilemma: To maintain control, their rudders must be able to exert force against water flowing past them. The slower they go, the less effective their rudders are. To drift is to have no control whatsoever. The solution, unnerving to the uninitiated spectator or passenger, is to speed downriver.

Ships' masters routinely turn their ships over to licensed river and harbor pilots, who are themselves captains specializing in maneuvering safely through the perils unique to their particular bodies of water. Pilots, in turn, often summon the help of tugboats, whose captains are experts in local navigation. Communicating by radio and telephone, they turn ships around in mid-stream, pushing them sideways against docks, or otherwise repositioning them. Powered by the same kind of diesel engines used in railroad locomotives, the biggest generating 3,600 horsepower—their captains may charge as much as $500 an hour for their services. While they work, they monitor the river to spot hazards and alert others.

Sandbars shift; what was a navigable channel last year may now be a treacherous shoal. Wind exerts massive force against tall ships. Rain and fog can reduce visibility to next to nothing. One of the eerie realities of being on the river is that a ship longer than two football fields can approach you from behind in virtual silence, its great engines muffled by distance and wind.

Every year off New Orleans's waterfront, approximately 6,000 large ocean-bound vessels and 120,000 towboats, pushing and pulling barges, pass by. If that traffic is blocked for more than a day or two, the channel

becomes like Times Square during afternoon rush hour. Deliveries are delayed; millions of dollars put at risk. The ripple effect is worldwide. The pressure on masters and pilots to perform perfectly is enormous; one misjudgment, one missed radio transmission, a misunderstanding, and an unblemished career can be ruined in seconds. A captain may have senior officers and crew members speaking a variety of languages, raising the risk of miscommunication.

"The perils of Algiers Point," wrote a *Houston Chronicle* reporter several years ago in a story about marine safety, "are obvious even to the untrained eye." In the vicinity of Algiers Bend is a 175-foot-deep hole, known to pilots as "the Boil." When the river is running high it can generate a whirlpool so big and so powerful that it can turn a ship 360 degrees.

Heading upriver from Algiers Point, a tanker and a tugboat pushing a barge face powerful, dangerous currents.

The Mississippi's temperature drops below 40°F in winter; even those with life jackets would quickly suffer hypothermia if forced to abandon ship.

Ships' masters communicate with blasts of their horns and telephone signal towers staffed by federal employees, themselves experienced river pilots who provide guidance. While all this is going on, there is lively traffic in conversation among the captains up and down the river. You can listen in; VHF radio channel 67 covers navigation along the Mississippi River.

It is a 24-hour, seven-day-a-week world, but when you board a vessel and venture out, you will quickly hear its key players looking out for you. ■

Students of chef Richard Bond (second from right) get hands-on instruction.

More places to visit in Algiers Point

HOUSE, GARDENS & GUMBO

If you'd like to learn the fundamentals of traditional New Orleans cooking, drop by the 1849 home of chef Richard Bond and his wife, Sue, and join one of their half- or full-day classes. The student body is limited to eight and reservations are required. You'll get your own apron and a lot of personal guidance in this hands-on short course. Subjects include technique, seasonings, and presentation. There's a bonus: You get to nibble while you learn. The Bonds also cater private affairs. Check their menus on the Internet at www.gumbo-gardens.com.

Map pp. 96–97 511 Seguin St.
504-362-5225 Closed Sun. $$

WILLIAM BURROUGHS HOUSE

For fans of the Beat Generation, this modest house is an important footnote to the saga of its footloose literary lions. For some months in 1948 and 1949, William S. Burroughs (1914–1997) lived here. His first novel, *Junkie,* and his second, *Naked Lunch,* widened the boundaries of contemporary literature with their rendering of the addict's world. After Burroughs left to join his occasional houseguests Jack Kerouac and Neal Cassady on the road, the same family has lived in the house, but they are not associated with its literary past. A historic marker in the yard confirms its Beat credentials, but please respect the owners' privacy.

Map pp. 96–97 509 Wagner St. ■

Abe's adventure on the river

In 1831, 22-year-old Abraham Lincoln left home to try to find his own way in the world. He was hired, along with two others, to guide a flatboat of produce to New Orleans. They ran aground on a milldam near New Salem, Illinois, but the future President's responsible handling of the incident led Salem merchant Denton Offutt to offer Abe a clerk's job in a store he planned to open. After Abe and his companions delivered their cargo to the Crescent City, he worked briefly as an apprentice pilot on Illinois' Sangamon River until Offutt's store opened. A year later he made his first run for state office, but lost. In 1834 Lincoln was elected to the state assembly and commenced his self-study of law. ■

The vintage St. Charles streetcar still clatters along St. Charles Avenue, conveying residents and visitors from the French Quarter through the fabled Garden District and beyond to Uptown, the city's preeminent residential district.

Garden District & Uptown

Alligators at Audubon Zoo

Garden District & Uptown

AFTER THE LOUISIANA PURCHASE OF 1803, NEW ORLEANS CAME UNDER A government bent on transforming the French-speaking city into an American one. As Yankees with capital and mercantile ambitions flowed in, the culture clash with European Creoles led to mutual antipathy. As a result, Anglo Americans set about creating their own New Orleans upriver from the French Quarter.

They encamped west of Canal Street and launched enterprises in today's Central Business District (see pp. 95–116). In what would become the Garden District and Uptown, they replaced French colonial plantation houses with classical revival ones facing broad avenues and surrounded by lush gardens.

A memorable and convenient way to tour the Garden District and Uptown is to ride the St. Charles streetcar (see pp. 128–131) upriver from the Central Business District and return via Magazine Street by the No. 11 bus (see pp. 144–145), hopping on and off to stroll the street's eclectic bazaar of shops, cafés, galleries, antique dealers, clothiers, and booksellers.

GARDEN DISTRICT

If you visit only one place outside the French Quarter, make it the Garden District. This peaceful and elegant neighborhood between St. Charles Avenue and Magazine Street runs from Jackson Avenue uptown to Louisiana Avenue. Nowhere has the city's vigorous preservation movement been more successful than here, reversing the erosion of its outlying neighborhoods by attracting enterprising home buyers charmed by the eccentricities of vintage architecture.

The district was laid out on the cane plantation of a Frenchwoman who was bought out by four New Englanders. They staked out large lots to attract wealthy buyers and incorporated the development in 1833 as the independent City of Lafayette. The wealthy came—mostly brokers and middlemen scheming in cotton, lending, insurance, shipping, and wholesaling. They commissioned impressive houses, favoring raised Greek Revival manses with galleries lavishly spider-webbed with cast iron. Shaded by magnolia, live oak, and palms, most were set amid the dense flowering gardens that gave the district its name.

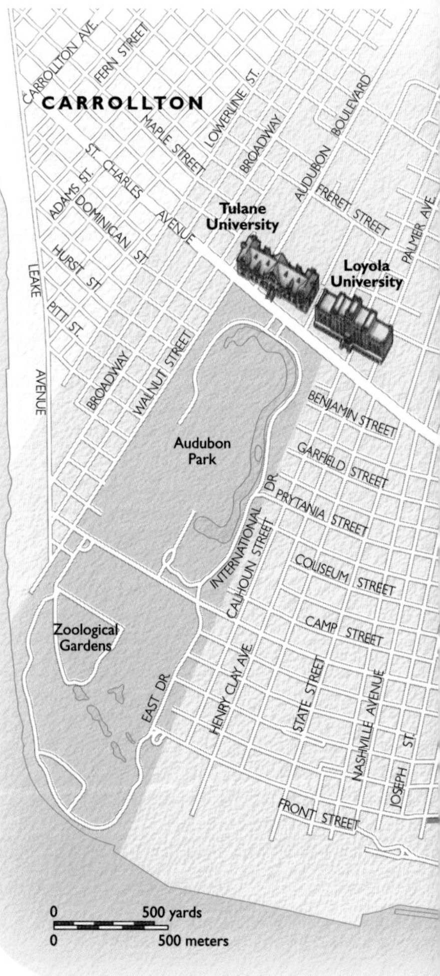

UPTOWN

Bounded by Louisiana Avenue, S. Claiborne Street, and the Mississippi River, Uptown reaches west beyond the Garden District to Carrollton. (The term "uptown" refers to everything upriver from Canal Street; "Uptown" refers specifically to the district upriver from the Garden District.) In Uptown you'll find the houses of New Orleans's long-established social elite—the old families; the kings and queens of Mardi Gras; and the leaders of its hoary krewes. It is a part of town where debutantes are still presented with pomp, circumstance, and calculation, and where rented tuxedos are rare.

Uptown is where 19th-century New Orleanians learned to relax after decades of commercial preoccupation. They established the Audubon Park and Zoo (see pp. 142–143), a favorite family recreation spot, and found room for the city's two most prominent private universities—Tulane (see pp. 140–141) and Loyola. Uptown ends in Carrollton, near the western reach of the great river crescent that embraces the Crescent City and gave it its nickname. ■

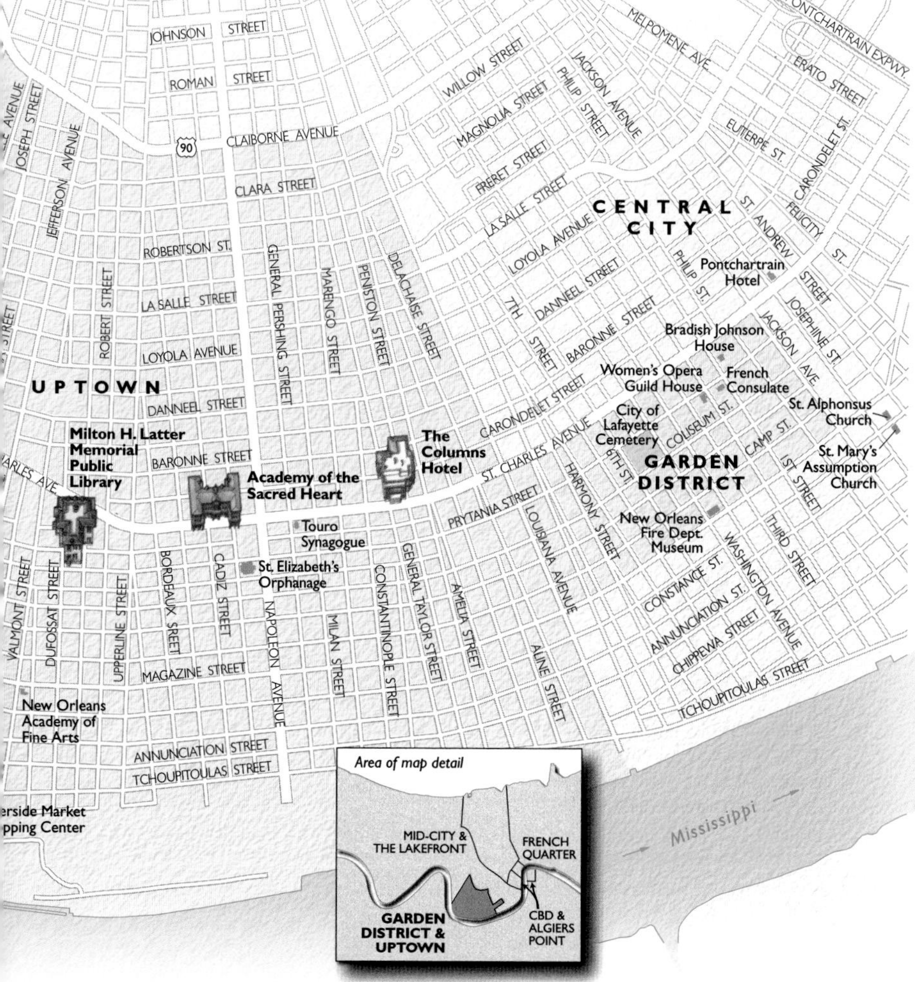

St. Charles streetcar line: an uptown tour

The oldest continuously running light-rail system in the world, rolling 24 hours a day along a 6.6-mile track, the St. Charles's first cars were pulled by mules starting in 1832.

This is not Tennessee Williams's *A Streetcar Named Desire*; that title referred to another line, no longer in service, which ran along Canal Street. But these old coaches, traveling the length of St. Charles Avenue and then some, from the Central Business District through the heart of the Garden District and Uptown, are to New Orleans what cable cars are to San Francisco. Even if you've walked the Garden District and toured Uptown, you should treat yourself to the 90-minute round-trip if for no other reason than to ride one of these vintage arch-roofed cars, teal-green coaches built in North Carolina in the 1920s. They are not air-conditioned, but details such as reversible wooden seats, brass handgrips, and windows that may be raised evoke 19th-century travel. The "Avenue" is one of America's grandest boulevards, and the sights, grouped here according to the nearest streetcar stop (the numbers of which are posted on signs in the neutral ground, the median islands in the street; see p. 99), are a living diorama of New Orleans history.

Make your excursion by daylight. After 7 p.m., cars arrive every 20 minutes until midnight, when they run every hour or so until morning. It is unwise to loiter at a car stop after dark. A one-way fare is $1.25 (exact change required), but you must pay another $1.25 each time you reboard. One-day and three-day visitor passes, costing $5 and $12 respectively, are good for unlimited riding on all Regional Transit Authority (RTA) bus and streetcar lines. Many hotels and stores, as well as tourist information kiosks, sell passes and provide schedules. For information call 504-248-3900.

STOP #1 Board the streetcar here, at St. Charles Ave. and Common St. in the Central Business District. If this stop is crowded, try boarding a block away, at Carondelet St. and Canal—the "Zero Stop."

STOP #3 Skyscrapers line Poydras Street from the Mississippi River to the Superdome. Most are barely a decade old, and many house oil companies and financial institutions. **One Shell Square,** the white tower at Poydras and St. Charles, is New Orleans's tallest skyscraper.

STOP #4 To your right is the Greek Revival-style **Gallier Hall** (see p. 103), designed by the senior James Gallier in the 1850s. It served as New Orleans's city hall until 1957, and now it is used for official fêtes. Gallier Hall faces **Lafayette Square** (see p. 103), the center of the early American enclave.

STOP #5 Leave the streetcar at this stop to visit the historic **Thirteen Sisters** (see p. 106). During the 1840s notables of the small

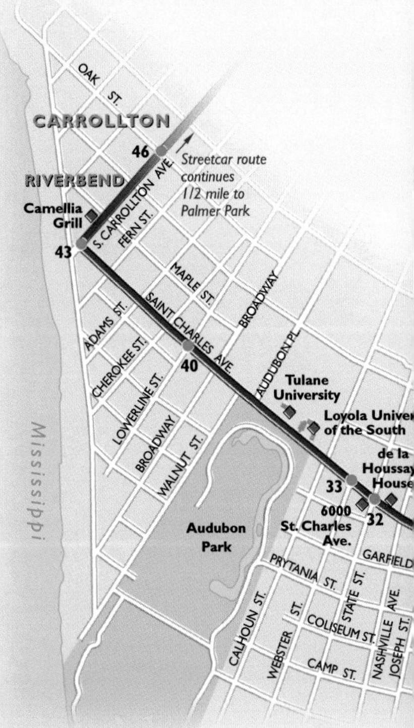

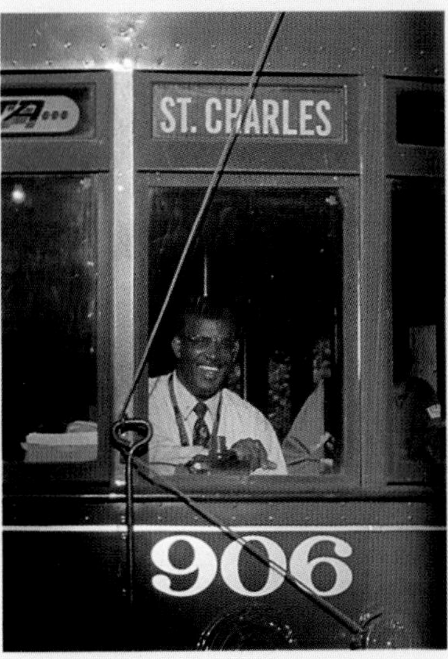

Electric power drives the St. Charles streetcars, built in the 1920s.

American community lived in townhouses built to Yankee tastes. A thriving arts community has taken root here.

STOP #7 Entering Lee Circle, you'll view the **Ogden Museum of Southern Art** (see p. 110), a showcase for regional creativity. The commander-in-chief of Confederate forces strikes a noble pose in bronze in the middle of the circle at the **Lee Monument** (see p. 115). Note that Lee gazes north from his lookout atop a tall white marble column—symbolizing, some say, his defiance toward the Union Army.

STOPS #8–11 This commercial stretch was redeveloped in the 1950s and 1960s.

STOP #13 On your right is the luxuriously refurbished **Pontchartrain Hotel** *(2031 St. Charles Ave. 504-524-0581 or 800-777-6193;* see p. 248). Built in 1926, it is the queen of uptown lodgings and is a socialite watering hole. This is also the stop for the **Official Visitors Center**

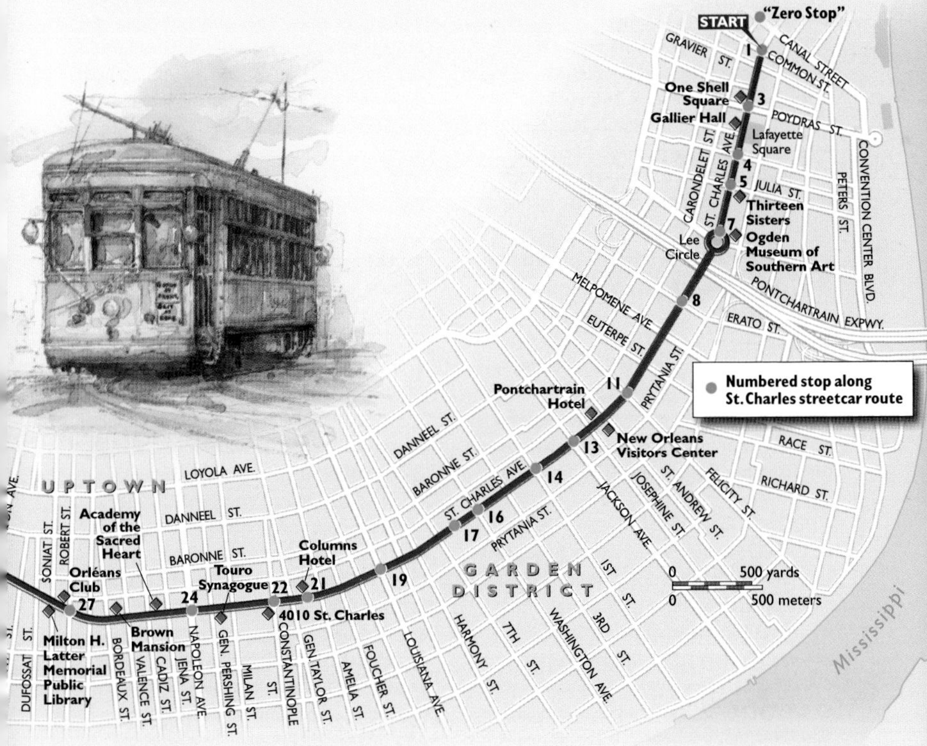

Averaging 9 miles an hour, the St. Charles line carries 20,000 passengers every 24 hours.

and the New Orleans Metropolitan Convention & Visitors Bureau *(2020 St. Charles Ave.).*

STOP #14 Hop off at First St. for a walking tour of the **Garden District** (see pp. 132–137). After, you can pick up the streetcar again at **STOP #16** or **#17,** flanking Washington Ave.

STOP #19 Above Louisiana Avenue are elegant, mostly residential blocks shaded by live oaks that reach nearly across the street.

STOP #21 The Columns hotel *(3811 St. Charles Ave. 504-899-9308 or 800-445-9308. Reservations required;* see p. 248) was built in the 1880s as a home for Simon Hernsheim, a Magazine Street cigar manufacturer. Louis Malle used the Victorian as a primary location for his 1978 film *Pretty Baby,* based on the life of Storyville photographer E.J. Bellocq. The porch is a delightful place to pause for brunch or a drink and to watch the parade along St. Charles.

STOP #22 The modest Queen Anne/shingle house on your left, at **4010 St. Charles,** was built by architect Thomas Sully for his family. Sully's was New Orleans's first large architectural firm, and from 1880 to 1905 he designed some two dozen houses built on St. Charles Avenue.

STOP #24 To your left, at 4238 St. Charles (at General Pershing St.), is **Touro Synagogue** *(504-895-4843),* a prominent Reform Jewish congregation here since 1909. Its pale brickwork, arcade of rounded arches, and dome give it an appealing Middle Eastern look.

STOPS #25–27 The buildings between Napoleon and Robert Streets are unusually attractive, especially the **Academy of the Sacred Heart,** a Catholic girls' school on your right at 4521 St. Charles, just beyond Jena Street. A couple of blocks up on your right, at 4717 St. Charles near Valence, is the limestone Richardsonian Romanesque **Brown Mansion,** the largest house on St. Charles. It was built by William Brown, a poor boy who started as a clerk in a Mississippi country store and worked his way up to corner the world cotton market from the New Orleans exchange. The house was completed in 1905 after three years of construction at a cost of $250,000. It is said to have been a wedding present to his wife, with the promise that it would be, as it is, the avenue's grandest home.

STOP #27 On your right at 5005 St. Charles (at Robert) is another nuptial gift, a lovely French Second Empire building with a mansard roof. It was built in 1868 by William Wynne for his daughter and remodeled in 1907 into its present appearance. In 1925 it became the **Orléans Club,** a women's social and cultural association.

On your left, at 5120 St. Charles between Soniat and Dufossat, is the **Milton H. Latter Memorial Public Library** *(504-596-2625. Closed Fri. & Sun.),* one of the avenue's few old residences open to the public. It mixes Mediterranean and prairie styles, the latter a creation of Chicago architects led by Frank Lloyd Wright. In 1948 real estate mogul Harry Latter and his wife, Anna, gave it to the city as a memorial to their son Milton, killed in World War II. The formal first-floor rooms are now reading rooms, their gorgeous details, including ceilings imported from France, preserved. Ask a librarian for a brochure

Tourists share the old Perley A. Thomas cars with everyday cross-town commuters.

describing the building's features and history. Among its owners was silent screen star Marguerite Clark (1883–1940), a rival of Mary Pickford in waiflike and ingenue roles. Clark retired here in 1921.

STOP #32 Known as the Wedding Cake House because of its extravagant decoration, the Georgian Revival **de la Houssaye House,** on your right at 5809 St. Charles at Rosa Park, is probably the avenue's most opulent. Dating from 1896, it was built for comfort as well; its huge bay windows and numerous porches and balconies bespeak leisure.

STOP #33 Thomas Sully was one of New Orleans's preeminent late 19th-century architects, and this 1895 corner-lot Georgian Revival beauty (on your left at **6000 St. Charles** at Webster) is one of his finest accomplishments. Note the "bow windows" on its State Street side.

STOPS #35–38 On your right at St. Charles and Calhoun, a collection of redbrick, terracotta-trimmed buildings identify the 19-acre campus of **Loyola University of the South,** established in 1904. Across the street to your left is **Audubon Park** (see pp. 142–143). The handsome limestone Richardsonian Romanesque buildings ahead on your right are the oldest at **Tulane University** (see pp. 140–141), whose narrow 110-acre campus runs north for about a mile. The building to the left is Tilton Hall, dating from 1901 and the home of the **Amistad Research Center,** a vast and important archive devoted primarily to African-American history and the civil rights movement.

STOP #40 Lowerline Street marks the boundary between Uptown and the district of **Carrollton.** It was first linked by rail to the Quarter by the New Orleans & Carrollton Railroad in 1835. Carrollton was annexed to New Orleans in 1874 but has maintained its own personality.

Approaching the end of St. Charles Avenue, look to the left to see the Mississippi River levee. Shortly after passing Fern Street, the streetcar turns right onto Carrollton Avenue.

STOP #43 The river's curve around Nine Mile Point gave this part of Carrollton the name **Riverbend.** This is a good place to stretch your legs with a stroll around Riverbend, where you'll find a nice mix of cafés, shops, and restaurants. One of the more appealing is the venerable **Camellia Grill** *(626 S. Carrollton Ave. 504-866-9573; see p. 250)*, an old-fashioned lunch counter joint known for its homemade pecan pies.

STOP #46 This is the place to stop off for **Oak Street,** Carrollton's main avenue. A dime store, shops, diners, and clubs recall small-town Southern life in the 1940s.

STOP #51 Leafy little **Palmer Park** and its arched portal have been here since Carrollton sprouted in the 1800s.

STOP #52 The end of the line. Access to the river is hard to find here because of railroad right-of-ways and private docks. If you're still in a streetcar state of mind, enjoy the 45-minute ride back to the CBD—you're certain to see things you missed on the upriver leg. If you're pressed for time, call for a cab pickup. ■

How to visit the Garden District

Women's Opera Guild House

Map pp. 126–127

2504 Prytania St.

504-899-1945

Open Mon. p.m. Sept.–May; guided tours by appt.

$; $$$ (guided tours)

Streetcar: St. Charles

THE GARDEN DISTRICT FLIRTS WITH VISITORS—ITS BEAUTY is alluring—but it has no significant historic buildings open to the public, and only a pair of minor museums. Exclusively residential, virtually all of its magnificent houses are privately owned, but architecturally worth even an outside glance.

Save for glimpses through tall windows, their stunning interiors—some with 22-foot ceilings and glittering crystal chandeliers, many decorated with period furniture, antique objets d'art, ornate wall coverings, and swaged, floor-length draperies—remain mostly private domains. What you can do is stroll the Garden District's jasmine-scented sidewalks, admiring the magnificent exteriors of these gems. Most visitors approach from a St. Charles Avenue streetcar stop, but the Magazine Street shopping district (see pp. 144–145) provides equally good access, particularly by car. (Keep in mind, however, that the Garden District street regulations strictly limit nonresident parking.) See pp. 134–137 for a guided walking tour of the neighborhood.

The only house open to the public is the **Women's Opera Guild House,** a Greek Revival townhouse completed in 1858 and remodeled in the 1880s to reflect the Queen Anne style popular at that time. The makeover into the Queen Anne style added its right-hand-side octagonal turret. In the 1960s the home's last owner, Nettie Seebold, bequeathed it to the Women's Guild of the New Orleans Opera Association, which keeps a small opera museum there. The interior is decorated with period furnishings, art, vintage stenciled wallpaper, and beautiful curtains.

There are vintage lodgings here and there—unheralded by signs, forbidden by zoning law. The century-old Queen Anne-style **Sully Mansion** *(2631 Prytania St. 504-891-0457)* has period decor including original stained-glass windows. The spacious **Josephine Guest House** *(1450 Josephine St. 504-524-6361 or 800-779-6361)* is a beautifully restored Italianate mansion dating from 1870 and furnished with period antiques. For other suggestions, consult New Orleans Bed & Breakfasts and Accommodations *(504-838-0071).* ■

Magnolias shade this pair of double-galleried St. Charles Avenue Victorians built in the 1880s.

New Orleans Fire Department Museum

FIRE WAS ONCE NEW ORLEANS'S WORST NIGHTMARE, more frightening than the Mississippi's flooding. Starting in 1850 this stolid two-story redbrick building—originally the City of Lafayette's fire department—sent its horse-drawn steam-powered gleaming brass pump wagon out its arched doorway in a clatter of hoofs.

Two years later, when the three local municipalities ended their experiment with independence and reunified, this firehouse became known as Chalmette Engine No. 23. It was the last to retire its teams of horses for a motorized fire truck. About a generation ago the station itself was put out to pasture, its crews moved to new and bigger quarters around the corner on Magazine Street. But those who knew it well—including New Orleans's cadre of retired firefighters who know it best—pushed for a full-scale refurbishment and its opening, in 1995, as a museum and educational center.

Fighting fires has never been easy or safe, and the vintage equipment displayed inside reveals not only how far we have come but also how little the task has changed. (In the end it still takes guts and determination, and a whole lot of water.) Chat with the docents, most of whom are retired firefighters with fascinating stories. The emeritus firemen explain how things like the 1838 Hunneman Hand Pump and the 1860 hand-drawn ladder truck were used. When it was fired up and pulled by a team of galloping horses, the 1896 Ahrens "2nd Class Steamer," all gleaming brass and nickel plate, thrilled people like nothing else.

The memorabilia are fascinating: old New Orleans Fire Department uniforms, citations, newspaper clippings, and logbooks documenting fire department personnel and New Orleans fires from 1891 to the present. Note the photographs, recalling the time when fire company members posed like rugby teams, arranged in poses that still radiate pride in their calling. One thing you'll not see in the old photos, however, is a black fireman. Activists noted in 1950 that while African Americans comprised a third of the city's population, none were firefighters. Outcry over such local employment discrimination spurred civic reforms presaging the civil rights movement. ■

New Orleans Fire Department Museum

- Map pp. 126–127
- 1135 Washington Ave.
- 504-896-4756
- Open Mon.–Fri.
- Donation
- Streetcar: St. Charles Bus: Magazine St.

Years of fighting Crescent City fires qualify these comrades to be docents at the New Orleans Fire Department Museum.

A walk in the Garden

This two- to three-hour stroll features some of the most interesting Garden District residences, including the only home open to the public.

Peering through the front gate of the Bradish Johnson House, at 2343 Prytania Street

You don't need a car to get here; you can hop aboard the St. Charles streetcar and take it to First Street (Stop #14), where the walk begins. At the end of your stroll, you can reboard at Washington Avenue (Stop #16). If you think you need more information about the area before starting out, however, consider alighting one stop earlier. Stop #13 is the stop for the recently opened **New Orleans Metropolitan Convention & Visitors Bureau** *(2020 St. Charles Ave.)*; here you will find informative brochures and helpful staff who can answer questions about the Garden District and the rest of New Orleans as well. The visitor center opens at 8:30 a.m. Monday through Saturday and at 10:00 a.m. on Sunday, which should allow you plenty of time to get your bearings and then enjoy a leisurely stroll through the district. It is strongly recommended that you make this walk in the morning, especially in summer, to avoid the midday heat. Be sure to take a break for lunch at the Commander's Palace Restaurant (see p. 137), two blocks from Stop #16.

The Garden District was created as an American retreat away from the noise and congestion of the French Quarter (not to mention as an escape from the tensions rising between Americans and French Creoles). But it still afforded easy access to the commercial sections where the fortunes necessary for achieving and sustaining the Garden life-style were made. Most of the houses you'll see were built between the 1830s and the 1880s; together they form what might be called a living encyclopedia of mid-19th-century architecture. The buildings cited here are splendid examples, and there are dozens of others that will no doubt strike your fancy as you mosey around the district.

Start at St. Charles Avenue and First Street, where the lovely home at **2344 St. Charles** ❶ typifies the Greek Revival style often seen in the district. Built in the 1850s, this house is notable for its tall windows, high ceilings, and set-back galleries that maximize ventilation and provide shelter from the sun and rain.

Go south on First to 2343 Prytania St., where the front garden of the **Bradish Johnson House** is shaded by magnolias and mimosas. This is the city's grandest expression of the French Second Empire style, a vogue of the 1860s and 1870s named for the reign of Napoleon III (1852–1870). This emperor undertook building programs that gave Paris its monumental structures and grand boulevards. (The Old Executive Office Building in Washington, D.C., is one of the finest examples of this style in the United States.) The Bradish Johnson

House was built in 1872 for a transplanted New Yorker whose sugar plantation made him rich. Note the mansard roof—made popular when Napoleon III added one to the Louvre. Since 1929 this has been the Louise S. McGehee School for Girls.

Across Prytania, at No. 2340 on the downtown-riverside corner, is the Thomas Toby House, more commonly called **Toby's Corner.** The Greek Revival plantation-style home dates from 1838 and is believed to be the oldest house in the Garden District. Thomas Toby, from Philadelphia, prospered as a wheelwright and used some of his fortune to have his house raised on brick piers as a precaution against flooding. Note the size of the lot—the four-per-block plan the subdividers specified to attract the wealthy.

Across the intersection on the uptown-riverside corner of Prytania and First, New Orleans's **French Consulate** occupies a formal brick Georgian Revival manse at 2406 Prytania. This structure was probably built in the 1880s, when the style, unused in America since the Revolutionary War era, enjoyed a brief encore. Walk another block toward the river to Coliseum Street and take a look at the beautiful Italianate **Joseph C. Morris House** *(1331 1st St.)*, also known as the Morris-Israel House. Morris made his money in rope—the term then was cordage—and had this three-level brick home built in 1869. The architecture of Italy's rural villas was appealing to many mid-19th-century American architects because it lent itself equally well to restraint or exuberance, depending on the wishes of their clients. Entrance towers, round-headed windows, arcaded porches, and balustraded balconies are among the many attractive features of the Morris House—here decorated with exquisite, locally cast ironwork.

In 1886 writer Mark Twain was a guest at several fancy dinner parties that were hosted by cotton broker and lender Joseph Carroll in his mansion at 1315 First Street. The **Joseph Carroll House** was built

Also see area map pp. 126–127
St. Charles Ave. & First St.
0.75 mile
2 to 3 hours
Commander's Palace Restaurant

NOT TO BE MISSED

- Toby's Corner
- Brevard-Wisdom-Rice House
- Women's Opera Guild House
- Commander's Palace Restaurant

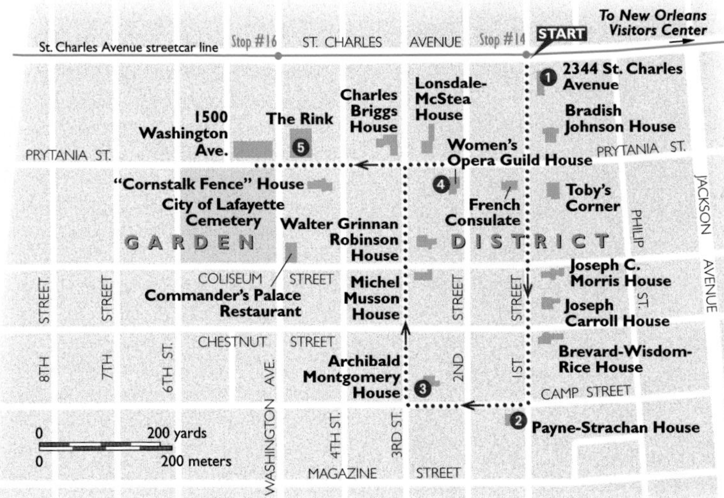

in 1869 of brick and stone in the Italianate style, its galleries enclosed by intricate ironwork. (Wander a few steps down Chestnut Street, to the right, for a look at the Carroll family's tree-bowered garden and pretty carriage house.)

The architect of the **Brevard-Wisdom-Rice House,** across the street at 1239 First, combined Italianate and Greek Revival styles in his 1857 design for merchant Albert Brevard. The house's fence of woven wire, manufactured in New York and of a type once widely used in New Orleans, is now rare. Subsequent owner, jurist John Minor Wisdom, added his surname to the house. In more recent years, it was the home of Crescent City native and novelist Anne Rice, who was raised in the Garden District and in Texas. After achieving great literary success with her tales of vampires, she returned to the district with her husband—artist and poet Stan Rice (now deceased)—and son. She has since sold the imposing house on First Street and moved to a nearby suburb.

The cast-iron Cornstalk Fence at 1448 Fourth Street dates from the mid-1800s.

Jefferson Davis came to the end of his life in 1889 while visiting family friends at the **Payne-Strachan House** ❷, at 1134 First Street, on the uptown-riverside corner of First and Camp. The patrician home, with its cast-iron Ionic columns, bay windows, and classical details, hews closely to the conventions of the Greek Revival style.

Walk uptown along Camp Street to the downtown-lakeside corner of Camp and Third Street, where you'll find the **Archibald Montgomery House** ❸. This ornate Italianate structure was commissioned by the Irish-born president of the Crescent City Railroad in 1868. Montgomery wanted decoration and formality, and he definitely got both. Note the decorative brackets and the columned porches, which are seldom seen on urban Victorians because of the typically narrow lots.

Walk two blocks north (toward Lake Pontchartrain) to the riverside-downtown corner of Third and Coliseum. Here at 1331 Third Street is the Italianate **Michel Musson House.** Credited to James Gallier, Sr., this building was completed in 1853 for New Orleans postmaster and Cotton Exchange president Michel Musson. His nephew was French Impressionist Edgar Degas, who bequeathed to his uncle immortality as the broker seen inspecting cotton in Degas's 1873 painting "A Portrait in an Office: The New Orleans Cotton Exchange."

On the lakeside-downtown corner of Coliseum and Third is a house that was built between 1859 and 1865; is it said to be the first in New Orleans to have been equipped with indoor plumbing. The **Walter Grinnan Robinson House** *(1415 3rd St.)* is also one of the biggest manses in the Garden District. Walter Robinson, a tobacco dealer, permitted his architect to tinker with convention by rounding the ends of the house's double gallery, a style attributed to James Gallier, Jr. See the handsome stables in the back, especially notable for having survived.

Continue north (toward the lake) and turn right on Prytania Street to view the **Women's Opera Guild House** ❹ *(2504 Prytania St. 504-899-1945),* a lovingly maintained, Greek Revival/Queen Anne confection. This is the only residence in the Garden District

currently open for tours, although the policy of the guild generally favors groups over individuals (see p. 132).

Backtrack on Prytania to Third Street, where on the downtown-lakeside corner the tall Italianate **Lonsdale-McStea House** stands as a monument to the tenacity of its builder. New York native Henry Lonsdale rewarded himself with this imposing mansion in 1856, some 19 years after the market in gunnysacks, over which he reigned supreme, collapsed. Undaunted, Lonsdale engineered his way back to the top by becoming the top coffee broker in New Orleans, a feat that enabled him to build this house. Unfortunately, the chaos following the Civil War ruined him again.

Across Third Street, the **Charles Briggs House—**also known as the Briggs-Staub House—occupies the uptown-lakeside corner lot at 2605 Prytania Street. This trophy, more than 150 years old, is the only Gothic Revival home in the Garden District; it was designed in 1849 by the indefatigable James Gallier, Sr. Charles Briggs, a native of London who prospered here in the insurance business, eschewed slaves for

In the Payne-Strachan House, former Confederate President Jefferson Davis died while visiting friends.

hired servants quartered in a matching, adjoining, freestanding clapboard residence. For some critics, the clean lines and restrained adornment of the Charles Briggs House make this home the most elegant residence in the district, and certainly another feather in Gallier's hat.

Walk one block west (uptown) on Prytania to Fourth Street, where at No. 1448 the 1859 Italianate-style **"Cornstalk Fence" House** commands the uptown-riverside corner lot. You'll probably find people with cameras crouching low to photograph the fanciful designs in the cast-iron fence surrounding this structure. The dominant motif of the fence—cornstalks—rises on posts incorporating iron pumpkins and garlanded with morning glories. The whole assemblage was manufactured in Philadelphia and shipped here, as was much of the ironwork in New Orleans. The house is also known as Colonel Short's Villa. It reflects aspects of Italian country estates, or villas,

Enjoying an outdoor Sunday jazz brunch at Commander's Palace Restaurant on Washington Avenue in the Garden District

and its Kentuckian owner, a wealthy middleman in local commerce, was an honorary Confederate colonel.

Continue west to the downtown-lakeside corner of Washington and Prytania. The place at 2727 Prytania Street began as the Crescent City Skating Rink in 1884, did time as a mortuary, and then served as an automobile repair shop until about 20 years ago; it is now a little retail center known as **The Rink** ⑤**,** whose tenants include the popular Garden District Book Shop *(504-895-2266)*. Author Anne Rice has made a policy of releasing the first signed copies of her works at this bookstore, which also has a good stock of writing by other local authors and books about New Orleans subjects.

The two-story Victorian residence across the street, at **1500 Washington,** has a colorful history. In the 1880s this building was the front section of the fashionable Southern Athletic Club, where boxer James J. "Gentleman Jim" Corbett, considered the inventor of the left hook, trained in a rear gymnasium (no longer existing) for his 1892 fight in New Orleans against world champion John L. Sullivan. The first recognized heavyweight to fight successfully under the Marquess of Queensberry rules, which ended the brutal bare-knuckle era of boxing, Corbett knocked out Sullivan in the 21st round.

The historically interesting **City of Lafayette Cemetery** (see p. 146) is across the street. And across from it, at 1403 Washington Avenue near Coliseum Street, is one of New Orleans's longtime favorite dining places, **Commander's Palace Restaurant** *(504-899-8221. Reservations advised)*. The restaurant occupies a turreted Queen Anne-style Victorian. Emile Commander opened an eatery here in 1880 and lived upstairs. Since the late 1960s, Commander's Palace has been operated to rave reviews by the Brennan family, one of the preeminent epicurean clans in New Orleans. Consider ending your walk here with a relaxing lunch before strolling back up Washington Avenue to Stop #16 of the St. Charles streetcar. ■

Ecclesiastical Square

AS IRISH CATHOLIC IMMIGRANTS BEGAN SETTLING THE Lafayette City/Irish Channel area upriver from the French Quarter in the 1840s, the Redemptorist Fathers built a complex of buildings that once occupied five adjacent city blocks and was known as Ecclesiastical Square. The cluster included an orphanage, nine school buildings, a gymnasium, three churches, a rectory and gardens, two convents, stables, and an institutional laundry.

Ecclesiastical Square
Map pp. 126–127
Constance St. between Josephine & St. Andrew Sts.

Still dominating the square are a pair of once important, still beautiful Roman Catholic churches from the mid-1800s.

St. Mary's Assumption Roman Catholic Church, completed in 1860, ministered to the Irish Channel's German Catholics. The baroque interior boasts stained-glass windows crafted in Munich. The Channel's Irish folk had their own spiritual house across Constance in the Italian Renaissance-style **St. Alphonsus Roman Catholic Church,** completed in 1855. Its twin square towers are unfinished; they are supposed to support spires. Both churches reflect the masonry trade that reached its zenith in New Orleans in the mid-1800s. The Irish dispersion from the Channel forced St. Alphonsus to close; it's now the deconsecrated St. Alphonsus Art and Culture Center, open for tours on some days, plus for occasional concerts and community events. ■

The thriving 19th-century masonry trade produced St. Alphonsus Church, an Italian Renaissance beauty.

Irish Channel

Originally part of the City of Lafayette, now adjoining and downriver from the Garden District, the Irish Channel sprouted as a working-class neighborhood populated by the mostly unskilled Irish immigrants who arrived en masse in the mid-1800s. The social divide was (and remains) Magazine Street. To the south lived the newcomers, whose low incomes from labor in waterfront brickyards, slaughterhouses, tallow houses, soap and leather factories, and sawmills meant modest one-story frame shotgun doubles—duplexes joined lengthwise under one pitched roof. After the Civil War, the Irish Channel evolved into a tough blue-collar Roman Catholic stronghold, united in its insularity until succeeding generations began to become part of the city's social mainstream. The Irish Channel is today mostly African American and Cuban American. In 1976 its neighborhoods bounded by Jackson Ave., Aline and Magazine Sts., and the river were designated a national historic architectural district. ■

St. Mary's Assumption Church
2030 Constance St.
504-522-6748
Donation
Bus: Magazine

St. Alphonsus Church
www.stalphonsus.org
2045 Constance St.
504-524-8116
Open Tues., Thurs., & Sat.
Donation
Bus: Magazine

Built of Indiana limestone, Richardsonian Romanesque-style Gibson Hall facing St. Charles Avenue is Tulane's signature building and administrative center.

Tulane University

TULANE BEGAN IN 1834 AS THE MEDICAL COLLEGE OF Louisiana. In 1847 it became a part of the newly established University of Louisiana, which also comprised a law department and collegiate department.

Tulane University
www2.tulane.edu
Map pp. 126–127
6823 St. Charles Ave.
504-865-5000
Streetcar: St. Charles

An 1883 bequest from merchant and real estate investor Paul Tulane rescued the bankrupt college, allowing it to move uptown from the Central Business District; in 1894 its first building, Randall Lee Gibson Hall (named for Tulane's partner in the planning), opened on St. Charles Avenue. The unveiling began a campus tradition of Richardsonian Romanesque buildings that remain Tulane's architectural trademark.

Tulane was originally a men-only institution. In 1886 another wealthy benefactor, Mrs. Josephine Louise LeMonnier Newcomb, founded **Sophie Newcomb College** in memory of her only daughter. It became Tulane's sister college, and the nation's first women's coordinate college adjoining the other's campus along Broadway Street and adopting the redbrick Georgian Revival style for its buildings.

Nearly 12,000 students, roughly 5,000 of them in graduate programs, are currently enrolled at Tulane's 110-acre campus.

Tulane receives highest marks for its excellent research libraries, of which the **Amistad Research Center** in Tilton Hall *(6823 St. Charles Ave. 504-865-5535. www.tulane.edu/~amistad. Open Mon.-Sat.)* is a shining example. It is one of the leading African-American history collections anywhere, housing some 10 million documents —90 percent of them the papers of business leaders, clergy, lawyers, artists, educators, authors, musicians, factory workers, and farmers. The remainder document the experiences of Puerto Ricans, Chicanos, Native Americans, Asian Americans, European immigrants, and Appalachian whites. The center has a superb collection of African and African-American art, pieces of which are displayed throughout the center's corridors (where visitors may roam). It includes works by virtuosos such as Ellis Wilson, Henry O. Tanner, Elizabeth Catlett, and Jacob Lawrence. Be sure to seek out Tilton Hall's beautiful windows, designed by Louis Comfort Tiffany for the building's opening a century ago.

The modernistic **Howard-Tilton Memorial Library** *(7001 Freret St. at Audubon St. 504-865-5605)* includes the incomparable **Hogan Jazz Archive** *(Jones Hall. 504-865-5688. Open Mon.-Fri.).* Located across the parking lot from the main library, it preserves oral history interviews, recorded music, photographs, sheet music, clippings, and other artifacts and materials shedding light on the cultural phenomenon of American jazz—particularly the New Orleans style. Its holdings are intended mainly for scholarly study, but its top-floor Special Collection reading room has changing displays of rare materials donated by Crescent City luminaries such as Nick LaRocca, Ray Bauduc, and Knocky Parker.

Also in Jones Hall is the fascinating **Southeastern Architectural Archive** *(Jones Hall. 504-865-5699. Open Mon.-Fri.),* a major research collection for studying "the built environment." Drawings, office records, and photographs relate primarily to the architectural and urban history of New Orleans from 1830 to the present. The archive is the South's largest collection of architectural drawings and building records; it focuses particularly on New Orleans and Louisiana and work by leading architects, including James Gallier Sr. and Jr., James Dakin, and Henry Howard.

Cross over to the Newcomb College campus to visit the new **Newcomb Art Gallery** in the Woldenberg Art Center, next to the Art Building on Newcomb Place *(504-865-5328. www.tulane.edu /~gallery. Closed June–Aug.).* Enter through the Woodward Way lobby to view the beautifully restored Tiffany triptychs, stained-glass ecclesiastical scenes taken from the windows of the college's former chapel. Beyond is a serene, spare space of soft white walls, natural pine floors, and filtering skylights that critics praise as one of the finest exhibition spaces in New Orleans. The works of modern masters, culled from other galleries as well as Newcomb's own collection, are showcased here on a rotating basis. Auguste Rodin, David Smith, and James van der Zee typify the quality of artists featured. Several rooms treat the American Arts and Crafts movement and permanently display decorative art designed by Newcomb's female students, featuring now rare Newcomb Pottery produced from 1894 to 1940. Graceful, earth-toned pieces in soft blue, green, and rose, they are considered among the 20th century's most significant American art potteries. ■

Curator Bruce Raeburn with cornet, Victrola, and other artifacts from the Hogan Jazz Archive, Tulane University

Audubon Park & Zoo

Audubon Park & Zoological Gardens

www.auduboninstitute.org

Map pp. 126–127

6500 Magazine St.

504-581-4629 or 800-774-7394

$$

Streetcar: St. Charles

Note: A free shuttle runs through the park. The *John James Audubon* riverboat *(fare)* makes one-way and round-trips from Aquarium of the Americas.

THESE VERDANT 340 ACRES WERE ONCE PART OF THE sugarcane plantation of Jean Étienne Boré, who in 1795 developed a commercially feasible technique for granulating sugar. Of those days only some very old oak trees survive in the vicinity of the zoo, planted by the Frenchman's son-in-law, who took over the land. The city purchased this tract in 1871, initially calling it Upper City Park.

In 1884–85 New Orleans staged the World's Industrial and Cotton Centennial Exposition here, but all the pavilions of that great event are gone. In 1886 the park was renamed in honor of artist and ornithologist John James Audubon, who resided in the French Quarter between 1821 and 1822.

Today people come here to relax on its sweeping lawns or picnic in the shade of thick-limbed spreading trees. They also walk, jog, in-line skate, bicycle its winding paths (outfitted with exercise stations), play tennis, ride horses, or try to keep their golf balls from dropping into the lagoons that flank the 18-hole **Audubon Park Golf Course** *(6500 Magazine. 504-865-8260. Greens fee)*. You can rent well-trained horses at **Cascade Stables** *(700 East Dr. 504-891-2246. Hourly fee, with guide)* for trail rides within the park. The horse barn and corral are located just east of the zoo, on a one-way side road leading to Magazine Street. Call for directions, as the facility is a bit hard to find. The park's 2-mile jogging path

Left: The park's broad pedestrian boulevards make it among the city's most popular places for family outings. Above: A young zoo visitor gingerly touches a baby alligator.

circles the golf course, skirting lagoons. There are ten excellent hard-surface (but unlighted) tennis courts at the back of the park off Tchoupitoulas Street *(504-895-1042)*.

ZOOLOGICAL GARDENS

The Zoological Gardens hold some 1,500 animals, many of which roam about in natural habitats. In the acre-and-a-half **Jaguar Jungle,** the great cats lounge in a rain forest setting amid copies of Mayan temple ruins while spider monkeys chatter to one another and sloths, Jabiru storks, and scarlet ibis watch. The stone carvings duplicate those found at Copán, Chichén Itzá, and other Middle American sites. This is a wonderful place for young children (accompanied by adults) to experience a semblance of jungle exploration. A trail winds into the forest, through dense fog and over a stream, beneath ancient archways and crumbling temple ruins to an archaeological dig. At the heart of the rain forest is **Jaguar Plaza,** where two of these animals, who were considered gods by the Maya, command a ruin.

Rare white leucitic alligators eye spectators with toothy grins from their pools in the 6.5-acre **Louisiana Swamp Exhibit,** one of the zoo's most popular attractions; it includes a re-creation of a 1930s Cajun swamp village. Kangaroos and wallabies hop and scuffle about in the **Australian Exhibit.** If you have young children, be sure to find your way to the **Embraceable Zoo,** where kids can touch and hold docile and well-supervised domestic animals.

No creature here, however, captivates more visitors than the fearsome Komodo dragon, the world's largest lizard; ranging from 6 to 9 feet long, it can weigh up to 200 pounds. Found only on three small Indonesian islands, this lizard is the stuff of nightmares, with a mouth full of sharklike serrated teeth, an appetite that drives it to swallow wild pigs whole, and an ability to outrun humans.

Check postings of daily activities. Events are scheduled throughout the day, including narrated feedings of giraffes, alligators, and komodo dragons, and there are lively talks by wildlife specialists and opportunities to pet live animals. ■

A romantic moment warms a Magazine Street coffeehouse.

Magazine Street

NAMED FOR THE FRENCH COLONIAL TOBACCO HOUSES *(magasins)* that once clustered at Magazine and Commons, the 6-mile-long thoroughfare runs from Canal Street in the Central Business District to Uptown's Audubon Park, making slight turns that mirror the curve of the Mississippi around New Orleans.

Magazine Street
Map pp. 126–127

To call it the city's premier shopping street sells it short, for its eclecticism—the sheer variety and range of its antique shops, furniture stores, galleries, boutiques, bookstores, newsstands, cafés, and restaurants—reflects New Orleans's multiple personalities as no other avenue in the city does.

The street is too long to walk conveniently. You should drive it, stopping where the flavor of the street strikes your fancy, or buy a pass that allows you to hop on and off the Magazine Street bus, which rolls along its entire length. Many stores occupy vintage shotgun houses, permitting you to enter and gain a sense of these quintessentially New Orleans buildings. Here is a sampling of what you'll find along the way from the zoo back to the Quarter:

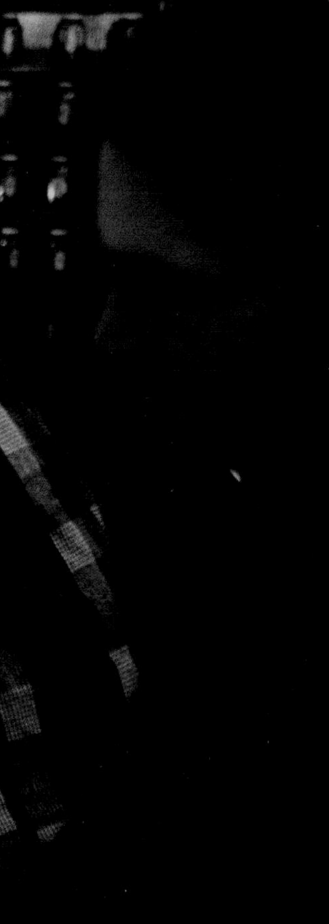

AUDUBON PARK TO NASHVILLE AVENUE

This six-block stretch charms visitors with its casual flair. Stop at **Taqueria Corona** *(5932 Magazine St. 504-897-3974)* if you're in the mood for a hearty lunch or dinner.

NASHVILLE AVENUE TO JEFFERSON AVENUE

Among the specialty shops lining this four-block section are **Scriptura** *(5423 Magazine St. 504-897-1555)*, an Italian stationer, and **Beaucoup Books** *(5414 Magazine St. 504-895-2663 or 800-543-4114)*, which is particularly strong in Southern literature and is a good place to buy unusual postcards.

JEFFERSON AVENUE TO NAPOLEON AVENUE

This stretch is thin on shopping but interesting for its variety of Victorian residences. The **Academy Gallery of the New Orleans Academy of Fine Arts** *(5256 Magazine St. 504-899-8111)* sells fine art, particularly works by local artists. If you have an appetite, have a look at **Casamento's Restaurant** *(4330 Magazine St. 504-895-9761. Closed May–July).*

NAPOLEON AVENUE TO LOUISIANA AVENUE

Along these 13 blocks are some of Magazine's finest dealers in objets d'art—paintings, antique furnishings, sterling silver, estate jewelry, lamps, Oriental rugs, fine porcelain, ceramics, handblown glass, iron furniture. If you visit only one stretch of Magazine, this is probably your best bet. Among the most eclectic collections is the stock at **Neal Auction Company** *(4038 Magazine St. 504-899-5329)*, one of New Orleans's leading auctioneers. A fine place to relax and dine just off Magazine is the reasonably priced **Cafe Atchafalaya** *(901 Louisiana Ave. 504-891-5271)*, which features Southern cuisine.

JACKSON AVENUE TO FELICITY STREET

Only four blocks long, this stretch of Magazine Street is well worth a visit for anyone who's interested in yesterday's treasures. Walk into **O. J. Hooter's Furniture Company** *(1938 Magazine St. 504-522-5167)* and discover a wealth of used and antique furnishings. If you happen to be hereabouts in mid-afternoon, make your way to the 1860s **St. Vincent Guest House** *(1507 Magazine St. 504-523-3411)* for tea. From here, catch the Magazine St. bus back to the CBD or French Quarter. ■

Stone carving adorns the Lafayette Cemetery "society tomb" of the elite Jefferson Fire Company No. 22, erected in 1852.

More places to visit in the Garden District & Uptown

CENTRAL CITY

Lakeside of St. Charles Avenue and upriver from Pontchartrain Expressway is interesting but depressed Central City, where antebellum houses survive. Irish immigrants settled here in the 1830s; working-class German and Jewish émigrés followed. Locals recommend sight-seeing from the Freret Street bus, from its start at Carondelet and Canal. Upriver from Canal, public housing attests to efforts to revitalize this district of many churches. Streets upriver from Napoleon Avenue are better off. Beyond Jefferson Avenue the fashionable University Section's residences are even more prosperous. Get off at Tulane University, cross the campus to St. Charles, and return by streetcar. If you tour by car, visit the double shotgun house at **2309-11 First Street.** Here, from 1887 to 1904, cornetist Buddy Bolden, creator of the first jazz band, enjoyed some of his most creative years. A 1915 gift, Andrew Carnegie's library at **1924 Philip Street** was for years the city's only public library open to African Americans. The galleried house at **2037 Carondelet,** built in 1859 for steamboat *Natchez* captain Thomas Leathers, retains its original carved entrance and stables. Map pp. 126–127 Roughly bounded by Pontchartrain Expwy., Louisiana, St. Charles, & Claiborne Aves. Guided tours offered by Le'Ob's Tours and Travel *(504-288-3478. $$$)*

CITY OF LAFAYETTE CEMETERY

A peaceful place in the center of the Garden District, this quintessential New Orleans cemetery was dedicated in 1833, when this part of New Orleans was the City of Lafayette. Wander the cemetery's broad avenues (intended to accommodate large funeral processions) and you'll find among the many aboveground crypts names reflecting every ethnic group in the old city, from German to West Indian.

One of the most interesting tombs here is a society monument built in 1852 for members of the Jefferson Fire Company No. 22. (Look for the stone carving of an old-fashioned fire engine atop it.) By the late 1850s the cemetery was crowded with free-standing tombs, and burial vaults were added to its surrounding walls. By the 1970s the place had fallen into such ruin that only a determined campaign by Garden District stalwarts thwarted a city plan to demolish the walls and their burial vaults and replace them with a chain-link fence. Save Our Cemeteries *(504-525-3377 or 888-721-7493)* leads informative walking tours of the cemetery on Mondays, Wednesdays, Fridays, and Saturdays at 10:30 a.m.

Map pp. 126–127 Bordered by Prytania St., Washington Ave., Coliseum St., & 6th St. Streetcar: St. Charles Ave. ■

Swampland in the 19th century, drained in the early 20th, Mid-City lacks the historical cachet of other districts. But its residents, from Esplanade Ridge to Lake Pontchartrain, enjoy a sense of forward-looking community far from the madding crowds of the Quarter.

Mid-City & the lakefront

Victorian-style "brackets" decorate the roof overhang of a Hagen Street shotgun house.

Mid-City & the lakefront

IN THE LATE 1800s, ATTENTION TURNED TO THE LOW-LYING SWAMPLAND lakeward of the Quarter, then known as the "back of town." Pumping stations were installed and the soggy plain was drained, and by the early 20th century it was a suburb. For a time, but only in a geographical sense, it was New Orleans's center, and thus known as Mid-City.

Brothers play an impromptu jazz duet on a New Orleans sidewalk.

Roughly bordered on the west and south by I-10's right angle through town, Mid-City's northernmost reach ends at the cluster of burial grounds known as the Cemeteries District. From there its downtown edge follows Conti Avenue to I-10 (here N. Claiborne Avenue), which runs from the vicinity of City Park to just lakeside of the area known as the Faubourg Tremé. (The Tremé—once a close-knit community of French-speaking Creole families—is an area beset with big-city problems. At night, visitors are advised not to walk alone there.) Mid-City's best feature, perhaps, is City Park. Big (at 1,500 acres) and bucolic, its premier attraction is the noteworthy New Orleans Museum of Art (see p. 154).

Notched between Mid-City's downtown edge and the nearby Esplanade Ridge district —bisected by Esplanade Avenue and extending from the French Quarter to City Park—is the Parkview District. This area is more often referred to by locals as Bayou St. John, after the historic waterway that flows through its southernmost section. An early 19th-century residential development, Bayou St. John's pretty streets of mostly bungalow and colonial revival houses in recent years have attracted those who fancy vintage architecture and enjoy the rigors of do-it-yourself restoration.

Above Mid-City, extending to Lake Pontchartrain, are the aptly named Lakeview and Lake Vista Districts. These were first developed in the 1800s as a waterside resort area with everything from high-priced casinos and luxury hotels for the wealthy to campgrounds and cabins for the budget-minded. The districts are now mainly residential.

To gain a sense of how the personalities of Mid-City and the lakefront differ from the older, better-known sections of New Orleans, drive Esplanade Avenue and Wisner Boulevard from the Faubourg Marigny north to Lakeshore Drive. Then return via Canal Boulevard and Canal Street. Visiting the historical sites featured in this chapter—old plantation houses, once isolated graveyards, hidden gardens, and the Lake Pontchartrain shore—will transport you from the lush romanticism of New Orleans's colonial era and the proud mercantilism of the Anglo-American 19th century to the social ferment of the unsung, everyday people.

Mid-City's collection of historical relics and public places spans New Orleans's social evolution from French colonial times to the Great Depression—from the oaks in City Park where duels were first fought in the 1700s to the Botanical Garden, a legacy of President Franklin Roosevelt's Works Progress Administration. Both City Park and the New Orleans Museum of Art were gifts from benefactors grateful to the city for the good fortune it bestowed upon them. The home where French painter Edgar Degas sojourned with relatives, along with Mid-City's grand 20th-century estates, testify to the unusual refinement that has characterized the area's mercantile elite. ■

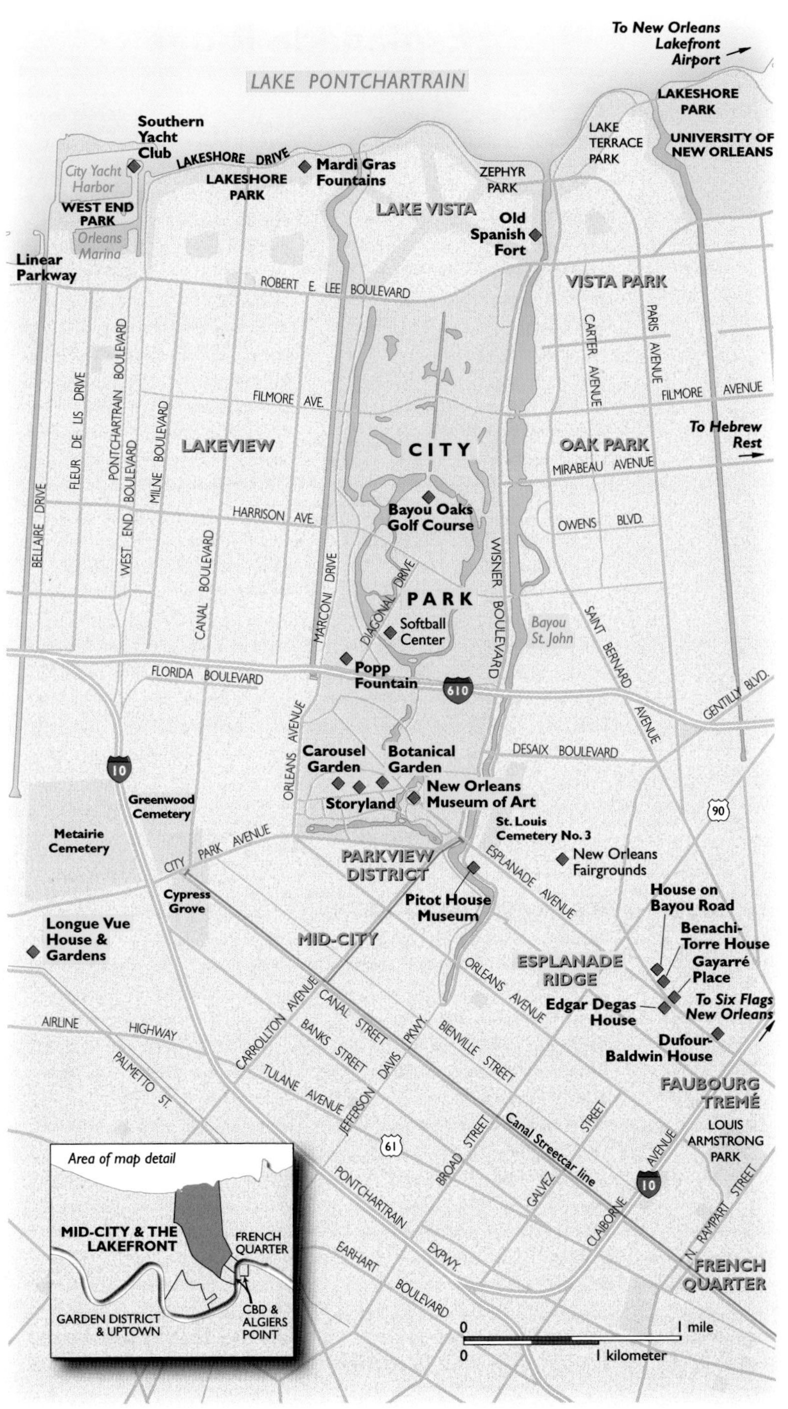
To New Orleans Lakefront Airport
LAKE PONTCHARTRAIN
LAKESHORE PARK
UNIVERSITY OF NEW ORLEANS
LAKE TERRACE PARK
Southern Yacht Club
City Yacht Harbor
LAKESHORE DRIVE
Mardi Gras Fountains
LAKESHORE PARK
ZEPHYR PARK
WEST END PARK
Orleans Marina
LAKE VISTA
Old Spanish Fort
Linear Parkway
ROBERT E. LEE BOULEVARD
VISTA PARK
CARTER AVENUE
PARIS AVENUE
FILMORE AVE.
FILMORE AVENUE
To Hebrew Rest
LAKEVIEW
CITY
OAK PARK
MIRABEAU AVENUE
BELLAIRE DRIVE
FLEUR DE LIS DRIVE
PONTCHARTRAIN BOULEVARD
WEST END BOULEVARD
MILNE BOULEVARD
HARRISON AVE.
Bayou Oaks Golf Course
OWENS BLVD.
CANAL BOULEVARD
MARCONI DRIVE
DIAGONAL DRIVE
PARK
WISNER BOULEVARD
Softball Center
Bayou St. John
SAINT BERNARD AVENUE
FLORIDA BOULEVARD
Popp Fountain
610
GENTILLY BLVD.
ORLEANS AVENUE
DESAIX BOULEVARD
Carousel Garden
Botanical Garden
10
New Orleans Museum of Art
Storyland
Greenwood Cemetery
90
Metairie Cemetery
St. Louis Cemetery No. 3
CITY PARK AVENUE
PARKVIEW DISTRICT
New Orleans Fairgrounds
ESPLANADE AVENUE
Cypress Grove
Pitot House Museum
House on Bayou Road
Longue Vue House & Gardens
MID-CITY
Benachi-Torre House
ESPLANADE RIDGE
Gayarré Place
ORLEANS AVENUE
Edgar Degas House
To Six Flags New Orleans
AIRLINE HIGHWAY
CARROLLTON AVENUE
CANAL STREET
BANKS STREET
DAVIS PKWY.
BIENVILLE STREET
Dufour-Baldwin House
PALMETTO ST.
TULANE AVENUE
JEFFERSON
FAUBOURG TREMÉ
LOUIS ARMSTRONG PARK
STREET
Canal Streetcar line
61
BROAD STREET
AVENUE
GALVEZ
CLAIBORNE
10
N. RAMPART STREET
PONTCHARTRAIN EXPWY.
EARHART BOULEVARD
FRENCH QUARTER
0
1 mile
0
1 kilometer
Area of map detail
MID-CITY & THE LAKEFRONT
FRENCH QUARTER
GARDEN DISTRICT & UPTOWN
CBD & ALGIERS POINT

Esplanade Ridge

Esplanade Ridge
Map p. 149

For 250 vintage square blocks, Esplanade Ridge stretches from the Faubourg Tremé and Louis Armstrong Park to City Park, embracing architecturally distinctive neighborhoods that developed over the course of the 19th century.

Early in the century, the Creole and shotgun cottages predominated. Later, along Esplanade Avenue, wealthy French Creoles who had abandoned the Quarter built grand houses, making it the most fashionable boulevard of French-speaking New Orleans. With the 20th century came period revival homes filling the blocks from Broad Street north to Bayou St. John.

Restoration is reversing decades of neglect, and some properties, although private residences, should be visited. Walk by the **Dufour-Baldwin House,** a double-galleried Greek Revival-Italianate property at 1707 Esplanade near Derbigny.

Where Esplanade crosses Bayou Road is **Gayarré Place.** Stop to admire the elaborate red pedestal, the city's preeminent example of cast decorative terra-cotta. It was salvaged from the World's Industrial and Cotton Centennial Exposition of 1884–85 in Audubon Park.

Follow brick-paved Bayou Road to No. 2257. The **Benachi-Torre House,** a two-story Greek Revival mansion, was built in 1849 for a Greek-American shipping magnate. It is a private residence, but from the Gothic Revival cast-iron front gate you can admire the house's ornate ironwork and graceful columns. At 2275 Bayou Road, a Creole plantation house built about 1798 has been refurbished and opened as a bed-and-breakfast inn. Known as the **House on Bayou Road** *(504-945-0992),* it is an authentic example of the city's earliest colonial architecture. ■

Bayou St. John

Bayou St. John
Map p. 149

When voodoo was widely practiced in New Orleans, believers assembled along the bayou on St. John's Eve at the summer solstice to dance themselves into a mystic trance in which a *loa*—or spirit—would replace one of the two souls that practitioners believe everyone carries within. The 4-mile arm of Lake Pontchartrain, which nearly reaches Mid-City's lakeside boundary, was considered a sacred "spirit gate"; through it came the loas whom believers invited not only into their homes but into their minds as well.

French plantations surrounded the inlet, each with a narrow frontage on the water. This enabled the landowners to ship products, beginning the bayou's career as a commercial highway—an era that ended in the 1930s when the Works Progress Administration landscaped its banks for recreation.

For a time in the 1880s, resort hotels, amusement parks, casinos, and theaters did a lively tourist trade along the bayou, in the vicinity of **Fort St. John.** The fort was initially a dirt redoubt established by the French during the early 1700s; it was built up into a full-fledged brick fortification during the Spanish era. Remnants, known as **Old Spanish Fort,** are still visible on the banks of the bayou near the intersection of Beauregard Avenue and Robert E. Lee Boulevard. ■

Opposite: A two-family, Eastlake-style shotgun double Victorian is reflected in Bayou St. John.

Thrill-seekers careen among oaks where duels were once fought.

City Park

IT IS AMERICA'S FIFTH LARGEST URBAN PARK, ITS 1,500 ACRES filled with Spanish moss-draped oaks—some more than 600 years old. Interrupting expansive lawns are quiet lagoons, fountains, and statues, recreational facilities, gardens, and lovely old buildings. This is where New Orleanians bring their kids for picnics, where locals jog and play tennis and golf, and where couples are married beneath one of the more than 250 live oaks that are registered historical landmarks.

City Park Visitor Center
www.neworleanscitypark.com
Map p. 149
1 Palm Dr.
504-482-4888
Streetcar: Canal 45
Bus: Esplanade

Unfortunately, much of the park no longer retains its parklike quality: I-610 slices through it, and the larger, lakeside portion is now occupied by four golf courses and a riding stable. Most visitors stick to the southern third. There you'll find the **New Orleans Museum of Art** (see p. 154), and the exquisite **Botanical Garden** (see p. 155).

Eight miles of lagoons meander throughout the park, rippled by swans, egrets, ducks, and geese. People also come to the bayou to try their luck at catching catfish, bass, and perch. The fishing season runs June through August, and permits are required *(available at the Timkin Center, across from the City Park Tennis Center, at 1 Dreyfous Dr. 504-483-9474)*. There is no equipment rental.

Young children will enjoy **Storyland,** a theme park with 26 storybook exhibits by Mardi Gras float-meister Blaine Kern (see p. 116). The kids can climb on and into Pinocchio's whale, Captain Hook's ship, and more. Afterward, visit the **William A. Hines Carousel Garden** to see a lovingly restored antique merry-go-round with 54 carved wooden animals. Only about 100 of these marvelous machines are left in America, and this is the only one in Louisiana. Next door, a permanent carnival makes noise with two miniature trains, a roller coaster, a tilt-a-whirl, and bumper cars.

On Marconi Drive at the corner of Zachary Taylor Drive, the 60-foot-high **Popp Fountain** shoots water 30 feet into the air in changing patterns. Take a walk around the wide promenade

surrounding the fountain, amid oaks, magnolias, cypresses, crape myrtles, camellias, and azaleas.

City Park caters to sports enthusiasts, too. The **Bayou Oaks Golf Course** *(504-483-9396. $$)*—actually four 18-hole courses under one banner—is the South's largest public golf facility, and the best place to swing a club within city limits. The Championship Course stretches beyond 7,000 yards. Relax afterward at the Bayou Oaks Clubhouse and Restaurant *(504-483-9395)* off Fillmore Avenue next to the Driving Range. The **City Park Tennis Center's** 21 hard courts and 15 clay courts, lighted for nighttime play, are ranked among the nation's 25 best municipal complexes.

DUELING OAK

More duels were fought in New Orleans than in any other American city, usually in the forests where City Park now stands. The Friends of City Park *(Timkin Center, across from City Park Tennis Center)* publishes a walking tour guide giving the history of these groves. ■

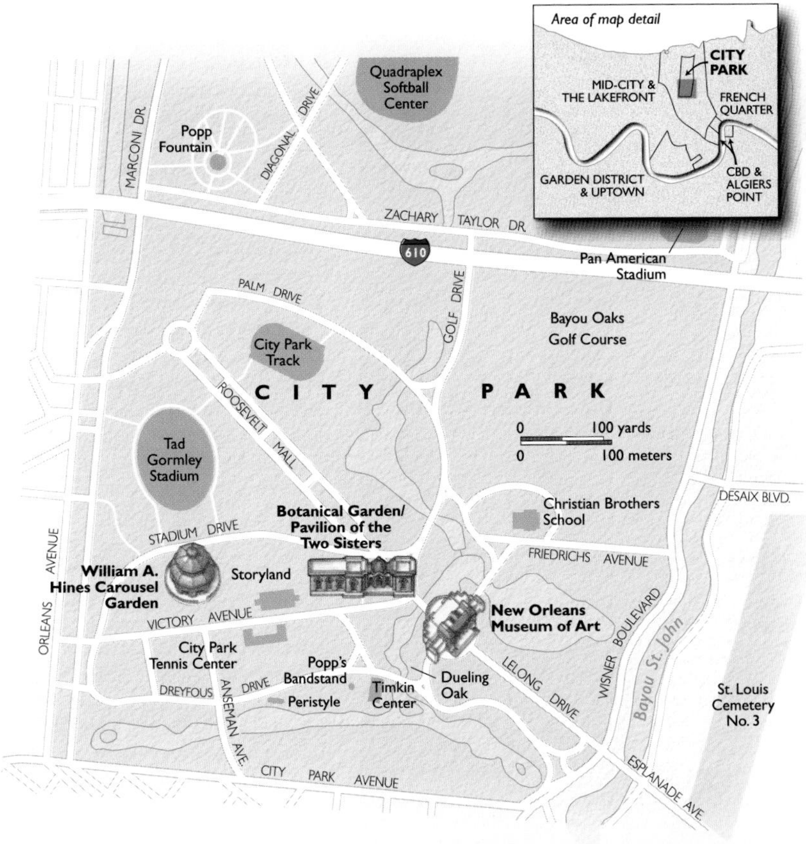

Area of map detail
CITY PARK
MID-CITY & THE LAKEFRONT
FRENCH QUARTER
GARDEN DISTRICT & UPTOWN
CBD & ALGIERS POINT
Quadraplex Softball Center
Popp Fountain
MARCONI DR.
DIAGONAL DRIVE
ZACHARY TAYLOR DR.
610
Pan American Stadium
PALM DRIVE
GOLF DRIVE
Bayou Oaks Golf Course
City Park Track
ROOSEVELT MALL
CITY PARK
0 100 yards
0 100 meters
Tad Gormley Stadium
Christian Brothers School
DESAIX BLVD.
STADIUM DRIVE
Botanical Garden/ Pavilion of the Two Sisters
FRIEDRICHS AVENUE
William A. Hines Carousel Garden
Storyland
ORLEANS AVENUE
VICTORY AVENUE
New Orleans Museum of Art
City Park Tennis Center
Popp's Bandstand
DREYFOUS DRIVE
Peristyle
Timkin Center
Dueling Oak
LELONG DRIVE
WISNER BOULEVARD
Bayou St. John
St. Louis Cemetery No. 3
ANSEMAN AVE.
CITY PARK AVENUE
ESPLANADE AVE.

New Orleans Museum of Art

New Orleans Museum of Art
www.noma.org
Map p. 149
1 Collins Diboll Circle
504-488-2631
$$
Streetcar: Canal 45
Bus: Esplanade

IT ALL BEGAN IN 1910 WHEN LOCAL BUSINESSMAN ISAAC Delgado quietly gave the city $150,000 for a "temple of art for rich and poor alike." His temple stands at the end of Esplanade Avenue inside City Park, where some 40,000 pieces reside in 46 permanent galleries.

There are European paintings and sculptures from the 16th through 20th centuries, 18th- and 19th-century American works, European and American prints, drawings, and photographs, and a large Asian art collection. Be sure to visit the **Lupin Foundation Center for the Decorative Arts** on the second floor, where you'll find one of the finest glass collections in the United States. Some objects date from 1500 B.C., illustrating the evolution of glassmaking from its origins in ancient Egypt to the present day. The **Latin American Colonial Art collection** offers a view of the Western Hemisphere seldom seen north of Mexico.

Also on the second floor are galleries exhibiting Louisiana-related art and artifacts. In the **Rosemonde E. and Emile Kuntz Rooms** you'll find a re-creation of an opulent Louisiana bedchamber, reflecting the lifestyle of wealthy French Creoles between 1800 and 1825. Another Kuntz exhibit presents the "Federal Parlor," decorated with early American furniture and objets d'art dating from circa 1790–1825. These include some made in Louisiana, conjuring up the world of uptown Garden District Anglo-Americans who prospered after the Louisiana Purchase.

For wonderful examples of 19th- and early 20th-century Louisiana paintings, look into the **George L. Viavant Gallery.** The **Entergy Corporation Gallery** has a grand collection of Newcomb Pottery. A gallery endowed by the ubiquitous art benefactor Frederick R. Weisman holds a splendid survey of contemporary Louisiana art—paintings, sculptures, and other media.

If time and weather permit, visit the **Besthoff Sculpture Garden** adjacent to the museum. On display among the magnolias, camellias, oaks, and pines are more than 40 extraordinary sculptures by such renowned 20th-century artists as Henry Moore and George Segal. ■

A patron ponders Denys Pierre Puech's "Amore et Psyche" at the New Orleans Museum of Art.

Hibiscus blooms at the classically styled greenhouse in City Park's Botanical Garden.

Botanical Garden

A CREATION OF THE WORKS PROGRESS ADMINISTRATION (WPA), the 10-acre Botanical Garden opened in 1936 as the City Park Rose Garden. It is a striking achievement in public garden design that charms visitors with its blend of classical and art deco styles.

A makeover in the 1980s included a new name, which is certainly more accurate: The garden contains more than 2,000 varieties of plants, shaded by live oaks, crape myrtles, sweet olives, and magnolias.

New Orleans's latitude mitigates the effects of seasonal changes, so although some displays peak in spring and fall, the region's mild winters enable many of the garden's tropical and subtropical plants to bloom all year. Small theme gardens illustrate the use of aquatic plants, ornamental trees and shrubs, and perennials—techniques you can definitely try at home.

The **Pavilion of the Two Sisters** is styled after a traditional European orangerie—an archaic term for a permanent greenhouse designed to permit year-round citrus growing. The views of the Botanical Garden from its many tall arched windows are photogenic and pleasing; this is a lovely place in which to linger. The moderne-style benches date from the 1930s. Tall French doors open out onto the pavilion's western terrace, where a walkway leads through the garden to the **Conservatory,** then to the **Parterre Garden.** On the pavilion's east side, French doors frame Enrique Alferez's sculptured moderne 1995 fountain in the azalea and camellia display.

Note the **Garden Study Center** near the lily pond. Its solid brick walls, slate roof, and copper gutters remind some of a rural English cottage, but it is a classic example of WPA architecture. Ask about hands-on horticultural demonstrations, usually held in the **Lath House** adjoining the Study Center. Its slatted design mixes sunlight and shadow to nurture seedlings and shelter light-sensitive plants.

Be sure to visit the library, which is filled with books about garden design and horticulture, and the Garden Gift Shop, both located in the Pavilion of the Two Sisters. ■

Botanical Garden

Map p. 149

Enter via Pavilion of the Two Sisters, on Victory Ave. behind New Orleans Museum of Art

504-482-4888

Closed Mon.

Streetcar: Canal 45
Bus: Esplanade

Spanish-accented gardens adorn Longue Vue House.

Longue Vue House & Gardens

THIS 8-ACRE ENCLAVE IS PROBABLY THE MOST INTERESTING 20th-century estate open to public view in Louisiana. Completed in 1942, the classical revival mansion was designed for cotton broker Edgar Stern and his wife, Edith Rosenwald Stern (daughter of Sears cofounder Julius Rosenwald).

Longue Vue House

- Map p. 149
- 7 Bamboo Rd.
- 504-488-5488
- $$
- Streetcar: Canal 42 Bus: Esplanade or Metairie

The Sterns valued comfort and liked to entertain, so asked their designer to make the house's late 18th-century Georgian-style interior both elegant and relaxing. They also spared no expense to ensure its durability: They instructed their architects to build the walls of concrete and to specify steel trusses for the roof.

What makes Longue Vue House exceptionally interesting is that it contains its original furnishings—an appealing if eclectic mixture of English and American antiques, French and Oriental carpets, modern art, exquisite fabrics, superb needlework, and fine creamware and pottery from British and European manufacturers. Some rooms serve as galleries with both permanent and changing exhibits.

Be sure to spend time outside in the formal garden, where perfectly manicured lawns are studded with live oaks, magnolias, camellias, azaleas, roses, sweet olives, crape myrtles, and oleanders. Gardeners embellish them seasonally with temporary displays of tulips, chrysanthemums, poinsettias, pansies, and Easter lilies.

Find the **Spanish Court,** the estate's largest garden, its trickling fountains and tiled walks inspired by the 14th-century gardens of the Alhambra in Granada, Spain. Then stroll through the naturalistic forest path in the **Wild Garden.** There are theme gardens here, too—one devoted to herbs, and one to evoke the spirit of Pan, the Greek god of pastures, flocks, and shepherds (a symbol of peace). ■

Cities of the Dead

AS NEW ORLEANS GREW, MORE CEMETERIES OPENED. THE tradition of ornate tomb building continued, most notably in Metairie and Greenwood near City Park, at St. Louis No. 3 on Esplanade Avenue, and at the Hebrew Rest burial grounds on Elysian Fields.

Metairie Cemetery
Map p. 149
5100 Pontchartrain Blvd.
504-486-6331
Streetcar: Canal 42
Bus: Metairie

Cypress Grove
Map p. 149
124 City Park Ave.
504-482-8983
Streetcar: Canal 42

METAIRIE CEMETERY

Reflecting its Anglo-American origins, Metairie Cemetery is landscaped and tree-shaded, and its tombs are ornate and architecturally diverse. This burial ground, a perpetual-care cemetery, was established in 1872 and has been spared the benign neglect afflicting some of the city's older cemeteries.

Visitors to Metairie are offered good maps and the use of cassette tape players and two recorded one-hour audiotapes for self-guided tours (the maps and tapes are free; a driver's license is required for deposit). One tape focuses on the politicians, statesmen, and soldiers buried here; the other celebrates the socially prominent and otherwise fortunate persons who are buried within these well-kept 150 acres. The cemetery office also offers an excellent guidebook for free.

Metairie's tombs are made from a variety of materials, including granite, marble, and brick. Some mimic Egyptian tombs, others Greek and Roman temples. The oldest belongs to the Duverje family and dates from about 1848. A marble sphinx guards the pyramidal Brunswig mausoleum, while angels embrace atop the Aldige family monument, built for a wife and daughter lost at sea. The great New Orleans architect James Gallier, Sr., who perished along with his wife when their passenger ship, bound from New York to New Orleans, sank in 1866, is interred here. Confederate Gen. Albert Sidney Johnston, whose bronze likeness ponders eternity from horseback atop the tumulus of the Louisiana Division of the Army of Tennessee, rests here as well.

Make sure to also visit the section of Jewish family tombs and the row of Italian-American society mausoleums along Avenue B.

CYPRESS GROVE

The entrance of Cypress Grove is the grandest of any New Orleans burial ground—befitting a cemetery founded in 1840 by the elite and politically influential men's club known as the Firemen's Charitable and Benevolent Association. At that time, firefighters were volunteers, and those who raised their hands climbed the social ladder as well. These proud all-male bastions chose monuments to impress: Just inside the portal to Cypress Grove (identified on some maps as the Firemen's Cemetery) are Egyptian pylons and sexton's quarters, reflecting a 19th-century vogue in funerary architecture.

What friends of New Orleans's cemeteries appreciate most about Cypress Grove—besides its many gray Massachusetts granite and marble mausoleums—is that it hasn't suffered insensitive refurbishing. Although it has had its share of vandalism and neglect, its original clamshell roads, once common in the Gulf South, have not been resurfaced. And it is shaded by a beautiful host of gnarled, old magnolias, live oaks, and, of course, many cypresses.

The most interesting tombs here are the oldest, grouped together just inside the gate. Note the Ferry tomb

A sphinxlike stone figure guards an Egyptian Revival tomb in Metairie Cemetery.

on your right as you drive in. Its broken marble column symbolizes a life cut short—a young fireman who perished in flames. Its designer was the Frenchman J.N.B. de Pouilly, the first architect of the St. Louis Cathedral. De Pouilly also designed pepper-sauce mogul Maunsell White's Greek Revival tomb in 1863, which is impressive in its dignity. Behind his monument on the parallel road is what appears to be a tiny church. It is the medieval revival tomb of the Slark family, a prominent mercantile clan, dating from 1868. Toward the front of the cemetery on the right-hand side is the cast-iron Greek Revival tomb of Charles Leeds. New Orleans's mayor from 1874 to 1876 and a manufacturer of decorative cast iron, Leeds had a fitting send off: He rests for eternity in this rusty iron fancy.

Greenwood Cemetery

- Map p. 149
- Canal St. & City Park Ave.
- 504-482-8982
- Streetcar: Canal 42

GREENWOOD CEMETERY

In 1852 the Firemen's Charitable and Benevolent Association opened this cemetery, filled with imposing tombs. Fronting on City Park Avenue is the monument of Lodge No. 30, Benevolent and Protective Order of Elks. Erected in 1912, it is topped by a heroic bronze elk. Nearby is the Gothic Revival Firemen's Monument of 1887, which includes a statue of a volunteer wielding a hose. In the corner closest to where City Park meets I-10, a white marble soldier stands atop the Confederate Monument. This tribute includes

busts of Generals Robert E. Lee, Stonewall Jackson, and Albert Sidney Johnston. It also includes a likeness of Leonidas Polk, the first Episcopal bishop of Louisiana who was made a general of the Confederacy; he was killed in action in 1864.

ST. LOUIS CEMETERY NO. 3

As you enter St. Louis Cemetery No. 3 from Esplanade Avenue, it makes a fine first impression. Its massive iron entrance gate is ornate, and its axial roads are paved and wide. Beautiful marble angels grieve atop the tombs just inside the gate, and the cemetery is better maintained than St. Louis Cemetery Nos. 1 and 2 (see pp. 87 and 88–89, respectively). But it is not as opulent or as ornate as its predecessors, and, ironically, the absence of decay denies it the gloomy charm of other burial grounds.

The front section holds the city's largest grouping of carved stone angels. Some remark slyly that the angels are weeping over the boxy, more modern tombs toward the back of the cemetery. But there are many priests and nuns interred here, so perhaps the simplicity of the stones is only appropriate. Others, however, such as members of the Hellenic Orthodox Community, endowed their final resting places with large and ornate tombs.

Unlike cemeteries Nos. 1 and 2, No. 3 does not have the tradition (rapidly fading) of relatives placing *immortelles*—wreaths made of black glass beads—at their loved ones' resting places.

HEBREW REST

One cemetery with three individual sections—Nos. 1, 2, and 3—this burial ground includes what is left of the city's first Jewish cemetery, Gates of Mercy. Dedicated in 1828 at Jackson Avenue and Saratoga Street, in the CBD, Gates of Mercy was the burial place of the first German Jewish immigrants who came to New Orleans following the 1803 Louisiana Purchase. Demolished in 1957, what remained of Gates of Mercy was moved to this site, where each cemetery, individually fenced and gated, occupies a full block. Start your visit at **No. 1,** which opened in 1860 and faces Elysian Fields Boulevard. Look for the name "Hebrew Rest" written in wrought iron over the large main gate. Cemetery **No. 2** opened in 1894 and **No. 3** in the early 20th century. The monuments therein, chiseled in English and Hebrew, constitute yet another thread in New Orleans's cultural tapestry. ■

St. Louis Cemetery No. 3

- Map p. 149
- 3421 Esplanade Ave.
- 504-482-5065
- Bus: Esplanade

Hebrew Rest Nos. 1, 2, & 3

- Map p. 149
- 2100 Pelopidas at Frenchman St.
- 504-861-3693
- Bus: Gentilly

Note: The records for Hebrew Rest Nos. 1, 2, and 3 are kept at Temple Sinai Reform Congregation, 6227 St. Charles Ave., 504-861-3693.

Voodoo

It is hard to say when the practice of voodoo first began, but it arose among the Fon, Yoruba, Kongo, and other people of Africa's Gulf of Benin, who believed spirits ruled nature and human activity. The Fon called it *vodun* and regarded it as a force with the power to affect life at any time, in any way.

Among the Fon, society was based upon family, kinship bonds, the tribe, and ethnicity. Each of these cultural spheres had its own ancestral and guardian deities, known as *vodu* or vodun. To win the favor and protection of these deities, followers held ceremonies that included dancing to the beat of drums and sacrificing cattle, sheep, or chickens. Priests, known as *voduno* or *huno,* interpreted the messages of the vodun for their followers.

Today voodoo's faithful are predominantly Haitian, a legacy of the African slaves brought to that country by the French between the 17th and 19th centuries. They melded their belief in vodun with the Roman Catholicism of the Europeans. Voodoo, as this hybrid belief is known, includes worship of a supreme god, or *bon dieu,* and a host of spirits called *loa,* who are often identified with Catholic saints. These spirits are more closely related to African gods, however, and may represent natural phenomena, such as fire, water, or wind. They are also believed to be the spirits of the dead. The loa fall into two main groups—the *rada,* typically helpful and benevolent, and the *petro,* who can be malevolent. When a loa takes possession of a believer, the possessed one exhibits behaviors corresponding, it is thought, to the nature of the particular spirit.

Voodoo came to New Orleans in the early 1700s with the arrival of African slaves. The connection between voodoo and Christianity was striking but superficial. By the mid-19th century, voodoo was being trivialized by dilettantes, for whom it was an exotic affectation, and popularized by hucksters, who published lurid accounts of orgiastic voodoo rites. Still, a considerable number of New Orleanians had lived with it for so long that small observances, such as voodoo charms, known as *gris-gris* (pronounced GREE-gree), were being used for good luck, better health, protection from misfortune, financial advantage, and romantic success. For most, simply having a charm was enough; the devout, however, knew that to be effective, a gris-gris had to be blessed with fire, water, earth, and air, and it must contain traditional ingredients whose number could not exceed 13. It was then up to the possessor to determine whether the powerful charm would be used for good or ill. Some frightened followers scrubbed their front stoops with brick dust as a protection against curses and consulted regularly with voodoo queens for advice.

The most esteemed voodoo queen in New Orleans was Marie Laveau, who called herself the Pope of Voodoo in the 1830s. Queen Marie was said to be the illegitimate daughter of a wealthy white planter and a mulatto. In her position as a hairdresser, Laveau listened carefully to her patrons' gossip; it enabled her to seem prescient as a fortune-teller among them. Her power was such that she was rumored to have eliminated rival queens by casting spells and using evil gris-gris. Through her public leadership of the Sunday slave gatherings at Congo Square, her savvy showmanship, and a pair of eyes that could hypnotize, Laveau came to symbolize all that was mysterious and powerful about the long-oppressed culture of New Orleans's African Americans. She retired in 1869, living another 12 years while other women attempted to follow in her footsteps—including, some say, her daughter. But none held sway as flamboyantly as she did.

Voodoo lives on in New Orleans. It is practiced in the Spiritual churches of the city, where elements of voodoo are intertwined with Catholicism and Pentecostalism. Followers observe the rituals of baptism and Holy Communion, as well as rites with obscure origins, but that are clearly closer to vodun than traditional Christianity. The churches' altars combine Christian and voodoo iconography, and ritualistic dancing is practiced in order to achieve communion with spirits. Catholic saints are venerated, along with the Native American leaders Sitting Bull and Blackhawk.

A voodoo priestess prepares for a ritual ceremony.

Nonmembers are seldom allowed to visit these churches; their congregations are devout and usually private. But one authentic house of worship, the Voodoo Spiritual Temple *(828 N. Rampart St. 504-522-9627)*, offers an open Thursday evening service. Visitors are greeted by Priestess Miriam, who presents an overview of the religion, answers questions, and previews the evening observance. *(Church open daily; African bone readings available for a fee.)* You need not feel shy or uncomfortable here. Nonpractitioners are welcome, and believers strive to dispel the stereotypes that obscure voodoo's fervent, if unconventional, spirituality.

Consider a visit to the New Orleans Historic Voodoo Museum *(724 Dumaine St. 504-523-7684;* see p. 93) to learn more about voodoo. ■

More places to visit in Mid-City

EDGAR DEGAS HOUSE

Although he lived here just a short time—for just over four months—this double-galleried 1854 frame house has come to be known as the Edgar Degas House. At age 38, the not-yet-famous French Impressionist painter left his native Paris to accompany his younger brother René back to Louisiana. (A New Orleans resident, René was in France on business.) After a ten-day Atlantic steamer crossing to New York and a four-day train trip south, Degas arrived to spend the winter of 1872–1873 with his mother's extended family.

Marie Célestine Musson had been born into the city's Creole aristocracy, and as a teenager Degas had grown close to several female Musson relatives who took refuge in France during the Civil War. (One of his finest portraits, now in the New Orleans Museum of Art, is of his cousin Estelle.) In addition to René, the painter's kinfolk in the city included younger brother Achille Musson; uncle Michel Musson, a partner in the Musson, Prestidge & Co. cotton brokerage; and various nephews and cousins.

"Everything attracts me here," Edgar Degas wrote of his stay in New Orleans.

At the time René was renting this house, it was flanked by a carriage house and stables, and a walled garden embraced it. Eighteen Musson relatives lived here together, and the painter was given a ground-floor back bedroom. Although he found the light too strong for outdoor painting, he wrote to a friend that "everything attracts me here." He painted much of what he saw—family portraits, children—including a series set at his uncle's firm. One, depicting three merchants and known as "Cotton Merchants," is among the most important works in the Fogg Art Museum in Cambridge, Massachusetts; another, titled "Portrait in an Office: The New Orleans Cotton Exchange," depicts 14 people, most identified as Mussons. The only painting of Degas' to be acquired by a museum during his life, it is today the preeminent painting in the Musée de Beaux-Arts in Pau, France. Michel Musson's building still stands in the Central Business District, at Perdido and Carondelet Streets.

Map p. 149 2305 Esplanade Ave. 504-821-5009 $$ Bus: Esplanade

PITOT HOUSE MUSEUM

Built in 1799, this is the oldest of the city's museum houses and the finest surviving residence from French colonial times. James Pitot, who served as the city's second mayor under American rule in 1804-1805, bought the West Indies-style plantation as a country home, and it served three succeeding French-American families as a working farm.

Saved from demolition and moved to its present location (the site of the first French settlement in the area) by the Louisiana Landmarks Society in the 1960s, the house is filled with period furnishings and art (be sure to visit the South Bedroom). Broad galleries surround the first and second floors; their shade and the many windows convey a sense of ease and relief from the heat.

Map p. 149 1440 Moss St. 504-482-0312 Open Wed.–Sat. $ ■

Lake Pontchartrain

In 1699 explorer Pierre le Moyne named this large body of water for the Count de Pontchartrain, minister of finance during the reign of France's "Sun King," Louis XIV. But the Choctaw-speaking people who lived alongside it captured its essence with the name Okwa-ta, or "wide water."

Lake Pontchartrain is definitely impressive—a pleasure-boating paradise some 40 miles long and 24 miles wide, with a surface area of 629 square miles. But in the strictest sense of the word, it is not a lake. Because it exchanges water with the Gulf of Mexico, Lake Pontchartrain is actually an estuary, part of the transition zone of a watershed draining some 4,700 square miles of land in 16 Louisiana parishes and 4 counties in Mississippi. From the Pontchartrain Basin, as it is known, rivers and bayous empty into Lake Pontchartrain and its connecting sister lakes, Maurepas and Borgne. The three lakes form a major estuarine system—one of the largest estuarine systems in North America—whose wetlands filter and purify their shared flow before it enters the Gulf of Mexico.

As the city of New Orleans grew, cutting

The steps of the Lake Pontchartrain levee offer a great place to relax.

The New Orleans Marina is one of several boating centers on the lakeshore.

of the lake's north-shore timber commenced, and ships carrying loads of lumber and charcoal plied the lake, joining those laden with bricks, shells, cotton, and oysters on their way to distant markets. By the 1800s, Madisonville on the north shore developed into the region's boatbuilding center (see p. 200), and by 1815, steamers were replacing sailing ships on the lake. In 1834, after selling his plantation to the city for development into the Faubourg Marigny, wealthy landowner Bernard de Marigny moved across the lake to Fontainebleau, his family's north shore plantation, and developed a resort in the town of Mandeville (see p. 198 & 199). The instantly fashionable Mandeville Hotel offered gambling, billiards, a bathhouse, and riding stables, and it was particularly popular in summer when those who could afford it crossed over by steamer for the cooler, breezier weather along the forested shore.

Around the mouth of Bayou St. John on the south shore, restaurants, casinos, and fancy hotels catered to the burgeoning elite of the city. In 1849 the exclusive Southern Yacht Club opened at West End, and the New Orleans lakeshore district straddled the boundary between Orleans and Jefferson Parishes. Soon the lake offered something for everyone, as campsites for the working-class folk sprang up, built on marshy islands in the lake and connected by wooden planks.

Today, lakeside recreation in New Orleans centers mainly along Lakeshore Park (see p. 165–166), which greens the levee-shouldered shoreline from the University of New Orleans campus to the City Yacht Harbor and West End Park at the end of Pontchartrain Boulevard. Here you can join the New Orleanians who come to walk, jog, bicycle, in-line skate, roller-skate, picnic, or simply relax. Kite flyers and wind surfers take advantage of the lake's frequent gentle breezes, and anglers descend the steplike face of the concrete levee to cast fishing lures into the water. Offshore, especially in evenings and on weekends, sailboats cut back and forth across the surface of the lake.

The neighborhood just west of the City Yacht Harbor—West End—is known for its seafood restaurants. Here the levee holding back Lake Pontchartrain's occasional storm tides stretches over 7 miles, providing a greater degree of solitude for strollers and bicyclists than is found east of the marina in Lakeshore Park.

About a quarter of Louisiana's population—roughly 1.5 million people—live in lakeside parishes. One unfortunate result of that population boom has been that pollution caused by street runoff, industrial drainage, and sewage has kept swimmers out of the water at New Orleans's Pontchartrain Beach since 1972. In 1989 the Lake Pontchartrain Basin Foundation *(504-836-2215)* was established. Its goal is to restore the health of the lake and its rivers and to protect the natural habitat of the Basin. With aggressive cleanup campaigns under way, some cautiously predict that it will not be many more years before residents and visitors alike will be able to plunge into Lake Pontchartrain without trepidation. ■

Along the lakefront

IN 1831 THE PONTCHARTRAIN RAILROAD LINKED DOWNtown with the lakeshore, and a resort strip called Milneburg developed where the main campus of the University of New Orleans now stands. Ever since, this part of Lake Pontchartrain's south shore has provided New Orleanians and visitors with the city's most convenient waterside getaway.

WEST END PARK

It is more of a wide grass median than a true park, but in local minds West End Park signifies the center of lakeshore recreation and the nautical ambience of its surroundings. Nearby are the **City Yacht Harbor;** the **Orleans Marina;** and the **Southern Yacht Club,** which though private sets a certain tone by virtue of the lovely road to its entrance.

To reach the park, take West End Boulevard from I-10 or I-610 to the lake, and lakeside of Robert E. Lee Boulevard turn left onto Lake Marina Avenue, which becomes Breakwater Drive and curves toward the lake. Take the first right and circle West End Park, which has an appealing boathouse community. Leave your car in the Orleans Marina parking lot and stroll along the marina's pier. It is surpassingly pleasant—you'll hear the cry of gulls and the slap of lines against hollow aluminum masts, and witness the stately coming and going of sailboats.

Just west is the **West End neighborhood,** known for first-class seafood houses. For an inexpensive, casual eatery with a good view of the water, stop in at **Bruning's** *(1924 West End Pkwy. 504-288-4521).* Or, just a short walk from the lake, try **Sid-Mar's** *(1824 Orpheum St. 504-831-9541).* This friendly restaurant prepares its fare in a variety of ways—from frying to broiling and steaming. There's hardly a nicer way to end a day on the lake than at the park, where you can show up casual (with shoes and a shirt) and relax with a plate of local fare.

LAKESHORE DRIVE & PARK

An outing along Lakeshore Drive is the perfect solution to a sudden longing to go somewhere that seems far away but takes little time to reach. The drive winds along the lake for about 5.5 miles, between West End Park and the New Orleans Lakefront Airport.

Wind-whipped waves slap the lakeshore.

Nearing City Park, eastbound from the yacht basin area, you'll come upon **Mardi Gras Fountains.** If you're fortunate and the city's maintenance budget permits, the fountains will spray streams of water that pulse and wane, jetting up 60 feet at times as floodlights render them gold, purple, and green, the traditional colors of Mardi Gras. Tiles laid in the walk bear the names, symbols, and coats of arms of the city's Mardi Gras krewes. Even if the water show

Evening on Lake Pontchartrain brings out boaters and sunset watchers.

is temporarily out of service, shade trees and picnic tables make this an inviting place to take a break from your driving tour.

In fact, there are numerous places to stop and enjoy scenery and ambience along Lakeshore Drive. Paralleling the drive is **Lakeshore Park,** a people-friendly, recreationally oriented, and gentle shoreline. There are many parking areas that make it convenient to stop on impulse and walk along the 5.5-mile levee, built in the 1930s, and admire the posh homes of the Lake Vista neighborhood. On weekends and holidays, weather permitting, people flock to the park's levees and picnic areas, which have public rest rooms and, usually, food stands open for business. Windsurfers launch from the seawall steps, descending to the lake where reliable breezes make for pleasant sailing. Anglers cast for catfish, bass, and perch, and hundreds bicycle along the delightful curving paths. Students from the nearby University of New Orleans come here to study under shade trees or at picnic tables, readers stretch out with books, joggers run by, and in-line skaters zip along the paths. Notably absent are swimmers. That's because the lake water, despite cleanup efforts, is still too polluted for safe immersion.

At park's end you'll come to the **New Orleans Lakefront Airport** (see p. 168), which offers good viewing of airplanes in action. It counts 160,000 to 175,000 take-offs and landings per year—the most of any airport in Louisiana.

From Monday through Thursday Lakeside Drive serves the workaday world by accommodating two-way traffic. Friday through Sunday, however, it becomes one-way, eastbound (downriver) from Paris Avenue, which intersects Lakeshore just east of Bayou St. John. To reach its western portions on these days, find West End Boulevard, which leads to the City Yacht Harbor and the Orleans Marina. From here you can bear

onto Lakeshore and travel the one-way section.

The facilities along the shore are open from 8 a.m. to 10 p.m., and they are well maintained and peaceful.

LINEAR PARKWAY

The most frequent activity along the south shore is touring by car. But close on its heels is walking, and arguably the most popular place to do it is the **Linear Parkway.** You'll see people walking at every speed, from a slow amble to power walking, along this greenbelt, which is threaded by a 7.5-mile path along the levee.

The parkway runs from West End Park—an area sometimes referred to as Bucktown, although you won't see it on maps—to the Williams Boulevard Boat Launch in Kenner. There are free public parking areas at both ends. You will probably not see the term "Linear Parkway" on New Orleans maps, either—most indicate only the levee and a dotted line—but it's there, winding upriver from the city's yacht basin, and it's hugely popular. People come here to watch the sun set and to picnic, although the absence of rest rooms, picnic tables, cooking grills, water fountains, and food stands requires that you bring everything you need. The tradeoff, however, is fair enough: In exchange for convenience you have a simple, natural getaway place, with lawns and trees, and a broad expanse of water stretching as far as the eye can see. As with any big-city public place, however, do your walking by day.

Bird-watcher's delight

About 2 miles west (upriver) of West End Park along the Linear Parkway, where the Causeway Bridge crosses the lake, a curious wildlife phenomenon takes place every evening from April through August. To witness it, you need only be on hand toward dusk, when for about 20 to 25 minutes, hundreds of purple martins—*Progne subis,* the largest North American swallow—take to the air from their roosts beneath the bridge. They're striking creatures; the male is purplish blue over its entire body, while the female is gray on the underside. And they're beneficial, too, because they feed on the wing—which you'll be witnessing here—and rid the air of pests.

The birds have adopted the bridge's understructure as a substitute for the tree cavities in which they commonly nest. The nightly summer show includes lots of jerky aerobatics and swallow calls that echo from the bridge. It ends quickly, as the martins return to their roosts. There is a viewing area set up to provide a good vantage point. ■

The Student Union at the University of New Orleans, where many attend evening classes

More places to visit along the lakefront

SIX FLAGS NEW ORLEANS

Thirty rides and a re-created French Quarter fill this 55-acre lakeside attraction, where music takes a rear seat to thrills like a 4,000-foot-long roller coaster. New Orleans's melodic heritage is celebrated at an old-fashioned dance hall built in the Cajun style and serving traditional Creole fare. First-rate musicians hold forth here from mid-afternoon until about 9 at night.

Map p. 149 ✉ 12301 Lake Forest Blvd., near I-10 & I-510 ☎ 504-253-8000 Daily early June–mid-Aug., weekends only mid-Aug.–Oct., closed rest of year $ $$$ Bus: Elysian Fields

NEW ORLEANS LAKEFRONT AIRPORT

When dignitaries assembled here in New Orleans on February 10, 1934, to cut the ribbon and inaugurate air service from its 3,000-foot runway, the crowd on hand to witness the opening of what locals called the Air Hub of the Americas numbered more than 10,000. Reporters rushed to their telephones to report on the architecture and decor of the art deco terminal, which symbolized New Orleans's new bid to be an international city. Those romantic days are gone—passenger traffic now goes to New Orleans International Airport—but Lakefront, which today caters to general aviation, is busier than ever. The old terminal has aged well, its fundamental lines still evident despite a host of minor modernizations. Try its modestly priced **Walnut Room** restaurant *(504-241-2561),* where the runway view from the dining room guarantees a ringside seat for the airport's 450-odd daily arrivals and departures.

Map p. 149 ✉ 6001 Stars and Stripes Blvd. ☎ 504-243-4010 Bus: Elysian Fields

UNIVERSITY OF NEW ORLEANS

UNO's two lakefront campuses opened in 1958 on the site of a former Naval Air Station. A flexible schedule suited to working students has garnered the largest enrollment—about 16,000 students—of any New Orleans-area college or university, and statewide it is second in size only to LSU Baton Rouge. UNO is known for its jazz studies program, headed by eminent pianist Ellis J. Marsalis, Jr. (father of musicians Wynton, Branford, and Delfeayo Marsalis). For performing arts, the **Kiefer UNO Lakefront Arena** is one of New Orleans' leading pop-music concert venues. *(Box office: 6801 Franklin St. 504-522-5555 or 800-488-5252)* UNO's parking lots are a good place to leave your car for a walk in adjoining **Lakeshore Park.** And if you play tennis, the east campus has six lighted tennis courts and a clubhouse, offering classes and public play. Free campus tours are available; call for an appointment.

Map p. 149 ✉ Lakeshore Dr. ☎ 504-280-6595 Bus: Elysian Fields ■

The parishes surrounding Orleans Parish are not mere suburbs but communities that grew up with their own histories, each reflecting its original natural setting, each a supplemental chapter in the saga of New Orleans.

Greater New Orleans

Statue of a boxer at Rivertown, Kenner

Evening falls in the Barataria bayous, once a pirates' haven.

Greater New Orleans

THE COMMUNITIES THAT SURROUND NEW ORLEANS—DOWNRIVER, upriver, and across Lake Pontchartrain—began mostly as outposts that served the city in some way. They were established as a first line of defense, as suppliers of food and building materials, as recreational getaways, or simply as sources of land for the city's expansion. Their histories, though less dense, go back just as far as that of New Orleans. That these places were once at the edge of the great wild is evident in their undisturbed tracts of forest and swampland. They are windows on the past, a reminder of what the Crescent City's founders faced 300 years ago when they walked ashore at the great bend in the Mississippi and made the decision to start clearing the canebrake.

KENNER

In 1682, when Robert Cavelier, Sieur de La Salle, voyaged down the Mississippi from the Great Lakes to the Gulf of Mexico, he claimed the Mississippi watershed for France. He staked that claim not at the downriver bend, where 30 years later New Orleans would be founded, but on the shore where Kenner's Rivertown stands today. The relics of Kenner's history have mostly been erased by urban sprawl, and many folks living downriver in Orleans Parish dismiss the community as an uninteresting suburb dominated by the New Orleans International Airport. Its lakeshore, however, includes the westernmost leg of the Linear Parkway, which begins in New Orleans's West End Park (see p. 165), and a handful of small but interesting museums devoted to science, history, and wildlife.

CHALMETTE

It took only one day—January 8, 1815—to forever place this bit of the Mississippi's east bank, 4 miles downriver from the French Quarter, in America's historical pantheon of important places. Here is where Andrew Jackson's ragtag militia defeated—some would say slaughtered—the unwisely commanded force of British redcoats sent to capture New Orleans, killing about 700 and wounding 1,300. The battlefield remains undeveloped; all you need is imagination to populate it with the two opposing armies who, tragically, clashed after the U.S. and Britain had struck a peace agreement. Civil War dead sleep here in a national burial ground, a quiet and somber reminder that, for all its innate hardships—disease, flooding, isolation—New Orleans's strategic location once caused presidents and kings to lose sleep over who would ultimately possess it.

NORTH SHORE OF LAKE PONTCHARTRAIN

The 23.9-mile Pontchartrain Causeway, the world's longest bridge, touches the north shore between the piney tourism-oriented lakefront towns of Mandeville and Madisonville. Subdivided in the 1830s as a retreat for the wealthy, Mandeville ended the 19th century as Lake Pontchartrain's preeminent resort; despite a recent influx in population, it still retains a distinctive air of leisure in its old broad streets and generously dimensioned lots. Timber and shipbuilding gave Madisonville its handsome vintage architecture.

Eight miles inland lies Covington, an upscale bedroom community with many 19th-century raised cottages and a well-kept vintage downtown filled with smart boutiques, shops, restaurants, and cafés—a civilized little town surrounded by wild swampland.

Lake Pontchartrain's North Shore is the fastest growing region in Louisiana. Although home to a quarter of the state's population, it is rich in natural places—bayous, swamps, forests, and marshlands enclosed and protected within the boundaries of state and federal preserves. As part of the vast Pontchartrain Basin, the watershed whose three large lakes drain into the Gulf, the north shore faces thoroughly modern challenges. It must manage urban sprawl, reverse the pollution of its lakes and wetlands, and remain a place where New Orleanians, who once voyaged across Pontchartrain to dally along its breezy, wooded shoreline, may still escape the intense urbanity of the old city. ■

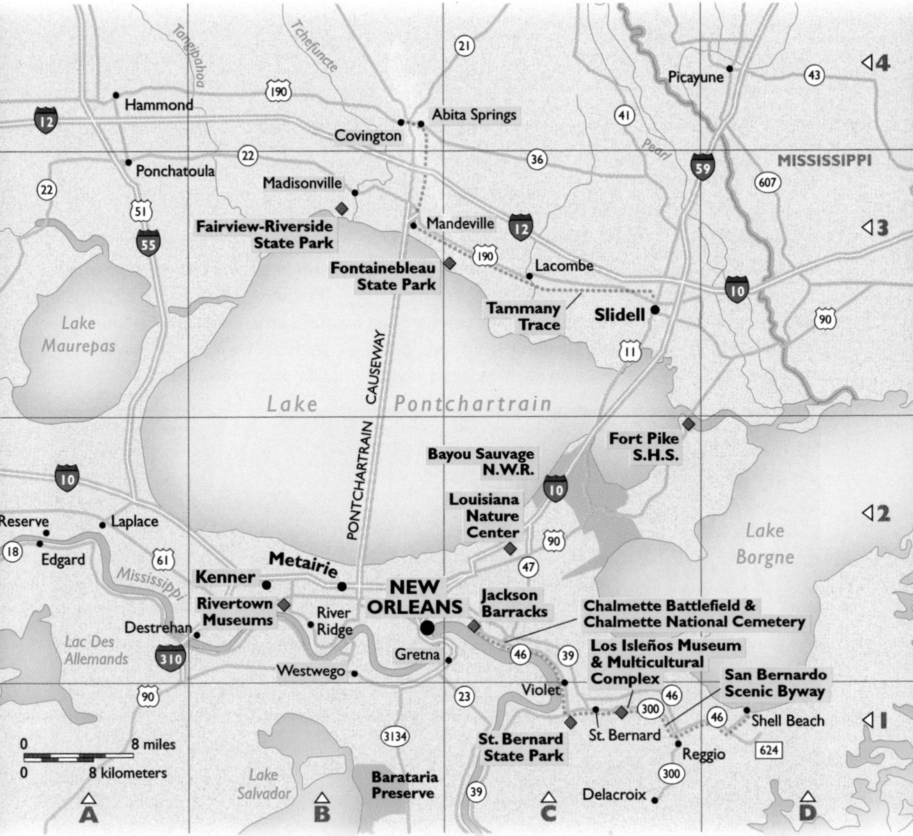

Kenner

Kenner
Map 171 B2

Kenner Convention & Visitors Center
2100 Third St., Unit 10, Kenner
504-464-9494
Closed Sat.–Sun.

ON EARLY FRENCH MAPS THIS WAS CANNES BRÛLÉE—"burnt cane"— inspired by the natives' practice of torching canebrakes to drive out wild game. By the 1720s plantations here were producing sugar, indigo, wheat, beans, and corn on coveted high ground, far enough above the Mississippi to escape its floods. In the late 1800s, immigrant Italian and German families planted farms, growing virtually every kind of vegetable, their "truck patches" dominating regional produce markets until the 1950s.

This might still be Cannes Brûlée had four brothers named Kenner not acquired Oakland, Belle Grove, and Pasture Plantations in the 1850s. This land comprised much of what became their namesake town, first known as Kennerville. Today, Kenner is Louisiana's fifth largest city.

About 10 miles from New Orleans via I-10, Kenner preserves and celebrates its past in **Rivertown,** a historic district bound by Airline Highway and Jefferson Highway. Here refurbished Victorian cottages house shops, offices, and restaurants, and a cluster of eight museums offers a variety of cultural entertainment.

The historical center is **La Salle's Landing,** which overlooks the place on the Mississippi where the explorer stepped ashore to assert France's ownership of the Mississippi Valley and its drainage basins.

Where Williams Boulevard meets Lake Pontchartrain in north Kenner, in a part of town known as Laketown, waves lap upon the lakeshore—an ideal spot to spread a towel and relax away from New Orleans's frenzy. Among the amenities here are a picnic and boat launch area. The **Treasure Chest Casino** *(5050 Williams Blvd. 504-443-8000)* offers gaming 24 hours a day, 7 days a week.

Kenner also features the outstanding **Rivertown Repertory Theatre** *(325 Minor St. 504-468-7272 or 504-468-7221),* where musicals, plays, and performances take place year-round. ■

Neon sketches Carnival watchers' traditional cry and begging hands at Kenner's Mardi Gras Museum.

Rivertown Museums

A space station prototype looms over a visitor to Space Station Kenner.

KENNER'S FAMILY-ORIENTED MUSEUMS CLUSTER IN convenient proximity along Williams Boulevard—among them the Mardi Gras Museum, Daily Living Science Center & Planetarium, Space Station Kenner, Louisiana Wildlife & Fisheries Museum, Cannes Brûlée Native American Exhibit of the Gulf South, Louisiana Toy Train Museum (see p. 204), and the Saints Hall of Fame Museum (see p. 204).

MARDI GRAS MUSEUM

Kenner boasts the impressive Mardi Gras Museum. Sprawling over some 10,000 square feet, its attractions include a re-created Mardi Gras street scene and a three-quarter-scale model of a traditional float onto which visitors may climb. You can also wander through a giant papier-mâché King Cake, or stroll along a timeline that marks events in the evolution of Mardi Gras. Fifteen TV monitors play simultaneously, each describing an aspect of the Carnival tradition. They show costume balls, floats and marching bands, French Quarter revelry, and the traditional Cajun Courir du Mardi Gras ("running of the Mardi Gras"), in which revelers on horseback visit rural homes to beg ingredients for a community gumbo fest later in the day. There are props, costumes, pages from designers' sketchbooks, Mardi Gras-themed artwork, miniatures of floats, and movie memorabilia from feature films depicting the event. Live demonstrations by Mardi Gras artisans are regularly scheduled.

DAILY LIVING SCIENCE CENTER & PLANETARIUM

This is one of those places that tend to fascinate kids to the degree that adults have to drag them away. Although designed to appeal to the young, the Daily Living Science Center is not a children's museum; it presents a common-sense approach to life's natural puzzles, with an emphasis on how things work. The scope of inquiry ranges from everyday life (How does the body work? What's hidden inside the walls of a house? How does an automobile's engine generate power?) to the mysteries of the natural world, such as hydrology

Rivertown Museums
www.kenner.la.us/rivertown.html
Map 171 B2
Purchase tickets for all museums at 415 Williams Blvd., Kenner, at the exhibition hall
504-468-7231
Closed Sun.–Mon.
$ per museum; multipass available

Mardi Gras Museum
415 Williams Blvd.

Daily Living Science Center & Planetarium
409 Williams Blvd.

Space Station Kenner
✉ 409 Williams Blvd.

Louisiana Wildlife & Fisheries Museum
✉ 303 Williams Blvd.

and how to track hurricanes. The questions go even further—all the way to the stars, which are explored from the museum's **planetarium** and **observatory.** Recline in one of the planetarium's 42 comfortable seats for the 30-minute tour of the galaxy, narrated live by astronomically savvy curators. (A question-and-answer period follows each show.) After dark on Friday and Saturday evenings, weather permitting, the observatory's huge telescope—one of the largest in Louisiana open for public stargazing—focuses on objects familiar and strange, an unforgettable experience for a youngster who has never put an eye to one of these great optical wonders.

This whooping crane has living relatives; other mounted birds at the Louisiana Wildlife & Fisheries Museum are extinct.

SPACE STATION KENNER

Life in orbit and traveling through space are themes of Space Station Kenner, an exhibit adjoining the planetarium. It showcases a full-size prototype of the NASA Space Station. You're free to enter the million-dollar mock-up, an orbiting outpost not much bigger than any of the caravels sailed to the New World by Christopher Columbus in 1492. But the awesome sense of discovery that compelled the mariner into the unknown is palpable in the cramped space inside this amazing assemblage. The historical exhibits tracing America's space effort put it in context. The space station is so popular that when you first arrive at the Daily Living Science Center, you should immediately obtain tickets that will specify your boarding time.

LOUISIANA WILDLIFE & FISHERIES MUSEUM

This unusual institution, a creation of the state's Wildlife and Fisheries Department, focuses on the natural

world surrounding urban New Orleans and the threats to its survival. It also recalls this area's aboriginal human pageant, nearly all traces of which time, aided by a warm, wet climate, has virtually erased.

Louisiana's list of native wild creatures is so long that no museum could possibly treat them all, but this one comes very close. Displays and exhibits feature 700-odd species, depicting some in re-created habitats. A 15,000-gallon freshwater **aquarium** is filled with better-known denizens of the state's underwater menagerie, including darting perch, sluggish bottom-feeding catfish, schools of minnows, listless bass, slithering eels, and surprisingly spry turtles.

Because of environmental concerns about the effects on wildlife from the oil industry, a key contributor to the state's economy, the museum has a permanent exhibition on offshore drilling. You'll find a detailed scale model of an offshore oil rig, with discussion on how exploration continues in the Gulf just off the Louisiana coast, despite the moratorium on oil and gas operations in Lake Pontchartrain. The juxtaposition of the rig with mounted animals from the collection of the Louisiana Wildlife and Fisheries Department is provocative, because the latter includes the passenger pigeon and the ivory-billed woodpecker. Examine these creatures closely—they are both beautiful—and remember them: They no longer exist on this world, driven to extinction by pollution, habitat destruction, and just plain carelessness.

CANNES BRÛLÉE NATIVE AMERICAN EXHIBIT OF THE GULF SOUTH

Outdoors, behind the museum, is a living history exhibition that you should not overlook. Interpretive Native American docents in traditional dress from the 1700s to present-day demonstrate ancient skills—making of dugout canoes, weaving palmetto leaves into huts, and creating decorative beadwork. Visiting artists perform the dances of the Houma, Choctaw, and other tribes who lived in these marshy regions, the domestic tasks required to maintain a household in the wild, and the cultural rituals that impart to tribal members a sense of their unique identity. Beyond the re-created village structures is a bayou setting, where plants and animals reflect the daily reality of village life. You can read about these vanished people, whose survivors were mostly assimilated into the region's African-American communities, but to see their world conjured up here is infinitely more satisfying and informative. ■

Cannes Brûlée Native American Exhibit of the Gulf South
☒ 303 Williams Blvd.

Cannes Brûlée docent Janie Luster holds a turtle shell mask.

Southern trees

Nothing gives southern Louisiana—and certainly New Orleans itself—the sense of the South more than its trees.

Live oaks *(Quercus virginiana)* Able to shade whole streets from the hard light that drove Edgar Degas indoors to paint, the live oak is unmistakable for its lovely gnarled branches spreading outward and dipping nearly to the ground. Its small, deep green, leathery leaves retain their color throughout the year—hence the name "live" oak. You'll find live oaks throughout the South on floodplains and barrier islands, in upland forests, swamp hammocks, sand dunes, pine woods, and pastures. Their wood is some of the heaviest, toughest, and most durable in America. (Live oak timbers were used in 1794 to build the legendary frigate U.S.S. *Constitution*—also known as "Old Ironsides.") The longevity of these trees is remarkable. One growing in Goose Island State Park near Rockport, Texas, is believed to be nearly 1,000 years old; some in New Orleans may be well beyond 600 years. In addition to the famed Dueling Oaks in City Park, splendid live oaks grow in Audubon Park, throughout the Garden District, and along St. Charles Avenue. One of the most emblematic images of the Old South is that of Oak Alley Plantation and its grand allée of live oaks dating back 300 years or more. And don't forget the Evangeline Oak in St. Martinville, thought to be the spot where the real-life heroine of Longfellow's epic poem *Evangeline* reunited with her lover after being separated during the Acadian exile, only to find he had married.

Southern magnolias (M*agnolia grandiflora)* The fragrance of the magnolia blossom—Louisiana's aromatic state flower—

Left: Live oaks frame the river view from Oak Alley's front porch. Above: Spanish moss is a symbol of the Deep South.

evokes warm summer nights, as evocative of romance as perfume. Even when it's not in bloom, the magnolia can be recognized by its pyramidal silhouette and imposing stature; some magnolia trees reach 100 feet high. The magnolia's leaves are dark green and glossy with a leathery feel, and its gorgeous, flamboyant, ivory-colored flower, which blooms in May, can be 10 inches in diameter. You'll find lovely old magnolias in Uptown front yards and just about everywhere else in southern Louisiana—except in swampland.

Crape myrtles *(Lagerstroemia)* Symbolizing the popular perception of Crescent City life as one of languor and ease, the flower of the crape myrtle arguably equals that of the magnolia. It explodes into color in May and June on trees ranging from 10 to 20 feet tall. The tree's trunk is the color of caramel, smooth, and sculptural. Its small oval leaves have a satiny sheen, and its crumpled petals remind some of old Mardi Gras party favors. The crape myrtle flourishes throughout the Gulf South. If you happen to be riding the St. Charles streetcar, keep an eye out for a beautiful cluster of crape myrtles near Stop #24, the Napoleon Avenue neutral ground. There is another splendid display in Jackson Square.

Palm trees Swaying palms, trademarks of the tropics, are right at home in the heat and humidity of southern Louisiana, reminding everyone that this corner of the world shares its latitude with Cairo and the Sahara. The region boasts some 15 different types of palms. Don't bother trying to sort them out by species; just enjoy their exotic appearance and the dry rustling of their fronds in the breeze—always a soothing sound at night. The smallest are the shrublike palmettos, rarely more than 3 feet tall. The grandest of all are the stately Canary Island date palms, some topping 80 feet. You'll find them decorating the Garden District, City Park, and Audubon Park. They also grow throughout Louisiana's southern lowlands.

Banana trees And when you sit down to a dessert of baked plantains, thank the local banana trees, which are not really trees, but herbaceous plants. They do an excellent imitation of a tree, however, and can grow to 15 feet. Short and exuberant looking, they testify that the tropics are not far to the south. ■

Jackson Barracks

Jackson Barracks
Map 171 C2
6400 St. Claude Ave., New Orleans
504-278-8242
Closed Sun.
Bus: St. Claude

ANDREW JACKSON'S VICTORY AT THE BATTLE OF NEW Orleans in 1815 made clear the tactical advantages of the place where he made his stand. A sugarcane field on a narrow flat between the Mississippi and a swamp, 4 miles downriver from the French Quarter, it left attackers with little room to maneuver. In the 1830s the Army established a garrison about a mile upriver, just off St. Claude Avenue, near Arabi.

Adopting a quadrangle layout frequently used on American military bases of that era, government architects built 15 strikingly handsome two-story redbrick buildings. White columns supported deep first- and second-floor galleries and peaked roofs. Originally called the U.S. Barracks, it was renamed Jackson Barracks in 1866 in honor of Old Hickory, America's seventh president, who had died in 1845.

Its location was close enough to the city to allow a quick response to civil disorder, particularly a slave rebellion, yet far enough from the French Quarter so that the cadre would not succumb to its temptations. In return for their isolation, officers were billeted in considerable comfort and style. The heavy construction of the two-story quarters with burly brick columns also made the buildings suitable as defensive positions in the event of close attack. Laid out between them and the Mississippi shore was the parade ground, roughly 300 yards long and 100 wide, bordered by quarters for commissioned officers.

Opened in 1836, the barracks complex was built to last, and it has. Its formal federal architecture has been altered slightly by Southern regional styles. When you walk up the steps, you are sharing moments with some of the young officers who trained here and now occupy history books: Robert E. Lee, Pierre Beauregard, George B. McClellan, and Ulysses S. Grant. Military officers still assemble here; these splendid buildings are used to billet the commissioned members of the Louisiana National Guard.

To reach Jackson Barracks from the French Quarter, follow Rampart Street east, which becomes St. Claude Avenue (La. 42) in Faubourg Marigny. Drive 3.2 miles downriver to Avenue E, turning right (toward the river). Follow E past Dauphine Street, then turn left (upriver) onto Lee Street and enter the post. The old section of interest to you is toward the river, surrounding the **Guerre Drive Loop,** which you may drive around. Observe posted speed limits. Visitor parking is beside Building 51, the Post Exchange.

JACKSON BARRACKS MILITARY MUSEUM

The old powder magazine flanks a modern building on Avenue C; both the old and the new display war souvenirs from the American Revolution to the Persian Gulf War, including weapons and medals from enemy soldiers and poignant items of human interest—letters home, recruiting posters, smart uniforms worn by young men long ago. Particularly affecting is a cutaway of a World War II barracks building that shows its tight-fitting quarters. ■

Opposite: A color guard at Jackson Barracks in Army uniforms of the late 1830s

John Landis's 1940 lithograph of Andrew Jackson's 1815 triumph, part of the Historic New Orleans Collection

Chalmette Battlefield & Chalmette National Cemetery

THIS UNIT OF JEAN LAFITTE NATIONAL HISTORICAL PARK and Preserve protects the location of the last battle of the last war between the United States and Britain. It is also the resting place of American soldiers who have fallen in battle from the Civil War through the years of the Vietnam conflict.

Chalmette Battlefield & Chalmette National Cemetery

Map 171 C2

8606 W. St. Bernard Hwy., Chalmette

504-281-0510

The end of the American Revolution in 1783 brought an uneasy accord with the British. Americans resented Britain's failure to withdraw from U.S. territory along the Great Lakes, their support of Native American resistance to westward expansion, and London's choke hold on maritime commerce, which reduced the U.S. treasury to near bankruptcy. Many in Congress demanded action. In 1812 and 1813, American forces invaded Canada; the invasion quickly faltered, however, and the tide turned. In August 1814, British troops invaded Washington, routed the government, and torched the White House. Desperate American counterattacks forced a retreat, leaving both sides worn out and with nothing to show for it. On December 24, British and American diplomats meeting in Belgium signed the Treaty of Ghent, ending the war.

In those days, however, news took weeks to cross the Atlantic, and communication with ships at sea was all but impossible. Unaware that the treaty was about to be signed, more than 50 ships carrying 10,000 veteran British troops from Jamaica deposited the soldiers east of New Orleans in mid-December.

The British force, led by Major General Sir Edward Pakenham, planned to hold New Orleans hostage for concessions of land.

Meantime, although there was a price on his head, French-born Jean Lafitte, an organizer and leader of pirates, offered to share with the Americans his in-depth knowledge of the bayous and swamps within the Bay of Barataria. Andrew Jackson, then a major general, warned against this initially, because 80 or so of Lafitte's "hellish banditti," as he called them, had just been imprisoned. Desperate for aid, Jackson finally conceded, exchanging the release of Lafitte's imprisoned men for maps and drawings of the bayous and assistance in manning batteries. This decision became an unquestionable advantage for the Americans.

Jackson led his force of regular recruits, militiamen, volunteers, and Baratarians 9 miles downriver, where on the night of December 23 they launched a surprise attack on the British. The Americans then retreated to the Macarty plantation on the upriver side of the Rodriguez Canal from the Chalmette plantation. This wide ditch traversed the narrowest strip of solid land between the British and New Orleans, about three-fifths of a mile wide.

Jackson chose this place for strategic reasons. On his right flank was the great moat of the Mississippi; on his left, beyond the planters' fields, was an impassable cypress swamp. This meant the British would have to attack head-on across crew-cut sugarcane fields that provided them no cover. Jackson's men deepened the canal and partially filled it with water. Behind it they built a shoulder-high rampart of mud and cotton bale thick enough to stop a cannonball. They set up their batteries behind it.

On December 28, the Americans repulsed an infantry attack on the breastworks and withstood a New Year's Day cannon bombardment. The British commander waited until the wet gray morning of January 8, then gave the order to attack in force. Only one British unit (there were Scots fighting as well) reached the American rampart; most were mowed down. As Pakenham rode forward to rally his troops, he was wounded twice before a bullet severed an artery in one of his legs. Ordering his successor to fight on, he died minutes later, at the age of 36. His senior officer wisely assessed the British situation as hopeless. The battle had lasted less than two hours, with the most intense fighting confined to about 30 minutes. The British suffered more than 2,000 casualties, including some 700 dead. The Americans reported 8 killed and 13 wounded.

News of the victory spread across the country before word of the treaty arrived, creating the misperception that Jackson's triumph had won the war. Coming as it did after a three-year conflict notorious for American military ineptitude and humiliating defeats, the public was predisposed to ignore the truth. The Battle of New Orleans restored American pride and unity and demonstrated the country's ability to hold on to the Louisiana Purchase. It made Jackson a national hero and a future President, and sparked a wave of migration and settlement along the Mississippi River.

VISITING CHALMETTE BATTLEFIELD

A 1.2-mile road, starting from the park entrance, highlights six places significant in the outcome of the 120-minute clash. Start at the **visitor center** *(504-281-0510),*

The Malus-Beauregard House's classical exterior belies shallow rooms within that facilitate ventilation.

where exhibits and an audiovisual program provide a background on the war, explaining the importance of southern Louisiana and New Orleans to the 39-year-old nation and chronicling the progress of the battle. The 28-minute film will make your visit more meaningful. Be sure to obtain the brochure including a map of battlefield sites, and ask about programs given by rangers before you depart. You may drive or walk, following your progress on the map; its text is keyed to the numbered sites along the route.

The **Malus-Beauregard House,** a columned residence designed by James Gallier, Sr., was built on the battlefield about 1833. It once belonged to René Beauregard, a judge and son of Confederate Gen. P.G.T. Beauregard. From the nearby levee, one can get a fine panorama of the battlefield and the Chalmette National Cemetery downriver.

Stop 1 visits Batteries 5 and 6, which, along with Batteries 7 and 8 to the northeast, anchored the left flank of Jackson's line. The cannon in Battery 5 are reproductions of two six-pounders.

Stop 2 includes Battery 4, which contained the largest American gun—a naval 32-pounder salvaged from an American schooner. It was manned by an artillery team supported by an African-American unit, the Battalion of Louisiana Free Men of Color. This position, with its powerful weapon, inflicted many casualties on the attackers.

When British troops attacking along the edge of the swamp were unable to reach the American line, General John Keane led a reserve force of 93rd Highlanders diagonally from **Stop 3** across the battlefield, but the American line directed their fire across the cane field, hitting the Scotsmen with an intense broadside. Four out of five of them fell.

You learn about the British perspective at **Stop 4.** Most of Pakenham's artillery was positioned downriver, in what is now the Chalmette National Cemetery (see p. 183). The guns' placement was unwise. An inadequate supply of gunpowder and shot so reduced their effectiveness that they did little to support the infantry assault. This becomes more evident at **Stop 5,** where you have a panoramic view of the battlefield from the British perspective. On your far left, by the river, one British column briefly overran the American rampart. On your far right, then the border of the swamp, is where the bagpipes of Keane's Highlanders were silenced. That General Pakenham would ride to the

When the first soldier was buried here in 1864, Old Glory held only 35 stars.

front of the line (**Stop 6**) in a desperate attempt to rally his troops for another assault was an indication of how badly the battle was going for them. It was here that Pakenham came into the sights of the rifleman whose bullet delivered his mortal wound.

CHALMETTE NATIONAL CEMETERY

A more somber monument—and a reminder of the saying that wars are understood best by those who do not return from them—is this burial ground adjoining the Chalmette Battlefield (Stop 4 on the auto route). Established in 1864, it is the resting place for the roughly 12,000 Union soldiers who died in Louisiana. Only one casualty from the Battle of New Orleans is buried here.

The graveyard's antiquated white marble headstones were the result of much deliberation by the Quartermaster General of the Army after the Civil War. Wooden markers and crosses, intended as a necessary means for locating graves and identifying the dead, were intended to be temporary, and were seen as an insufficient expression of gratitude from the nation for which the men had died. The solution was the incised marble marker seen here by the thousands, about 4 inches thick and standing about a foot high.

Unknown soldiers

In 1870 the Quartermaster General reported to Congress that the remains of 299,696 Union soldiers had been laid to rest in 74 national cemeteries. Of them, 173,109 had been positively identified. Unknowns numbered 143,446—42 percent of the recovered dead. Roughly half of those interred in the Chalmette National Cemetery are unknowns. ■

Larger ones commemorate casualties of the Spanish-American War, World Wars I and II, and the Vietnam War, but the basic style remains consistent.

This area figured importantly in the Civil War. Here in 1862 Confederate forces tried but failed to stop Union naval ships commanded by David Glasgow Farragut from proceeding upriver. Ordered by the Navy Department to capture New Orleans, Farragut reached the city on April 25. Six days later, the Union army occupied it, and the lower Mississippi was again open to Federal forces. Foreign nations disposed to helping the Confederacy backed off, and Farragut was promoted to rear admiral, the first in the U.S. Navy to hold that rank. ■

Los Isleños Museum & Multicultural Complex

WHEN THE AMERICAN REVOLUTION BROKE OUT, SPAIN feared that Britain might seize New Orleans for military advantage.

Los Isleños Museum displays reproductions of formal clothing worn by Isleño settlers.

Los Isleños Museum & Multicultural Complex

- Map 171 C1
- 1357 Bayou Rd., St. Bernard
- 504-682-0862
- Closed Mon.–Wed.
- $

To bolster its small military garrison in the delta country, Spain drafted hundreds of Canary Islanders—tenacious provincials known as "Isleños"—from its seven isles off the North African coast to settle locations strategic to New Orleans's defense. These included the Bayou des Familles (which flows through the Barataria Preserve, see pp. 194–195) and the labyrinthine waterways of St. Bernard Parish.

Mostly soldiers, farmers, and fishermen, the émigrés adapted to the difficult terrain much in the way the Acadians did, living an isolated existence that has preserved Isleño language and culture. In St. Bernard, a community still predominantly Spanish, many locals continue to speak the settlers' original dialect. They also sing decimas (a complex 16th-century Spanish folk song genre characterized by a ten-line stanza), celebrating their Canary Island heritage with neighbors in the outlying fishing villages of Delacroix, Reggio, and Yscloskey. Today the Isleños still work the lower delta's lands and waters as trappers, hunters, crabbers, shrimpers, and fishingboat builders.

The 21-acre Los Isleños Complex is a living history museum comprising several different buildings—with several more in the works—that represent the lives of Canary Island descendants. Here, **Los Isleños Museum** is housed in a Creole cottage (ca 1840). The home of a local Isleño businessman between the 1940s and 1980s, it displays old photographs, household items, and period clothing, including 18th-century hats and shoes made on the islands. The **Estopinal House** is furnished and decorated in the manner of the 1920s, '30s, and '40s, complete with family memorabilia and photographs, children's toys, and kitchen appliances. Typical Isleño dances and cooking demonstrations are held in the village. Woodcarving classes are offered on Saturday mornings.

Located near St. Bernard State Park (see p. 187), the **Canary Islands Descendants Museum & Library** *(600 St. Bernard Pkwy., Braithwaite, 504-682-1010. Closed Mon.–Wed.)* assists visitors in tracing their Spanish and Isleño roots by computer. ■

An 1875 fire gutted the mansion Pierre Denis de la Ronde built in 1805 to rival Versailles.

San Bernardo Scenic Byway

THIS 17-MILE ROUTE RUNS FROM JACKSON BARRACKS (see pp. 178–179) to Shell Beach via La. 46 and La. 300. Cutting through the delta's vast wetland bayou country east of the Mississippi, passing through shrimping and ocean-fishing hamlets, it spotlights historical sites—especially those related to Isleño culture.

San Bernardo Scenic Byway
Map 171 C2, C1, & D1

St. Bernard Parish Tourist Commission
204 Cougar Rd., Arabi
504-278-4200 or 504-278-4242

In Arabi, the **Old Arabi Historic District** *(along parts of Angela, Mehle, & Esteban Sts.)* includes several old structures dating from the mid-1800s, when the area flourished.

Farther on, the byway passes through **Chalmette,** site of the Battle of New Orleans (see pp. 180–183). Just downriver, stop by the ruins of the **de la Ronde plantation house,** which the British temporarily used as a headquarters and hospital during the 1815 battle.

In St. Bernard the **Los Isleños Museum & Multicultural Complex** (see p. 184) surveys this region's Spanish-speaking culture. Several doors away, the **Ducros Museum** *(1345 Bayou Rd. 504-682-2713. Closed Fri.–Sun.)* occupies an early Creole cottage, thought to date from about 1800, and recounts other aspects of local history.

Roadside markers on La. 46 east of St. Bernard describe the pre-Civil War sugarcane industry and grand plantation houses that once flanked this road. In Kenilworth a rare survivor, the columned, white **Kenilworth Plantation House** *(Private),* completed about 1819, typifies the French colonial houses of southern Louisiana's rural elite. **Contreras** was once the Contreras Plantation, birthplace of heroic Confederate general P.G.T. Beauregard, whose postwar years in New Orleans inspired Frances Parkinson Keyes's novel *Madame Castel's Lodger.* In the early 19th century, **Verret** was the pastoral empire of Marial Verret, a sugar planter. His neighbor Auguste Reggio's plantation, on the Bayou Terre Aux Boeufs, begat **Reggio,** on La. 300 south of the byway. Like **Delacroix,** also on La. 300, this sleepy hamlet is known for its ishing charters. In any of these towns, where fishing boats line the shored-up banks of canal-like bayous, you'll find little picnic-table eateries serving up home-style crawfish, shrimp, and oyster dishes. ■

Audubon Louisiana Nature Center

IT IS NOT NECESSARY TO VENTURE INTO THE WILD WHEN you have a hands-on museum such as this nearby. Although suited to children, it will enthrall adults as well. Its curators call it an "urban nature center" that examines Louisiana's many wild habitats—particularly its hardwood forests and freshwater wetlands. The idea is to experience them up close, and that you'll do when you explore the botany center, a butterfly garden, and nature trails that wind through 86 acres of bottomland hardwood forest.

A black-crowned night heron strolls and a water lily blooms at the Audubon Louisiana Nature Center.

Elementary school science classes go here on field trips, and it's easy to see why: The staff is well trained and adept at describing the surroundings to children. The **nature trails** are a getaway all by themselves. This is not an educational trudge past trees with labels on them; it is rather a genuinely natural environment where animals live and dart about. Some are elusive, while others are perhaps more curious about you than you are about them. To enhance the experience, the center will provide a naturalist pack, complete with

Audubon Louisiana Nature Center
www.auduboninstitute.org
Map 171 C2
Nature Center Dr. in Joe W. Brown Memorial Park, New Orleans
504-246-5672
Closed Mon.
$

binoculars, magnifying glasses, field guides, dip nets, and activity guides—all free of charge.

The **Botany Center** specializes in living displays of the rich and varied flora of Louisiana. Even more suited to the youngsters, perhaps, is the **Discovery Loft.** It is designed to demystify the natural world by allowing visitors to touch and examine objects fast disappearing from urban lives, such as bones and animal hides and furs. Adjacent to the Botany Center is the **Butterfly and Hummingbird Garden,** where visitors and wildlife alike are attracted to the year-round blooms.

When you feel the need to sit, consider taking in one of the several shows at the **Planetarium,** in the Judith W. Freeman Astronomy Center. "Planet Patrol" is designed specially for children. The center's gift shop specializes in educational books and toys and in science and nature-themed gifts. ■

St. Bernard State Park

IN 1699, SOME 20 YEARS BEFORE HE FOUNDED NEW Orleans, Jean Baptiste Le Moyne, Sieur de Bienville, happened to be downriver at a point where the Mississippi, flowing south, abruptly turns northwest. In charge of a small group of scouts, he was dismayed to see a contingent of English explorers sailing upriver, undoubtedly of a mind to make land grabs for their own king.

St. Bernard State Park

Map 171 C1

Off La. 39 at 502 St. Bernard Hwy., Braithwaite

504-682-2101 or 888-677-7823

This was not an era of fair play. Bienville told the British scouts that they were lost. He said the Mississippi was farther west and the French had built a very large military outpost to protect several French settlements to the north. Though they were not lost, the Englishmen were apparently uncertain enough about their whereabouts to take Bienville at his word and turn around, leaving this unsettled region to the French and this bend in the river to be known forever after as **English Turn.**

At the tip of the turn sprawls St. Bernard State Park, one of the most popular close-to-town outdoor recreation spots on the east bank. Its 358 acres are only 18 miles from the French Quarter, and its many improvements make for convenient and comfortable camping.

Within the park are man-made lagoons and wetland habitats, best accessed by a winding nature trail that crosses a narrow waterway over a low short bridge of logs, built in the manner of early settlers. From the trail, you'll catch glimpses of turtles, alligators, raccoons, rabbits, possums, squirrels, and dozens of species of birds, including ruby-throated hummingbirds and northern cardinals. This is a great place to introduce children to the outdoors. Ask rangers about special nature walks and campfire talks.

A half mile south of the park entrance stands a levee from which you can look across the river **Twelve Mile Point.** Its wild-looking shore of live oak and magnolia forest suggests what the New Orleans riverbank looked like before the Europeans arrived. On many road maps the 126-acre park beyond is identified as English Turn Wilderness Park. It is used by the Louisiana Nature Center for educational programs reserved for scouts and students; it is not open to the public. But do not fret: Your side of the river is far more comfortable. ■

Bayou Sauvage National Wildlife Refuge

Bayou Sauvage NWR

Map 171 C2

15 miles E of New Orleans, off I-10 E. Take Irish Bayou exit, turn left and cross I-10, & left again onto gravel road before US 11 bridge.

U.S. Fish & Wildlife, Southern Louisiana Refuges: 985-882-2000

This refuge bills itself as the wildest part of New Orleans, and the U.S. Fish and Wildlife Service wants to keep it that way. Only 20 minutes by car from downtown, this is America's largest urban wildlife refuge. Its wetlands offer one of the best bicycle adventures in southeastern Louisiana—a 10-mile round-trip through pristine wetlands and along Lake Pontchartrain's shore, a tangled natural habitat where endangered species like the bald eagle and piping plover nest.

The **Bike Pathway** is paved and level, routed to bring you as close as possible to the places where these and other creatures roost and feed. Most of the path follows the top of the hurricane-protection levees surrounding over half of the marsh and swampland that make up the refuge. Originally built to hold back storm surges, they now artificially maintain the wetland system.

You can walk or bike the pathway, of course, but not drive on it. Either way you will get a close-hand look at the natural transition zone between freshwater marsh and the brackish lake, where egrets, herons, gulls, and pelicans attract veteran birders.

Between April and July, thousands of migratory waterfowl and songbirds stop over at the marshes. Come September, the skies fill with all kinds of ducks, splashing down en masse to begin their winter stay. Full-time residents like alligators and turtles can be easily spotted if you scan the marsh and bayous.

Headgear, insect repellent, and drinking water are recommended. Call the U. S. Fish and Wildlife Service's Southeast Louisiana Refuges program office to ask about free canoeing tours offered every weekend. ■

Fort Pike State Historic Site

Fort Pike State Historic Site

Map 171 C2

Off US 90, 23 miles E of New Orleans

504-662-5703 or 888-662-5703

$

Andrew Jackson's brilliant victory over the British in the Battle of New Orleans nevertheless revealed the inadequacy of American coastal defenses. Congress, determined to protect the burgeoning economy of the lower Mississippi River Valley, commissioned the building of updated Gulf Coast fortifications.

To protect New Orleans, President James Monroe lobbied for the building of a sextet of brick-stone-and-concrete forts at points then strategic to the city's defense. Most have crumbled away, but Fort Pike, begun in 1819 and completed in 1826, survives as a bulky ghost of 19th-century warfare.

Named in honor of explorer-soldier General Zebulon Montgomery Pike, it was designed to withstand attack from land or sea. Pointed fortified corners, extending out from the walls and known as bastions, created deadly intersecting fields of fire over its land approach, and a curved wall faces the water. There would be more to see here—officers' quarters, a general merchandise store—had not retreating Confederate troops, who held it briefly during the Civil War, torched it in 1862. Museum exhibits show the installation in full flower, surrounded by wooden service buildings—including a bakery, repair shops, a blacksmith—mostly located outside the fort's walls. ■

Opposite: A lazy afternoon on the dock at Bayou Sauvage

Managing the Mississippi

About halfway to the Gulf of Mexico on its 2,350-mile journey from Minnesota's Lake Itasca, the Mississippi River merges with the Missouri River, taking on the flows of the Yellowstone, the Cheyenne, the Sioux, and the Platte. In Illinois, it picks up the Ohio River, which carries the runoff of the Allegheny, the Kentucky, the Cumberland, the Tennessee, and the Monongahela. The Arkansas joins in farther downriver.

All told, the Mississippi collects water from more than 100,000 rivers and streams, draining a 1,246,000-square-mile area that includes parts of 31 states and two Canadian provinces. A watershed reaching west to Idaho, north into Canada, and east to New York, it touches 41 percent of the continental United States. By the time the Mississippi reaches New Orleans its peak flow freights about one million cubic feet of water per second—or 3.5 million gallons, roughly enough to fill a major football stadium in fewer than 15 seconds.

During heavy rainfall seasons or rapid snowmelts upriver, runoff can double, overwhelming the capacity of the river's natural channel. For this reason the lower Mississippi Valley floodplains range from 40 to 70 miles wide. During the awful 1927 flood—the river's worst in recorded history—it reached 80 miles across in some places.

At New Orleans, the Mississippi's annual average high-water mark is 14 feet above mean sea level. St. Louis Cathedral, however, is 7 feet below that, at about 7 feet above sea level. The upper right-hand corner of the Quarter is a mere 2 feet above sea level, and the riverside boundary of the University of New Orleans campus on L.C. Simon Boulevard is 5 feet *below* sea level—roughly 6 feet below the level of Lake Pontchartrain a few hundred yards north.

When New Orleans was founded, the river's potential for serious flooding was ignored. But early on, action had to be taken to fight its forces. By 1727, a mile-long, 18-foot-wide levee snaked along the settlement's shore. After the disastrous 1927 flood, the need for a safety valve was obvious. In 1931, in St. Charles Parish, about 33

Forming a natural bowl, parts of New Orleans are below the level of the Mississippi River and Lake Pontchartrain. During heavy rains, pumping is necessary to keep the city from flooding.

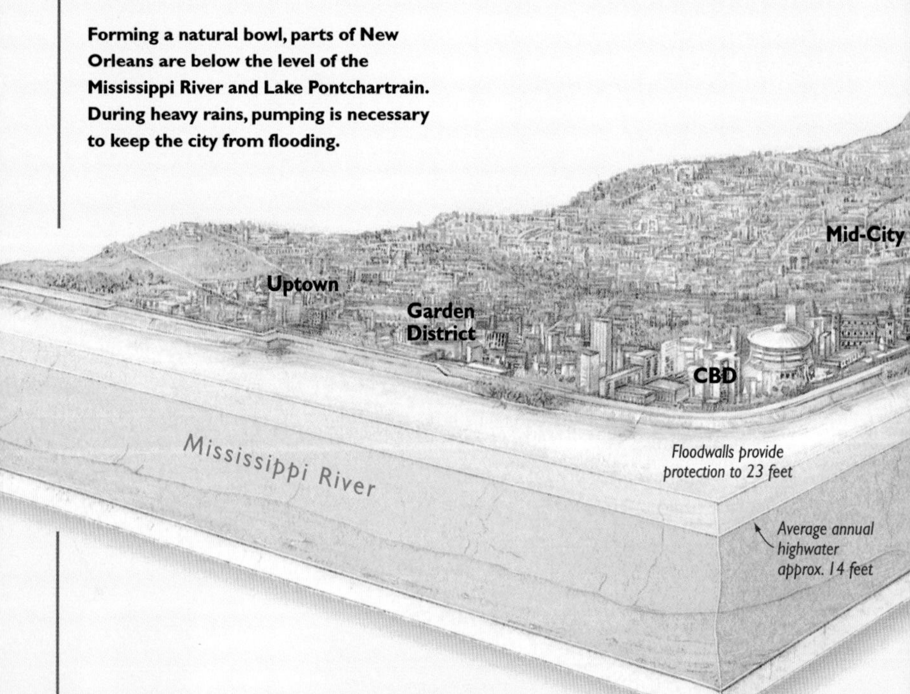

miles upriver from Canal Street, the Bonnet Carré Spillway was constructed to protect downstream communities by diverting water from the Mississippi into Lake Pontchartrain. Operated by the U.S. Army Corps of Engineers, the spillway has been opened eight times—the first time in 1937, the last in 1997—releasing a massive muddy torrent rumbling 8 miles north into the lake, which then empties into the Gulf.

In New Orleans, where riverfront real estate is limited—railroad right-of-ways, wharves, and warehouses claim much of it—an 8.2-mile flood wall extends from Audubon Park to the Inner Harbor Navigation Canal, just over a mile downriver from the Quarter. The 2-foot-thick concrete wall encloses a vertical sheet of metal driven 20 to 25 feet into the ground. To permit vehicular access to the river, massive floodgates swing on huge hinges, roll sideways, or lift vertically to open.

In the last 5,000 years, the Mississippi has cut at least five different routes to the Gulf of Mexico, each leaving a delta of alluvial silt. Drawn seaward by gravity, it drops over 1,400 feet along its journey, slamming against riverbanks, eventually eroding through the necks of land enclosed by circular bends. Its current channel system is believed to be about 500 years old. In the 1950s it became apparent that the Mississippi was diverting an increasing amount of its water into the Atchafalaya River, which branches off from the Mississippi about 300 river miles upstream from the Gulf. In 1900, roughly 6 percent of the river's flow was lost to the Atchafalaya; by 1950, the diversion claimed 25 percent. If nothing had been done, today the main stem of the Mississippi would be flowing miles west of New Orleans, putting it out of business as the world-leading port in total bulk tonnage handled.

The decision was made to place barriers at the end of the Atchafalaya to limit the loss of Mississippi water. Called the Old River Control Structures, the rationale was compelling. The barriers would protect the region's nearly 300-year history of farming and industry, preserve the communities that derive their livelihood and culture from the river's current path, and protect the vast wildlife refuges that have grown up around it. The stream has been harnessed to human endeavors, although it can never be truly tamed. ■

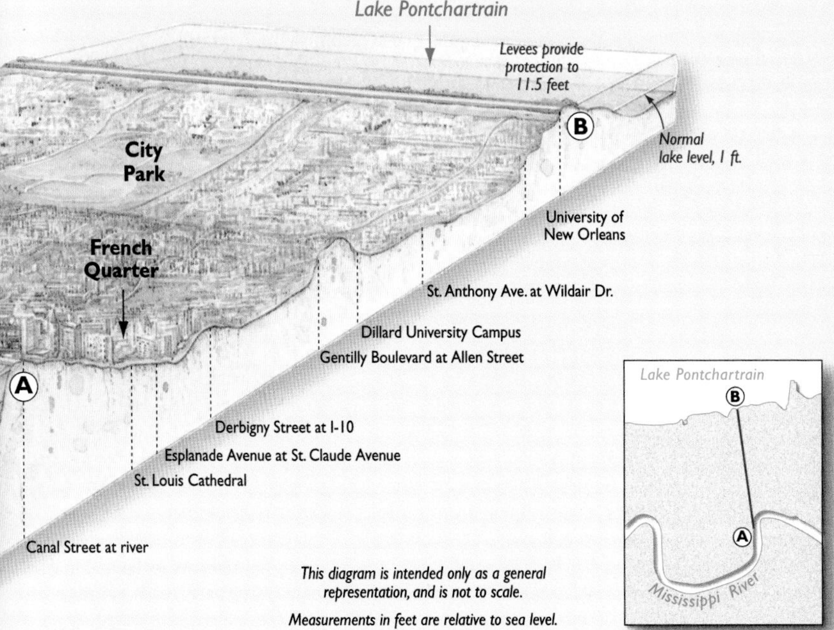

This diagram is intended only as a general representation, and is not to scale.

Measurements in feet are relative to sea level.

Gretna

Gretna
Map 171 C2

Gretna Visitor Center
Huey P. Long Ave. at 2nd St., Gretna
504-363-1580 or 888-447-3862
Center open but attractions closed Mon.

DIRECTLY ACROSS THE MISSISSIPPI OPPOSITE NEW Orleans's Central Business District, this pleasant little city, founded by German-American settlers in 1836, enjoys a relative peacefulness. That's why people living on the west bank often call it Best Bank.

Gretna's old section fronts on the river, running inland to about Sixth Street. Its heart lies between Lafayette Street and Huey P. Long Avenue, neighborhoods with many shotgun-style homes and late-vintage Victorians—Italianate, Queen Anne, and Edwardian styles in particular. The **Gretna Historical Complex** *(209 Lafayette St. 504-362-3854. Closed Sun.–Mon.; $)* preserves the **Kittie Strehle Home,** a Creole cottage where an immigrant family who arrived in the 1840s raised nine children. The **David Crockett Fire Museum** occupies the city's first firehouse, a 19th-century survivor whose prize is an obsolete steam-powered water pumper from the 1870s. Wander in on your own or ask about tours of the **Gretna Green Blacksmith Shop,** a new addition where you can view demonstrations. Three blocks away, the Old Southern Pacific Railroad Depot houses memorabilia.

The city's history is most interestingly recounted by the **German-American Cultural Center** *(519 Huey P. Long Ave. 504-363-4202. Closed Sun.–Tues.; $).* In 1721 Germans settled along the Mississippi River 30 miles above New Orleans. The area was soon dubbed the German Coast (or, as the French on the other side of the lake insisted on calling it, *La Côte des Allemands*). The first wave was mostly farmers who made their living supplying produce to New Orleans. The colonial settlers were assimilated into the city's Franco-American sphere through intermarriage with the French Catholics and by changing their names—from Heidel to Haydel, Himmel to Hymel, Zweig to LaBranche, and Zehringer to Zeringue. By 1850 the city's census counted more Germans than French. The center's historical exhibits are mainly personal ones, more focused on family life and the *Gemütlichkeit* that held the émigrés together in a new land. ■

Founded in 1841 and named in honor of the Alamo hero, Gretna's Steam Fire Company No. 1 is said to be the oldest continuously functioning volunteer fire department in the United States. Its firehouse dates from the late 1850s.

Westwego

FRONTING ON THE MISSISSIPPI ACROSS FROM UPTOWN, Westwego's proximity to wetlands, picturesque bayous, and placid lagoons recalls the French Quarter in the days when only swampland lay beyond Rampart Avenue. Recent residential development has given the little town a more contemporary appearance than most in this region, but its adjacent wilds remain seductive and offer one of the most pleasant getaway spots within sight of New Orleans.

As its boosters are quick to point out, Westwego adjoins a lovely urban state park, **Bayou Segnette,** where wetlands offer boating, birding, fishing, and jogging. All this was once swampland; the cutting of drainage canals permitted saltwater intrusion from the Gulf of Mexico and creating marshes in which plants and animals—including alligators, armadillos, possums, raccoons, even mink and nutrias—flourish. Birders know it for sightings of red-tailed hawks, Mississippi kites, red-winged blackbirds, bald eagles, and cardinals swooping among its Spanish moss-draped cypress trees.

This is pretty terrain, but difficult to explore except by shallow-draft boat. That is why boaters are usually lined at Bayou Segnette's launching area just riverside of Lapalco Boulevard (which runs through the park). Bayou Segnette winds south into a watery maze that you could spend years exploring, although most people bring their skiffs and canoes just to paddle off somewhere for solitude and a picnic, or to cast for bass, catfish, bream, perch, redfish, and trout. Come evening, joggers lope along a marked 5.4-mile path that skirts woods and waterways.

The park is a fine place for camping with kids. There is a playground, the picnic areas are comfortable, overnight campsites have water and electrical hookups, and rest rooms are nearby. Twenty vacation cabins raised on piers and with screened porches front on the bayou. These contemporary versions of old Cajun-style cabins are air-conditioned, but it's a lot more fun to cool off in the overnight area's pool *(closed Mon.; $$).* ■

Mimicking old-time Cajun swamp houses, many modern Westwego houses are built on piers over water.

Westwego
Map 171 B2

City of Westwego Tourist Information Center
www.jeffparish.net/westwego.html
10 Westbank Expwy., Westwego
504-436-0812

Bayou Segnette State Park
7777 Westbank Expressway, Westwego
504-736-7140 or 888-677-2296; 877-226-7652 (reservations)
$

Barataria Preserve

Jean Lafitte National Historical Park & Preserve, Barataria Preserve

Map 171 BI

6588 Barataria Blvd., Marrero

504-589-2330

IN THE EARLY 1800s THIS REGION WAS THE DOMAIN OF Jean Lafitte's "hellish banditti," a feared place of trackless swamplands where cutthroat pirates were said to have piled up booty. Anyone without a phalanx of bodyguards ought not have ventured here.

Today the Barataria region some 8 miles south of New Orleans is a point of departure for fishermen trawling for shrimp and oysters, and it is recognized as one of North America's most productive estuarine wetlands. The boundaries of the Barataria Preserve, one of six physically separate sites of the Jean Lafitte National Historical Park and Preserve, enclose some 20,000 acres of the upper Barataria Basin. This is a wilderness of hardwood forests, bald-cypress swamps, and freshwater marshes choked with subtropical vegetation and teeming with wildlife, including the American alligator, largest reptile on the continent.

The Barataria Preserve (in Marrero) is named for the great bay to the south, which is linked to Lake Salvador by the delta's labyrinthine waterways. The site preserves a representative example of the delta's environment that includes natural levee forests, bayous, swamps, and marshes. It is not a pristine wilderness; there is evidence of prehistoric settlement, and since the 1700s the region has seen farming, plantation agriculture, logging, commercial trapping, fishing, hunting, and oil and gas exploration. But it remains wild nevertheless. This quickly becomes apparent when you strike out on Barataria's 8 miles of hiking trails, which include about 2.5 miles of boardwalk, to visit the various biological zones of the preserve.

There are also 9 miles of bayous and canals open for exploration by canoe, but they are closed to motorized boats.

Stop at the **visitor center,** where exhibits include a bayou museum and a 25-minute film, "Jambalaya: A Delta Almanac," depicting the natural and human history of the region. Ranger-guided walking tours leave daily at 2 p.m. from the head of the **Coquille Trail.** Every Sunday morning, rangers lead canoe treks into the surrounding swamplands, a wonderful way to comfortably explore this otherwise impenetrable world. (The tours are free but reservations are required. Rent canoes just outside the preserve.) If you don't have time to explore, enjoy

a little serenity and a leisurely snack at outdoor tables in the **Pecan Grove Picnic Area** and by the **Lower Kenta Canal** and **Twin Canals.** If you have a valid Louisiana state fishing license, you might even try to catch your meal.

Go exploring along the footpaths of Barataria Preserve and you'll find hardwood forests growing on the high ground of the natural levees created over hundreds of years by the ever changing course of the Mississippi River. Live oaks dominate the driest elevations; on the backslopes of the levees the forest is taken over by palmetto.

In the area of the preserve where water stands most of the year, the canopied wetland forest, composed mostly of bald cypress, creates the familiar picture most people associate with the notion of a swamp. Beyond that you'll see flat treeless marshes—the eastern reach of one of the largest expanses of floating freshwater marsh in the world.

The subtropical climate of the region, which is warm and humid with abundant rainfall, combines with the rich alluvial soil deposited by the Mississippi River to produce an explosion of life. The marshes are alive with crawfish, while the tangled mass of vegetation around and above you teems with exotic birds and huge-winged butterflies. Although many of the creatures that dwell here are nocturnal and wary by nature, during the daylight hours you're still quite likely to encounter several interesting ones. These include mammals such as gray squirrels, swamp rabbits, and even the lumbering nine-banded armadillo. All of them keep their distance, but herons, egrets, ibises, and other birds will likely be prancing nonchalantly in the shallows while feeding.

Ripples in the placid water at your feet can mean turtles, frogs, or snakes. Bring binoculars to observe American alligators from a safe distance; they are easily mistaken for old logs when they lie motionless on a bank, sunning themselves. ■

A boardwalk winds through Barataria's wilderness, where Jean Lafitte's cutthroats once lurked.

Swamp ecosystem

Bottomland hardwood swamps are wetlands where the water table is at, near, or above the surface of the land, and in which only plants able to withstand having their roots submerged for extended periods can survive. Typically swamps are dominated by woody plants, primarily trees and shrubs. In the southeastern United States you'll find bald cypress, tupelo, black willow, cottonwood, oak, and maple trees.

Many people associate swamps with stagnation. In fact, the water in a healthy swamp is rich in oxygen and nutrients, even though it may be tea colored or dark brown because of the presence of organic acids, such as tannic acid, from decaying vegetation.

Because their terrain is so difficult to cross—at the Battle of New Orleans, Andrew Jackson's left flank required no defense beyond that provided by a cypress swamp—they often have been dismissed as worthless, save for harvests of red swamp and white river crawfish, and cypress, one of the finest and most durable of woods. In truth, however, these wetlands produce a disproportionate share of North America's waterfowl and wildlife. In Louisiana alone, wetlands are home to a myriad amphibians, snakes, alligators, songbirds, wading birds, raptors, beavers, otters, bobcats, black bears, basin deer, and more than 100 species of fish.

Swamps are also crucial to water storage and quality. A 6-inch rise in a 10-acre marsh amounts to 1.5 million gallons, while wetland plants absorb excess nitrogen and phosphorus from effluents, in many places reversing pollution generated by faulty sewage systems. The United States once had some 215 million wetland acres; today less than half that remains, and loss rates are running as high as 32 square miles—more than 20,000 acres—per year. ■

Barred
owl
Bald eagle
Rat
snake
Yellow-bellied
sapsucker
Cypress
Cypress
Tupelo
Button
bush
Bear
Deer
Egret
Wood duck
(male & female)
Red slider
Crawfish
Alligator

North Shore

While New Orleans swelters in summertime, breezes rustle the cypresses and live oaks across Lake Pontchartrain, along its northern shore. New Orleanians have escaped to this refreshing place since the early 1800s—first by boat, then train, and finally, with the completion of the Causeway Bridge in 1956, by car.

The man responsible for developing the north shore into a resort destination was Bernard Xavier de Marigny de Mandeville. In 1834 the bold businessman inherited a fortune from his father, Pierre Enguerrand Philippe de Mandeville Ecuyer, Sieur de Marigny. The Marigny family had once owned about a third of the land that became New Orleans. De Marigny's prosperous plantation, Fontainebleau, sprawled across about 9 acres of Lake Pontchartrain's northern shoreline, on the site of what is today Fontainebleau State Park. To be invited across the lake to sojourn at Fontainebleau—to escape the sultry summer heat with swims in the cool lake waters and dine at the de Marigny table—was to be anointed one of the Creole elite.

De Marigny envisioned how New Orleans would grow and how its wealthiest residents would need country places. He saw a profit in their need; so he bought about 5,000 acres of land and had Louis Bringer, the surveyor general of Louisiana, draw up plans for the luxury town of Mandeville. Like the design of Bringer's Faubourg Marigny in New Orleans, everything was executed to his precise order. Streets were wide and lots were huge, and no obstructions were permitted between the lake and the streets fronting it. Before long, a community of summer houses faced the lake. Although barely inhabited during the Civil War, by the late 19th century Mandeville was the lake's premier resort. Its cachet was enhanced by the romantic ritual of the steamship-ferry crossing from New Orleans, which ended in the 1930s. Twenty years later, the opening of the Causeway Bridge made the north shore a convenient commute; today the parishes surrounding Mandeville's once isolated plantation are growing at an amazing speed.

A cluster of places, however, retain their air of leisure—including Mandeville, Madisonville, Covington, and Abita Springs. In each of these communities, restored historic buildings breathe new life with small cafés, little restaurants, galleries, and trendy shops that lure New Orleanians for a day or weekend getaway, seemingly far away from the city's bustle. ■

Pier posts provide flood protection for Mandeville's historic lakefront house, "Hightide."

Mandeville

THE 24-MILE DRIVE ACROSS THE CAUSEWAY BRIDGE DELIVERS you to this quiet waterfront community. Shaded by a lush canopy of live oaks, quaint cafés and charming restaurants seem like they should be seasonal businesses even though, in this temperate clime, the season is always high.

From the causeway northbound just after reaching land, a right turn onto Florida Street and another right will take you to **Old Mandeville** and Lakeshore Drive, a mile-long row of 19th-century summer houses. Among these private gems, admire **Moore House "Hightide"** at 1717 Lakeshore Drive and the **Morel-Nott House** at 2627 Lakeshore Drive. Airy and comfortable, they evoke a different era.

New Orleanians often cross the bridge to dine in Mandeville. Among the more popular restaurants known for their fine Louisiana-style cuisine is **Benedict's Restaurant** *(1144 Lovers Ln. 985-626-4557).*

On the east side of town, beside Bayou Castine, the 400-acre **Northlake Nature Center** *(23135 US 290. 985-626-1238)* offers a pleasing stroll through mixed forest dominated by pines and hardwoods. Bullfrogs and birds inhabit a quiet marsh, and beavers have backed up a large pond.

FONTAINEBLEAU STATE PARK

Just south of Mandeville, these 2,800 acres are watched over by the ruin of a sugar mill that de Marigny built in 1829. The planter named his plantation, Fontainebleau, after the forest near Paris once reserved for the pleasures of French kings. De Marigny lived like one here until 1852.

There is no more pleasant spot on Pontchartrain's shores to while away time than in the shade of the park's old oaks, watching sailboats and windsurfers. The naturally sandy beach, a fine place for kids to play, makes for comfortable sunbathing. Swimming is allowed in the lake, but as an alternative during summer a big lakeside pool is open six days a week *(closed Mon.).*

Bring your walking shoes. The park is bordered on three sides by water—by the lake, Bayou Cane, and Bayou Castine—a mix of wetlands, mixed hardwood forest, sloughs, and open fields supporting an astonishing variety of trees and shrubs, and over 400 different species of animals and birds. (If you're a birder, check at the park office for the "Fontainebleau Birding Guide," and ask about ranger-guided walks.)

An old railroad bed through the park is part of the **Tammany Trace,** a pathway for bicycling, strolling, horseback riding, and in-line skating that will eventually run 31 miles from Covington to Slidell (see p. 204). A separate nature trail has interpretive signs offering ecological insights.

This is a favorite getaway for New Orleanians who enjoy sleeping under the stars. You have a choice of improved sites—complete with barbecue grills and picnic tables—or unimproved sites, for those who prefer to go on wilderness-style outings. ■

Mandeville
Map 171 B3

Mandeville City Hall
www.ci.mandeville.la.us
3101 E. Causeway Approach
985-626-3144
Closed Sat.–Sun.

Fontainebleau State Park
Map 171 C3
2 miles SE of Mandeville on US 90
985-624-4443 or 888-677-3668 or 877-226-7652 (campsite reservations)
$

Schooners like these at Madisonville's Wooden Boat Festival once supplied New Orleans with much of its food and lumber.

Madisonville

A LATE 19TH-CENTURY TIMBER BOOM BROUGHT PROSPERity to this riverside hamlet, founding a tradition of relaxed living today reflected in its pleasure boat marinas, vacation houses, and dockside restaurants. Situated on the Tchefuncte River, Madisonville is a frequent choice among New Orleanians hankering for a weekend drive and a good meal in a small-town setting.

Madisonville
Map 171 B3

Madisonville Town Hall
403 St. Francis St.
985-845-7311
Closed Sat.–Sun.

Lake Pontchartrain Basin Maritime Museum
985-845-9200

The town's tree-cutting days are long gone, as is its shipbuilding industry, which peaked during World War I. Tourism has taken their place. This evolution is traced at the **Madisonville Museum** *(201 Cedar St. 985-845-2100 or 985-845-7311. Closed Sat.–Sun.)*. Old photographs, maps, antiques, and vintage miscellany recount the Civil War era here, when Federal troops smashed into town. Other exhibits survey regional wildlife and display local archaeological finds.

Park downtown where La. 22 crosses Water St., which parallels the Tchefuncte, and explore the oak-shaded, four-block riverfront. Here you'll find appealing shops and eateries—**Morton's Seafood** *(702 Water St. 985-845-4970)*, a longtime favorite, serves local catches.

On the last weekend in September, 30,000 people crowd this part of the riverbank for the Wooden Boat Festival, where about 100 vintage watercraft are displayed. The event raises funds for the new **Lake Pontchartrain Basin Maritime Museum** *(985-845-9200)*. Its interactive multimedia exhibits are designed to examine the immigration and maritime commerce that built Madisonville and spurred New Orleans's growth.

For a scenic and historic lake view, drive south on La. 1077 about 1.5 miles to the Tchefuncte's mouth. On the west bank, accessible only by boat, stands the 30-foot-tall brick **Tchefuncte River Lighthouse,** built in 1868. ■

Fairview-Riverside State Park

WHEN YOU SEE THE OLD HOUSE FRANK OTIS BOUGHT AND restored for his summer home in the 1930s, the possibilities of north shore life become apparent. Built in the 1880s as part of a lumber camp, it faces the quiet stream of the Tchefuncte, where logs, lashed together to form temporary barges, were once floated down to the lake.

Fairview-Riverside State Park

Map 171 B3

119 Fairview Dr.

985-845-3318 or 888-677-3247); 877-226-7652 (campsite reservations)

$

Otis, a mahogany importer and New Orleans native, called it Fairview–Riverside, a name true on both counts. Set back among spreading oaks, its galleries screened for long evenings of conversation after dark, it is the epitome of a Southern house—gracious, inviting, and designed for conviviality.

The house and 99 acres of land that are now enclosed by the park were Frank Otis's legacy to the state of Louisiana in 1962, following his death. Recently refurbished, his manse is now open for tours. That alone makes the three-minute drive from Madisonville worthwhile. But when you see the park, with its picnic tables in the cool shade of huge oaks, you will probably want to linger a while.

Anglers cast in the crystalline waters of the Tchefuncte for bass, white perch, bluegill, and bream. Where the river meets Lake Pontchartrain, others vie for channel catfish, redfish, and speckled trout. The stream's clarity and the absence of underwater obstructions make it one of the most popular waterskiing areas on the lake.

This all grew out of the New Orleans tradition of crossing the lake for bucolic retreats—at your country place, if you were prosperous like Frank Otis, or more likely in a rented weekend tent cabin elsewhere along the shore. Camping is still popular today.

Take time for a stroll along the Tchefuncte, one of Louisiana's prettiest rivers. It makes a sharp bend here, rounding the point of land beyond the travel-trailer camp—a lovely spot to spread out a picnic blanket, read a book, or watch the breeze stir the gray-green garlands of Spanish moss overhead. ■

A magnolia flower in Fairview-Riverside State Park. Louisiana's state flower since 1900, the magnolia survived a 1950 ouster attempt by the Louisiana Iris Society.

Covington artist Stephen Hasslock puts finishing touches on a pitcher.

Covington

THIS VERY HANDSOME LITTLE CITY OF 8,000, SITUATED 8 miles north of the causeway's landfall, is best known for a 28-square-block historic old town district adjoining the Bogue Falaya River. It has attracted a number of aesthetically minded residents, who account for its thriving arts community, the quality of its antique and collectible stores, galleries, restaurants, sidewalk cafés, and bookstores, and a busy civic schedule of public concerts and festivals.

Covington
Map 171 B4

St. Tammany Parish Tourist & Convention Commission
68099 La. 59
985-892-0520 or 800-634-9443

Event information
985-892-1873 (Covington Downtown Development Council)

Founded on the Fourth of July in 1813 by businessman John Wharton Collins, Covington was called Wharton until 1816. Then the state renamed it in honor of Leonard Covington, a general who won glory in the War of 1812. It has been the seat of government for St. Tammany Parish since circa 1820. Always esteemed as a vacation spot, after the causeway linked the north shore with New Orleans in 1956, it immediately became the city's most desirable bedroom community as well.

Take a stroll around the oak-shaded old town, where many buildings date from the 1880s when Covington was an agricultural shipping center for cotton, sweet potatoes, and sand. Nowadays you will find delicacies such as strawberries and pecans at the **Farmer's Market,** held Wednesdays and Saturdays on the lawn of City Hall at 609 N. Columbia Street.

The **Old Railroad Depot** at 503 N. New Hampshire Street is a relic of flush times that ensued after the East Louisiana Railroad connected Covington with the rest of the state in 1888.

Long-time residents cherish memories of the former **Champagne Grocery** at 427 N. Columbia, founded in 1919 and in business for more than 60 years. Have a look at the century-old

Seiler Building at 434 N. Columbia, once the address of a lavish oyster bar, whose patrons lined up in front of carved mahogany bars. In 1999 this restoration, along with the conversion of the old hotel building at 407 N. Columbia into stylish offices, won Covington an annual Louisiana Main Street Award in a competition with 29 other cities.

Representing the prosperity of former times is the **Covington Bank & Trust Building** *(308 N. Columbia St.),* the city's oldest mercantile edifice. One of the oldest businesses hereabouts is the **H.J. Smith and Sons Hardware and Museum** *(308 N. Columbia St. 985-892-0460),* built in the mid-1870s. Its exhibits display artifacts of Covington history. The **Patecek Building** at 301 Columbia Street was built after what is locally remembered as the Great Fire of 1898. It is a splendid example of Victorian era mercantile construction.

The **Southern Hotel Building** at 428 E. Boston Street was completed about 1907 and is now the St. Tammany Court House annex. Nearby, peek into **Hasslock Studios** *(334 N. Vermont St. 985-893-6648),* where Stephen Hasslock and his crew create colorful, meticulously painted ceramic dinnerware.

Where Columbia Street meets the river you'll find the **Columbia Street Landing,** once crowded with schooners and steamers. The dock hosts the free evening Sunset at Landing Concert Series, which occasionally features well-known musical stars.

One of downtown's prettiest structures is **Christ Episcopal Chapel** at 120 N. New Hampshire Street, dedicated in 1846. You can get a broad sampling of local artists' work by visiting the **St. Tammany Art Association Art House** at 320 Columbia Street *(985-892-8650).* Exhibits, changed monthly, display up to 100 works.

At the end of New Hampshire, on the Bogue Falaya River, is **Bogue Falaya Park,** the city's main venue for outdoor arts and crafts shows, festivals, and concerts. ■

Signs direct shoppers in old Covington.

Abita Springs

A WELL-PRESERVED, FORESTED 19th-CENTURY RESORT town—it has but one traffic light—Abita Springs is once again a favorite escape for New Orleanians.

The **UCM Museum** (Unusual Collections and Miniatures, pronounced "you-see-'em") features weird, witty, contemporary folk art. It occupies an old-time service station, an early-century Louisiana Creole cottage, a rustic exhibition hall, and the House of Shards—a cottage fancifully decorated with thousands of pieces of tiles, pottery shards, mirrors, and glass.

The popular **Abita Brewery** has been producing pilsners and ales since 1986 and offers interesting tours. Its restaurant on the town square, the **Abita Brew Pub** *(72011 Holly St. 985-892-5837)* is a casual eatery serving its microbrews and good lunches and dinners daily. Humble though Abita Springs is, its new, highly praised restaurant **Artesia** *(21516 La. 36. 985-892-1662;* see p. 252), which serves fine French cuisine in a beautiful two-story Creole home dating from the 1880s, is not. ■

Abita Springs
Map 171 B4

St. Tammany Parish Tourist & Convention Commission
See p. 202

UCM Museum
22275 La. 36
985-892-2624
$

Abita Brewery
21084 La. 36
Covington
985-893-3143
Closed Mon.–Fri.

Yesterday's toys are today's collectibles in the Louisiana Toy Train Museum.

More places to visit in Greater New Orleans

LOUISIANA TOY TRAIN MUSEUM

Belle Grove Plantation owner Philip Minor Kenner (1808–1862) had the advantage of farming on Kenner's relatively high ground, which kept his fields dry when the Mississippi flooded surrounding lowlands. He knew which tracts escaped the deluges, and when surveyors came looking for a new route between New Orleans and Jackson, Mississippi, Kenner pointed out the advantages of his property and sold a right-of-way to the railroad.

That link, and the community's dominance of southern Louisiana produce markets for the ensuing century, made the little rural community particularly dependent upon rail commerce, and the citizenry more fond of it than those in other towns. A charming little vestige of Kenner's past is this little museum, a part of the Rivertown Museums (see pp. 173–175). The focal point is, of course, toy trains. There are exhibits in which miniature depots are lighted, flag stops work, and switches divert model trains; some of them permit kids to try their hands at running a railroad. A nod to contemporary electric toys is the red clay track outdoors, where kids can operate radio-controlled model cars.

519 Williams Blvd., Kenner (purchase tickets at 415 Williams Blvd.) 504-468-7231 Closed Sun.–Mon. $

SAINTS HALL OF FAME

If you appreciate professional football in general, and the New Orleans Saints in particular, this little collection, part of Kenner's Rivertown Museums (see pp. 173–175), will hold interest. New Orleanians are fierce fans; hence this place, which displays memorabilia—jerseys, sports page clippings, souvenir tickets, autographed footballs, busts of team heroes and Hall of Famers, photographs—and big-screen videos of past seasons' glories. Most interesting, probably, is an actual professional locker room (without players scuffing around in towels and shower shoes). A field goal-kicking machine lets you try your skill at what is often one of the game's most excruciatingly high-pressure moments.

415 Williams Blvd., Kenner 504-468-7231 Closed Sun.–Mon. $

TAMMANY TRACE

This walking, jogging, in-line skating, and biking trail makes a 31-mile journey along what was once the route of the Illinois Central Railroad from Covington to Slidell, passing through Abita Springs, Mandeville, and Lacombe. A beautiful corridor through dense forest and marshland, every mile brings a bridge, mostly old timber spans. No motorized vehicles are allowed; a horse trail *(horse rentals weekends only)* parallels the trace.

The trace runs along the north shore of Lake Pontchartrain from La. 21 in Covington to Slidell, largest city in St. Tammany Parish. An information center occupies a caboose at the Tammany Trace Trailhead between Abita Springs and Mandeville. Rangers patrol the trail during open hours to provide assistance.

800-43-TRACE ■

From early on New Orleans was privileged, supplied by upriver plantations and defended by outlying fortresses. It was, and to some extent remains, an island of Creole culture amid the rural Cajun empire; it is second only to Baton Rouge as the region's political center.

Excursions

A Grand Isle beach house

Excursions

NEW ORLEANS'S PECULIAR SOPHISTICATION—ITS MIXED HERITAGE, antique architecture, international commerce, elaborate social traditions, ever evolving music and cuisine, and Southern-style urbanity—is all the more remarkable when viewed in the larger geographical context of southeastern Louisiana. Here, the landscape of dark bayous and steamy swamps seems as wild as it must have been when the first Europeans ventured into it, and in any case utterly unlike the old city at its center.

You will need an automobile, because public transport outside New Orleans is virtually nonexistent. But all these excursions are easily done—as long as you have a detailed road map. Each trip requires at least a day; taking two eliminates the need to rush.

UPRIVER PLANTATIONS

The great rural mansions that dot the Mississippi River between New Orleans and Baton Rouge (see pp. 208–211) evoke the culture that built New Orleans. They are at once fascinating and sad, captivating historical relics no longer surrounded by quiet fields. Development—sometimes industrial—and levees ensure their survival but block the view from their porches. Although each plantation has a unique aspect, all relied upon slave labor, an inequity so profoundly wrong yet so integral to these places' existence and

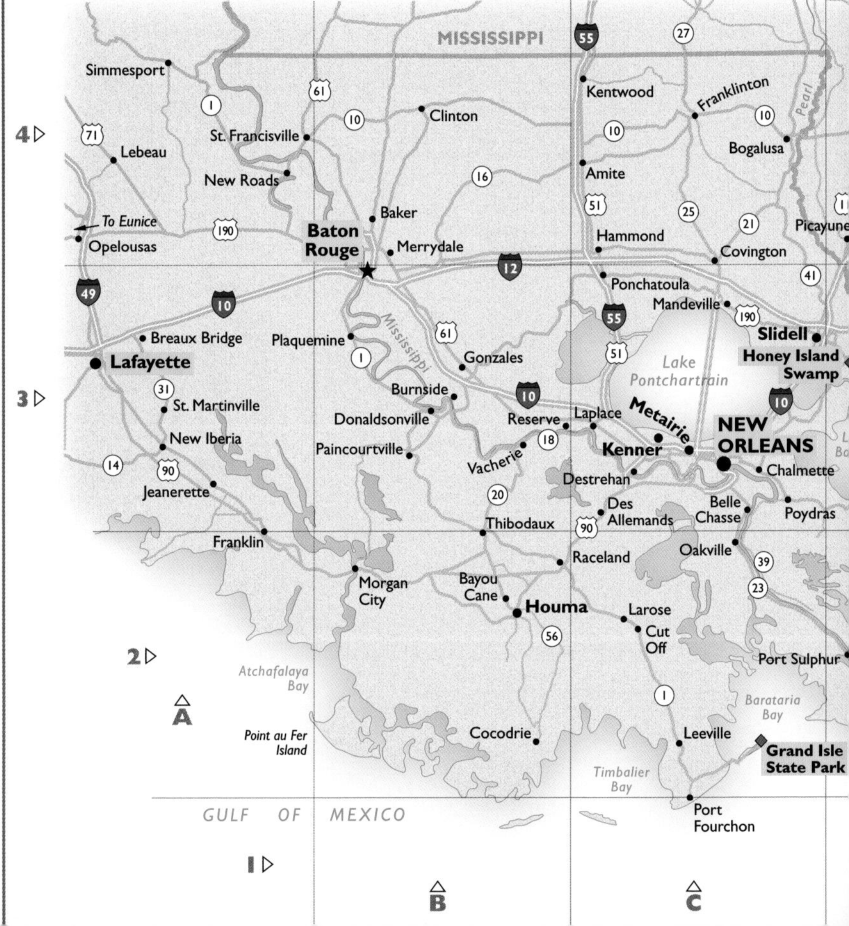

prosperity that they cannot be visited without a constant awareness of it. Implicit in their auras of privilege is the great catastrophe of the Civil War, an event that haunts the plantations like a ghost.

BATON ROUGE

The capital of the rest of Louisiana, New Orleans's partner in Mississippi River commerce anchors the state's famously flamboyant political pageant some 75 miles to the northwest. Baton Rouge (see pp. 212–217) could not be more unlike New Orleans. It seems like an older cousin who opted for a career in politics and commerce and left the Bohemian life to its downriver relative.

THE GULF

Once the first line of defense against foreign intrigues up the Mississippi, battered barrier islands along the Gulf and the shoreline they protect are now under attack by the sea itself. Northeast of New Orleans across the Mississippi state line is the westernmost reach of the Gulf Islands National Seashore (see pp. 218–219), featuring white-sand beaches, green waters, salt marshes, bayous, and the ruins of a fort.

SWAMPLANDS

Wrapped in misunderstanding and myth, the wetlands surrounding New Orleans are natural labyrinths. To become lost in them is so easy it is almost imperative that first-time visitors enter them in the company of a knowledgeable guide. Comparisons to Eden are inevitable, and appropriate too, for these are environments that resist cultivation and development, and they can only be filled, not "improved." One of the best destinations within easy reach of New Orleans is the Honey Island Swamp (see p. 220).

THE DELTA

This great alluvial plain is a rural kingdom unlike any other in America. Scruffy, unaffected, and hardworking, its villages are welcoming places—many founded two centuries ago by Cajuns and Canary Islanders, whose cultures still thrive. Stock up your car with water, tune your radio to local stations (the music will be twangy and countrified), and don't let hand-lettered signs put you off from sampling the local fare (seafood, mostly). The wild lands that flank the roads are vast, great wetlands swarming with migratory waterfowl, which depend on outlying places like this for safe nesting. Among the most intriguing places you'll visit is Fort Jackson (see p. 221). Another is Grand Isle, reached by a scenic drive through the Cajun heart of the delta (see pp. 222–225).

CAJUN COUNTRY

West of New Orleans lies the heart of Acadia—Louisiana's rural French-Canadian region—settled in the 1700s and still hallmarked by the language, culture, and cuisine of its resourceful émigrés. Acadia's capital is Lafayette (see pp. 228–230), where monuments and festivals celebrate Cajun life. Small-town renditions of it play in nearby communities like Eunice, St. Martinville, and Breaux Bridge. ■

Great River Road plantations

Destrehan Plantation

www.destrehanplantation.org

13034 River Rd., Destrehan

985-764-9315

$$

RELICS OF A VANISHED ERA, THESE GREAT ESTATES OF SELF-styled aristocrats were worlds unto themselves: Privileges in these rural fiefdoms included the buying and selling of people. Though fatally flawed and historically doomed, the genteel way of life here remains the enduring symbol of the antebellum South.

In essence private colonies set up for agricultural enterprise, the plantations were generally complexes of outbuildings resembling small villages. Typically there were stables, dairy barns, workshops, blacksmithies, slaves' cabins, storage sheds, and general stores. Not quite self-sufficient, the plantations relied upon Mississippi River traffic to bring them what they could not produce, and to carry away their products: cotton and rice, hemp, indigo, tobacco, sorghum, corn, peanuts, potatoes, and sugar. Primitive roads in horseback days meant isolation; when guests came, they tended to stay for extended periods.

Destrehan's original thin French Creole-style wooden columns were replaced in 1840 with these of plastered brick.

Some of the most beautiful, most historic, and best preserved plantations in Louisiana lie in the Mississippi bottomlands between New Orleans and Baton Rouge, along what is called the Great River Road. Signed with a distinctive pilot-wheel icon, the road is actually two separate routes, one on each side of the Mississippi and linked by bridges, permitting motorists to visit nearly all of these grand old estates with a minimum of backtracking.

DESTREHAN PLANTATION

The plantation house closest to New Orleans (25 miles), Destrehan is the oldest surviving in the lower Mississippi Valley. Originally a French colonial completed in 1787—its two stories and double galleries reflect a style common then in the West Indies—it was remodeled in 1840 along Greek Revival lines. Credit its longevity to the hand-hewn cypress wood used in its construction and to its insulation, a mixture of Spanish moss and horsehair known as *boursillage.* What makes the history of this plantation unusual is that the house was built by Charles Pacquet, a free man of color. Its interior is simply furnished with period pieces.

ORMOND PLANTATION

A mile west of Destrehan, Ormond traces back to a 1790 land grant awarded by the Spanish Governor

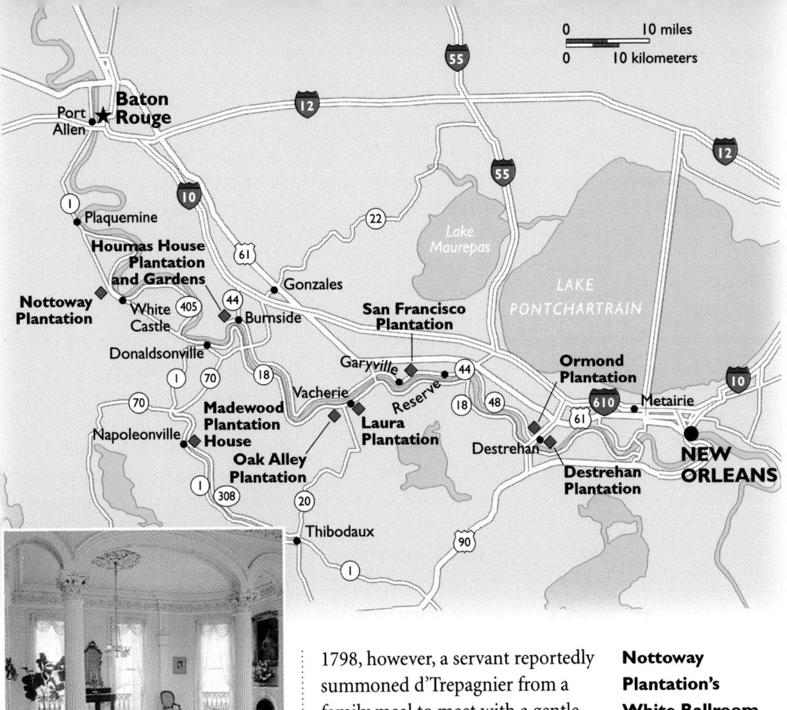

Nottoway Plantation's White Ballroom

of Louisiana to Pierre d'Trepagnier, who distinguished himself while fighting against the British during the American Revolution. He established himself here and grew indigo and then sugarcane. This is a beautiful "Louisiana Colonial" that, like Destrehan, was modeled after sugar plantations of the West Indies. Ormond was meant to last, its builders using massive cypress studs filled in with bricks—the *briquettes-entre-poteaux* or "bricks-between-posts" style seen in old New Orleans.

The d'Trepagniers were well connected socially, frequently entertaining French and Spanish notables in their lovely home. In 1798, however, a servant reportedly summoned d'Trepagnier from a family meal to meet with a gentleman wearing the uniform of a Spanish official. The planter left with the visitor and never came back. No trace of him was ever found, but ghost stories hint of his return to Ormond.

Apparitions aside, this is a pleasant place to explore. The view from the second-floor gallery is nothing less than palatial, the tea room is charmingly formal, and the gun room, with its collection of bottles and pictures of past owners, is personal and appealing. Three rooms, all furnished with antiques, are available for overnight guests (see p. 255).

SAN FRANCISCO PLANTATION

One of the most unusual great houses along the Mississippi, this colorful plantation was built in 1856 by Edmond Bozonier Marmillion. It has been carefully restored to historical accuracy by its former owner, Marathon Oil Company (which operates the nearby refinery). San Francisco's

Ormond Plantation
www.plantation.com
✉ 13786 River Rd., Destrehan
☎ 985-764-8544
$ $$

San Francisco Plantation
www.sanfranciscoplantation.org
✉ On River Rd. (La. 44), Reserve
☎ 985-535-2341 or 888-322-1756
$ $$

Laura Plantation
www.lauraplantation.com
2247 La. 18, Vacherie
225-265-7690
$$

Oak Alley Plantation
www.oakalleyplantation.com
3645 La. 18, Vacherie
225-265-2151 or 800-44ALLEY
$$

unique blend of Victorian, classical, and Gothic architecture reminds some visitors of a Mississippi riverboat; in fact, New Orleans novelist Frances Parkinson Keyes penned a family saga here entitled *Steamboat Gothic.* Pay particular attention to the ceiling frescoes and to the faux marbling over cypress that decorates the woodwork and fireplace mantels throughout the house.

LAURA PLANTATION

Farther west on the River Road, cross over the Mississippi via Veteran's Memorial Bridge. Turn right on La. 18 and in 4 miles look for this Creole confection. It was built in 1805 and owned for some 190 years by two different Creole families. Among the dozen historic buildings here are two manor houses, Creole cottages, barns, and four slave cabins.

For four generations Laura Plantation was managed by women. The slaves here were Senegalese, whose folklore included the *Brer Rabbit* stories. Tales told by the slaves were translated from French in 1896 by writer Joel Chandler Harris, and for decades beloved by Southern kids.

The last woman owner was Laura Lecoul Gore, whose memoirs describing the lives of 19th-century Creole women, slaves, and children provide many of the interesting details recounted in the guided tours. Laura herself, however, grew weary of running such a huge agricultural operation; she sold the plantation in 1891 to marry and move north to St. Louis.

OAK ALLEY PLANTATION

Not far upriver from Laura Plantation on La. 18 sprawls this Greek Revival masterpiece. Ringed with 28 columns, Oak Alley is probably the most photographed of all Southern plantations. It was the home of a wealthy Creole

Oak Alley's sheltering trees once framed a Mississippi River view, now blocked by a levee.

sugar planter named Jacques Telesphore Roman, who purchased the plantation in 1836 as a summer house for his family. Roman's wife, Clina Pilie, christened the plantation house Bon Sejour—"pleasant stay." Passing travelers, noting its grand avenue of live oaks (now thought to be nearly 300 years old), took to calling it Oak Alley.

You can leisurely explore the grounds on your own using a map provided when you purchase your ticket, but do take the guided house tour, which lasts about 35 to 40 minutes and is conducted by docents wearing period clothing. An onsite restaurant, housed in a 19th-century cottage not far from the mansion, offers Cajun and Creole fare for breakfast and lunch. Try a beignet for breakfast and later indulge in some red beans and rice, jambalaya, or maybe even some fried alligator nuggets, followed by a slice of pecan or buttermilk pie.

Overnight guests stay in one of the plantation's comfortable 20th-century cottages (see p. 257). Each provides what management calls "a respite from those noisy three T's of the modern world: telephones, telephones, and traffic."

HOUMAS HOUSE

Just upriver is Houmas House, so handsome it has appeared in motion pictures (the most notable being *Hush, Hush, Sweet Charlotte* starring Bette Davis). It is actually two houses, one built in the 1790s and connected by a carriageway to the main house, a columned white Greek Revival edifice dating from 1840 and filled with period antiques. Houmas has a freestanding spiral staircase and beautiful landscaping.

MADEWOOD PLANTATION HOUSE

Luxurious when built in 1846 for Col. Thomas Push, and just as luxurious today, 21-room Madewood Plantation *(4250 La. 308, Napoleonville. 985-369-7151 or 800-375-7151. $$)* resembles a Greek temple. Tall ceilings with ornate medallions and chandeliers, and cornices with elaborate dentils are some of the elegant finishing touches inside. Overnight guests stay in one of the main house's sumptuous bedrooms (see p. 257).

NOTTOWAY PLANTATION

No plantation in the region can rival the architecture of this 64-room palace *(30970 La. 504, White Castle. 225-545-2730. $$)* for sheer grandeur. Built in 1859 and decorated with 22 columns, it has a lavish interior made bright by 200 windows. The original slate roof is still in place, and original crystal chandeliers still glitter in the ballroom. B&B accommodations include 13 guest rooms and a first-class restaurant (see p. 257). ■

Houmas House Plantation & Gardens

www.houmashouse.com

40136 La. 942, Burnside

225-473-7841, 225-473-9830, or 888-323-8314

$$

Baton Rouge

Baton Rouge
Map 206–207 B3

Baton Rouge Area Convention & Visitors Bureau
www.batonrougetour.com
730 North Blvd.
225-383-1825

MORE THAN 228,000 PEOPLE LIVE IN LOUISIANA'S CAPITAL city, 80 miles northwest of New Orleans. It has its superlatives: America's fourth largest port city; home to Louisiana State University and Southern University, the latter the nation's largest historically African-American university. But its citizens prefer to speak of things that make Baton Rouge so hospitable: It has clean, well-lighted streets, many attractions and historic sites, convenient parking, and first-class restaurants featuring French, Cajun, Creole, and traditional Southern cuisine.

State Capitol Welcome Center
At the Capitol, State Capitol Dr. at 3rd St.
225-342-7317

A statue of politician Huey Long, Jr., marks his grave in front of the Capitol he built.

There have been attempts to change the city's name, but given the story of how it was acquired, replacing it would seem a shame. On March 17, 1699, a French expedition led by Pierre Le Moyne, whose title was Sieur d'Iberville, got its first glimpse of Baton Rouge's bluffs and landed by a small river flowing into the Mississippi. The stream separated the hunting grounds of the Bayagoula from the Houma Indians, who lived on the bluffs above. Marking the boundary was a 30-foot-tall pole to which were attached the heads of fish and bears, sacrifices dripping with blood, put there by the tribes. The sight of the "red stick"—*baton rouge*—gave Le Moyne his name for this place.

Arriving from New Orleans via I-10, don't cross over the Mississippi; instead, bear right as you approach the business district and Metro Airport exit, and take I-110 north. About a mile beyond the I-10/I-110 split, take the Capitol Access Road exit, which deposits you near Baton Rouge's towering **State Capitol Building**—a good place to begin your tour of the city.

Park your car in the lot in front of the Capitol, and walk across the 27 acres of landscaped grounds to the 34-story, 450-foot-high limestone-and-marble building, constructed in 1932–33. The 48 broad granite steps you'll mount as you approach the entrance were quarried in Minnesota, one for each of the states in the Union then; at the top, two additional steps have been added to represent Alaska and Hawaii. The building's architectural style is art deco, and most people consider it Gov. Huey Long, Jr.'s monument to himself. It was built during Long's brief but unparalleled choke hold on state politics, an era that still provokes heated debate among both historians and

the general public. Long was criticized for spending five million Depression-era dollars to build the Capitol. But in fairness to him, the use of heroic architecture in public buildings was a federal policy at the time, the notion being that heroic dimensions instilled confidence among Americans, whose faith in government was badly shaken by the nation's economic malaise. And the fact is, this is one of America's most distinctive and impressive state capitols, as well as the tallest. The House and Senate chambers inside are open for viewing, and the finest overlook of Baton Rouge and the Mississippi is from the 27th-floor **Observation Tower,** which takes in a 7-mile stretch of the river.

Long's bombastic oratory and

Huey Pierce Long, Jr.

Considered a foe of corporate interests as an attorney and state official, while governor from 1928 to 1932 Long championed reforms that benefited the poor rural folk, who became his most ardent supporters. He gave books to schoolchildren, built roads and bridges, and repealed the poll tax. Critics denounced his dictatorial rule and powerful political machine. As a U.S. senator he won a national following with his radical Share Our Wealth scheme—taxing the wealthy to provide every family with a $5,000 homestead allowance. ■

anti-rich economic schemes appealed to many in those desperate times and won him a national following after his election to the U.S. Senate in 1932. By 1935 he was powerful enough to be taken seriously as a third-party presidential candidate. That year, however, on September 8, on the first floor of the State Capitol, he was mortally wounded in a still-mysterious shooting some blame on a lone assassin, a New Orleans physician who was immediately shot to death by Long's retinue of bodyguards. Others believe the bodyguards engineered the assassination and that the hapless doctor was perhaps a dupe. In any event, a display case filled with historical information stands on the spot. Long is buried in front of the building beneath a 12-foot bronze statue of himself.

It is a short walk from the Capitol to the imposing **Old Arsenal Powder Magazine** *(State Capitol Grounds, State Capitol Dr. at Capitol Access Rd. 225-342-0401),* which dates from the 1830s and now is filled with exhibits that focus on the city's historically strategic high ground above the Mississippi.

Opposite the Capitol across Third Street is another historical archive, the **Pentagon Barracks** *(225-387-2464),* which were constructed in 1819–1823 to quarter Federal troops posted here to defend the city. Among ranking officers and officials who visited here at one time or another were future Presidents Abraham Lincoln, Zachary Taylor, and Ulysses S. Grant; future Confederate leaders Robert E. Lee and Jefferson Davis; and the Union Army's blond-tressed George Custer, whose flamboyant career would end a few years later at the Battle of the Little Big Horn in Montana. The military base to which these facilities belonged was Fort New Richmond, the site of the only Revolutionary War battle to occur outside of the original 13 Colonies.

Huey Long made his reputation as an orator in the **Old State Capitol** *(100 North Blvd. at River Rd.S. 225-342-0500. Closed Mon.; $),* a gorgeous, castlelike structure topping a knoll above the Mississippi. Completed in 1849, it served as Louisiana's seat of government until 1862, when Union forces seized and burned it. (Look in the Senate Chamber for a portion of the wall left unrepaired.) The Confederate legislature exiled itself to Opelousas, then Shreveport. In 1879 Baton Rouge citizens raised money to repair the Capitol, and a state constitutional convention made the city Louisiana's permanent seat of government. In 1882 the lawmakers moved back into the building, meeting here until Huey Long cut the ribbon for his new capitol in 1932. The old statehouse has been restored to its original grandeur. It serves as Louisiana's film and video archive and features interactive multimedia exhibits. One in particular is extremely well done: "Louisiana: The Story is Here" surveys the state's tumultuous political and social sagas. The "Huey Long Assassination" exhibit is also intriguing, with film clips, old radio reports, and musical recordings that conjure up the sound and fury of Louisiana's unique public pageant.

Even these high-tech exhibits, however, cannot convey local political history with the peculiar intimacy achieved by the display of Huey Long's red silk robe and other personal items at the **Old Governor's Mansion** *(502 North Blvd. 225-387-2464. Tours Tues.–Fri.; $).* Long built this grand Georgian manse in 1930 and was

Opposite: Huey Long, Jr., climbed these 150-year-old steps in the Old State Capitol to political power and then ordered the building's replacement.

The Louisiana Naval War Memorial Museum displays a World War II-era P-40E Warhawk.

Louisiana State University Rural Life Museum
rurallife.lsu.edu
✉ 4600 Essen Ln., off I-10
☎ 225-765-2437
$ $

the first of nine governors to reside here. Recently retired, it was replaced by a new residence for the state's chief official located nearby; the old building now serves as home to the Foundation of Historical Louisiana.

It's a bit of a walk downriver to the **Louisiana Naval War Memorial** *(305 River Rd. S. at the base of Government St. www.usskidd.com. 225-342-1942. $$)*. The premier attraction is the World War II Fletcher Class Destroyer U.S.S. *Kidd*, rated by naval historians as one of the best preserved warships of that era. The museum is a memorial to men and women killed in action, in particular those from Louisiana, and its model ship collection is the South's biggest. There is a restored P-40E Warhawk and a carrier-based A-7E Corsair jet fighter from the Vietnam era. Be sure to find the re-creation of a gun deck aboard the U.S.S. *Constitution*—the famed frigate from the War of 1812.

The nearby **Louisiana Arts & Science Center** *(100 River Rd. S. 225-344-5272. Closed Mon.; $)* occupies a reconstructed train station and mounts changing art exhibitions. Permanent exhibits include a vintage five-car railroad train, an Egyptian tomb display with mummies, and two hands-on areas for children—one called the "Discovery Depot" and another, the "Science Station."

A short walk away, adjacent to the Centroplex at River Road, is Baton Rouge's main tourist dock, the **Riverfront Landing Facility.** This is a fine place to watch the coming and going of passenger-carrying paddle wheelers, including the oft-photographed *Samuel Clemens* and the former *Baton Rouge Belle,* now occupied by the Argosy Casino.

LOUISIANA STATE UNIVERSITY RURAL LIFE MUSEUM

Well worth the drive from downtown is this remarkable place dedicated to depicting the South's agrarian world in the 1700s and 1800s. The outdoor complex preserves a fascinating collection of vintage buildings, many moved

here from within and outside the state. Others are historically accurate re-creations, and all are furnished as they would have been in their respective high periods. Among the structures are an overseer's house, a blacksmith shop, an open kettle sugar mill, and a plantation commissary and church. While you're here, visit the 25-acre **Windrush Gardens,** located beside the overseer's house. Classical statuary fills the semiformal garden, which features an old-fashioned citrus greenhouse. The garden honors the late Steele Burden, considered one of America's outstanding landscape architects.

LOUISIANA STATE UNIVERSITY

If time permits, from downtown take Highland Road downriver to the beautifully landscaped, 2,000-acre campus of Louisiana State University. Overlooking the Mississippi and shaded by hundreds of live oaks, this is Louisiana's flagship educational institution, a sprawling community of 31,000 students and some 3,000 faculty and staff. LSU is a leader in agricultural research, has a nationally recognized interior design program, and is widely known as the publisher of *The Southern Review,* one of the English-speaking world's most highly regarded literary journals. The **LSU Museum of Art** *(225-578-4003),* located in the 175-foot-high Memorial Tower on Memorial Drive, permanently exhibits original 17th- through mid-19th-century period rooms from England and America, New Orleans-wrought silver, Newcomb College crafts, and more.

Four and a half miles south of LSU via Highland Road is the **Hilltop Arboretum** *(11855 Highland Rd. 225-767-6916. Guided tours),* a 14-acre living museum of Louisiana plants, including century-old oaks spreading over winding paths. Cross the old footbridge over the ravine to reach the Cathedral, a green canopy of trees creating a softly lighted shelter. If there is a breeze, the bamboo grove will rustle and creak. Come autumn, wildflowers bloom in the tallgrass meadow. ■

An old-fashioned Cajun swamp boat takes shape at the Louisiana State University Rural Life Museum.

LSU Visitor Information Center

www.lsu.edu

✉ Highland Rd. & Dalrymple Dr.

☎ 225-578-5030

Note: Obtain directions, a free campus map, & a free parking permit at the information center.

Mississippi's coast draws the beach-minded from Louisiana, where sandy shores are few.

Gulf Islands National Seashore

LOUISIANIANS JOKE THAT THE STATE'S FINEST OCEAN beaches are in Mississippi. They're speaking of Mississippi's contribution to the Gulf Islands National Seashore, a 150-mile-long system of barrier islands running from Gulfport, Mississippi, to the Florida Panhandle.

Gulf Islands National Seashore
Map 206–207 E3

Davis Bayou area
www.nps.gov/guis
3500 Park Rd., Ocean Springs, MS
228-875-0821

It takes some doing to reach the isles off Gulfport—an 85-mile drive from New Orleans via I-10 and US 90, then an hour-long trip on a ferry. Your reward, however, includes the finest beaches on the Mississippi Gulf coast, wild barrier islands offering tranquil solitude, warm ocean swimming and bodysurfing in pellucid water, and an old coastal fortress predating the Civil War.

Mississippi's Gulf Islands National Seashore has two separate units—one on the mainland and the other offshore. The mainland facility, the **Davis Bayou area** in Ocean Springs, is a shoreline park surrounding the bayou's mouth, which opens out onto the Gulf. This is a multipurpose recreational green popular with families, with a visitor center, shade trees, trails for walking and bicycling, a swimming beach, and a boat-launching ramp. If you just want to relax for a spell beside the water, claim one of the picnic tables, which have fire grills for cookouts.

Four barrier islands—**West** and **East Ship, Horn,** and **Petit Bois—**compose the offshore unit of the seashore's Mississippi component. West Ship is the seashore's only island with extensive visitor facilities—including shaded picnic areas, showers, Gulf beach snack bar, beach chair and umbrella rentals, and ferry service. Those seeking pristine wilderness, with beaches, lagoons, and maritime woodlands in a wholly natural state, should consider East Ship, Horn, or

Petit Bois. Primitive camping *(228-875-9057)*, permitted year-round on these three, is an unforgettable experience; charter boat services provide access. You will gaze up at pitch-black skies so filled with stars, meteor streaks, and speeding satellites that you will find it hard to close your eyes.

WEST SHIP ISLAND

When you troop down the gangway onto West Ship's pier, you will be greeted by the bulky Fort Massachusetts. You will also immediately see why this island is one of the South's favorite getaways. Nearly 4 miles long,West Ship is an arc of wind-sculptured dunes fringed with sea oats. Like other barrier islands, it was built up by wave action and anchored by vegetation. White-sand beaches divide the Mississippi Sound from the clear green waters of the Gulf of Mexico. In 1969, Hurricane Camille howled through here with 200-mile-an-hour winds pushing a 30-foot storm surge. When it was over, Ship Island had been split into 555-acre West Ship Island and 362-acre East Ship Island.

If you prefer less wind and calmer surf, unroll your beach blanket on West Ship's Mississippi Sound shore, where the ferry docks. Calm weather brings somnolence to both sides of the island, but typically the south-facing Gulf beach has stronger breezes and higher waves. To get to the less frequented Gulf side, take the wooden boardwalk from the ferry landing across the island, here one-third of a mile long. The planked path leads through a scruffy but delicate wild garden of wind-bent grasses and sea oats, which shouldn't be trod upon (They are what anchor the island's sand.)

Don't swim alone on any of the islands, especially on the Gulf side, and watch out for stinging Portuguese man-of-war jellyfish.

Visiting Fort Massachusetts

Burly and forbidding, the fort *(228-875-9057)* is remarkably well preserved—although its wooden outbuildings have long since disappeared. Its outer walls are up to eight feet thick, built to take punches. The high walls make for cool shade and a windbreak—an excellent picnic spot. In the courtyard-like interior, you can see the massive masonry arches required to support the colossal weight of solid steel guns.

You're free to explore the batteries on your own. There is interpretive signage; however a ranger-led tour is recommended for its historical and technical insights. A visitor center is located in the guard room. ■

West Ship Island
www.msshipisland.com

- Ferry from Gulfport Small Craft Harbor, at US 90 and US 49 in Gulfport, MS
- Departures March–Oct. at 9 a.m. & 12 p.m. (June–Aug. only), returning 2:30 p.m. & 5 p.m.
- 228-875-0821
- $$$ (for ferry)

Note: No reservations; tickets on sale one hour before sailing. No oversize coolers, no glass permitted on Ship Island; no pets.

Island history

Named in 1699 by French colonials impressed with its protected deep-water anchorage, Ship Island had a strategic importance that became apparent in the War of 1812, when 60 British ships carrying 10,000 troops rendezvoused offshore for the invasion of New Orleans. Construction on the fort began in 1859. During the Civil War federal engineers added 40 outbuildings to serve some 18,000 Union troops massed here for the push on New Orleans. Although the fort was also the headquarters of David Farragut's daring campaign to capture New Orleans, it went without a name until admiration for the widely reported exploits of the Union blockade ship *Massachusetts* inspired someone with the necessary authority to name it after the vessel. ■

Honey Island Swamp

AS SOUTHEASTERN LOUISIANA'S SWAMPLAND ACREAGE IS steadily lost to development, opportunities to see pristine examples of these environmentally essential wetlands diminish. Preservation efforts have recently focused on a tract lying 37 miles northeast of New Orleans across Lake Pontchartrain, on the West Pearl River. Honey Island Swamp encompasses nearly 250 square miles of a virtually primordial land, including an unusually complex ecosystem within the Nature Conservancy's 586-acre White Kitchen Marsh Preserve.

A diamondback water snake dwells in Honey Island Swamp. Up to four feet long, the nonpoisonous creatures feed on fish and frogs.

Honey Island Swamp

- Map 206–207 D3
- Across Lake Pontchartrain via I-10; where US 90 and US 190 meet, look for Nature Conservancy's dark green sign.
- 225-338-1040 (Nature Conservancy, Louisiana office, for preserve information, plus advice on special boat tours)

Named for a popular roadside inn that once stood nearby, **White Kitchen Marsh Preserve** is the most accessible corner of Honey Island Swamp. An elevated boardwalk extends out over the vast freshwater marsh, from which you can watch the goings-on of this mystical, sun-dappled place. A complex forest of bald cypress, water tupelo, swamp black gum, and black willow trees rings the marsh, with live oak and slash pine on higher ground. Like most protected wetlands, this is a fecund wildlife refuge considered to be one of Louisiana's premier bird-watching sites. It is a roosting ground for bird species including the American bald eagle—there are nests within sight of the observation platform—and also great blue herons, yellow-crowned night herons, white ibises, and great egrets. The swamp also teems with alligators, otters, and beavers, creatures that are not shy about approaching visitors peering down at them from the wooden walkway. More elusive are deer, bears, wolves, feral hogs, and minks. Regardless of whether or not you encounter the swamp's resident creatures, you will not soon forget the remarkable serenity that prevails in this watery wilderness.

The Conservancy does not permit boating or offer tours in the White Kitchen Marsh Preserve; however, several tour concessions run motorized, flat-bottomed boat trips through other portions of the swamp. Guides on Honey Island Swamp Tours *(504-242-5877 in New Orleans, 985-641-1769 in Slidell. www.honeyislandtours.com)*, provide narrations on the natural history and ecology of Louisiana swamps. Mr. Denny's Voyageur Tours *(985-643-4839)* offers canoe excursions on the Pearl River. ■

Spanish moss

The greenish tufts draping Honey Island Swamp's tree limbs are neither Spanish nor moss. *Tillandsia usneoides* is an epiphyte—a plant that uses other plants only for physical support. Unlike parasites, it does not feed on hosts; it absorbs nutrients and water from the air. French colonials dubbed it "Spanish beard"; in retaliation the Spanish called it "French hair." ■

A guard opens Fort Jackson, challenged but never conquered by Union forces.

Fort Jackson

TO CIVIL WAR BUFFS, FORT JACKSON IS A SACRED PLACE, for here is where a Union gambit succeeded in splitting the Confederacy by taking control of the Mississippi and capturing New Orleans. Construction of the riverside brick-and-concrete fortress, named for Andrew Jackson, took ten years, ending in 1832. A small museum has historical displays.

Fort Jackson, backed by its smaller companion across the river, Fort. St. Philip, seemed impregnable. Twenty-foot-thick walls ran between high bastions, creating a star-shaped pentagon surrounded by a moat. Dozens of cannon and huge arsenals of gunpowder and shot made it capable of punishing artillery volleys. But Union strategy required that the Mississippi be closed to Rebel ships; the forts had to be defeated somehow.

In April 1862 Adm. David G. Farragut arrived with the 18-ship West Gulf Blockading Squadron. After a week of artillery salvos failed to silence the forts' guns, Farragut camouflaged his ships with river mud and felled trees, and tried to sneak past both strongholds under cover of darkness. The camouflage confused Rebel gunners enough so that their barrages failed to halt Farragut and several of his fleet, which took possession of New Orleans on April 28; the rest of his fleet continued to battle the forts until after New Orleans fell; only then did the forts surrender.

Walk the perimeter of the fort, then ascend to the top open-air gun deck, where cannon would have aimed at the Mississippi. Explore the interior, where the practical requirements of military architecture do not diminish the gracefulness in the archways and vaulted ceilings. ■

Bird haven

The drive from New Orleans to Fort Jackson takes you into the heart of the Mississippi River Delta, one of the largest freshwater estuaries in the lower 48 states and a refuge for hundreds of thousands of wading birds, waterfowl, and shorebirds. So vital is it as a wintering ground for migratory birds that early in the 20th century the federal government designated the tip of the Mississippi's alluvial plain the Delta National Wildlife Refuge *(215 Offshore Shipyard Rd., Venice. 985-534-2235)*, a watery Eden accessible only by boat. ■

Fort Jackson

- Map 206–207 D2
- 56 miles S of Gretna via Herbert Harvey Dr., off La. 23
- 985-657-7083
- $ Donation

Mississippi River Delta drive

The Lower Mississippi Delta country includes some of the newest land in North America: The ground beneath New Orleans is only about 2,500 years old. But when you drive west and south from the city, from New Orleans to Grand Isle, you enter a region that looks older and, in fact, is geologically much older. Here is a plain laid down around an earlier channel of the Mississippi. For over 200 years this rugged land has belonged to Cajuns, renowned for their seafood and exuberant music. Passing through their little towns, this drive takes you to land's end at Port Fourchon, then east to the settlement of Grand Isle, the most popular barrier island off the Louisiana coast.

Beachcombers stroll at Grand Isle State Park, the island's best swimming and picnic area.

From New Orleans, take I-10 west to I-310, and follow it to US 90, exiting to the right toward Raceland. Proceed southwest through Paradis and Des Allemands to the Bayou Lafourche (lah-FOOSH) waterway. Cross the high bridge over the bayou, take the Lockport-Thibodaux exit, and head for the **Lafourche Parish Visitor Center** ❶ at US 90 and La. 1 *(4484 La. 1 in Raceland. 985-537-5800 or 877-537-5800)*. Here you can learn more about the bayou, ask about tours, and inquire about the best places to shop for crafts, souvenirs, and folk art. If you're a birdwatcher, be sure to ask about the Grand Isle Loop Birding Trail.

As you travel south on La. 1 from the visitor center, you pass through the towns of Mathews, Lockport, and Larose, humble communities with low skylines broken only by an occasional Catholic church steeple.

About 2 miles south of Larose, you cross the Intracoastal Waterway lift-span bridge. From this point the bayou begins to widen, with sugarcane fields giving way to seafood and oil enterprises. Only three netmakers still work in Lafourche Parish—look for their shops along the roadside in Cut Off, Galliano, and Golden Meadow. Peek in to watch men preparing nets for use on shrimp boats. Fishermen moor along the bayou, cleaning, repairing, and maintaining their vessels; feel free to stop and chat with them.

In **Cut Off,** on the right side of La. 1 before you reach W. 79th Street, watch for the 1893 **Curole House.** The raised Creole cottage is the oldest surviving house south of the Intracoastal Waterway, having survived the hurricane of 1893.

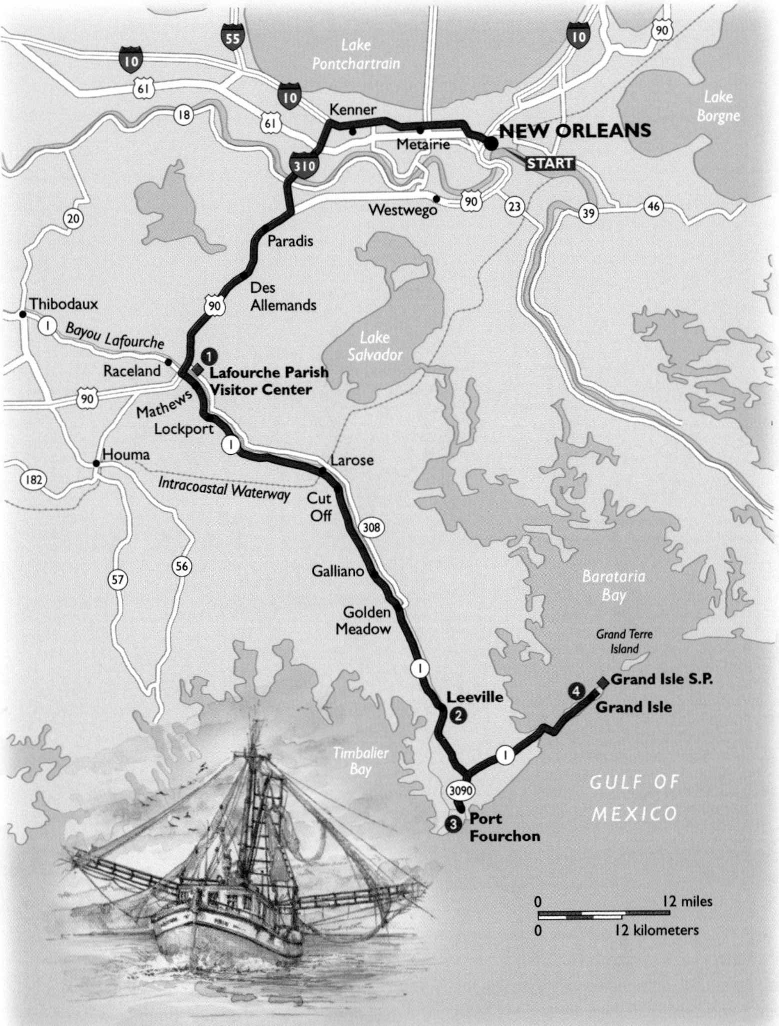

In the vicinity of **Golden Meadow,** admire the yard statues that mark the locals' devotion to Catholicism. If you're hungry, **Randolph's Restaurant** *(806 S. Bayou Dr. 985-475-5272),* a favorite in Golden Meadow since the 1930s, serves Cajun-style seafood.

Farther south on La. 1, watch for shrimp docks along the bayou operated by wholesale dealers. Some 10 miles beyond Golden Meadow, La. 1 crosses Bayou Lafourche at **Leeville 2,** a busy shrimping community crowded with oil support installations.

See area map pp. 206–207
- New Orleans
- 110 miles one-way
- 2.5 hours
- Grand Isle

NOT TO BE MISSED

- Peregrine falcon-watching in the Port Fourchon area
- Grand Isle

Where La. 1 intersects La. 3090, check for peregrine falcons perched on the roadside microwave tower. Perhaps the world's most amazing raptor, these crow-size birds hit prey in midair at speeds above 200 mph. An adult has a dark gray back and crown, dark streaks on a pale chest and abdomen, and a broad dark stripe dropping from its eyes. For a better chance of seeing one, turn right onto La. 3090 or A.O. Rappellet Road (locally dubbed Fourchon Road). In 3 miles you'll come to **Port Fourchon** ❸, with camping and surf fishing along 4 miles of public beach. Just past the turn onto Fourchon Road, look for wintering peregrine falcons on the nearby transmission tower or farther down the road atop the water tower. About a quarter mile ahead is a large lagoon to the west (right)—a roost for as many as 1,000 American white pelicans and populations of roseate spoonbills and reddish egrets. A good vantage point is on the dead-end dirt road that goes west along the north side of the lagoon.

Return to La. 1 and turn east (right) toward **Grand Isle** ❹, Louisiana's southernmost island community. A beach ridge created by the action of waves from the Gulf, it once enjoyed a reputation as a romantic place. In *The Awakening* (1889), a short story by New Orleans novelist Kate Chopin, a married woman's life takes a dramatic turn during her summer sojourn there. Linked to the mainland by a causeway bridge, the island is home to a group of year-round residents—mostly

Shrimp boats leave Grand Isle at dusk in search of "pink gold."

fishermen and offshore oil-rig workers and their kin, who share it with a seasonal influx of summer folk.

People come to Grand Isle to relax in rented cabins, motels, or flamboyantly painted summer cottages raised on piers; to swim and body surf; and to stroll downtown in the evening to dine in one of many good reasonably priced seafood joints. Among the most popular is **Cigar's Cajun Cuisine restaurant and bar** *(1119 La 1. 985-787-3220),* a low-slung white building with bright blue awnings and a locally famous seafood platter.

Many also come for bird-watching, this being Louisiana's only barrier island with sizable woods accessible by road. The woods make it a stopover vital to the migratory songbirds of the eastern United States.

A popular birding spot is **Grand Isle Woods** *(off La. 1)*—but be aware the understory is mostly poison ivy. These groves are mostly private; but owners indulge birders as long as their vehicles do not block the neighborhood's narrow lanes. Although several roads connect with the forest, Chighizola Lane takes you past some of the area's lovely old houses. Try parking at the Sureway Market and walking north to woods along the shell road—some ten acres said to be the island's best birding spot.

Thousands more people come here to fish: Over 280 species live in these waters. You will see charter boats lined up to take people out into the Gulf to find big fish like snapper and marlin. Surf fishermen cast for speckled trout throughout the year and for redfish in fall and winter. Others work closer to shore in search of tarpon, croaker, and drum. During the annual Tarpon Fishing Rodeo in July *(Grand Isle Tourist Commission 985-787-2997),* the island takes on a spring-break quality in marked contrast to its reputation as a quiet retreat with no nightlife.

Visitors are sometimes disappointed to find that access to much of the beachfront is blocked by private land. Fortunately, at the eastern end of the island is **Grand Isle State Park** *(985-787-2559 or 888-787-2559, 877-226-7652 for camping reservations. $),* with picnic tables, a 400-foot fishing pier, a swimming area and bathhouse, peaceful lagoons and ponds, and a primitive campground with spots for 100 families. Visitor center exhibits trace Grand Isle's history, including the reason why the early 19th-century ruins of Fort Livingston loom on **Grand Terre Island** across the Barataria Pass channel. President James Monroe commissioned the forlorn, mosquito-tormented outpost to protect the Barataria approach to New Orleans. The observation tower doesn't seem high when you are looking up at it from ground level, but the view of the coastline from the top of the tower is splendid. You'll see the maze of inlets and channels where pirate Jean Lafitte hid out in the early 1800s. ■

The Cajuns

The name is synonymous with southern Louisiana, where Cajun music and cooking, and the mellifluous lilt of accented Cajun English are charming vestiges of a 200-year saga of French émigrés who found their way here in the late 18th century.

The Acadians came primarily from rural areas in western France and in 1604 started settling in the province of Acadie, or Acadia—today's Nova Scotia. They lived comfortable lives as farmers and fishermen, but throughout the 17th century Acadia was a rope in the tug-of-war between French and British colonial interests. Through the Peace of Utrecht in 1713, the French ceded Acadia's mainland portion to the British, then lost Cape Breton Island. In 1755, as war neared between France and England, British authorities demanded that the Acadians renounce their Roman Catholic faith and swear allegiance to the Crown. When the Acadians refused, the British expelled somewhere between 6,000 and 10,000 Acadians—a mass exile known as *Le Grand Dérangement,* lamented in Henry Wadsworth Longfellow's poem *Evangeline.* The British eventually allowed some Acadians to return, but meanwhile, in the late 18th century, they encouraged New Englanders, refugee Loyalist fishermen from the United States, evicted Scottish Highlanders, Germans, and Irish to settle on lands previously held by the Acadians, making a return to the Acadian past impossible.

The exiled Acadians were shipped to the New England Colonies, others to the West Indies or back to France, and many wandered for years before learning that they were welcome in the predominantly French territoryof Louisiana. By 1790, about 3,000 to 4,000 Acadians had settled in the wetlands along the lower Mississippi River. They cleared small farms, trapped fur-bearing animals, gathered moss, and raised sugarcane, cotton, and corn. Others settled on the prairies to the east and started cattle ranches and planted rice. They improvised a rough but comfortable domestic architecture of daubed or half-timbered houses with gable roofs, mud chimneys, and outside stairways leading to attics. Still others found a life in the swamplands, where they fished and trapped, and acquired from their Indian neighbors the name by which they are known today, a corruption of the archaic French pronunciation of Acadian, which sounded like "Ah-ka-jun." Their cabins, raised above the water on posts, created an architectural style and an enduring Cajun trademark.

The Cajun territory today remains about the same as what it was then: a triangle of 22 parishes whose base is Louisiana coastline and whose apex is in the central part of the state near Alexandria. The region's principal city, Lafayette, is its unofficial capital.

The Cajuns intermarried with their American, Spanish, Indian, and African-American neighbors, but they stayed true to their Roman Catholic faith and developed their own dialect—an archaic form of French laced with words taken from English, German, Spanish, and various Indian tongues. The Cajun traditions of rural outdoor labor have evolved into a dominance of not only the oystering and shrimping trade, but also the state's labor force for oil and gas exploration.

Cajun cooking, countrified and hearty, arose from the realities of rural, unrefrigerated living, and it is incarnated today on the menus of New Orleans's best and earnestly traditional Creole restaurants as jambalaya, gumbo, turtle sauce piquante, andouille sausage, boudin (a pork and rice sausage), soft-shell crab, myriad shrimp dishes, crawfish étouffée, crawfish bisque—the list goes on. An excellent introduction is a recently published cookbook by New Orleans's best known culinary ambassador, Chef Paul Prudhomme's *Louisiana Tastes : Exciting Flavors from the State That Cooks.*

Today, there are over 170 groups producing recordings of Cajun and zydeco music. From the scratchy old soundtracks to contemporary CDs, from the bands with old-style with fiddles, accordions, and triangles to the contemporary Cajun bands with drums and guitar, the themes of rural life and love's ups and downs persist; the lyrics weaving French and English together. ■

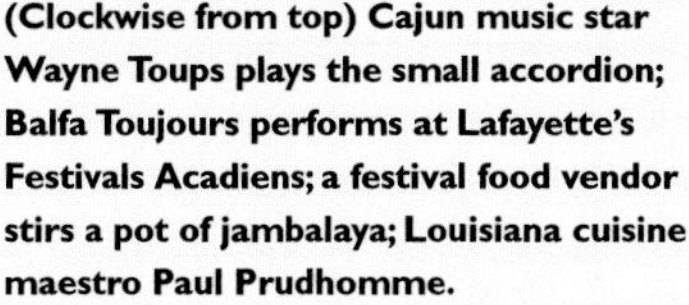

(Clockwise from top) Cajun music star Wayne Toups plays the small accordion; Balfa Toujours performs at Lafayette's Festivals Acadiens; a festival food vendor stirs a pot of jambalaya; Louisiana cuisine maestro Paul Prudhomme.

Lafayette & Cajun Country

Lafayette
Map 206–207 A3

Lafayette Convention & Visitors Commission
1400 N.W. Evangeline Thruway, Lafayette
337-232-3737

ACADIAN CULTURE—ITS LANGUAGE, MUSIC, AND CUISINE especially—is inextricably woven into the fabric of Louisiana life. New Orleans's human heritage is too complex for any one theme to dominate its personality, but the city of Lafayette, about 128 road miles west of New Orleans, and neighboring communities—Eunice, St. Martinville, and Breaux Bridge in particular—define themselves by their French-Canadian heritage. Lafayette proclaims itself the capital of Acadia, a region more often referred to simply as Cajun Country.

To visit Lafayette in a day, take I-10 to and from New Orleans. If you can overnight in Lafayette, consider driving west from New Orleans on US 90, which takes you past St. Martinville. Take a good road map, as there are opportunities to parallel US 90 on lesser roads that pass through rural hamlets shaded with live oak, and rustic fishing villages alongside swamps and bayous.

LAFAYETTE

Introduce yourself formally to Cajun Country in downtown Lafayette. You can't miss the stolidly Romanesque **Cathedral of St. John the Evangelist** *(914 St. John St.),* consecrated in 1913. Its formal cemetery, with the aboveground crypts typical in this region, holds the tomb of Lafayette founder Jean Mouton. Adjoining the church is the **St. John Oak,** a venerated elder in the registry of the Louisiana Live Oak Society, thought to be about four centuries old.

Walk two blocks east on Main Street to the **Lafayette Courthouse** *(800 Buchanan St. 337-233-0150. Closed Sat.–Sun.),* where a permanent photographic exhibition documents regional history. Leave the courthouse via the Lafayette Street entrance and stroll two blocks south to the **Lafayette Museum** *(1122 Lafayette St. 337-234-2208. Closed Mon.; $).* The archive occupies a handsome townhouse dating from 1800, built by city founder Mouton. One of its galleries exhibits historical objects and furnishings from the era of Acadian settlement, and typifies Acadian architecture. The museum's main section focuses primarily on how the Civil War affected this region.

Just south of town you'll find Louisiana's finest official celebration of Cajun life, the **Jean Lafitte National Historical Park and Preserve's Acadian Cultural Center** *(501 Fisher Rd. 337-232-0732 or 337-232-0961).* The center presents the Acadian saga—a historical melodrama of the first order—using many audiovisual interpretive displays that trace the French-speaking settlers' dramatic odyssey from Canada in the mid-1700s. A must-see is the 45-minute historical documentary, "The Cajun Way: Echoes of Acadia," which depicts the Acadians' *Grand Dérangement* from Nova Scotia. Other displays point out the distinguishing aspects of Acadian culture—its architecture, music, and language especially, along with the Cajun approach to farming, domestic life, religion, foodways, and dress.

A theme park it is, but **Vermilionville** *(300 Fisher Rd. 337-233-4077 or 866-992-2968. $$),* which adjoins the Acadian Cultural Center, is also a living history village, with more than 20 old-style Cajun buildings that re-create the appearance of a 19th-century Acadian hamlet. Thrice daily, tour

Opposite: Dry-land farmers and ocean fishermen in Canada, the Acadians who settled in Louisiana's wetlands switched to trapping, hunting, and freshwater fishing.

This warning is common in bayou country, where the reptiles occasionally sun themselves on rural roads.

Breaux Bridge
Map 206–207 A3

Bayou Teche Visitors Center
314 E. Bridge St., Breaux Bridge
337-332-8500 or 888-565-5939
Closed Sat.–Sun.

St. Martinville
Map 206–207 A3

St. Martinville Tourist Information Center
215 Evangeline Blvd., St. Martinville
337-394-2233

guides lead groups through the village and point out the nuances that distinguish this branch of Louisiana's French-speaking folk from New Orleans's Creoles. There are midday cooking demonstrations—you can also sample Acadian cuisine at Vermilionville's old-fashioned restaurant—and performances of traditional Cajun music in the old music hall.

EUNICE

In the town of Eunice, some 40 miles northeast of Lafayette via I-49 and US 90, historical and cultural exhibits at the **Jean Lafitte National Historical Park and Preserve Prairie Acadian Cultural Center** *(250 W. Park Ave. 337-262-6862)* survey the world of the Acadians who settled farther west, beyond the Atchafalaya River Basin, on southwest Louisiana's lush grasslands. Known as the Prairie Acadians, they took up farming and raised cattle, developing lifestyles in marked contrast to their wetland cousins. The center's program includes demonstrations of old-fashioned Cajun skills such as spinning wool, weaving, and preparing food.

BREAUX BRIDGE

Ten miles east of Lafayette on Bayou Teche, this quintessentially Cajun community bills itself as the Crawfish Capital of the World. It hosts a brisk antique trade and has nicely appointed lodgings and several fine eateries and art studios. The best known restaurant is probably the **Café des Amis** *(140 Bridge St. 337-332-5273)*, a friendly, day-long banquet house occupying an old downtown mercantile building. Resist the urge to order familiar things; look for exotica like okra gumbo and crawfish-topped eggplant wheels. Breaux Bridge is a musical town—Cajun music, of course—and some of the best hereabouts is heard at **Mulate's** *(325 Mills Ave. 337-332-4648 or 800-422-2586)*, a restaurant-dance hall that is sometimes too popular. If the appreciative crowd is spilling out onto the sidewalk here, try **La Poussière** *(1215 Grand Point Rd. 337-332-1721)*, a venerable Cajun dance palace.

ST. MARTINVILLE

It's thought that Henry Wadsworth Longfellow based his epic 1847 *Evangeline* on the story of Emmaline LaBiche. Emmaline and her lover, Louis Arceneaux, were separated during the tumultuous ejection of the Acadians from Canada. For three years she searched for him; she finally found him beneath what is now called the **Evangeline Oak,** only to discover he had married. A statue of Evangeline strikes a wistful pose behind the rectory of **St. Martin de Tours Church.** During the French Revolution, the town swelled with aristocratic refugees, who built European-style manses and attended grand balls. They are responsible for the settlement's nickname, Petit Paris. This historical footnote is the primary theme of the *très petit* **Petit Paris Museum** *(103 S. Main St. 337-394-7334. $)*. ■

Travelwise

Esplanade Avenue fruit stand

TRAVELWISE INFORMATION

The best source of visitor information is the **New Orleans Metropolitan Convention and Visitors Bureau** at 2020 St. Charles Ave., New Orleans, LA 70130; www.neworleanscvb.com. Call 800/672-6124 and ask to be sent the "Official Visitor's Packet," which includes a calendar of events, kids' activities, and a handy Visitor's Guide—all for free.

For up-to-the-minute news about New Orleans, including weather forecasts and current entertainment listings, check out the NOLA Live (short for New Orleans, LA) Web site at www.nola.com.

PLANNING YOUR TRIP

WHEN TO GO/CLIMATE

New Orleans's climate is subtropical, meaning mild winters (average lows in the mid-40s) and hot, humid summers (average highs over 90°F). Spring and fall are basically nonexistant. Rain is common year-round, with an average of 5 inches per month. Most rain falls in summer, when light afternoon showers are nearly a daily occurrence.

The high season for visitors is generally September through May, with most people smart enough to avoid the city during June, July, and August. However, there are some great hotel deals to be had in summer, if you can brave the heat.

Average daily temperatures are slightly cooler in September, ranging from 70°F to 88°F. The remaining months average highs/lows are as follows:

October–79°F/59°F
November–70°F/50°F
December–64°F/45°F
January–63°F/43°F
February–64°F/45°F
March–72°F/52°F
April–79°F/59°F
May–84°F/64°F

WHAT TO BRING

Light clothing is recommended most of the year, with the addition of a coat or jacket during winter. As tourists often spend a lot of time walking around the French Quarter, comfortable shoes are also a good idea.

TRAVELING TO NEW ORLEANS

BY PLANE

The **New Orleans International Airport** is approximately 12 miles west from New Orleans, in the suburban city of Kenner (900 Airline Hwy., Kenner, LA 70062. 504/464-2650 or TDD 504/463-1057). It is served by the following passenger airlines:

Air Canada 888/247-2262
AirTran 800/825-8538
American 800/433-7300
Continental 800/525-0280
Delta 800/221-1212
JetBlue 800/538-2583
Northwest/KLM 800/225-2525
Southwest 800/435-9792
United/Lufthansa 800/241-6522
US Airways/MetroJet 800/428-4322

The smaller **New Orleans Lakefront Airport** primarily serves private planes. Located in the city along the shore of Lake Pontchartrain, the airport can accommodate planes as large as 757s. Call Aviaport customer service at 504/242-9496.

BY TRAIN

Three major Amtrak lines stop in New Orleans at Union Passenger Terminal (1001 Loyola Ave.) The *City of New Orleans* arrives daily from Chicago. The *Crescent* is another daily run coming from New York and Washington, D.C. The *Sunset Limited* arrives from Los Angeles on Tuesdays, Thursday, and Sundays. For reservations, call 800/872-7245.

BY BUS

Greyhound buses also provide service to New Orleans via Union Passenger Terminal. Fares and schedules: 800/231-2222.

GETTING INTO THE CITY

FROM THE AIRPORT

The flat taxi rate from the airport to downtown is $28 for up to two people and $8 for each additional passenger (with a five-person limit). Pick up a taxi right outside of the baggage claim area.

Airport Shuttle is the official transportation company providing shuttle service to and from the airport. Tickets cost $13 each way and can be purchased at the Airport Shuttle information desk, staffed 24 hours. Vans arrive and depart the airport every 10 minutes. Call 504/592-0555.

Louisiana Transit buses run between the airport and Tulane University (in Uptown) from 6 a.m. to 6:30 p.m. for $1.60 fare. Buses run approximately every 10 minutes during the peak hours of 6 a.m. to 9 a.m. and 3 p.m. to 6 p.m. and about every 23 minutes the rest of the day. Call 504/818-1077.

Greyhound buses are also available at the airport with tickets being sold by the driver. For fares and schedules call 800/231-2222.

FROM UNION PASSENGER TERMINAL

Union Passenger Terminal, where trains and buses arrive, is located on the edge of the New Orleans Central Business district—just a short bus or cab ride from the French Quarter.

GETTING AROUND

Those planning to spend most of their time in the downtown area may want to forego driving. Take a streetcar or a cab. It's easier.

BY PUBLIC TRANSPORTATION

BUSES & STREETCARS

The Regional Transit Authority (RTA), 2817 Canal St., runs New Orleans's buses and streetcars. The St. Charles line runs from Canal Street downtown to Carrollton Avenue uptown. The Riverfront streetcar line runs along the edge of the French Quarter and can provide respite for tired feet. And the newest line, the Canal Street, runs from the river to City Park. For the exact fare of $1.25, this is a cheap way to tour the city's most beautiful neighborhoods. VisiTour Passes, which cost $5 for one day or $12 for three days, allow unlimited ridership on streetcars and buses. They are available at hotels and shopping areas. For bus schedules, call the RTA at 504/248-3900.

FERRY

The Canal Street Ferry carries cars and passengers between downtown and Algiers Point, directly across the Mississippi River, several times each day. The last ferry leaves Canal Street at midnight. Pedestrian passengers are free, and cars pay $1 on the inbound from Algiers Point.

BY TAXI CAB

Good luck hailing a cab in New Orleans. It is usually easier to catch one queued up in front of a hotel or call ahead. The city's largest taxi company is United Cab at 504/522-9771.

BY CAR

New Orleans possibly could be the pothole capital of North America. When traversing its streets, be careful. Also, moving violation fees can be quite steep so try to follow the law. First, those sitting in the front seat as well as all children under 13 years of age are required to wear seat belts. The speed limit on most undivided streets is 25 mph with divided streets allowing 35 mph.

Parking can sometimes be difficult, especially during special events such as Carnival. Always look for signs listing parking restrictions. Towable offenses include parking on parade routes, in certain areas during rush hours, on medians, within 20 feet of a crosswalk or within 15 feet of a fire hydrant.

If a car is towed, it can be found at the auto pound, 400 N. Claiborne Ave., on the edge of the Central Business District. Call 504/565-7450 and know the following: make and color, license plate number, and where car was parked. Caution: Do not attempt to walk to the auto pound. Although it may be in relatively close proximity, it is not in a safe neighborhood.

The drinking age here is 21, and open containers are not allowed in automobiles. (Open glass or metal containers are also not allowed to be carried around on city streets. Just ask for a "go cup"—a plastic cup that is perfectly acceptable, even when filled with liquor.)

Car rentals

The following car rental agencies are located at or near the airport:

Alamo 504/469-0532
Avis 504/464-9511
Budget 800/527-7000
Dollar 866/434-2226
Enterprise 504/468-3018
Hertz 504/468-3695
National 504/469-0532
Rainbow 504/468-2990
Thrifty 504/463-0800

PRACTICAL ADVICE

In the past decade, New Orleans has seen drops in every category of crime. Most tourist areas are relatively safe. Authorities recommend staying with the crowds and not wandering off to deserted streets, especially at night. In general, follow the common sense rules of traveling:

Don't leave valuable belongings in your car. Don't leave any items under the seat or in the trunk.

If accosted, give the perpetrator whatever is demanded. Do not resist. Afterward call 911 emergency.

Keep your wallet in a front pocket; hold your purse close. Don't carry large amounts of cash. Leave unneeded credit cards at home.

Be mindful of the people around you. If someone seems suspicious or makes you nervous, move away from them.

Do not leave your bags unattended. Do not give them to anyone other than airport or hotel personnel or a taxi driver.

EMERGENCIES & HEALTH CARE

USEFUL NUMBERS

- Police, ambulance, or fire emergency 911
- American Red Cross 504/620-2205
- Alcohol abuse helpline 800/395-3400
- New Orleans Health Department 504/565-6900
- Travelers Aid 504/525-8726

In need of a doctor? The following numbers are for physician referral services at area hospitals.

Doctors Hospital of Jefferson 800/968-3638

East Jefferson General Hospital 504/456-5000
Lakeland Medical Center 504/245-4806
Lakeside Hospital 504/780-8282
Meadowcrest Hospital 800/968-3638
Memorial Medical Center 800/968-3638.
Ochsner Medical Institutions 504/842-3155
St. Charles General Hospital 800/968-3638
Touro Infirmary 504/897-7777
Tulane University Medical Center 504/588-5800

Walgreens operates 24-hour prescription service at the following New Orleans-area store:
4421 Airline Dr., Metairie, 504/836-2316

TRAVELERS WITH DISABILITIES

Those with disabilities may have some trouble when visiting New Orleans's many historic buildings, as they are not covered by the Americans with Disabilities Act and therefore may not be handicapped accessible. It's best to call ahead.

Services for the disabled can be found through:
American Red Cross 504/620-2205
Catholic Deaf Center 504/891-2673 or 504/949-4413 (TDD)
Davisson Mobility 504/433-3786
Lighthouse for the Blind 504/899-4501
Specialized Transportation Services, LIFT 504/827-7433

ANNUAL EVENTS

JANUARY

Nokia Sugar Bowl
Louisiana Superdome, 1500 Poydras St., tel 504/525-8573
One of college football's biggest post-season games, the Sugar Bowl is played on or around Jan. 1 at the Louisiana Superdome.

FEBRUARY

Carnival, tel 800/672-6124
New Orleans biggest event of the year falls during February or March (depending on when Easter is). The final day of Carnival is Mardi Gras (Fat Tuesday), which always takes place the day before Ash Wednesday. (Traditionally, Mardi Gras is the last day of debauchery and self indulgence before the solemn Lenten season.)

The season officially begins the day that the Christmas season officially ends, on the Feast of the Epiphany (Jan. 6); also known as Kings' Day, it celebrates the three wise men's arrival at Bethlehem following the birth of the Christ child. At this time, Mardi Gras krewes, the clubs that produce the season's street parades, begin hosting private balls. The public portion of the festivities, for the most part, take place during the two and a half weeks leading up to Mardi Gras, when parades make their way through the city on virtually a daily basis. Many visitors come to town for the final four or five days of the season, which includes the weekend immediately preceding Fat Tuesday. Then, "super krewes" Bacchus and Endymion put on Carnival's most extravagant parades.

MARCH

Tennessee Williams/New Orleans Literary Festival
Tel 504/581-1144
This three-day literary festival, featuring events which take place all around the downtown area, includes panel discussions, theater and musical performances, poetry readings and a book fair.

New Orleans Spring Fiesta Association
Tel 504/581-1367 or 800/550-8450
This mid-month French Quarter event features guided tours of historic homes.

St. Patrick's Day
Tel 800/672-6124
Everyone in New Orleans is Irish on St. Patrick's Day. Two prominent parades highlight the celebration, in which float riders throw traditional Hibernian fare of cabbages, carrots and potatoes. One promenade takes place in New Orleans's Irish Channel neighborhood the Saturday before St. Patrick's Day; the other is in the suburb of Metairie the following Sunday.

APRIL

Crescent City Classic
Tel 504/861-8686
This 20-year-old 10K foot race, which begins at Jackson Square in the French Quarter, draws 20,000 participants including world-class runners. It is followed by a festival in City Park (where the race ends), featuring live music, food, and sports gear for sale.

French Quarter Festival
Tel 504/522-5730
This free three-day mid-April event, which draws more than a quarter-million people, offers over 100 hours of musical entertainment on stages throughout the Vieux Carré; popular New Orleans food and libations also available.

New Orleans Jazz and Heritage Festival
Tel 504/522-4786
This two-weekend long festival (the last week of April and first week of May) is one of the city's most popular. Its draws big-name entertainment and devoted fans from around the country. Held at the Fair Grounds racetrack, it offers continuous entertainment on a dozen stages.

MAY

Greek Festival
Tel 504/282-0259
Held each Memorial Day weekend at Holy Trinity Cathedral, the oldest Greek Orthodox Church in America, this festival offers tasty Greek treats including souvlaki, Athenian salad, and gyros—with

ouzo to wash it all down. A 5K race and tours of the church add to the festivities.

JUNE

Great French Market Tomato Festival
Tel 504/522-2621
Ripe and meaty Creole tomatoes are the star of this show held the first Sunday in June. Cooking demonstrations, local delicacies, and crafts featured.

Reggae Riddums International Arts Festival
Tel 504/367-1313
Reggae, calypso, and other island sounds can be heard above the crowds enjoying jerk chicken, rice and peas, and other island favorites during this three-day, early June event.

JULY

New Orleans Wine and Food Experience
Tel 504/529-9463
Held for four days at various venues in the second week of July, this charitable event boasts tastings of more than 400 wines, cuisine from 100 of the city's best restaurants, seminars, and open houses at art galleries and antique shops.

Essence Music Festival
Tel 504/522-5555
More than 160,000 people attend this early July event organized by the publishers of *Essence* magazine. Top soul, blues, jazz, and hip-hop artists perform at this Superdome extravaganza; it also includes empowerment seminars.

SEPTEMBER

Southern Decadence
Tel 504/522-8047
This gay French Quarter happening is highlighted by a flamboyant parade of drag queens through Vieux Carré streets, with no one knowing exactly where the entourage will end up; it takes place the Sunday afternoon before Labor Day.

OCTOBER

Art for Arts' Sake
504/528-3805
This posh, early month affair officially opens the local visual arts season with wine and cheese open houses at a variety of galleries in the French Quarter, Warehouse District, and Uptown.

New Orleans Film Festival
Tel 504/523-3818
Sponsored by the nonprofit New Orleans Film Society, this mid-month event offers premieres of regional and other independent films, cocktail parties, panel discussions, and a film competition at various venues around town.

Gumbo Festival
Bridge City, Tel 504/436-4712
This festival features every type of gumbo imaginable, plus other local delicacies. Held the second weekend in October in the Gumbo Capital of the World, nearby Bridge City.

Jeff Fest
Tel 504/838-4389
This family-oriented mid-month event takes place at Lafreniere Park, in the New Orleans suburb of Metairie. Three stages feature classic rock, Latin, zydeco, blues, and more music. Dancers, magicians, jugglers, and crafts add to the mix.

NOVEMBER/DECEMBER

Celebration in the Oaks
Tel 504/483-9415
The highlight of this nightly event, which begins the night after Thanksgiving and runs through year's end, is thousands of sparkling lights hanging from the towering live oak trees in City Park. Drive through or park and tour the lights on the park's train, then enjoy the roller coaster and other rides. Santa stops by nightly.

A New Orleans Christmas
Tel 504/522-5730
This coordinated, citywide event, which takes place from the beginning of December through Christmas, celebrates the season with a French Market tree-lighting ceremony, candlelight caroling, traditional French reveillon dinners, holiday musical performances, and walking tours.

Christmas Eve Bonfires
Tel 504-522-5730
Upriver from New Orleans, residents of the River parishes still celebrate the Cajun tradition of building holiday bonfires along the levee to light the way for Papa Noel (Santa Claus). Take the hour drive or relax on a riverboat to watch the blazing glory.

New Year's Eve
Tel 504/522-5730
Festivities take place throughout the French Quarter with most revelers gathering at midnight to watch the dropping of a lighted ball atop Jax Brewery at midnight.

FURTHER READING

A Streetcar Named Desire, by Tennessee Williams (1947). This play set in New Orleans won the Pulitzer Prize in 1947.
The Awakening, by Kate Chopin (1899, reprinted 1995). A woman comes into her own while summering at Grand Isle.
The Battle of New Orleans, by Robert Vincent Rimini (1999). The story of the battle that turned the tide of the War of 1812.
Interview with the Vampire, by Anne Rice (1977). This Gothic tale set in French Louisiana explores immortality, death, and evil.
Literary New Orleans, edited by Judy Long (1999). The Big Easy has inspired some of the world's most accomplished writers.
New Orleans Then and Now, by Marini and Richard Campanella (1999). Survey of the city between 1847 and 1998, with hundreds of historical photos.
Voodoo Child, by Michael Reaves (1999). A fictional thriller set in New Orleans.

HOTELS & RESTAURANTS

Quixotic and diverse, New Orleans offers as many types of accommodations and dining possibilities as there are moods and atmospheres to be enjoyed in this city of lively traditional jazz, multicultural gastronomy, and 24-hour bars.

HOTELS

Whether opting for the romance of the French Quarter and and neighboring Faubourg Marigny, the Spanish oak-draped gentility of the Garden District and Uptown, the quietude of tree-lined Mid-City, the urban pulse of the Central Business District, or the artsy air of the Warehouse District, the Big Easy has hotel accommodations with tariffs to fit nearly every budget. In fact, the rates in New Orleans hotels—many of which have hosted presidents, celebrities, pop stars, and literary figures—compare more than favorably to many of the world's other major tourist destinations. They are renowned for Southern hospitality, European-style personal service, and, depending on the property, award-winning fine dining and/or legendary bars.

A boutique hotel or luxurious ultra-modern high-rise? An up-on-the-roof Mississippi River view or a lush bougainvillea-framed courtyard? The Old World charm of antiques and Oriental rugs or the sweeping grandeur of a polished marble lobby of crystal chandeliers? Balcony breakfasts or terrace dinners? Maybe a mix of all of the above? Whatever the preference, New Orleans didn't forget that the vast majority of visitors view their hotel as much a part of the experience as the town's attractions and restaurants.

Unless otherwise noted, all properties have air-conditioning, elevators, and nonsmoking rooms.

RESTAURANTS

New Orleans knows how to whip up a tour de force of earthly culinary delights. In fact, few places in the country can match the Big Easy's multicultural heritage as reflected in the melting-pot cooking traditions brought by the French, Spanish, Africans, West Indians, Irish, Italians, Germans, and, most recently, Latin Americans and Vietnamese. Even fewer can boast this city's near-staggering spectrum of restaurants, and travelers aren't likely to go broke while enjoying some of the best food the city has to offer, typically served with a friendly smile and in generous portions. Seafood rules the kitchens here thanks to the abundance of shellfish, finfish, and bivalves harvested virtually year-round from surrounding local waters and the nearby Gulf of Mexico. But fresh produce, poultry, and beef featured in both traditional and imaginative new recipes also help set the Crescent City restaurant dining table.

Unless otherwise noted all restaurants are air-conditioned and offer nonsmoking seating. All restaurants are open daily unless indicated otherwise.

L = lunch
D = dinner

CREDIT CARDS

Many hotels and restaurants accept all major credit cards. Smaller ones may accept some, as shown in their entry. Abbreviations used are:

AE=American Express
DC=Discover Card
MC=Mastercard
V=Visa.

ORGANIZATION

Hotels and restaurants indicated are listed by price category, then alphabetically. Hotel restaurants—some famous in their own right—are listed with their parent hotel.

PRICES

HOTELS

An indication of the cost of a double room without breakfast is given by **$** signs.

$$$$$	$225+
$$$$	$175–$225
$$$	$125–$175
$$	$85–$125
$	Less than $85

RESTAURANTS

An indication of the cost of a three-course dinner without drinks is given by $ signs.

$$$$	Over $50
$$$	$35–$50
$$	$15–$35
$	Under $15

FRENCH QUARTER

HOTELS

HOTEL MAISON DE VILLE
$$$$-$$$$$
727 TOULOUSE ST., 70130
TEL 504/561-5858 or 800/636-1600
FAX 504/528-9939

This place is for the birds. At least that's what John James Audubon thought when he lived here while illustrating part of his *Birds of America.* One of the most historic and certainly romantic hotels in New Orleans offers 16 rooms and 7 cottages. Restored 18th-century slave quarters and half-timbered Creole cottages have exposed brick walls, fireplaces, antiques, four-poster beds, and high ceilings. An award-winning menu, accented by pan-seared loin of pork with calvados, and New Zealand rack of lamb with cannelini beans, mushroom, and eggplant on a polenta cake, is served up at the Parisian-style **Bistro restaurant** (see p. 240). Sit on red-leather banquettes among French Impressionist-style prints.

23 P Valet All major cards

OMNI ROYAL ORLEANS
$$$$-$$$$$
621 ST. LOUIS ST., 70140
TEL 504/529-5333 or 800/843-6664
FAX 504/529-7089
Oh, the ultra luxury—and views—guests encounter at this historic property that has wooed European travelers for decades with its wrought iron balconies, 19th-century English and French antiques, and gilt-mirror lobby of chandeliers and brass—all nearly as handsome as the marble stairway. Amenities ranging from hair dryers and goose-down pillows to babysitting are just part of the package. The rooftop pool offers unsurpassed views of the French Quarter's St. Louis Cathedral and the Mississippi River. **The Rib Room** (see p. 242) is the place to see and be seen for lunch.
346 P Valet All major cards

SONIAT HOUSE
$$$$-$$$$$
1133 CHARTRES ST., 70116
TEL 504/522-0570 or 800/544-8808
FAX 504/522-7208
Even if Brad Pitt hadn't stayed here, this well-known romantic retreat and honeymoon haven would remain a mega-hit among travelers who appreciate the peace and privacy of an intimate country inn coupled with the luxury of a boutique hotel. Silk curtains, antique Oriental rugs and furnishings, linen-draped and canopied four-poster beds with 200-thread-count percale sheets, and bathroom telephones accent the 33 rooms and suites of this 1829 Creole townhouse hotel two blocks from the round-the-clock carnival of Bourbon Street. Sumptuous, Southern-style, white-linen breakfasts are served around the tree-shaded courtyard lily pond. No elevator.
33 P Valet AE, MC, V

CHATEAU SONESTA HOTEL NEW ORLEANS
$$$-$$$$$
800 IBERVILLE ST., 70112
TEL 504/586-0800 or 800/766-3782
FAX 504/586-1987
Some of the pleasantly furnished rooms have balconies overlooking Bourbon Street; all feature data port telephones, armoires and high ceilings. The European-style lobby literally sparkles from the reflection of chandeliers on the polished marble floors. The **Clock Bar** and three restaurants including the popular **Red Fish Grill** (see p. 242), owned by Ralph Brennan of the city's famous restaurateur family, keep this well-known property on locals' lists of places to visit on a regular basis.
251 P Valet All major cards

DAUPHINE ORLEANS
$$$-$$$$
415 DAUPHINE ST., 70112
TEL 504/586-1800 or 800/521-7111
FAX 504/586-1409
Savvy travelers staying here often opt for one of the 14 Dauphine patio rooms with exposed brick walls and furnished with Jacuzzi tubs, chandeliers, and armoires. Lush ferns hang in a tropical courtyard of beautiful trees entered through French double doors. Welcome cocktails and hors d'oeuvres. Complimentary newspapers and continental breakfast. Only in New Orleans could a motor hotel boast as part of its colorful history the fact that in the 1850s the world's oldest profession was practiced in what is now the bar.
111 P Valet All major cards

MAISON DUPUY HOTEL
$$$-$$$$$
1001 TOULOUSE ST., 70112
TEL 504/586-8000 or 800/535-9177
FAX 504/566-7450
Respite from the blare of Bourbon Street two blocks away is one of the reasons this lovely hotel stays on the short list of smart travelers keen on convenient location but without the noise. Guest rooms were given a major facelift several years ago during renovation and today feature 19th-century furnishings, local art, and, in some cases, balconies with a view of the hotel's lush courtyard.
200 P Valet All major cards

SOMETHING SPECIAL

OLIVIER HOUSE HOTEL
$$$-$$$$$
828 TOULOUSE ST., 70112
TEL 504/525-8456
FAX 504/529-2006
A trio of historic 1836 townhouses with individually and tastefully decorated guest rooms, plus a cottage, set the backdrop for discrete Southern romance. A large sunken bath off the bedroom of an 18th-century Creole cottage helps No. 114 earn its moniker as the honeymoon suite, which features a private brick courtyard. A living room fountain bathed by skylight sunrays casts a serene spell over the garden suite, No. 112, tucked in the back of the courtyard.
42 P AE, MC, V

PRINCE CONTI HOTEL
$$$
830 CONTI ST., 70112

TEL 504/529-4172
or 800/366-2743
FAX 504/636-1046
The **Bombay Club** tucked off of the carriageway is probably one of the most pleasant—and pleasantly untouristed—bars in the French Quarter. But don't let this locally popular and subdued watering hole, modeled after a British gentlemen's club, or its restaurant's menu of uncomplicated Creole dishes exert undue influence. Simple touches such as drive-in parking and valet laundry have helped this antique-furnished European-style pension, half a block from Bourbon Street, earn a well-deserved loyal following.
53 P All major cards

W NEW ORLEANS FRENCH QUARTER
$$$-$$$$$
316 CHARTRES ST., 70130
TEL 504/581-1200 or 800/448-4927
FAX 504/523-2910
If guests like the valet parking, free newspaper, and 24-hour coffee at this recently remodeled boutique hotel, with spacious, traditionally furnished rooms, they'll love the fact that they can get breakfast, lunch, and dinner room service from the award-winning, Ralph Brennan-owned **Bacco restaurant** (see p. 240), located on the ground level. Try the foie gras pizza with caramelized Chianti onions; roasted Portobello mushrooms and mozzarella; or the house-specialty crawfish ravioli with sundried-tomato pesto butter sauce. Carriage house suites with balconies embody the European-style intimacy of this fountain courtyard property near Jackson Square and Royal Street's antique shop and art gallery corridor.
98 P Valet All major cards

BIENVILLE HOUSE HOTEL
$$-$$$$
320 DECATUR ST, 70130
TEL 504/529-2345 or 800/535-7836
FAX 504/525-6079
It's hard to beat the location of this Creole-style manor house—it's on one of the main drags in the French Quarter, across the street from Jax Brewery and nearby Royal Street's antique corridor. Recent renovations have spruced up the lobby and added four sundecks and a tropical courtyard. Courtyard- and Decatur-view balconies accent some rooms. The contemporary Creole cuisine at long-time local chef Greg Sonnier's new **Gamay** restaurant is already drawing good reviews.
83 P Valet All major cards

BOURBON ORLEANS
$$-$$$$$
717 ORLEANS ST., 70116
TEL 504/523-2222 or 800/521-5338
FAX 504/571-4666
Antique writing desks, Chippendale furnishings, and canopied king beds help put guests at this historic hotel, the site of legendary 19th-century quadroon balls, in the lap of Creole luxury. Some rooms have balconies. But even amenities like marble bathrooms with TVs and phone, free newspaper, and oversize towels have a hard time competing with the rooftop French Quarter views and the serene courtyard, with pool, where Barataria pirate Jean Lafitte once strolled.
216 P Valet All major cards

HOTEL MONTELEONE
$$-$$$$
214 ROYAL ST., 70130
TEL 504/523-3341 or 800/535-9595
FAX 504/528-1019
Even the famous—and revolving—**Carousel Bar** and its whimsical clown-fist wall-mounted lighting takes a back seat to the chiming 1909 mahogany grandfather clock towering over a lobby of drop-dead European elegance. Opened in 1886, this still family-owned and operated landmark walks the walk luxury-wise with furnishings that include four-poster canopied beds, separate vanity and dressing areas, and armoires.
600 P All major cards

LE RICHELIEU
$$-$$$
1234 CHARTRES ST., 70116
TEL 504/529-2492 or 800/535-9653
FAX 504/524-8179
Mickey Rooney and Paul McCartney have signed the guestbook of this historic Greek Revival rowhouse. A former macaroni factory, the motor hotel features cozy rooms and suites, some with balconies overlooking Chartres Street or the courtyard pool. Decorated in Victorian style and furnished with brass ceiling fans, percale sheets, and reproduction furnishings, this refreshingly quiet property tucked on the edge of the French Quarter is only a short walk from the hubbub of Bourbon Street and Jackson Square. Don't forget to ask owner Frank Rochefort about the hotel's colorful history.
86 P All major cards

PLACE D'ARMES
$$-$$$
625 ST. ANN ST., 70116
TEL 504/524-4531 or 800/366-2743
FAX 504/571-2803
Old New Orleans architecture is a key feature of this small, informal hotel located in adjoining 18th-century row houses and the old slave

quarters behind the houses. It's a stone's throw from Jackson Square and the heart of the French Quarter. Free continental breakfast. Lush courtyard with pool.
78 Valet All major cards

THE SAINT LOUIS
$$–$$$$
730 BIENVILLE ST., 70130
TEL 504/581-7300 or 504/535-9706
FAX 504/679-5013
All the individually decorated rooms of this French-Creole oasis, located half a block from Bourbon Street, are furnished with French antiques and separate vanity areas. Some have courtyard wrought-iron balconies and walk-in closets. Complimentary morning newspaper. Guests can do far worse than to start off their morning with a breakfast of spiced bloody Marys, eggs Benedict, and steaming grits in the palm-flanged Mediterranean courtyard of this elegant hotel's award-winning **Louis XVI Restaurant.**
81 Valet All major cards

CORNSTALK HOTEL
$–$$$
915 ROYAL ST., 70116
TEL 504/523-1515
FAX 504/522-5558
The complimentary breakfast and free morning newspaper are by no means the only reasons to stay at this eye-catching Queen Anne Victorian landmark. It is popular among tourists and locals alike for its unusual ornate iron fence of pumpkin vines, morning glories, and stalks of ripe corn. Canopied beds, chandeliers, fireplaces, and stained-glass windows in some or all of the 14 individually furnished rooms have made this property a hit among honeymooners for years. Porch and communal balcony overlook Royal Street. No elevator.
14 AE, MC, V

HOTEL VILLA CONVENTO
$–$$$
616 URSULINES ST., 70116
TEL 504/522-1793
FAX 504/524-1902
Jimmy Buffet once stayed here. But even guests who have never been to Margaritaville enjoy this Creole townhouse built in 1833 on land bought from Ursuline nuns and, ironically, rumored to be the House of the Rising Son. Some of the individually decorated rooms in this four-story landmark, located a block and a half from the energetic French Market and Café du Monde, have original brick walls, four-poster beds, balconies, high ceilings, and views of the French Quarter. Mornings include coffee and tea.
25 All major cards

LAMOTHE HOUSE
$–$$$$
621 ESPLANADE AVE., 70116
TEL 504/947-1161 or 800/367-5858
FAX 504/943-6536
This Victorian double-townhouse mansion on the edge of the French Quarter will quicken the pulse of any bed-and-breakfast fan who relishes the idea of finding a homemade praline on her pillow each night and free continental breakfast in the morning. All rooms have private baths; some feature four-poster canopied beds, armoires and marble-top dressers.
30 All major cards

RESTAURANTS

K-PAUL'S LOUISIANA KITCHEN
$$$$
416 CHARTRES ST.
TEL 504/524-7394
Most people know that New Orleans chef Paul Prudhomme is routinely credited with launching the nationwide Cajun food craze back in the '80s. But not everything served inside this recently renovated and expanded 1834 structure is heavily seasoned with the de rigueur bayou spice— cayenne pepper—and blackened. Fans of open kitchens can also watch cooks prepare a daily changing menu of such Prudhomme standbys as bronzed salmon with roasted-pecans-and-jalapeño sauce; stuffed and smoked soft shell crawfish; heavenly smoky chicken-andouille gumbo; and the casual restaurant's understandably famous—and sumptuous—sweet potato pecan pie, served with chantilly cream. Reservations required.
200 Closed Sun.
All major cards

ANTOINE'S
$$$–$$$$
713 ST. LOUIS ST.
TEL 504/581-4422
Seems everyone from Mark Twain to the Duke and Duchess of Windsor have broken bread inside this fifth-generation, near mythological Creole dining institution. Opened in 1840, it is the home of *pompano en papillote*, as well as oysters Rockefeller, created for the nation's then-wealthiest family. Today it is regarded primarily for its encyclopedic French-language menu of beef and fish specialties. Try the oysters Rockefeller; speckled trout poached in white wine sauce with fresh shrimp; grilled pompano with sautéed lump crabmeat; or bacon-wrapped lamb medallions. Locals opt for the red Annex room in back.
1000 Closed Sunday
AE, MC, V

SOMETHING SPECIAL

ARNAUD'S
$$$
813 BIENVILLE ST.
TEL 504/523-5433

Classic haute-Creole dining is underscored by such traditional favorites as oysters Bienville with shrimp and mushrooms; crisply fried trout meunière; and shrimp Arnaud served with the restaurant's famous homemade remoulade sauce. Beveled glass windows and overhead fans are part of a massive restoration undertaken by owner Archie Casbarian in the late 1970s to return this block-long fine-dining enclave of twelve 18th- and 19th-century buildings to its former glory. Café brulot—flamed with cinnamon sticks, cloves, and orange and lemon rind with brandy and Grand Marnier—is an after-dinner New Orleans tradition not to be missed. Sunday jazz brunch.

350 P Closed Sat. L All major cards

BACCO
$$$
310 CHARTRES ST.
TEL 504/522-2426

This award-winning Tuscan-style trattoria casts an amorous spell on diners even before they fall in love with such signature nouveau Italian dishes as foie gras pizza (topped with caramelized onions and wood-roasted Portobello mushrooms), crawfish ravioli, and Vermouth-steamed mussels. From the Venetian chandeliers and color-stained concrete floors to the vaulted ceilings and hand-painted murals, its design by owner Ralph Brennan, of the city's legendary Brennan restaurant family, is the most visually interesting eatery on his roster. Sunday brunch.

200 P All major cards

BAYONA
$$$
430 DAUPHINE ST.
TEL 504/525-4455

Over the years hotshot proprietor-chef Susan Spicer's travels have stamped her "New World cuisine" passport with an eclectic mix of sure-to-please house specialties bearing her signature culinary savoir faire. Among them are sautéed salmon with choucroute and gewurztraminer sauce; grilled duck breast with pepper jelly; roasted garlic soup; eggplant caviar and olive tapenade; lamb loin with herbed goat cheese and zinfandel sauce; and Southwestern-style grilled shrimp with black-bean cakes. Another signature of the award-winning Spicer's long-time stint as one of New Orleans best-known chefs is the romantic courtyard and intimate indoor dining offered at her 200-year-old, European-style Creole cottage restaurant.

120 P Valet Closed Sat. L, all Sun. All major cards

BELLA LUNA
$$$
914 N. PETERS ST.
TEL 504/529-1583

This beautiful fine-dining restaurant's scenic Mississippi riverfront views from the French Market are guaranteed to flavor chef Horst Pfeifer's continental-Creole dishes with *amore*. Hands-down appetizer winners are the duck confit quesadillas and smoked-salmon tartar topped with white-truffle-oil sour cream and cavier. The crawfish and crab cakes are a must. Other must-tries: pecan-crusted pork chop with Abita beer sauce; housemade fettuccine tossed tableside with truffles; and blackened mahi mahi on creamy maque choux. Dinner only.

220 P Valet All major cards

PRICES

HOTELS

An indication of the cost of a double room without breakfast is given by $ signs.

$$$$$	$225+
$$$$	$175–$225
$$$	$125–$175
$$	$85–$125
$	Less than $85

RESTAURANTS

An indication of the cost of a three-course dinner without drinks is given by $ signs.

$$$$	Over $50
$$$	$35–$50
$$	$15–$35
$	Under $15

BISTRO AT HOTEL MAISON DE VILLE
$$$
727 TOULOUSE ST.
TEL 504/528-9206

Die-hard courtyard romantics looking for a nouvelle Parisian dining experience will find all that and more at this smart bistro-style enclave at the **Hotel Maison de Ville** (see p. 236). It is decorated by ceiling fans, Impressionist-style paintings, beveled-glass mirrors, and white table linens, all set against attractive red-leather banquettes. Award-winning chef Greg Picolo has captured the hearts of locals with his New Zealand rack of lamb, grilled shrimp with andouille sausage and Creole tomato sauce, mussels *bruxellois*, and spinach salad with andouille vinaigrette. Well-known for its excellent wine list.

40 All major cards

BRENNAN'S
$$$
417 ROYAL ST.
TEL 504/525-9711

For an unforgettable taste of world-class New Orleans history, this intimate, poised, pink-stucco landmark,

founded by Owen E. Brennan, Sr., in 1946, boasts a litany of time-honored staples. Try the deliciously thick if not old-fashioned turtle soup; eggs Benedict, Sardou, or Hussarde; redfish Jaime with lump crabmeat; and, of course, the restaurant's famous—and original—flaming bananas Foster dessert. Breakfast at Brennan's is almost as famous as *Breakfast at Tiffany's.* Diners also love this lush courtyard restaurant for its 50,000-bottle wine cellar, rated by *Wine Spectator* magazine as among the best in the world. Sunday brunch.
550 P All major cards

CAFÉ SBISA
$$$
1011 DECATUR ST.
TEL 504/522-5565

The inside mezzanine balcony offers a voyeur's bird's-eye view of the ground-floor action around the bistro-style 1903 mahogany bar. Opened at the turn of the 20th century, this wood-paneled dining nook across from the French Market serves up one of the tastiest Sunday brunches in town, with turtle soup, poached eggs on crabcakes with hollandaise, poached eggs with gravlox, eggs Sardou, and zesty Creole omelettes with spicy andouille sausage. Sunday jazz brunch. Reservations recommended. Smoking at bar only.
230 Closed L All major cards

THE COURT OF TWO SISTERS
$$$
613 ROYAL ST.
TEL 504/522-7261

Brunch or dinner anytime inside this venerated Creole establishment is a sure bet. But the main reason locals bring out-of-town guests here is for the jazz brunch, amid the fountains and flickering gas lamps of one of the city's prettiest and most romantic courtyards. Best loosen your belts for the walloping, 60-item, all-you-can-eat buffet that includes everything from hot-boiled shrimp and fresh-made eggs Benedict to seafood and vegetarian pastas and crepes Suzette. Brunch daily. Reservations recommended.
555 Closed L All major cards

GALATOIRE'S
$$$
209 BOURBON ST.
TEL 504/525-2021

The 1990s renovation of this venerated Creole dining den added second-floor seating, a waiting area for customers, and an overall fresh look. Founded in 1905, it is a popular Friday lunch hangout for politicians, dowagers, and debutantes. If possible, go with a local who has his or her own waiter—it helps. What remains largely unchanged at this embodiment of New Orleans gustatory hedonism is a menu of famous Galatoire's standards: crabmeat maison, shrimp remoulade, grilled pompano meunière, oysters *en brochette* and, of course, trout amandine. Jacket required for dinner and Sunday.
225 Closed Mon. All major cards

MR. B'S BISTRO
$$$
201 ROYAL ST.
TEL 504/523-2078

It's hard to know what tasty regional Creole dish to order at this sparkling, bistro-style, highly popular addition to the Brennan family's growing list of award-winning gourmet New Orleans restaurants: The Gumbo Ya Ya (chicken-and-andouille gumbo)? Barbecue shrimp (served with French bread for dipping in the peppery butter sauce)? Crawfish-and-shrimp spring rolls? Hickory-grilled Gulf fish? Pasta jambalaya? Good luck! Sunday jazz brunch. Reservations recommended.
245 P Closed Sun L All major cards

NOLA
$$$
534 ST. LOUIS ST.
TEL 504/522-6652

A hip clientele flocks to New Orleans chef and Food Channel star Emeril Lagasse's energetic eatery for both the innovative menu of fresh ingredients as well as the exposed-brick, Soho-style ambience. Among best bets are the crab cake with chili aioli, fresh crab cake with fire-roasted beurre blanc sauce, duck with andouille spoon bread, and Vietnamese-style seafood salad with fresh watercress and ginger-lime veal glaze.
200 P Closed Sun. L All major cards

PELICAN CLUB
$$$
312 EXCHANGE ALLEY AT 615 BIENVILLE ST.
TEL 504/523-1504

Though not as well known as other local restaurants of the same league, this stylish venue should not be overlooked; the menu of intriguing Louisiana-Asia fusion flourishes. Good examples: escargots with crawfish and mushrooms, paella-style jambalaya, almond-and coconut-crusted tilapia with shrimp and pineapple; and pan-fried fish with roasted jalapeño hollandaise.
140 P Closed L All major cards

PERISTYLE
$$$
1041 DUMAINE ST.
TEL 504/593-9535

France's Provençal cooking traditions receive a respectful nod with a menu laced with winners like pan-roasted veal sweetbreads with roasted garlic, grilled filet with mushroom-orzo croquette,

and leek-stuffed tomato in sauce Lyonnaise. Chef-proprietor Anne Kearney, who studied under Emeril Lagasse, has decorated her bistro-style, split-level dining room with banquettes, antique mirrors, tiled floors, and a pair of huge murals painted in the 1920s. Reservations required.
64 P Closed Sat.–Thurs. L, all Sun. & Mon. All major cards

THE RIB ROOM

$$$
621 ST. LOUIS ST.
TEL 504/529-7045

This is a local power-lunch favorite on the ground floor of the **Omni Royal Orleans hotel** (see p. 237). It owes its stalwart reputation to the French rotisserie in the dining room, which turns out all that mouth-watering English-cut prime rib, chateaubriand, and filet mignon. The expanded dinner menu features grilled seafood specialties. Light years from your typical hotel restaurant. Romantic at night with windows looking out on Royal Street. Reservations recommended.
131 P All major cards

MIKE ANDERSON'S SEAFOOD OF NEW ORLEANS

$$
215 BOURBON ST.
TEL 504/524-3884

Former All-American LSU football legend Mike Anderson rarely needs to punt thanks to his 60-item, be-true-to-your-school menu of homestyle Cajun touchdowns, such as gumbos, étouffées, bisques, fried and broiled seafood platters, and po-boys. This bouncy, refreshingly casual eatery and oyster bar also tackles a handful of noteworthy house specialties that include turtle soup, oysters Rockefeller and Bienville, jumbo shrimp broiled in sherry, and fresh broiled snapper with fresh mushrooms and sautéed lump crabmeat. Raw oyster special Sunday through Thursday 11:30 a.m. to 6 p.m. Smoking at bar only.
180 All major cards

RED FISH GRILL

$$
115 BOURBON ST.
TEL 504/598-1200

Fun makes the world go 'round at this whimsical Ralph Brennan eatery. It is festooned with hand-painted tables in seafood designs, three-foot mirrored oysters, and metal palms. Likewise, a good-times menu of nouveau Southern comforts features shiitake-and-grilled-shrimp quesadillas, shrimp remoulade with fried green tomatoes, crabmeat-stuffed shrimp, sweet potato catfish, and spring rolls with chicken prepared on the state-of-the-art kitchen's wood-burning grill. Smoking at bar only. Sunday brunch.
210 All major cards

TUJAGUE'S

$$
823 DECATUR ST.
TEL 504/525-8676

Opened in 1856, this grandfather of classic New Orleans dining and the city's second oldest restaurant has entertained its share of U.S. presidents and foreign heads of state. Come hungry—the six-course-only dinners, built around beef brisket and filet mignon, are a mouthful. Reservations suggested.
220 All major cards

ACME OYSTER HOUSE

$
724 IBERVILLE ST.
TEL 504/522-5973

Since 1910 this noisy, crowded, classic Big Easy oyster shrine has been shucking the raw bivalves and consistently ranked as among the city's best to a loyal following of locals, celebs, and international visitors alike. Other New Orleans staples include deep-fried oysters, oyster po-boys (or stuffed any way you like), bounteous seafood platters, and red beans and rice. Bar stocks a good selection of cold beers perfect for downing a dozen on the half shell.
100 All major cards

BENNACHIN

$
1212 ROYAL ST.
TEL 504/486-1313

The daring menu crafted by Cameroon and Gambia natives Alyse Njenge and Fanta Tambajang, respectively, is a heartwarming tribute to the centuries-old West African influenced legacy of traditional Creole cookery found in New Orleans and throughout the Caribbean. "Bennachin" is the Gambian word for jambalaya. African music and colorful paintings depicting village life sets the mood for a Mandinka and Bassa language menu, with English translations, rich in poultry, fish and lamb. Among winners are *nsouki ioppa* (a smoky-flavored West African gumbo), *kembel-ioppa* (sautéed lamb strips in ginger-garlic sauce), and *akara* (black-eyed peas). Many dishes come with *mbondo cone* (coconut rice).
50 Closed L Sat. All major cards

SOMETHING SPECIAL

CAFÉ DU MONDE

$
800 DECATUR ST.
TEL 504/581-2914

This legendary and oldest surviving outdoor French Market coffee stand, located across the street from Jackson Square and St. Louis Cathedral, is the place to be, especially in the wee hours of the morning when the French Quarter is yawning awake. Creamy café au lait and hot beignets, dusted with

powdered sugar, are hallmarks of this must-see canopied landmark open 24-7 and known for its after-hours caffeine nightcaps and early morning jolts of chicory. No alcohol.
400 Cash only

OLD COFFEE POT
$
714 ST. PETER ST.
TEL 504/524-3500
Unless it's a hot summer day, opt for the cozy, tree-shaded courtyard in back in which to enjoy one of the city's best Creole breakfasts—served at all hours, they are the mainstay of this 1894 eatery. Sure-fire hits include Benedict-style eggs Jonathan (with ham, tomatoes, and raw oysters), eggs Conti (poached in white wine sauce with fresh chicken livers, served over buttermilk biscuits), Rockefeller omelette (stuffed with creamed spinach, oysters, herbs, spices, and cheese), and *callas* (Creole rice cakes with Vermont maple syrup). Breakfast daily.
120 All major cards

PORT OF CALL
$
838 ESPLANADE AVE.
TEL 504/523-0120
Two of the main reasons locals and tourists in-the-know get their buns to this noisy, nautically themed neighborhood eatery is for its legendary, freshly ground mega-burgers, served alongside fist-sized baked potatoes loaded with the works. Also specialty pizzas and good steaks, especially filet mignon and strip sirloin. Bar patrons keep the oldies jukebox cranked up weekend nights. Smoking.
60 AE, MC, V

QUARTER SCENE
$
900 DUMAINE ST.
TEL 504/522-6533
Breakfast and after-hours draw a loyal clientele of artists and bon vivants to this cozy, bustling establishment. No alcohol, but customers are welcome to bring their own. Brunch is a mainstay thanks to a charitable menu of local favorites ranging from po-boys and thick gumbo to seasoned corned-beef hash and eggs Beauregard with tasso and black olives. Breakfast daily.
54 All major cards

FAUBOURG MARIGNY

HOTELS

CLAIBORNE MANSION
$$$–$$$$$
2111 DAUPHINE ST., 70116
TEL 504/949-7327
FAX 504/949-0388
www.claibornemansion.com
Discerning travelers, including artist LeRoy Neiman, have appreciated the fact that this 1859 three-story Greek Revival mansion—meticulously restored and luxuriously appointed by owner Cleo Pelleteri—is tucked in Faubourg Marigny a few discrete blocks away from the thrills and spills of the French Quarter. And no one has ever complained about the delicious breakfasts still prepared in the original open-hearth kitchen. A gorgeous oak tree-framed courtyard, where complimentary evening cocktails and hors d'oeuvres are served, is surrounded by individually decorated rooms and suites with queen-size beds and marble bathrooms. The No. 11 double-parlor suite features a grand piano, a palatial bathroom, and a separate living area with medallion ceilings.
7 P AE, MC, V

RESTAURANTS

PRALINE CONNECTION
$
542 FRENCHMEN ST.
TEL 504/943-3934
The melt-in-your-mouth cornbread that accompanies most meals, including baked or crispy fried chicken and to-die-for sweet barbeçue ribs, is a hallmark of this eatery's unsurpassed homestyle Creole soul food. Try the soft shell crabs. A hip, friendly wait staff dressed in wild-patterned ties and fedoras give this casual corner restaurant, accented by ceiling fans and black-and-white tile floors, just the right rakish tilt. Save room for a dessert of bread pudding with praline sauce.
75 All major cards

CBD & ALGIERS POINT

HOTELS

JW MARRIOTT
$$$$$
614 CANAL ST.
TEL. 504/525-6500
The contemporary exterior of this 30-story glass tower bordering the French Quarter belies the Old New Orleans feel of its interior decor with wrought iron accents and murals depicting the city's musical roots. Rooms in this AAA four-diamond property offer views of the French Quarter, the Mississippi River or the downtown business district. Amenities include cable TV, upscale toiletries, in-room coffee/tea, free local calls and a morning newspaper. A French-inspired restaurant, the Midi (serving breakfast, lunch and dinner), gives a nod to the ancestry of both the

city and the hotel that was previously part of the Le Meridien chain.
494 P All major cards

WINDSOR COURT HOTEL
$$$$$
300 GRAVIER ST., 70130
TEL 504/523-6000 or 800/262-2662
FAX 504/596-4513

Afternoon tea accompanied by live harp music in the first-floor lobby's Le Salon and a six-million-dollar art collection aren't the only touches of refinement inside this British-style luxury property. Bay windows or private balconies offering spectacular views are standard in all guest rooms, including 264 spacious suites with separate living areas and Italian marble bathrooms. The award-winning **Grill Room** (see p. 247) offers five-star continental dining accented by such winners as grilled sweetbreads on a rosemary skewer with chick-pea hummus and huckleberry-orange chutney; and sweet potato and walnut ravioli with sautéed fois gras.
324 P All major cards

HOTEL INTER-CONTINENTAL NEW ORLEANS
$$$$–$$$$$
444 ST. CHARLES AVE., 70130
TEL 504/525-5566 or 800/445-6563
FAX 504/523-7310

A charming garden courtyard landscaped with musical sculpture helps soothe the restless traveler staying at this downtown high-rise on the St. Charles Avenue streetcar line and a short walk from the Warehouse District. People with allergies can opt for one of the environmental rooms that feature special air-filtration systems. Minibars and separate dressing areas are standard, while the 40 deluxe guestrooms and suites feature posh amenities such as Jacuzzis, and marble baths, as well as continental breakfast and complimentary cocktails in the lounge. Also on the premises is New Orleans chef Willy Cohn's popular **Veranda** (see p. 247) restaurant.
482 P Valet All major cards

HYATT REGENCY NEW ORLEANS
$$$$–$$$$$
500 POYDRAS ST., 70113
TEL 504/561-1234 or 800/233-1234
FAX 504/587-4141

This immense hotel's business center and outdoor pool attract a roster of devoted guests who understand the importance of mixing work with relaxation. Shopaholics, however, are thrilled to learn this 32-story atrium hotel is connected to the New Orleans Centre shopping complex, with Macy's and Lord and Taylor's. Travelers staying in one of the traditionally furnished rooms, each featuring a complement of amenities, can take the hotel's free shuttle to the French Quarter. Nighttime, the **Top of the Dome Steakhouse** (504-599-4826), the city's only revolving rooftop restaurant, offers first-rate prime rib as well as a bird's-eye view of downtown New Orleans.
184 P Valet All major cards

WYNDHAM NEW ORLEANS AT CANAL PLACE
$$$$–$$$$$
100 IBERVILLE ST., 70130
TEL 504/566-7006 or 800/996-3426
FAX 504/533-5120

Across from the Aquarium of the Americas on the edge of the French Quarter, on the 11th floor of the upmarket Canal Place Shopping Centre, this luxurious mega-luxury hotel has two-story window panoramic views and a marble lobby chockablock with antiques. Afternoon tea.
437 P Valet All major cards

PRICES

HOTELS
An indication of the cost of a double room without breakfast is given by $ signs.

$$$$$	$225+
$$$$	$175–$225
$$$	$125–$175
$$	$85–$125
$	Less than $85

RESTAURANTS
An indication of the cost of a three-course dinner without drinks is given by $ signs.

$$$$	Over $50
$$$	$35–$50
$$	$15–$35
$	Under $15

COURTYARD BY MARRIOTT
$$$–$$$$
124 ST. CHARLES AVE., 70130
TEL 504/581-9005 or 800/321-2211
FAX 504/581-6264

With a nod to history, the Veranda Hotel that graced this site from 1839 to 1855 has been faithfully re-created, complete with atrium columns and iron trellis balconies with St. Charles Avenue views. This six-story hotel of spacious guestrooms is located in the Central Business District on the streetcar line and a short walk from the French Quarter.
140 P Valet All major cards

FAIRMONT HOTEL
$$$–$$$$$
123 BARONNE ST., 70112
TEL 504/529-7111 or 800/635-2303
FAX 504/522-2303

www.fairmont.com/new orleans/
During the holidays, the block-long lobby of gilded columns and red Oriental rugs in this venerated 16-story hotel, enjoyed over the decades by eight U.S. presidents, is decorated like a winter wonderland. But sophisticated travelers anytime of year will understand why this historic property—and its legendary **Sazarac Bar,** home of the famous bourbon drink of the same name invented in 1859—is a long-time favorite among locals. Amenities include spacious rooms with marble bathrooms, oversized towels, and new tile floors. Tennis courts at the rooftop resort. Arthur Hailey used the Fairmont as the model for his novel *Hotel.*
700 P Valet All major cards

HOLIDAY INN DOWNTOWN SUPERDOME
$$$–$$$$
330 LOYOLA AVE., 70112
TEL 504/581-1600 or 800/535-7830
FAX 504/522-0073
All that jazz best describes the decor of this downtown hotel with telephones and voice mail, hair dryers and mini-safes in all rooms and suites. In the lobby guests discover complimentary morning coffee and evening ice cream, as well as original mural art of such New Orleans jazz legends as Louis Armstrong and Buddy Bolden. If that isn't enough, the marvelous, exterior, 150-foot mural of a clarinet painted by local artist Robert Dafford should be a tip-off to travelers that they are visiting the birthplace of jazz.
296 P All major cards

INTERNATIONAL HOUSE
$$$–$$$$$
221 CAMP ST., 70130
TEL 504/553-9550 or 800/633-5770
FAX 504/553-9560
From the forged-steel front desk to guest rooms decorated with 19th-century style armoires and black-and-white photos of jazz legends, this artfully designed boutique hotel, located inside a 12-story, turn-of-the-century, beaux arts building, is making a name for itself among domestic and international travelers. Double-headed glass showers and a private telephone number direct to each room are just a few of the flourishes. Fall under a love spell at **Loa,** the hotel's candlelit bar named for the divine spirits of voodoo, order a Flambeau drink of spiced rum and Grand Marnier.
119 P Valet All major cards

LAFAYETTE HOTEL
$$$–$$$$$
600 ST. CHARLES AVE., 70130
TEL 504/524-4441 or 800/524-4441
FAX 504/523-7327
In many ways this historic five-story hotel dripping with Old World charm embodies the sentiment behind the saying that New Orleans is America's most European city. Whether it's the wrought-iron balconies, the French mahogany front desk, or the individually decorated rooms furnished with gilt mirrors and marble baths, this property located adjacent to the Warehouse District offers a splendid retreat from the rattle and hum of New Orleans's urban pulse. Football legend **Mike Ditka's** restaurant of the same name on the ground floor offers a pigskin-themed menu of Souper Bowls and Training Table pot roasts, among other dishes.
44 P Valet All major cards

OMNI ROYAL CRESCENT HOTEL
$$$–$$$$$
535 GRAVIER ST, 70130
TEL 504/527-0006
FAX 504/523-0806
A European-style lobby with Oriental rugs and objets d'art and the classic New Orleans cuisine in **Christino's** (504-571-7500) are only a couple of the benefits of staying at this boutique hotel in the heart of the Central Business District. Others include the skyline views from the rooftop pool and guest rooms with bedside cassette players, cotton bathrobes and slippers, marble baths, and fine linens.
98 P Valet All major cards

THE PELHAM
$$$–$$$$$
444 COMMON ST., 70130
TEL 504/522-4444 or 888/211-3447
FAX 504/539-9010
One of the best features of this luxury European-style boutique hotel is the 10-foot windows overlooking Canal St. in each of the well-appointed guestrooms. The rooms are furnished with marble baths, four-poster beds, exposed brick walls, and antiques. Whether it's the complimentary newspaper delivered each morning to your room, fine soaps, or plush robes, the emphasis is on amenities.
60 P Valet All major cards

THE RITZ-CARLTON
$$$–$$$$$
921 CANAL ST., 70112
TEL 504/524-1331 or 800/241-3333
FAX 504/523-7310
The New Orleans edition of this worldwide luxury property is located inside the historic—and renovated to the tune of 200 million dollars—Maison Blanche beaux arts shopping landmark. Amenities in this property include minibar, in-room safe,

terry robes, and marble bath, plus a two-story, 20,000-square-foot fitness center and spa with 16 rooms. **Victor's** fine-dining restaurant offers a Creole-continental menu.
452 P Valet All major cards

W NEW ORLEANS
$$$–$$$$$
333 POYDRAS ST., 70130
TEL 504/525-9444 or
800 522-6963
FAX 504 568-9312
One of the newest faces on the block is this renovated and renamed financial district property. Fine linens, 27-inch TVs, and plush down comforters are some of the amenities offered at this 23-story high-rise within easy walking distance of the Warehouse District, the Mississippi River, and the French Quarter.
423 P Valet All major cards

WYNDHAM RIVERFRONT HOTEL
$$$–$$$$
701 CONVENTION CENTER BLVD., 70130
TEL 504/524-8200 or
800/996-3426
FAX 504/524-0600
This international chain's reputation for luxury and pleasantly furnished accommodations is alive and well at this property bustling with New Orleans hospitality. Wheelers and dealers will like the extra long phone cords, 100-watt work-friendly lighting, and oversized desks in each room. Located on the fringes of the trendy Warehouse District, it is within easy walking distance of the French Quarter.
202 P Valet All major cards

LE PAVILLON HOTEL
$$–$$$$$
833 POYDRAS ST., 70112
TEL 504/581-3111
or 800/535-9095
FAX 504/620-4130
European and American antiques accent the luxuriously appointed guestrooms and suites of this stylish and white-columned landmark to Old World charm. It is beloved by locals for the spectacular Bohemian crystal chandeliers hanging in the lobby. Complimentary shoeshine and 24-hour room service. Sumptuous dining in the **Crystal Room** is all the more gracious thanks to a marble fireplace and massive gilt columns.
226 P Valet All major cards

MAISON PIERRE LAFITTE
$$–$$$
108 UNIVERSITY PLACE, 70112
TEL 504/527-5800
FAX 504/527-5802
Theatergoers will find this modest-size property worth its weight in gold for convenience alone: The Orpheum Theatre is across the street. Tiffany lamps, armoires, and double beds grace guest rooms. Travelers with a yen for lofts have seven from which to choose, each featuring exposed ceiling beams and circular metal staircases. Free coffee available in the small lobby.
17 All major cards

THE AMBASSADOR
$–$$$$$
535 TCHOUPITOULAS ST., 70130
TEL 504/527-5271 or
888/527-5271
FAX 504/527-5270
Tucked in the heart of the trendy Warehouse District and three blocks from the French Quarter, this modest-size hotel is within easy walking distance to a host of galleries and untouristed restaurants and nightclubs. Created by renovating three 19th-century coffee warehouses, the hotel features oversize rooms accented by hardwood floors and furnished with four-poster wrought-iron beds. Phones, voice mail, and fax/modems, 24-hour lounge, in-room safes.
165 P Valet All major cards

ROSEWALK HOUSE
$–$$
320 VERRET ST., ALGIERS POINT 70114
TEL 504/368-1500 or
888/368-1500
FAX 504/366-9168
This Victorian-style bed-and-breakfast in historic Algiers Point offers guests a romantic nighttime view of the New Orleans skyline. Guestrooms have private baths, cable TV, and complimentary Creole breakfast in the formal dining room and morning newspaper. One room features an antique bed, fireplace, and second-floor view of the Algiers belltower. Garden-framed courtyard patio.
4 MC, V

SLEEP INN
$–$$$
334 O'KEEFE AVE., 70112
TEL 504/524-5400 or
888/524-8586
FAX 504/524-5450
This new, 129-room, downtown property, located only blocks from the French Quarter, has a lot to offer amenity-wise, including free breakfast and newspaper, on-site parking, and laundry facilities. Like a growing number of budget-friendly properties, this well-landscaped hotel has a business center for dealmakers on the move.
129 P All major cards

RESTAURANTS

EMERIL'S
$$$$
800 TCHOUPITOULAS ST.
TEL 504/528-9393
Even if the flagship restaurant

of bam-master celebrity chef Emeril Lagasse's culinary empire has, as some say, gotten too big for its own apron, the cutting edge of nouveau Creole cuisine rarely takes a detour inside this one-time factory. For proof start with the smoked trout dumplings and then move smartly to the andouille-crusted redfish, the seared fois gras with duck confit, or one of the always satisfying specials. Decor features polished hardwood floors and abstract oil paintings. Smoking at bar only.
250 Valet Closed Sat. L, all Sun. All major cards

GRILL ROOM
$$$$
WINDSOR COURT HOTEL
300 GRAVIER ST.
TEL 504/522-1992 or 800/262-2662
Tucked on the second floor of the elegant **Windsor Court Hotel** (see p. 243), this impeccable, world-class culinary oasis, ranked as one of the finest restaurants in the United States, never fails to dazzle even the most discriminating gourmet. It's also one of the most beautiful dining venues in the city. Seared foie gras, grilled sweetbreads on a rosemary skewer with chick-pea hummus and huckleberry-orange chutney, and white sturgeon with braised leeks are just the beginning of the ever changing French-continental menu by Alsace-Lorraine native and executive chef Rene Bajeux. He has been named a Master Chef of France, one of only 50 U.S. chefs to hold that title. For dessert order the crème brulée. Arrive early to enjoy a pre-dinner cocktail in the Polo Lounge. Reservations required.
150 Valet All major cards

RESTAURANT AUGUST
$$$$
301 TCHOUPITOULAS ST.
TEL. 504/299-9777
FAX 504/299-1199
Housed in an historic Italianate building that echoes the opulence of 19th century New Orleans, Restaurant August serves contemporary French food with an emphasis on fresh local ingredients. Within a year of its fall 2001opening, Restaurant August was named to *Conde Nast Traveler*'s list of Top-50 new eateries, worldwide. The menu of local-boy Chef John Besh remains true to his Creole roots, but also draws on his international experience including stints in Germany and the South of France. The wine list was named one of the ten best in the country by *Food & Wine* and *Condé Nast* called the bread pudding with whiskey ice cream "the best dessert in town." Dress code is "smart casual" and reservations are highly recommended.
84 Valet Closed Sun. All major cards

SOMETHING SPECIAL

PALACE CAFÉ
$$$
605 CANAL ST.
TEL 504/523-1661
Owner Dickie Brennan, Jr., of the city's famed Brennan restaurateur family, keeps earning well-deserved national kudos for this two-story Parisian-style brasserie, tucked in the century-old landmark building once occupied by Werlein's Music. Sit upstairs at one of the window tables overlooking Canal Street and enjoy chef Guy Martin's house specialties: crabmeat cheesecake, turtle soup, molasses glazed oven-roasted duck, or shepherd's pie updated with garlic mashed potatoes and veggies. Live blues Sunday brunch. Reservations recommended.
250 Valet Closed Sat. & Sun. L All major cards

RIVERVIEW
$$$
555 CANAL ST.
TEL 504/581-1000
This casual, 41st-floor restaurant—the highest in town—in the **New Orleans Marriott,** offers a bewitching nighttime view of the city. Its Creole-continental menu specializes in pan-seared salmon with fried oysters and veal chop stuffed with Fontina cheese, prosciutto, and sage cream.
150 Valet Closed Sun. & Mon. L All major cards

VERANDA
$$$
444 ST. CHARLES AVE.
TEL 504/525-5566
The enclosed, atrium-style gas lamp courtyard may be a reproduction of its French Quarter counterparts a few blocks away. But when summer hits with a vengeance, this lush oasis in the **Hotel Inter-Continental New Orleans** (see p. 244) is ideal for enjoying a sumptuous Sunday champagne jazz brunch. The setting is appealing for dinners, complemented by long-time local chef and native German Willy Cohn's vegetable and polenta lasagna and his famous crab cakes with fresh mozzarella. Sunday brunch.
150–200 Valet All major cards

BON TON CAFÉ
$$
401 MAGAZINE ST.
TEL 504/524-3386 or 888/524-5611
Restaurant owners and descendants of south Louisiana residents Alvin and Alzine Pierce liberally laced the traditional Cajun menu of this long-time culinary

nook with generations-old Acadian cookery. Today the Pierce's nephew Wayne and his wife, Debbie, carry on the family tradition of flawless authenticity with, among other dishes, crabmeat au gratin, crawfish served four ways (étouffée, fried, omelette, and bisque), oyster jambalaya, and shrimp Creole. Exposed brick walls and wrought-iron chandeliers make for nice ambience.
110 All major cards

LEMON GRASS CAFÉ
$$
217 CAMP ST.
TEL 504/523-1200

In recent decades the Vietnamese community has become one of the newest members of New Orleans's proud ethnic melting pot. And, thanks to proprietor-chef Minh Bui, who learned to cook at his family's postwar café outside Saigon, this spirited establishment is perhaps the city's best example of how well nouveau Creole flourishes can rev up the French-Vietnamese cooking traditions. Good examples include chicken and coconut milk curry soup, grilled lemongrass beef with papaya, and lacquered duck. Reservations recommended.
60 Closed L, all Sun. & Mon. All major cards

LIBORIO CUBAN RESTAURANT
$$
321 MAGAZINE ST.
TEL 504/581-9680

Pulsing Latin music accompanies traditional Cuban dishes such as the tantalizing garlic roasted pork, Cubano sandwich (pork, ham, Swiss cheese, and pickles on pressed grilled French bread), green-fried plantains, and boiled yucca with garlic sauce. Probably the only place in town that stocks Honduran Port Royal beer, an excellent accompaniment to the earthy Spanish-African cooking traditions born on the Caribbean's largest island.
80 Closed Sun.–Mon. D All major cards

GARDEN DISTRICT & UPTOWN

HOTELS

THE PONTCHARTRAIN
$$$
2031 ST. CHARLES AVE., 70140
TEL 504/524-0581 or 800/777-6193
FAX 504/529-1165

Stylish luminaries ranging from Truman Capote and Lillian Hellman to Frank Sinatra and Anne Rice have graced this Moorish-style grande dame hotel and its landmark blue canopy since it opened in 1927. Antiques, artwork, and king- and queen-size beds can be found under the 12-foot ceilings of all rooms; suites come equipped with kitchenettes and separate living and dining/entertaining rooms. Eighteenth-century London gates enclose a garden courtyard. Many of the city's movers and shakers can be found yawning awake over breakfast in the ground-floor coffee shop directly across from the **Bayou Bar,** a favorite for locals.
119 Valet All major cards

BEAU SEJOUR
$$–$$$
1930 NAPOLEON AVE., 70115
TEL 504/897-3746 or 888/897-9398
FAX 504/891-3340

European and Louisiana-country antiques grace the five gracious and tastefully decorated guest rooms, with private baths, of this 1906 home. The tropical patio is the ideal setting for the complimentary continental breakfast; the balconies and porch provide the view du jour for the dozen Mardi Gras parades that roll down Napoleon Avenue during Carnival season. Amenities include cable TV and phones.
6 All major cards

THE COLUMNS
$$–$$$
3811 ST. CHARLES AVE., 70115
TEL 504/899-9308
FAX 504/899-8170

To stay in this recently renovated and romantic St. Charles Avenue landmark in the heart of Uptown is to know the enduring charms of one of the city's prettiest hotels. But the recent addition of private baths, armoires, and other modern touches to the cozy guest rooms and suites with high ceilings tell only part of the story. The Victorian bar on the first floor of this four-columned hotel, seen in the movie *Pretty Baby,* is also one of the city's most popular watering holes. Or, guests can relax on the veranda and watch the streetcar roll by under a canopy of stately oaks.
20 AE, MC, V

PRICES

HOTELS
An indication of the cost of a double room without breakfast is given by **$** signs.

$$$$$	$225+
$$$$	$175–$225
$$$	$125–$175
$$	$85–$125
$	Less than $85

RESTAURANTS
An indication of the cost of a three-course dinner without drinks is given by **$** signs.

$$$$	Over $50
$$$	$35–$50
$$	$15–$35
$	Under $15

PARK VIEW GUESTHOUSE
$$
7004 ST. CHARLES AVE., 70118
TEL 504/861-7564 or 888/533-0746
FAX 504/861-1225

It's easy to take a walk on the wild side while staying at this Victorian jewel: Audubon Zoo is directly across the street. Most of the rooms inside this pink three-story former residence have baths, and many feature special touches such as armoires and four-poster beds. Audubon Park, St. Charles Avenue's streetcar, and a picturesque canopy of live oaks, not to mention Loyola and Tulane Universities, are right outside the front door. Simply put, location makes this hotel a winner.

22 All major cards

PRYTANIA PARK HOTEL
$$–$$$
1525 PRYTANIA ST., 70130
TEL 504/524-0427 or 800/862-1984
FAX 504/522-2977

Built in the 1850s, this cozy Greek Revival boutique hotel is tucked like a secret in the Garden District. Original European-style millwork, high ceilings, hand-carved English-pine furninishings, and spacious marble dressing areas are hallmarks of the guest rooms. Lofts with circular metal staircases, armoires, and four-poster beds accent some of the rooms. All come equipped with microwaves, refrigerators, and ceiling fans.

62 P All major cards

GARDEN DISTRICT HOTEL
$-$$$$$
2203 ST. CHARLES AVE.
TEL. 800/205-7131 or 504/566-1200
www.gardendistricthotel.com

Walk out of this three-diamond hotel and climb aboard the St. Charles Avenue streetcar to explore the historic Garden District or to enjoy a short ride to the French Quarter. Decorated in traditional New Orleans-style, the spacious rooms come with a complimentary weekday newspaper, in-room coffee/tea maker and 24-hour room service. The lobby restaurant, **Lulu's in the Garden,** has garnered a lot of positive press for its tasty "comfort food" cuisine. (See p. 250.) Located just two miles from downtown, this stately Clarion hotel offers special Internet-only rates on its Website that can make it an excellent choice for the traveler on a budget.

133 P Valet All major cards

RESTAURANTS

BRIGTSEN'S
$$$
723 DANTE ST.
TEL 504/861-7610

One of the city's most charming pockets of "brilliantly creative" nouvelle Creole cuisine awaits visitors to this bistro-style, renovated shotgun cottage of intimate, individually decorated dining rooms. Regulars count on surprises from the award- and accolade-winning chef Frank Brigtsen's ever changing menu: perhaps grilled rabbit tenderloin served on tasso Parmesan grit cakes, sesame-encrusted foie gras, or blackened yellow fin tuna. Reservations recommended. Nonsmoking only.

60 Closed L and Sun.-Mon. D All major cards

SOMETHING SPECIAL

COMMANDER'S PALACE
$$$
1403 WASHINGTON AVE.
TEL 504/899-8221

Could any life truly be complete without breaking bread at least once inside this glorious Garden District bastion of internationally acclaimed Creole fine dining? Its kitchen has been graced by a generation of New Orleans' best ever chefs, ranging from Emeril Lagasse to Paul Prudhomme. From shrimp remoulade, cane-smoked salmon, and rack of lamb to roasted quail and pan-seared foie gras, executive chef Jamie Shannon's Creole-continental menu keeps this Victorian palace of culinary excellence at the top of the dining wish list for locals and out-of-town visitors alike. In 1974, the city's equally legendary Brennan family of restaurateurs bought this establishment, first opened in the 1880s to cater to the staid, English-speaking Anglo-Saxons settling in the Uptown section of New Orleans, far from the French-speaking, freewheeling Creoles of the French Quarter. Saturday and Sunday live jazz brunch. Reservations required.

350 P Valet All major cards

EMERIL'S DELMONICO
$$$
1300 ST. CHARLES AVE.
TEL 504/525-4937

Five casually trendy dining rooms redecorated in contemporary style and a menu retooled with Creole classics by owner and super-star chef Emeril Lagasse have kept locals flocking to this century-old restaurant since it reopened in 1998. Try the slow-roasted chicken Delmonico, veal Marcelle sautéed with crab and topped with hollandaise, and filet mignon with fried oysters. Sunday Jazz brunch. Reservations recommended.

220 P Valet Closed Sat.. L All major cards

CAFÉ ATCHAFALAYA
$$
901 LOUISIANA AVE.
TEL 504/891-5271
Out-of-town diners lucky enough to stumble upon local legend Iler Pope's not-to-be-missed neighborhood eatery are greeted at the table by the Mississippi native's famous homemade jalapeño cheese bread. From there it's all uphill, thanks to the long-time chef's winning homestyle menu of "rather Southern specialties," such as the pork chop stuffed with andouille cornbread, chicken and dumplings, fried chicken livers with pepper jelly, and crabmeat- and shrimp-stuffed soft shell crab meunière. Brunch Saturday and Sunday.
70 Closed Sun. D, all Mon. MC, V

CLANCY'S
$$
6100 ANNUCIATION ST.
TEL 504/895-1111
Cozy, stylish, hip, and vivacious best describe this neighborhood corner bistro. For quiet, opt for an upstairs dining room decorated with floor-to-ceiling wine racks and Jazzfest posters. Signature best bets: veal liver Lyonnaise, filet mignon with Stilton and red wine demi-glace, smoked soft shell crab, and smoked shrimp with ginger. Reservations recommended.
110 Closed Mon. L, all Sun. All major cards

LULU'S IN THE GARDEN
$$
2203 ST. CHARLES AVE.
TEL. 504/586-9956
At this casual Uptown restaurant, located in the **Garden District Hotel,** Chef Corbin Evans keeps the food simple, but delicious—reinventing mostly Southern childhood comfort foods with a sophisticated and fun flair that would make anyone want to eat their vegetables. Evans gained a following while creating in the kitchen of Lulu's original French Quarter location where meals started with a plate of grilled vegetables. From aioli-dripping french fries or fried chicken salad with red onion rings and buttermilk-herb dressing to spice-crusted tilapia with lobster mashed potatoes and corn fritters—this menu leaves diners satisfied, and usually, coming back for more. Open for breakfast, lunch (Tuesday-Friday), dinner (Wednesday-Sunday) and Sunday brunch. Reservations recommended.
40 Valet All major cards

MAT & NADDIE'S
$$
937 LEONIDAS ST.
TEL. 504/861-9600
It may be hard to spot this charming restaurant tucked just off River Road, because it looks much like all the other 150-year-old wood-frame houses in this quiet Carrollton neighborhood. But step inside and find a casually elegant atmosphere, whether seated in the softly lit dining room or on the inviting outdoor patio. The food is mostly a sort of modern Creole—not quite as heavy and even featuring vegetarian fare—with a bit of Southeast Asian dishes thrown in the mix. However, for the most part, these disparate influences are kept separate rather than being fused, so diners can enjoy choices from Vietnamese spring rolls to baked oysters Bienville. Open for lunch Monday-Friday, dinner Thursday-Saturday. Seating is limited in this popular restaurant. Reservations recommended for dinner.
72 Street Closed Sun. All major cards

PASCALE'S MANALE
$$
1838 NAPOLEON AVE.
TEL 504/895-4877
The legendary home of the hands-down best barbecue shrimp in town has kept this Creole-Italian dining landmark—owned and operated by the same family since 1913—on the lips of loyal locals. Never mind that the dish is misnamed—the large shrimp aren't really barbecued but rather baked and served with doughy French bread for dunking in the spicy butter sauce. Other winners include the oysters—served raw, Bienville-, or Rockefeller-style.
180 Closed Sat.–Sun. L All major cards

SOMETHING SPECIAL

UPPERLINE
$$
1413 UPPERLINE ST.
TEL 504/891-9822
Long-time restaurateur and bon vivant JoAnn Clevenger's rotating collection of artwork is only one of the reasons locals love to dine at the affable host's bistro-style 1877 townhouse. Others include her summer-long "festival" of creative garlic dishes and a year-round award-winning nouveau Creole menu highlighted by Louisiana oyster stew, barbecued crawfish, duck gumbo, and shrimp curry. Sunday brunch. Reservations recommended.
85 Closed L. Dinner only Wed.–Sun. All major cards

CAMELLIA GRILL
$
626 S. CARROLLTON AVE.
TEL 504/866-9573
The sometimes lengthy lines of tourists and college students who've stepped off the streetcar at the Riverbend intersection of Carrollton and St. Charles

Avenue attest to the popularity of this century-old diner best known for its hamburgers with grilled onions, mocha freezes, and chili omelettes. The white-columned institution's open grill and counter-stool-only seating are part of the charm. Popular late-night spot, since it stays open till 3 a.m. on weekends. No alcohol served.
29 Cash only

MID-CITY & THE LAKESHORE

HOTELS

SOMETHING SPECIAL

DEGAS HOUSE
$$$$$
2306 ESPLANADE AVE., 70119
TEL 504/821-5009 or 800/755-6730
FAX 504/821-0870
French Impressionist artist Edward Degas lived with relatives for a short time in this Esplanade Ridge Historical District mansion and began no fewer than 20 works later completed following his return to Paris. Guest rooms in this bed-and-breakfast are named for Degas family members and include cable TV, phones, private baths, and antiques. Complimentary breakfast (a traditional Creole breakfast on weekends) is served in the sun-lit room believed to be Degas' studio. A third-floor attic features spacious, Parisian-style garret rooms each with double or queen-size beds.
4 P MC, V

BENACHI HOUSE
$$
2257 BAYOU RD., 70119
TEL 504/525-7040 or 800/308-7040
FAX 504/525-9760
Tucked on picturesque Bayou Road minutes from City Park, this 19th-century Greek Revival home and historical landmark is accented by 14-foot ceilings with decorative medallions, antique mahogany and rosewood furnishings, Rococo chandeliers, black-marble mantels, as well as artifacts from the backyard unearthed by the state's archaeological society. Guest rooms feature private baths and are named for each of the children of original owner Nicholas M. Benachi, the Consul of Greece who constructed the home in 1858. Romantic, tree-shaded grounds with walkways and terraces.
4 All major cards

ESPLANADE VILLA
$$
2216 ESPLANADE AVE., 70119
TEL 504/525-7040 or 800/308-7040
FAX 504/525-9760
Rich Victorian colors and 19th-century antiques accentuate the timeless beauty of this 1880 Italianate home and present-day bed-and-breakfast featuring five guest suites, three of which have small private porches overlooking tree-lined Esplanade Avenue. All suites have separate sitting rooms and private tiled baths with cast-iron Victorian tubs and pedestal sinks.
5 All major cards

BEST WESTERN PATIO MOTEL
$–$$$
2820 TULANE AVE., 70119
TEL 504/822-0200 or 800/270-6955
FAX 504/822-2328
Complimentary coffee, free shuttle service to the French Quarter, and secured enclosed parking are part of the package of amenities at this motel tailor-made for travelers looking for value without blowing their budget.
75 P All major cards

RESTAURANTS

CHRISTIAN'S
$$$
3835 IBERVILLE ST.
TEL 504/482-4924
Only in New Orleans would visitors find a renovated, former Lutheran church, built in 1914, pulling duty as a consistently popular French and Creole dining den; it is surrounded by Gothic-style stained-glass windows, and a bar is located on the spot of the one-time crying room. This historic Mid-City landmark is named for co-founder Christian Ansel. For two decades he and his partner, Hank Bergen, have lured faithful followers with a heavenly menu of local favorites, such as oysters en brochette, cold smoked soft shell crab, and oyster-stuffed filet mignon. Reservations recommended.
110 Closed Sun.–Mon. All major cards

GABRIELLE
$$$
3201 ESPLANADE AVE.
TEL 504/948-6233
From grilled loin of lamb and grilled rabbit tenderloin to jerked pork rib chop with cheese-stuffed peppers over dirty rice, the daily-changing menu by proprietors and long-time New Orleans chef team Greg and Mary Sonnier have earned a local loyal following over the years. Mirrored panels and oversized windows accent the cozy and romantic fine-dining venue.
64 Closed Sun. & Mon. AE, MC, V

CAFÉ DEGAS
$$
3127 ESPLANADE AVE.
TEL 504/945-5635
Named after the Impressionist artist who lived nearby for a short time, this casual, sometimes breezy, always charming covered-deck restaurant lures a mostly

movers-and-shakers crowd enamored of the eatery's classic French bistro-style menu. The wait staff is happy to help translate the French-language menu and specialties board. Hits include omelettes, sautéed escargots Bourguignon, liver mousse-stuffed quail, and roasted boneless duck breast with orange sauce.
70 All major cards

DOOKY CHASE
$$
2301 ORLEANS AVE.
TEL 504/821-0600
Long-time New Orleans chef and TV cooking show personality Leah Chase consistently dishes up some of the city's best Creole soul food. The restaurant opened in 1941 in Tremé, a historic district originally settled by free people of color and today the oldest African-American neighborhood in the United States. One wall features stained-glass panels depicting life in black New Orleans. No one ever goes to bed hungry after eating Chase's homestyle cooking hits such as fried chicken, crawfish étouffée, oyster-stuffed chicken breast, red beans and rice, and gumbo. Popular lunch buffet features all of the Creole classics.
200 All major cards

JOE'S CRAB SHACK
$
8000 LAKESHORE DR.
TEL. 504/283-1010
The name gives a pretty good indication of what to expect from the West End location of this seafood restaurant chain. And while the affordable food is decent, the overhead music lively and the atmosphere fun, the real value of Joe's can be summed up in three words: location, location, location. The eatery's large raised patio overlooks Lake Pontchartrain, offering one of the city's best perches for sitting back, sipping a cocktail and watching the brown pelicans glide over the sailboats as the sun goes down. The specialty, of course, is crab, served in a number of varieties year-round. Also look for other seafood dishes, as well as steak, chicken, salads and daily specials on the extensive menu. But whatever the dining choice, don't miss the sunset.
400 P All major cards

RALPH'S ON THE PARK
$$$-$$$$
900 CITY PARK AVENUE
504/488-1000
This historic building was built in 1860 as a coffeehouse and concession stand for adjacent City Park. Today, proprietor Ralph Brennan (of the famous Brennan restaurant clan) oversees this fine dining restaurant serving Louisiana French cuisine. With excellent service, tasteful decor and a picturesque view of the park's moss-draped live oaks, diners enjoy such delicacies as steamed mussels and fennel, grilled herb-crusted lamb chops, and veal short ribs—all expertly prepared by Chef Gerard Maras, formerly of Mr. B's Bistro. Private parties take place on the restaurant's second floor and include use of the exterior balcony. Dress code is smart casual. Reservations recommended.
130 P Valet AE, MC, V

BRUNING'S
$
1924 WEST END PARK
TEL 504/282-9395
This family-style window restaurant of simple decor overlooking scenic Lake Pontchartrain in West End opened in 1859 and has weathered its share of natural disasters until Hurricane George in 1998. The original restaurant was destroyed and is being rebuilt; the current address is a temporary site next door. A homestyle menu of specialties such as whole broiled flounder and whole fried trout are augmented by a roster of local favorites, including boiled crabs and crawfish, oysters on the half shell, fried chicken, and heaping fried seafood platters.
100 All major cards

PARKWAY BAKERY & TAVERN
$
538 HAGAN AVE. AT TOULOUSE ST.
504/482-3047
It was a bakery until the 1920s, when this Mid-City became known for its po-boy sandwiches. Right off Bayou St. John, it is the place scores of locals spent most of the last century enjoying that particular New Orleans staple. Parkway re-opened in 2004 and hoards of hungry diners can be found there daily, happily devouring large quantities of fresh French bread stuffed with mayo-dripping roast beef, hot ham and cheese, crispy fried oysters or tongue-on-fire hot sausage. Wash it all down

PRICES

HOTELS
An indication of the cost of a double room without breakfast is given by **$** signs.

$$$$$	$225+
$$$$	$175–$225
$$$	$125–$175
$$	$85–$125
$	Less than $85

RESTAURANTS
An indication of the cost of a three-course dinner without drinks is given by $ signs.

$$$$	Over $50
$$$	$35–$50
$$	$15–$35
$	Under $15

with an Abita beer and try a Hubig's pie for dessert. Passersby can't miss the building decked out in mustard yellow, ketchup red and pickle green, with a sign that proudly proclaims, "Good food. Cocktails." Covered patio dining is also available.
100 Street All major cards

GREATER NEW ORLEANS

ABITA SPRINGS

ARTESIA
$$$
21516 LA. HWY. 36
TEL 985/892-1662
Sip a pre-dinner cocktail in one of the rocking chairs on the veranda before stepping inside this elegant restaurant and former country inn, built in 1895, to enjoy some of the north shore's best testimonials to French-Creole fine dining. Not surprisingly, hotshot chef John Besh is raking in national kudos thanks to a menu whose consistently good highpoints include crab soup, three-way fois gras (smoked, seared, and parfait), and roasted young duck with rosemary honey. Sunday brunch.
100 P Closed Sat. L, Sun. D, all Mon.–Tues. All major cards

CHALMETTE

ROCKY AND CARLO'S
$
613 ST. BERNARD HWY.
TEL 504/279-8323
Check your heart-healthy diet at the door of this culinary tribute to Sicilian and New Orleans-style home-cooked gluttony and prepare to binge—you won't be alone. Sunday afternoons are best for enjoying the frenzy of local families who show up to wolf down this cafeteria-style landmark's famous house specials: king-size portions of Wop Salad, fried chicken, smothered pork chops, roast beef po-boys, and, of course, fresh-baked, piled-high macaroni and cheese. Wash everything down with another local tradition—Barq's root beer.
60 P Cash only

CROWN POINT

RESTAURANT DES FAMILLES
$$
HWY. 45 & HWY. 3134
TEL 504/689-7834
Overlooking Bayou des Familles, from which this eatery derives its name, is one of the consistently best restaurants in town. A menu chockablock with shrimp, crab, and finfish dishes includes My Mom's Shrimp Balls, served in a light tomato sauce over rice; Cajun Spaghetti (My Mom's Shrimp Balls served over angel hair pasta); soft shell crab topped with artichoke bottoms; alligator sauce piquant; and grilled crab cakes Barcelona topped with Béarnaise and served with Brabant potatoes. No one leaves hungry.
150 P Closed Mon. All major cards

GRETNA

CHINA BLOSSOM
$$
1801 STUMPF BLVD.
TEL 504/361-4598
Count on tasty, straight-forward Asian fare and solid service at this relaxed restaurant, one of the best known—and most popular—Chinese restaurants on the west bank. Best bets include pot stickers, soft shell crab with crawfish sauce, spicy flaming chicken, and Ming steak.
120 P Closed Mon. All major cards

KIM SON
$
349 WHITNEY AVE.
TEL 504/366-2489
The New Orleans area's best inexpensive Vietnamese food, cooked in traditional clay pots or chargrilled, is found amid the pleasant decor of this eatery just 10 minutes across the Crescent City Connection bridge from downtown. Start off with the Imperial or Spring rolls—or, better yet, both—and hot-and-sour fish soup, then dive into one of the always-tasty claypot-cooked fish dishes, or the curry chicken with coconut.
100 P Closed Sun. AE, MC, V

PUPUSERIA DIVINO CORAZON
$
2300 BELLE CHASSE HWY.
TEL 504/368-5724
The large framed photographs of Mayan ruins hanging on the walls of this colorful, relaxed eatery are the first clues that the Salmeron family of El Salvador is proud of its Central American roots. But the real tip off is the time-honored—and amazingly inexpensive—menu of native dishes, spearheaded by the laudable national food of El Salvador: the *pupusa*, a doughy cornmeal tortilla fattened measurably by cheese, beans, or pork (or combination), and topped with shredded lettuce and salsa. Other Salvadoran must-eats include *yuca con chicarron*, a hearty mix of boiled cassava and meaty fried pork rinds topped with homemade salsa, and fried plantains served with luscious cream and velvety refried beans. Mexican dishes also served.
60 Closed Sun. MC, V

KENNER

LE PARVENU
$$$
509 WILLIAMS BLVD.
TEL 504/471-0534
This cozy cottage tucked in the Rivertown Museums district of Kenner sets the stage for long-time chef Dennis Hutley's first-class Creole-continental menu. Highlights include cold crabmeat-and-artichoke appetizer; mirliton, shrimp, and crab bisque; sizzling duck l'orange; and rosemary-crusted lamb chops with cider-mint sauce.
70 Closed Sun. D, all Mon. All major cards

LACOMBE

SOMETHING SPECIAL

LA PROVENCE
$$$$
25020 US 190
TEL 985/626-7662
It's hard to tell which is more popular around these parts—Provence native and long-time chef-owner Chris Kerageorgiou, or his marvelous country French restaurant tucked amid the forests of pine-studded rural Lacombe. But one thing is certain: Long-time fans of one of the north shore's best restaurants can't get enough of both the affable chef or his infinitely pleasing menu of specialties underscored by quail gumbo, lamb sausage, thyme-marinated quail, duck l'orange, and sweetbreads braised in port wine.
120 Closed Mon.–Tues. All major cards

LAFITTE

VICTORIA INN & GARDENS

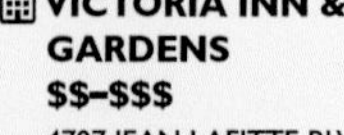

$$–$$$
4707 JEAN LAFITTE BLVD., 70067
TEL 504/689-4757
FAX 504/689-3399
The beautifully landscaped grounds of this West Indies-style Victorian charmer include a private pier extending out into Bayou Barataria (once the fields of this former indigo plantation), an iris pond, and garden. Amenities include complimentary breakfast, evening hors d'oeuvres and cordials, and use of paddle boats and pirogues (Cajun-style canoes) for exploring the local waters. All of the eight rooms and six suites inside this three-story home, 8 miles south of the Barataria Preserve, have garden views and feature antiques, private baths, TV, and telephone. Suites have Jacuzzi or oversized bath, VCR, and coffeemaker; some have canopied beds. Massage services available.
14 P All major cards

VOLEO'S
$$
NUNEZ ST., HWY. 45
TEL 504/689-2482
The Cajun-German menu can be traced to the Volion family's Bavarian roots. But the family-style eatery's moniker is the nickname of son-chef David "Voleo" Volion, who honed his culinary chops under Cajun cookmeister Paul Prudhomme for more than a decade. On mild days and evenings opt for a porch table overlooking Bayou Barataria. Best bets include the can't-miss flounder Lafitte in crawfish sauce and K-Paul's Original Pasta Diane—shrimp, crawfish, and oysters sautéed in garlic butter sauce and served over angel hair pasta. Hungry Jacques should opt for the lederhosen-popping Bavarian platter of pan-fried bratwurst and knackwurst, served with sweet-sour red cabbage, sauerkraut, German fried potatoes, and hot baked bread.
48 P All major cards

BOUTTE'S BAYOU RESTAURANT
$
BOUTTE ST. & HWY. 45
TEL 504/689-3889
One of the best reasons for dining at this family-owned restaurant, open since 1971, is the second-floor open-air balcony (closed weeknights) overlooking the steady stream of skiffs and shrimp boats plying Bayou Barataria. A homestyle roster of standard Cajun dishes runs the gamut from crawfish etouffée and gumbo to mouth-watering soft shell crab and fried flounder.
100 P Closed Mon. All major cards

MADISONVILLE

FRIENDS ON THE TCHEFUNCTE
$$
407 ST. TAMMANY ST.
TEL 985/845-7303
Watching the sunset and moonrise while dining on the dock of this seafood eatery overlooking the Tchefuncte River and its steady stream of pleasure boats is one of the most visually pleasurable experiences on the north shore. Strong suits include straightforward fried oyster, shrimp, or combo seafood platters and original fish dishes.
225 P Closed Mon. All major cards

MANCHAC

MIDDENDORF'S
$$
30160 HWY. 51
TEL 985/386-6666
For as long as anyone can remember, this unfussy family-style seafood eatery, founded in the 1930s and 45 minutes from New Orleans near Manchac, has served up some of the best cornmeal-battered crispy catfish anywhere. Other homestyle favorites include barbecued oysters, fried seafood platters,

and bread pudding.
175 P Closed Mon.
All major cards

MANDEVILLE

TREY YUEN
$$
600 CAUSEWAY BLVD.
TEL 985/626-4476
The Wong brothers have been luring a steady stream of loyal diners living on both shores of Lake Pontchartrain to their attentively decorated, first-class Chinese restaurant ever since it opened in 1981. Favorites include any of the seafood, duck, and beef dishes. Try the pot stickers, hot and sour soup, and lobster with black bean sauce.
207 P Closed Sat. L
All major cards

EXCURSIONS

BATON ROUGE

BATON ROUGE MARRIOTT
$$–$$$
5500 HILTON AVE., 70808
TEL 225/924-5000
FAX 225/925-1330
All guest rooms in this luxury property conveniently located at the I-10 and College Drive interchange, are furnished with one king-size or two double-size beds, cable TV with in-room movies, two telephones with data ports and voice mail, and irons and ironing boards. Other amenities include same-day valet, complimentary parking, and *USA Today*. On-site restaurant serves Creole cuisine.
300 P All major cards

EMBASSY SUITES BATON ROUGE
$$–$$$
4914 CONSTITUTION AVE., 70808
TEL 225/924-6566
FAX 225/927-2816
All guest rooms are two-room suites furnished with king-size or double beds, TV, vanity with sink, wet bar, armoire, microwave, small refrigerator, and dual-line telephones with data ports. Amenities include free parking and morning newspaper, complimentary cooked-to-order breakfast served in the garden setting of an eight-story atrium, and sauna/steamroom. On-site restaurant features award-winning Memphis barbecue.
223 P
All major cards

JUBAN'S
$$$
3739 PERKINS RD.
TEL 225/346-8422
No question this Baton Rouge fine-dining establishment opened in 1983 and accented by rustic French decor serves some of the best French-Creole cuisine in town. Owners Mirian Juban and Carol Juban oversee a menu that satisfies even hard-to-please local palates. Best bests include pan-seared Creole duck breast with sugarcane glaze and fried plantains, and Hallelujah crab—a seafood-stuffed, deep-fried soft shell crab topped with "Creolaise," a delicious mix of Creole mustard and hollandaise. Reservations recommended.
175 Closed Sat. L, all Sun. All major cards

MAISON LACOUR
$$$
11025 N. HARRELL'S FERRY RD.
TEL 225/275-3755
Amour sets the mood inside this 1920s French country cottage, ideal for close encounters of the romantic kind. Highlights of the French menu prepared by chef Michael Jetty, who trained under Jacqueline Greaud, include *soupe Jacqueline* (veloute of Brie, jumbo lump crab, and asparagus), broiled salmon filet served with three-mustard sauce, quail stuffed with veal, pork, and wild mushrooms in Madeira sauce, and grilled tenderloin with Béarnaise, and jumbo lump crab with hollandaise and shrimp in garlic butter sauce.
50 Closed Sat. L, all Sun. All major cards

DESTREHAN

ORMOND PLANTATION
$$
13786 RIVER RD., 70047
TEL 985/764-8544
FAX 985/764-0691
Well-appointed second-floor bed-and-breakfast rooms—two with one double bed; one with two twins—offer guests a taste of the oldest French West Indies-style Creole plantation on the Mississippi River (it was built between 1787 and 1830). Amenities include plantation tour; bottle of wine and a fresh fruit and cheese tray served in the evening; and plantation-style breakfast on the porch or in the restaurant dining room.
3 P AE, MC, V

DONALDSONVILLE

BITTERSWEET PLANTATION BED & BREAKFAST
$$$$
404 CLAIBORNE AVE., 70346
TEL 225/473-1232
FAX 225/473-1161
"Come home for dinner, then stay the night" is the motto and for good reason: On the second floor above the popular **Lafitte's Landing Restaurant** (see below), are two suites. Each is furnished with 19th-century antiques, king-size bed, TV, VCR, stereo/CD player, full bath, and refrigerator. Luxe amenities in the larger suite include a Jacuzzi, walk-in shower, fireplace, and treadmill.
2 P All major cards

LAFITTE'S LANDING RESTAURANT AT BITTERSWEET PLANTATION BED & BREAKFAST
$$$
404 CLAIBORNE AVE.
TEL 225/473-1232
The menu at this popular plantation-home restaurant owned by John Folse is accented by historical recipes passed down through the family that once owned Bittersweet Plantation. They range from PaPoo's turtle soup to Andrew Ginger's red velvet cake. But where Folse really earns his kudos as one of Louisiana's most imaginative chefs and ambassadors of local cuisine is with his original creations: chilled crabmeat lasagna, tuna Napoleon (tuna layered with garlic mashed potatoes and spinach Rockefeller on sundried tomato basil cream), and Louisiana tiramisu with Creole cream cheese and Community Coffee reduction. Sunday brunch. Reservations recommended.
88 P Closed L, Sun. & Mon. D All major cards

GOLDEN MEADOWS

RANDOLPH'S
$–$$
806 S. BAYOU DR.
TEL 985/475-5272
For more than half a century this landmark—it is the oldest restaurant on Bayou Lafourche—has been serving family-style, stick-to-your-ribs Louisiana favorites to locals and travelers alike. Decorative dinner plates from states visited by owner Randy Cheramie hang on the walls of the main dining room. But the plates that arrive on the dinner tables of this comfortable eatery are filled with strictly homegrown Cajun winners such as gumbo and fried seafood. Not to be missed is the cold-smoked soft shell crab with roasted red pepper beurre blanc, or the filet mignon Bordelaise stuffed with Boursin cheese, seared, roasted, and laced with wine sauce. The Sunday lunch special of fried chicken and chicken gumbo hasn't changed since 1946, when the restaurant opened.
98 Closed Mon.–Tues. DC, MC, V

GRAND ISLE

BRIDGESIDE CABINS & MARINA
$–$$$
2012 HWY. 1, 70358
TEL 985/787-2418
FAX 985/787-2146
It's not just the comfortable, fully furnished, two-bedroom cabins right on the beach that make this unfettered property a shoreline winner. Guests can also use the private lighted piers for fishing or strolling. Amenities include full kitchen, private bath, linens, and a pavilion for boiling seafood caught that day or purchased at a local grocery.
25 P All major cards

SUN & SAND CABINS
$
LA. 1 & SHELTON LN., 70358
TEL 985/787-2456
Located across the highway from the beach are these clean two-bedroom cabins, each with two double and two single beds, kitchenettes, private bath, linens, and private screened seafood "house" for boiling seafood.
7 cabins P AE, MC, V

CIGAR'S CAJUN CUISINE
$–$$
1119 HWY. 1
TEL 985/787-2188
Most people agree Cigar's is the hands-down best restaurant on Grand Isle. Opened in 1985, this informal eatery's reputation can be traced to a solid menu of Cajun classics such as gumbo and jambalaya, as well as house specialties like corn-shrimp-crab soup, blackened red snapper, and Italian-style baked shrimp. No miracles, just good down-home cooking at fair prices.
82 All major cards

PRICES

HOTELS
An indication of the cost of a double room without breakfast is given by $ signs.

$$$$$	$225+
$$$$	$175–$225
$$$	$125–$175
$$	$85–$125
$	Less than $85

RESTAURANTS
An indication of the cost of a three-course dinner without drinks is given by $ signs.

$$$$	Over $50
$$$	$35–$50
$$	$15–$35
$	Under $15

LA PLACE

BULL'S CORNER
$-$$
1036 WEST AIRLINE HWY.
TEL. 985/652-3544
FAX 985/653-3544
Those who find themselves in LaPlace, a small town in St. John the Baptist Parish (near the New Orleans airport), should also hope to find themselves hungry, because a meal at Bull's Corner is not to be missed. This comfortable restaurant specializes in prime steaks (from a crusty filet mignon to a dry-aged sirloin strip) as well as fresh Louisiana seafood, for lunch and dinner. But the extensive menu also offers salads, chicken, vegetarian entrees and burgers. All breads, sauces, salad dressings and desserts are made from scratch in-house. Portions are generous and the able staff offers

excellent service. This is where New Orleanians eat when they're in LaPlace.
130 P All major cards

NAPOLEONVILLE

MADEWOOD PLANTATION HOUSE
$$$$$
4250 HWY. 308, 70390
TEL 985/369-7151 or 800/375-7151
FAX 985/369-9848

Keith and Millie Marshall's elegant queen of the bayou plantation home is a wonderfully restored two-story Greek Revival mansion constructed in 1818 on Bayou Lafourche. Amenities include a library wine-and-cheese hour followed by a candlelit Cajun-style dinner prepared by Madewood's cooks and served with other guests in the plantation dining room, morning coffee in bed, and a Southern breakfast. Some guests opt for a more secluded stay in one of three informal suites in Charlet House, a beautifully restored raised cottage built in the 1820s on the plantation grounds, which features a family cemetery and carriage house. Madewood lured Hollywood to its breezy gallery and massive white columns for the filming of *A Women Called Moses*, starring Cicely Tyson.
8 All major cards

VACHERIE

SOMETHING SPECIAL

OAK ALLEY PLANTATION
$$
3645 HWY. 18, 70090
TEL 225/265-2151
FAX 225/265-7035

One of the most heart-lifting views in all Louisiana can be enjoyed by standing at the wrought-iron gates of this 1839 antebellum plantation mansion and gazing down its quarter-mile twin rows of 14 evenly spaced, 300-year-old live oak trees. Running a close second for weary travelers seeking a retreat of quietude are the bed-and-breakfast Creole cottages located on the spectacular—and famous—grounds, namely because they have no TVs or telephones. Cottages sleep five to eight people each and feature full-size and pull-out beds, living and dining rooms, private baths, full kitchens; most have screened porches. Amenities include breakfast served at the plantation's restaurant.
5 P All major cards

VENICE

VENICE CABIN RENTALS
$$–$$$
237 SPORTS MARINA RD., 70091
TEL 985/534-9357
FAX 985/534-9323

Each cabin features one large room with full-size futon, two sets of bunk beds, and two twin beds in the loft. Amenities include fully equipped kitchenette, TV, linens, private bathroom with shower, and an outdoor barbecue pit and picnic table.
4 cabins All major cards

VENICE INN
$–$$
42660 HWY. 23
TEL 504/534-7703

How low can you go? Located near the southernmost tip of the Louisiana delta is this no-frills restaurant best known for rib-eye steaks, grilled and fried seafood, pork chops, and chicken fried steak sandwiches. And, yessir, that really is chicken Cordon Bleu on the menu. Good selection of salads and side dishes. Clientele includes a mix of offshore oil riggers as well as local and out-of-state sports fishers.
65 All major cards

WHITE CASTLE

NOTTOWAY PLANTATION
$$$–$$$$$
30970 HWY 405, 70786
TEL 225/545-2730
FAX 225/545-8632

Bed-and-breakfast guests at this Greek Revival mansion completed in 1859 have a choice of staying in original bedrooms in the main house, the boys' or girls' wing, or the overseer's cottage. The master bedroom suite features 19th-century furnishings that belonged to original owner John Hampton Randolph. Amenities include complimentary tour, refreshments upon arrival, early morning wake-up call with hot coffee and sweet potato muffins, and a full plantation breakfast. Rooms are furnished with mahogany four-poster, and antique brass queen-size or antique Victorian double beds. Some offer views of the Mississippi River, gardens, or reflection pond.
13 P All major cards

RANDOLPH HALL AT NOTTOWAY PLANTATION
$$$
30970 HWY 405
TEL 225/545-2730

Touring the largest antebellum plantation below the Mason-Dixon line could make anyone peckish. Fortunately, this ode to genteel meals is located on the premises of Nottoway Plantation and aptly defends the honor of established Louisiana-style Southern cookery. Plenty of simple Cajun dishes—red beans and rice, fried catfish, jambalaya, and crawfish etouffée. Reservations suggested.
250 All major cards

SHOPPING

Shopping can be an interesting experience in New Orleans, where a wide array of unusual, unique, or just plain weird shops can be found. There's a shop that specializes in antique porcelain dolls *and* rare buttons; a business where customers can taste different brands of hot sauces for as long as they can stand it; a place where rag rugs are loomed while you wait; and a bakery that makes tasty treats for dogs. Most of these spots are located downtown (in and around the French Quarter) or Uptown. They are listed alphabetically by area. Listings of malls also appear for those who would rather hit national retailers.

FRENCH QUARTER

ANTIQUES & COLLECTIBLES

Civil War Store, 212 Chartres St., tel 504/522-3328. Collectibles from the War Between the States include pistols and Confederate money.
Dixon & Harris of Royal, 237 Royal St., tel 504/524-0282 or 800/848-5148. Boasts the largest selection of tall case clocks in America.
French Antique Shop Inc., 225 Royal St., tel 504/524-9861. Among Royal Street gems, the store primarily carries 19th-century French antiques.
M.S. Rau Antiques, 630 Royal St., tel 504/523-5660 or 800/544-9440. One of the area's best antique shops, M.S. Rau brims with both Old and New World treasures, including an impressive collection of antique music boxes and rare walking canes.
Rothschild's Antiques, 241 Royal St., tel 504/523-5816. Find chandeliers made between 1880 and 1920.
Royal Antiques Ltd., 309 Royal St., tel 504/524-7033. Mostly 18th- and 19th-century European antiques. A second location operates at 715 Bienville St., tel 504/524-7033.
Shops at Trois Rues, 335-339 Chartres St., tel. 888/333-5733 or 504/299-1650. This complex of specialty shops includes: Antiques and Small Pleasures, specializing in European antiques; The Green Pirogue, a gift shop with unique Cajun and Creole products; and La Boucherie, an upscale coffee house.

ART

Daska Roth, 332 Chartres St., tel 504/523-0805. This Quarter shop specializes in handmade metal and fused glass Judaica.
Entertainment Gallery, 537 Royal St., tel 504/588-1777. This store specializes in modern re-creations of 19th-century French street posters.
A Gallery for Fine Photography, 322 Royal St., tel 504/568-1313. Nineteenth- and 20th-century black and white photography is the specialty; it also carries a good selection of art books.
Thomas Mann Design, 1812 Magazine St., tel 504/581-2113. Featuring the artwork of Thomas Mann (and other artists), including brass, copper, nickel, and sterling jewelry.
Royal Cameo Glass, 322 Royal St., tel 504/522-7840. Hand-blown glass cameo artwork, including pieces by noted artists Paul Cunningham and Kelsey Murphy.

BOOKS

Arcadian Books and Prints, 714 Orleans St., tel 504/523-4138. This second-hand bookstore carries thousands of French-language books on a variety of subjects, as well as English-language books covering regional subjects.
Crescent City Books Inc., 204 Chartres St., tel 504/524-4997. Rare and used scholarly works are the specialty.
Faubourg Mariny Bookstore, 600 Frenchmen St. at Chartres St., tel 504/947-3700. The South's longest continuously operating gay and lesbian bookstore carries novels, magazines, and erotic photography (as well as novelty items) targeted to or written by homosexuals.
Faulkner House Books, 624 Pirate's Alley, tel 504/524-2940. William Faulkner lived in this 19th-century house while penning his first novel *Soldiers' Play.* Today, it is a used and rare bookstore specializing in local authors and, of course, a complete collection of Faulkner's works.

CLOTHES

California Drawstrings, 812 Royal St., tel 504/523-1371. For travelers who find the clothes they brought a tad warm, this French Quarter shop carries an array of lightweight cotton and linen clothing.
Fleur de Paris, 712 Royal St., tel 504/525-1899 or 800/229-1899. Always artful window displays draw customers into this boutique specializing in decidedly feminine hats created on the premises with ribbons and lace from around the world.

FOOD, GROCERIES, & COOKING

Central Grocery Co., 923 Decatur St., tel 504/523-1620. Try a traditional muffuletta sandwich at the counter of this French Quarter Italian grocery. Also on hand is a full selection of Mediterranean foods.
French Market, Decatur St. at Esplanade Ave. Fresh produce has been sold at the site of this open air French Quarter market since colonial times. Find a variety of produce, plus regional canned and bottled foods and spices.
New Orleans Famous Praline Co., 300 Royal St., tel 504/525-3370. Practically everything needed to re-create local delicacies, including recipe books, ingredients, utensils, and boxed mixes.
New Orleans School of Cooking & Louisiana General Store, 524 St. Louis St. tel. 800/237-4841. Located in a renovated

molasses warehouse, visitors can take a classes in Creole and Cajun cooking taught by experts. The Louisiana General Store sells (and ships) Louisiana cookbooks, condiments, and a private brand seasoning, mixes, and snacks.
The Praline Connection, 542 Frenchman St., tel. 800/392-0362 or 504/943-3934. The small candy shop and retail store inside this Creole soul food restaurant provides a little taste of New Orleans in the form of sweets, spices, recipes and a variety of meal starters to take home. Also at 907 South Peters St.
Southern Candymakers, 334 Decatur St., tel 504/ 523-5544. Five different varieties of pralines top the menu, which also includes freshly made fudge toffee and lots more.

HOME & GARDEN

American Aquatic Gardens, 621 Elysian Fields Ave., tel 504/ 944-0410. This block-long outdoor shop features beautiful water gardens, display pond kits, statuaries, and fountains. Parking and shipping available.
Arius Art Tiles, 504 St. Peter St., tel 504/529-1665. Specializing in handpainted ceramic tiles from Santa Fe, this Jackson Square shop also carries a line of New Orleans motif tiles.
Louisiana Loom Works, 616 Chartres St., tel 504/566-7788. A wide variety of handmade rag rugs are created here. Custom orders welcome.
Rendezvous Enterprises, 522 St. Peter St., tel 504/522-0225. Fine linens including sheets, tablecloths, mens handkerchiefs, and parasols are the specialty of the house. Also clothes and accessories for children.

MALL

Jackson Brewery Millhouse, (aka Jax Brewery), 600 Decatur St., 504/566-7245. Featuring more than 50 specialty shops and restaurants, this mall located across from Jackson Square offers local goodies in the form of Mardi Gras gifts, hot sauces, and Cajun cooking classes.

SPECIALTY SHOPS

The Cigar Factory 415 Decatur St., tel. 800/550-0775 or 504/568-1003. Customers can sit and smoke one of the numerous varieties of all hand-rolled cigars or watch these premium stogies being created.
Esoterica, 541 Dumaine St., tel 504/581-7711 or 800/353-7001. This occult shop carries books on witchcraft along with macabre accessories, including candles, incense, pentagram jewelry, and handmade brooms.
Hové Parfumeur Ltd., 824 Royal St., tel 504/525-7827. The oldest perfume manufacturer in the city offers more than 50 proprietary fragrances and oils.
The Kite Shop, 542 St. Peter St., tel 504/524-0028. This Jackson Square shop carries a wide array of kites, including those of handpainted silk, which no kite lover would want to miss.
Little Shop of Fantasy, 517 Rue Saint Louis, tel. 504/529-4243. Those who forgot their Mardi Gras costumes at home can find original, handmade masks created by 40 different artists, using feathers, leather, papier-mâché, fabric and metal. Accessories include boas, fans, wings, tiaras, and capes.
Louisiana Music Factory, 210 Decatur St., tel. 504/586-1094. This record store specializes in jazz, blues, Cajun, zydeco, R&B and Dixieland. Look for CDs, tapes, LPs, 45s, 78s, videos, books, posters, T-shirts, and sheet music.
The Quarter Stitch Needlepoint, 630 Chartres St., tel 504/522-4451. Needlepoint lovers won't want to miss this full-service shop featuring New Orleans patterns created by local artists.
Three Dog Bakery, 827 Royal St., 504/525-2253. Find feeding dishes, greeting cards, gift baskets, cookbooks, and, of course, fresh-baked tasty treats for the canine in your life. Among the specialties is the popular line of Bark 'N Fetch all-natural cookies in cheese and herb, vegetable beef and peanut butter flavors.

CBD & ALGIERS POINT

ART

Arthur Roger Gallery, 432 Julia St., tel. 504/522-1999. This gallery is generally credited with starting the renaissance that has transformed the Warehouse District into one of the city's premier art showcases and remains the gallery by which others are measured. Exhibits feature the best of local and world-reknown artists.
Contemporary Arts Center, 900 Camp St.,tel. 504/523-1216. More than 10,000 sq. ft of space hosts rotating exhibits year-round including everything from local schoolchildren's paintings to Dale Chihuly glass sculptures.
Jonathan Ferrara Gallery, 841 Carondelet St., tel. 504/522-5471. This artist-owned contemporary gallery features cutting-edge works by local, national and international artists including paintings, sculpture, glass, metal works, photography, mixed media and installation art.
New Orleans GlassWorks & Printmaking Studio, 727 Magazine St., tel. 504/529-7277. Visitors can watch free demonstrations of Venetian-style glass-blowing at this studio dedicated to glass sculpture and casting, lamp-working, stained glass, printmaking, and bookbinding. See exhibits of emerging and established artists, and shop in the adjoining ArtWorks Gallery.
YA/YA, 601 Baronne St., 504/ 529-3306. A non-profit arts and social service organization that empowers talented inner-city youth, by teaching them to create and sell art. At their studio/gallery, young artists work in various media including furniture design, fabric screen-printing, and computer graphics—most for sale to the public.

FOOD, GROCERIES, & COOKING

Crescent City Farmers Market, 700 Magazine St., tel 504-861-5898. Local growers offer fresh produce every Saturday morning 8 a.m. to noon, rain or shine.

MALLS

New Orleans Centre, 1400 Poydras St., tel 504/568-0000. Located next to the Superdome, this 60-shop mall features popular upscale retailers Macy's, Victoria's Secret, and Lord & Taylor. Caution: lunchtime is busy.
Riverwalk Marketplace, 1 Poydras St. tel 504/522-1555. Here, chains join local offerings such as the Tabasco Country Store and Evan's Creole Candy. However, 140 stores aside, the mall's biggest highlight is the view from the food court. Sit, relax, and watch the ships make their way down the Mighty Mississippi.

GARDEN DISTRICT & UPTOWN

ANTIQUES & COLLECTIBLES

As You Like It Silver Shop, 3033 Magazine St., tel 504/897-6915 or 800/828-2311. A beautiful variety of silver pieces and sets are purveyed here.

ART

Anne Pratt Designs, 3937 Magazine St., tel 504/891-6532. Latin American and Caribbean ethnic art.

BOOKS

Beaucoup Books, 5414 Magazine St., tel 504/895-2663 or 800/543-4114. Oddly, this shop with a French name specializes in Spanish books—by Latin authors.
Great Acquisitions Bookstore, 8200 Hampson St., tel 504/861-8707. More than 10,000 books on a variety of subjects stocked by a retired English professor.
Maple Street Book Store, 7523 Maple St., tel 504/866-4916. This charming, well-stocked independent bookstore is a favorite among locals.
Maple Street Children's Book Store, 7529 Maple St., 504/861-2105. Next door to the grown-up version, this kids' shop features a number of local children's books as well as traditional favorites and new national releases.

CLOTHES

On the Other Hand, 8204 Oak St., tel 504/861-0159. More than 3,000 stylish selections of clothing can be found on any given day at this consignment shop.
Yvonne La Fleur, 8131 Hampson St., 504/866-9666. Designer La Fleur creates unique, upscale women's apparel.

FOOD, GROCERIES, & COOKING

All Natural Foods & Deli, 5517 Magazine St., tel 504/891-2651. Visitors who have overdone it with traditional New Orleans cuisine may want to visit here for the vegetarian deli and organic produce.
Martin Wine Cellar, 3827 Baronne St., 504/899-7411, 714 Elmeer St. in Metairie, 504/896-7300. This is where locals shop for the best selection and prices on wine and liquor. Also, check out the gourmet deli for lunch.

HOME

Belladonna, 2900 Magazine St., tel 504/891-4393. The first floor of this popular day spa boasts upscale bath and beauty products, as well as fine quality linens.
New Orleans Cypress Works, 3110 Magazine St., tel 504/891-0001. Rustic cypress furniture is custom-made.
Orient Expressed Imports, 3905 Magazine St., tel 504/899-3060. Imported art including beautiful Asian pottery, as well as an exclusive line of hand-smocked children's clothing, make an unusual but winning combination.
Wicker Gazebo, 3715 Magazine St., tel 504/899-1355. Highlights include handmade wicker furniture fashioned with sturdy European willow.

MUSIC

Musica Latina, 4226 Magazine St., tel 504/895-4227. Latin music lovers won't want to miss this impressive selection.

SPECIALTY SHOPS

The Bead Shop, 4612 Magazine St., tel 504/895-6161. Customers can create their own bead jewelry or buy some of the ready-made pieces here.
Dos Jefes Uptown Cigar Shop, 5535 Tchoupitoulas St., tel 504/891-8500. An impressive selection of cigars and related gift items.
Mignon Faget Ltd., 3801 Magazine St., tel 504/891-7545. Artist Faget finds inspiration for her jewelry designs in architecture and nature.
Scriptura, 5423 Magazine St., tel 504/897-1555. This upscale stationery store carries fine writing paper, sealing wax, and custom-made seals.

GREATER NEW ORLEANS

MALLS

The Esplanade, 1401 W. Esplanade Ave., Kenner, tel 504/465-2161. Near the airport, this mall is the last, best bet for buying souvenirs. Look for Macy's, Dillard's, Mervyn's and 135 other specialty shops and restaurants.
Lakeside Shopping Center, 3301 Veterans Blvd., Metairie, tel 504/835-8000. Lakeside has long been a regional shopping mainstay. Look for familiar national chains including Disney, Old Navy, Banana Republic, and Nine West.

ENTERTAINMENT & ACTIVITIES

New Orleans offers a wide variety of fun for visitors. Those interested in the arts will discover a small but respectable performing arts scene, while spectator sports fans can usually find a game to watch. All kinds of tour operators will bring you to the cradle of jazz, swamps, and bayous, and more. And, of course, nightlife hops with a combination of virtually free flowing libations and hot jazz.

CASINOS

Bally's Casino Lakeshore Resort, 1 Stars & Stripes Blvd., tel 800/572-2559. 1,200 slots, 40 games, three restaurants, sports cocktail lounge, live entertainment, deck, and Commodore Club.

Boomtown Casino, 4132 Peters Rd., Harvey, tel 504/366-7711. 1,200 slots, 50 games, two restaurants, lounges, live entertainment, 3-D motion theater, arcade.

Harrah's Casino, Canal St. at the river, New Orleans, tel 800/427-7247. 3,000 slots, 100 games, 250-seat buffet, 144-seat Jazz Court, 1,950 parking spaces,

Treasure Chest Casino, 5050 Williams Blvd., Kenner, tel 800/298-0711. 1,000 slots, 50 games, three restaurants, lounges, and live entertainment.

DANCE

Delta Festival Ballet, 3838 N. Causeway Blvd., Metairie, tel 504/836-7166. New Orleans-only resident dance company performs throughout the year and with the New Orleans Opera Association.

New Orleans Ballet Association, Mahalia Jackson Theatre of the Performing Arts, 801 N. Rampart St., tel 504/522-0996. Presents varied professional guest companies.

FILM

Canal Place Cinema, Canal Place shopping center, 333 Canal St., tel 504/363-1117. This four-screen Landmark theater on the third floor of an upscale shopping center at the edge of the French Quarter is often the only place here to see independent and foreign-language films.

New Orleans Film Festival, 843 Carondelet St., tel 504/523-3818. Organizes the annual film festival.

Prytania Theatre, 5339 Prytania St., tel 504/891-2787. The state's only remaining single-screen theater shows current Hollywood releases.

MUSIC

Cathedral Concerts, Christ Church Cathedral, 2919 St. Charles Ave., tel 504/895-6602. Sunday afternoon concerts covering everything from baroque to jazz followed by talks between audience and performers.

Louisiana Philharmonic Orchestra, Orpheum Theater, 129 University Place, tel 504/523-6530. Professional symphony orchestra.

New Orleans Opera Association, Mahalia Jackson Theatre of the Performing Arts, 801 N. Rampart St., tel 504/529-2278. Presents four full opera productions each season.

Trinity Artist Series, Trinity Episcopal Church, 1329 Jackson Ave., tel 504/522-0276. Various performances by local and touring musicians, as well as yearly Bach-a-thon, a 24-hour non-stop concert performed on J.S. Bach's birthday, March 21.

NIGHTLIFE

544 Club, 544 Bourbon St. at Toulouse Street, 504/568-9127. Located in the heart of the French Quarter, this club features traditional New Orleans musicians nightly.

Bombay Club, 830 Conti St., tel 504/586-0972 or 800/699-7711. This elegant club is one of the places to be seen sipping martinis and listening to a jazz quartet.

Cat's Meow, 701 Bourbon St., tel 504/523-2788. Karaoke is the highlight with more than 1,000 recorded songs.

John Wehner's Famous Door, 339 Bourbon St., tel 504/522-7626. Bourbon Street's oldest live music club offers live rhythm and blues, dancing.

House of Blues, 225 Decatur St., tel 504/529-2624. Hear big-name touring groups and popular local bands.

Mid City Lanes Rock 'N Bowl, 4133 S. Carrollton Ave., tel 504/482-3133. Bowling and live music on two stages make this a popular nightspot.

O'Flaherty's Irish Pub, 514 Toulouse St., tel 504/529-1317. Authentic Irish pub with live entertainment and traditional Irish food.

Pat O'Brien's, 718 St. Peter St., tel 504/525-4823. Home of the Hurricane and a relaxed tropical patio environment in which to enjoy it.

Preservation Jazz Hall, 726 St. Peter St., tel 504/522-2841. This French Quarter institution is a must-see for all visitors. Professional jazz musicians, some of whom have been playing for more than 50 years, perform 30-minute sets nightly. There is always a line to get in and it is worth the wait.

Snug Harbor Jazz Bistro, 626 Frenchmen St., tel 504/949-0696. One of New Orleans's premier jazz clubs—the place where professional musicians go to hang out.

Tipitina's, 233 S. Peters St., tel 504/895-8477. One of the city's original live music club's French Quarter location offers nightly New Orleans music.

OUTDOOR ACTIVITIES

BOATING

Jean Lafitte National Historical Park & Preserve, Barataria Preserve, 6588 Barataria Blvd., Marrero, tel 504/589-2330. Canoes can be rented near the entrance and used to explore 9 miles of swamp.

FISHING CHARTERS & SERVICES

Bourgeois Charters, 2724 Sievers Dr., Marrero, tel 504/341-5614. Fish in the waters trafficked by Jean Lafitte and his pirates. Groups depart the Sea-Way Marina in Lafitte aboard one of Capt. Bourgeoise's 22-foot boats into the bayou for fly- and spin-fishing for speckled trout, drum and flounder.

Capt. Nick's Wildlife Safari, 102 Arlington Dr., Luling, 504/361-3004. Flat-bottom and bay boats take groups of 2 to 30 into the inland saltwater marshes, where redfish, flounder, and drum are caught. Shuttle vans from downtown hotels available.

Charter Boat Teaser, 2625 Fawnwood Dr., Marrero, tel 504/341-4245. Capt. Mike Frenette helms a 31-foot boat to the mouthwaters of the Mississippi River for blue marlin, blackfin and big eye tuna, grouper, barracuda, trigger fish, and Jack Crevalle, as well as to inland marshes and passes for large-mouth and striped bass.

City Park Fishing, City Park, 1 Palm Dr., New Orleans, tel 504/483-9371. For those who want to stay in the city, bass, catfish, and perch can be found in the lagoons of City Park. Fishing permits are required and obtained at the rear of the park's concession building. Each spring, look for City Park's Big Bass Fishing Rodeo, the oldest fresh-water fishing contest in the country.

Escape Charters, 210 Blackfin Cover, Slidell, 985/643-5905. Capt. Tim Urson, Sr., takes passengers aboard his 25-foot Privateer to fish off of Black Tank, Snake, and Lonesome Islands, Batteldore Reef in Lake Borgne, and Black Bay.

Fishing Guide Services, 7301 Downman Rd., New Orleans, tel 504/243-2100. Capt. A.D. "Dee" Geoghegan specializes in light-tackle saltwater fishing in Breton Sound, Chandelur Isle, and the Louisiana marsh aboard his 26-foot open-hull boat.

Fishunter Guide Service Inc., 1905 Edenborn Ave., Metairie, 504/837-0703. The father-son team of biologists, Capt. Nash Roberts III and Capt. Nash Roberts IV, leads year-round light-tackle fishing in the shallow, interior marshes and bays that border New Orleans.

GOLF

Audubon Park Golf Course, 6500 Magazine St., tel. 504/212-5290. This Denis Griffiths-designed course features contoured fairways, manicured Tif Eagle greens, four lagoons and exquisite landscaping on a par 62, 4,189-yard layout, set among hundred-year-old oak trees in Uptown's Audubon Park.

Bayou Oaks Golf Courses, City Park, tel 504/483-9396. The South's largest municipal golf facility offers four 18-hole courses.

Bayou Oaks Driving Range, City Park, tel 504/483-9394. Lighted, 100-tee driving range.

Belle Terre Country Club, 111 Fairway Dr., LaPlace, tel 985/652-5000. A Pete Dye-designed course 35 minutes from New Orleans.

Eastover Country Club, 5889 Eastover Dr., tel 504/245-7347. Recently given top ratings by *Golf Digest* as an outstanding public course, Eastover offers 36 holes.

Lakewood Country Club, 4801 General DeGaulle Dr., tel 504/393-2610. Former site of a PGA tour stop, the course sits ten minutes from downtown.

Oak Harbor Golf Club, 201 Oak Harbor Blvd., Slidell, tel 985/646-0110. Opened in 1992, the club's golf carts now feature the Parview GPS system for accurate distances.

HORSEBACK RIDING

New Orleans Equestrian Center, 1001 Filmore Ave., tel 504/483-9398. Riding camps for kids, private lessons are available.

TENNIS

City Park Tennis Center, City Park, tel 504/483-9383. The South's largest public tennis facility offers 36 lighted courts and racquet rentals.

SPECTATOR SPORTS

Fair Grounds Race Course, 1751 Gentilly Blvd., tel 504/944-5515. Horse racing on America's third oldest thoroughbred racecourse.

New Orleans Hornets, New Orleans Arena, 1501 Girod St. (adjacent to the Superdome), tel. 504/301-4000. NBA basketball.

New Orleans Saints, Louisiana Superdome, 1500 Poydras St., tel 504/731-1700 or 800/488-5252. Professional football.

New Orleans Zephyrs, Zephyr Field, 6000 Airline Dr., Metairie, tel 504/734-5155. Triple-A baseball.

Nokia Sugar Bowl, Louisiana Superdome, 1500 Poydras St., tel 504/525-8573 or 800/488-5252. College football.

THEATER

Contemporary Arts Center, 900 Camp St., tel 504/523-1216. Two theaters present works by established and emerging playwrights.

Le Petit Théâtre, 616 St. Peter St., tel 504/522-2081. The oldest continuously operating community theater in the country presents a full season of plays and musicals.

Rivertown Repertory Theatre, 325 Minor St., Kenner, tel 504/468-7221. A 300-seat theater producing mostly traditional shows.

Saenger Performing Arts Center, 143 N. Rampart St., tel 504/525-1052. Beautiful 1927 theater presents touring Broadway productions and special events.

Southern Repertory Theatre, 7214 St. Charles Ave., tel 504/861-8163. An Actors' Equity house presenting mostly Southern-themed plays.

TOURS

Cradle of Jazz Tours, 6010 Charlotte Dr., tel 504/282-3583. The city's only jazz history and landmark tour, led by journalist and jazz aficionado John McCusker.

French Quarter Walking Tours, 523 Saint Ann St. at Jackson Sq., tel 504/523-3939. Two hours.

Gray Line of New Orleans, 2 Canal St., 504-569-1401. Offers city, plantation, and swamp tours. City tours begin at Tujague's Restaurant, and takes in a jazz club, stroll down Bourbon St., and café au lait and beignets at Café du Monde. Includes dinner & gratuity, admission to night club, cocktail, coffee & beignets, and return transportation locally via taxi. For ages 21 and older.

Gretna Historical Society, 209 Lafayette St., Gretna, tel 504/362-3854. Escorted tours of the old German town of Gretna, across the Mississippi River from New Orleans, including Louisiana State Fire Museum, two 1840s Creole cottages, and a comprehensive historic exhibit.

Hidden Treasures Tours, 1915 Chestnut St., tel 504/529-4507. The only motor tour that shows the interior of a 19th-century mansion, monuments honoring women, Lafayette Cemetery, and homes of noted female authors.

Jean Lafitte National Historical Park and Preserve, French Quarter Visitor Center, 419 Decatur St., tel 504/589-2636. Free walking tours conducted by park rangers. Reservations required.

Laid Back Tours, 625 Hagan St., tel 504/488-8991 or 800/786-1274. Unique tours conducted on three-wheeled recumbent bicycles that are comfortable, stable and appropriate for almost any body type and fitness level. Includes City Park, Bayou St. John, the Garden District, and others.

Le'Ob's Tours, 4635 Touro St., tel 504/288-3478. Three-hour, African-American heritage driving tour.

New Orleans Tours, 4220 Howard Ave., tel 504/592-0560. Nine different motorcoach tours, including nightlife.

Old Ursuline Convent and St. Marys Church, 1100 Chartres St., New Orleans, tel 504/529-3040. Tour the oldest building in the Mississippi Valley and the only one dating from the French Colonial period.

Royal Carriages Inc., 1824 N. Rampart St., 504/943-8820. Narrated half-hour carriage ride through the French Quarter.

Southern Elite Tours, 4020 St. Charles Ave., tel 504/482-1530. Offers Gospel music tour itineraries.

Steppin' Out Tours, 4761 Major Dr., tel 504/246-1006 or 888/557-7465. Personalized van tours of the French Quarter, Garden District, and cemeteries, including Longue Vue House and Gardens, featured on A&E's "America's Castles."

CEMETERY & GHOST TOURS

Ghost Tours of New Orleans, 1335 Kentucky St., tel 504/524-0708. England's former hunter of ghosts combines Victorian magic and mind reading with historical tours of the haunted French Quarter.

Haunted History Tours, 97 Fontainebleau Dr., tel 504/861-2727 or 888/644-6787 Haunted sights, cemeteries, voodoo, vampires, and more. Theatrical, historical, and entertaining.

Historic New Orleans Walking Tours' Cemetery/ Voodoo Tour, 334-B Royal St., tel 504/947-2120. Stroll through the past and present of this fascinating city viewed through St. Louis Cemetery No. 1 with Robert Florence, author of *New Orleans Cemeteries* and *City of the Dead,* and one of New Orleans's top-rated guides (tours of St. Louis Cemetery No. 2 also available). Hear the humorous, tragic, and inspiring stories of numerous legendary New Orleanians and see many compelling burial locations, including the tomb of voodoo queen Marie Laveau.

Le Monde Creole French Quarter Courtyards & Cemetery Tour, 940 Royal St., tel 504/568-1801. Discover the social and cultural history of New Orleans through the history of five generations of one Creole family. Visit private courtyards in the French Quarter and St. Louis Cemetery No. 1.

Magic Walking Tours, 941 Bourbon St., tel 504/588-9693. Daytime cemetery tours leave from Pirate's Alley Café (at rear of St. Louis Cathedral). Nighttime haunted house tours leave from Lafitte's Blacksmith Shop, 941 Bourbon St., and end at the Funky Butt jazz club.

New Orleans Historic Voodoo Museum & Tour Co., 724 Dumaine St., tel 504/523-7685. See voodoo-inspired art, altars, rituals, and psychics in this unique museum. Ghost, graveyard and vampire tours also offered.

Sin City Tours, 940 Royal St., tel 504/566-1639. Offering daily walking tours of the historic French Quarter and St. Louis Cemetery No. 1.

RIVER TOURS

New Orleans Steamboat Company, 2 Canal St., tel 504/586-8777. Two-hour narrated day cruises and dinner jazz cruises on the sternwheeler *Natchez;* cruises between the aquarium and the zoo on the *John James Audubon.*

Creole Queen, 690 Port of New Orleans Place, tel 504/524-0814. Three-hour narrated cruises on a paddle wheeler.

Cajun Queen Riverboat, 690 Port of New Orleans Pl., tel 504/524-0814. Hour-and-a-half cruise on a reproduction 19th-century steamboat.

SWAMP TOURS

Airboat Tours by Arthur, 4333 Hwy. 306, Des Allemands, tel 800/975-9345. Twenty minutes from the city, explore Bayou Gauche by airboat.

Cajun Critters Swamp Tours, 645 11th St., Westwego, tel 800/575-5578. On Bayou Segnette, five minutes from Bayou Segnette State Park on the west bank of Jefferson Parish. The two-hour tour narrated by the captain includes Cajun legend and lore.

Cypress Swamp Tours Inc., 501 Laroussini St., Westwego, tel 504/348-8833 or 800/633-0503. On the west bank of Jefferson Parish, guides explore indigenous swamps in all-weather Lafitte skiffs. Gift shop and café.

Gator Swamp Tours, Inc., Hwy. 90, Slidell, tel. 504/649-1255 or 800/875-4287. Small boats maneuver easily through the still waters of Honey Island Swamp and marsh. Abundant wildlife.

Honey Island Swamp Tours, 106 Holly Ridge Dr., Slidell, tel 504/242-5877 or 504/641-1769. On the Pearl River 30 minutes north of New Orleans, this popular swamp tour is led by ecologist Dr. Paul Wagner.

Jean Lafitte Swamp Tours, Rte. 1, Box 3131, Marrero, tel 504/689-4186. Approximately 45 minutes from New Orleans on the west bank of Jefferson Parish, this tour explores swampland with a 60-passenger flatboat.

New Orleans Swamp Tours, 610 S. Peters St., Ste. 100, New Orleans, tel 504/236-3143 or 800/445-4109. In-city private swamp tour located in Bayou Sauvage National Wildlife Refuge, located near Jazzland Theme Park. See alligators and other swamp life aboard 60-passenger boat that travels through the 23,000 acre refuge and bird sanctuary.

Swamp Monster Tours, 108 Indian Village Rd., Slidell, 504/641-5106 or 800/245-1132. Two-hour narrated tour through the scenic Honey Island Swamp aboard the *Swamp Monster.* A relaxing journey through the back woods. Reservations appreciated.

CAJUN COUNTRY TOURS

The following tours take place a couple of hours away from New Orleans.

Baratarian Island Queen, 666 La. 45, Lafitte, tel 504/689-4524 or 800/511-2930. See the heart and soul of Louisiana on a tour that explores swamps and marshes, as well as cypress trees and alligators.

Cajun Tours of Terrebonne, 709 May Ave., Houma, tel 504/872-6157. Experience plantations, swamps, and Indian/Cajun fishing villages while enjoying picnics, seafood boils, and Cajun music.

Torres Cajun Swamp Tours, 101 Torres Rd., Thibodaux, tel 504/633-7739. The Bayou Boeuf area offers some spectacular scenery. Native Cajun guide Roland Torres has made his living in the area's swamps.

INDEX

Bold page numbers indicate illustrations.

ILLUSTRATIONS CREDITS

All photos/illustrations are by Philip Gould, except for the following:

9, The Historic New Orleans Collection, accession no. 1974.80
10-11, Richard Cummins/CORBIS
20–21, The Historic New Orleans Collection, accession no. 1970.1
23, The Historic New Orleans Collection, accession no. 1991.34.5
24, The Historic New Orleans Collection, accession no. 1974.25.10.40
25, The Historic New Orleans Collection, accession no. 1953.149
28–29, The Historic New Orleans Collection, accession no. 00.35
30–31, The Historic New Orleans Collection, accession no. 1941.1
32, Hogan Jazz Archive, Howard-Tilton Memorial Library, Tulane University
35 (upper), Hogan Jazz Archive, Howard-Tilton Memorial Library, Tulane University
38 (left), George Daniell/Photo Researchers, Inc.
38 (right), Bettmann/Corbis
42–43, Erich Lessing/Art Resource, NY
52–53, The Historic New Orleans Collection , accession no. 1948.3
63, Richard Nowitz/Folio, Inc.
80, Hogan Jazz Archive, Howard-Tilton Memorial Library, Tulane University
82, Hogan Jazz Archive, Howard-Tilton Memorial Library, Tulane University
110–111, courtesy of the Ogden Museum of Southern Art
111, courtesy Jerry Strahan
138 New Orleans Metropolitan Convention & Visitors Bureau/Richard Nowitz
180, The Historic New Orleans Collection, accession no. 1950.25

One of the world's largest nonprofit scientific and educational organizations, the National Geographic Society was founded in 1888 "for the increase and diffusion of geographic knowledge." Fulfilling this mission, the Society educates and inspires millions every day through its magazines, books, television programs, videos, maps and atlases, research grants, the National Geographic Bee, teacher workshops, and innovative classroom materials. The Society is supported through membership dues, charitable gifts, and income from the sale of its educational products. This support is vital to National Geographic's mission to increase global understanding and promote conservation of our planet through exploration, research, and education.

For more information, please call 1-800-NGS LINE (647-5463) or write to the following address:

National Geographic Society
1145 17th Street N.W.
Washington, D.C. 20036-4688 U.S.A.

Visit the Society's Web site at www.nationalgeographic.com.